THE MOUNTAIN WILL DECIDE

FIVE DUSTY JOURNEYS IN TIBET

KAREN SWENSON

The Mountain Will Decide

Copyright © 2022 by Karen Swenson

All rights reserved.

Published by Red Penguin Books

Bellerose Village, New York

ISBN 978-1-63777-256-0, 978-1-63777-362-8

Red Penguin Books

No part of this book may be reproduced in any form or by any electronic or mechanical means, including information storage and retrieval systems, without written permission from the author, except for the use of brief quotations in a book review.

IN MEMORY OF SONAM AND MY OTHER FRIENDS IN TIBET

May they be granted the nation they desire,
and become again citizens of paradise.

Contents

Introduction	vii
PART I	1
PART II	15
PART III	45
PART IV	115
PART V	225
PART VI	341
PART VII	463
PART VIII	579
About the Author	589
Also by Karen Swenson	591

Introduction

PART I

2006, The Inner *Khora*

The high valley opens its grey, stone-filled lap. There is no green here where the air is thin and clear; little grows. On the right a big, barren tor tops a ridge like a Stonehenge altar. Cold fingers the xylophone of my ribs through my down jacket as I walk this landscape graying into dawn. I turn 70 in three weeks. If at day's end I'm alive, I may be the first American woman of my age to complete the inner pilgrimage of Tibet's, and the Himalayas' holiest mountain, Kailash. In the cleft between the altar and lower ridges glows a luminous patch

Mount Kailash among her clouds.

of cloud. Kailash is behind that roseate glow. The cloud shreds like wet Kleenex, exposing a snowy curve of mountain, a white round of breast.

Rigsum, my guide, cries out, "See her? Did you see her?" voice vivid with our shared joy. She, elemental, ascetic creates in us a mélange of awe, fear, and joy.

I try to silence my yearning for a repeat of my encounter with her on my 1999 trip, knowing that wanting that recurrence is greedy, knowing that transcendent experience was a one time only, probably, unrepeatable gift.

The cloud closes. She is gone.

Ugly Darchen and an inexplicable sign.

5:15 AM. In my guesthouse in Darchen, no light glimmers through the room's one window, ecstatically draped by a ruffled, fringed orange, nylon curtain, which looks onto the windowed corridor connecting all the guesthouse rooms. All is silent and dark until my headlamp beam glances off the butter-yellow walls, the yawning unzipped mouth of my daypack, clothes set out the night before, and on the four beds between them a jumble of equipment from my unloaded backpack. By torchlight I floss, brush with water from the thermos but don't wash my face, remembering Rigsum's hesitant confession, unsure how the Western women I was guiding would respond, that he never washed his face before doing the *khora* or climbing to high altitude. The natural oil on your skin will provide a thin layer of protection against dry air and sun. I put cream and 70% sunscreen on my unwashed face—at 20,000 feet I will need as much natural and unnatural protection as I can get.

I pull on clothes and my down jacket. It's cold, under 30 degrees Fahrenheit. I walk, picking out the path with my flashlight, to the outhouse, a roofless, raised mud-brick cube with four holes to squat over and a superb view of Gurla Mandata, the mountain lying long and languorous, a bride in the wedding dress of her snows. The view, down into the hole, is of spiky mountains of feces, which dry to dust in this arid climate.

Darchen from above, looking out to Gurla Mandata.

The dark above, barred with gray streamers of cloud, is flecked with stars. I pour the contents of my piss pot, a blue, plastic, former detergent bottle, down one of the holes, walk back to the shiny, chromed barrel of water in the corridor to rinse it out. A girl from the guesthouse family gave me the bottle, accompanied by sound effects and pelvic motions, after I told Rigsum I wasn't crossing the courtyard to trip over a chained dog, purportedly vicious, to get to the outhouse in the middle of the night.

Darchen at its best, littered, dusty but true to its mud brick walls.

The kitchen is dark except for two candles. Rigsum and my driver, Jigme, are finishing their ablutions, combing their hair, packing rain gear, in case.

During four days of perfect weather, I have sat about or walked, my body struggling to adjust to 16,000 feet at the garbage-strewn village of Darchen, starting point for both outer and inner *khora*, because Jigme, a handsome twenty something, in youthful love of speed, had driven the pot-holed, dirt roads from Zangmu, on the Tibet-Nepali border, to Darchen in two days, rather than four, leaving me, in the rear seat, white and shaken like a dry martini as P.G. Wodehouse would say. I could have insisted he slow down, but I knew he and Rigsum wanted to hang out in Darchen with their fellow guides and drivers as well as chat up the pretty waitresses in all the ubiquitously lousy Darchen restaurants.

Darchen, the town from which one begins the 33 mile *khora*, pilgrimage path, around Mt. Kailash.

We had all worried as the days, during which my body, passing through the various stages of altitude sickness, struggled to adjust to 16,000 feet, went beaming by. In dust between guesthouse rooms and family restaurant, I'd gaze at Kailash framed by her dark ridges and wonder if, once I had acclimatized, it would still be beaming. Bad weather might cancel my trek or make it a deadly encounter with the mountain.

On every trip to Tibet, I must become accustomed to the altitude. It is the first hurdle I encounter on each journey and the symptoms and their sequence are always the same. Altitude hits in three stages. First the headache; it arrived in the middle of the first night in Nyalam, the town after Zangmu on the way from the border between Nepal and Tibet. Expecting it, I had set out my Tylenol bottle to grope for in the dark when I woke, head thrumming, the engine of a laboring ocean liner. Altitude makes the brain swell, thus the headache. With age the brain shrinks causing the headache to be less severe. This may or may not be comforting information.

Arriving in Darchen, I went through stage two—blood scabs in my nose, days of lassitude, feeling like a pale Victorian lady wasting away from TB. There is no pain, just a general feeling of physical exhaustion. The only sensation I know of that is at all similar is the physical malaise one experiences the day before a serious case of the flu hits.

In the final stage, I am totally physically and mentally miserable, head roiling with negativity: "What am I doing here? Why Tibet where there are no hot showers, no good food, everything is uncomfortable? At 70, I'm climbing through ice to 20,000 feet? Why would I do this? I'm mental. I'm scared. Can I climb to 20,000? We'll have bad weather, hail, golf-ball size. I'll have a heart attack. There will be a rock-fall from the side of the mountain. I'll die."

At this point I remember Dawa, the guide on my first Kailash trip, who, when I told him my age, then 59, shook his head and said in a voice dismal as Edgar Allan Poe's Raven, "Too old. Too old." Fear spews black sediment clouds in my brain. I try to block it with a paperback on meditation I've smuggled in from Nepal, a, forbidden-in-Tibet, picture of the Dalai Lama on the cover.

As I know from experience, on day four, despite a residue of fear, I'm okay. I walk to a monastery/school on the edge of Darchen, "womaned" by Swiss teaching English and basic medical facts; the school is attached to a hospital next door funded by Swiss and Tibetans in exile who are now living in Switzerland. In a court, jumbled with building materials, I talk to a blonde young woman with sparkling spectacles, a noteworthy detail in this dusty environment.

She has done the inner *khora* and has a theologian's grasp of the dispensation of twelve circuits for one that can be acquired in the Year of the Water Horse. The text might be misinterpreted, she says. Perhaps one should circumambulate the mountain twelve times in the Year of the Water Horse. But, she admits, traditionally you are credited for twelve circumambulations for one in the Year of the Water Horse, allowing you to do the inner *khora*.

The Chinese and Tibetan lunar/solar calendars have twelve divisions, like the Western zodiac, each assigned to an animal—rat, ox, tiger, rabbit, dragon, snake, horse, sheep, monkey, rooster, dog, and pig. Their zodiac, however, besides having twelve "months" also has cycles of twelve years in which each year has its animal and an attribute—water, fire, wood, earth. 2002 was, in the Tibetan calendar, the Year of the Water Horse. I had circumambulated Kailash in 2002 and, therefore, had acquired the dispensation.

No one checks before you do the inner *khora* to see if you have done the requisite twelve; you are on the honor system. The more *khoras* you accomplish, the closer you are allowed to the mountain because you have become, at least in theory, purer.

"What was the inner *khora* like? How was the path?" I ask, wanting reassurance about the physical difficulties ahead.

"There's a bad area, falling rocks, soft ice. But I tell no more because you imagine," she says in her stilted German-Swiss accent.

"True," I agree. She's already provided adequate imaginative material.

"Anyway, the mountain will decide," she finishes with a smile.

Does this refer to the theological point of my right to do the inner *khora* or to the pilgrim's relationship to the mountain or to the success or failure of completing the *khora*? All are welcome—Hindus, Jains, Bönpos, Buddhist, and unbelievers—but the mountain's power is recognized. She can ease your journey or she can decide to kill you.

6:00 AM. The kitchen flickers with candles. Rigsum scoops *tsampa*, ground roasted barley, from his bag into my bowl, adds a dollop of yak butter, which has a stronger flavor than cow butter, a flurry of grated yak cheese, finally pouring in yak butter tea. As I mash this to a slurry with a spoon, two men enter the kitchen, burnished, brown faces glowing in candlelight, the whites of their eyes, their gleaming teeth, like neon flashes in the dark. Rigsum introduces me to my "helpers." In the event, his designation is accurate. Diffidently, with polite deference, they accept cups of yak butter tea.

I sit in the back seat of the four-wheel drive, a "helper" on either side of me, one older, short, and squarely built, the perfect physique for mountain walking. At altitude, you don't want height, you want breadth. The other is younger, leaner, with a moustache, a bony face, a straw hat and the vague expression Tibetans often assume when not sure of what they are dealing with.

They look like Native Americans to whom they are possibly related. Those who went over the land bridge between Siberia and Alaska came from this part of Asia. A grim thought—this genetic line, first annihilated by us on the one continent are now likely to be wiped out by the Chinese on another.

We drive up the hill I've walked the last four days while trying to acclimatize, headlights sweeping prayer flags at cliff edge. We turn into the stream, driving in its bed. The older porter tells Jigme, who is driving faster than seems sensible under conditions of darkness and a stream-bed, that he's overshot the turn. Jigme reverses into a great slushing rattle of stones and water, turns to Selung Monastery, a reddish, mud-brick box that in daylight fades into the hill behind, a sail of prayer flags beside it.

Selung Monastery the starting point of the inner *khora*.

The men pound on the door, shout—no response. Finally a monk comes; they ask him to watch the car. As we start, I hand my daypack to the older porter, tell Rigsum to explain that I walk slower than anyone they have ever walked with. The two "helpers" smile and nod politely. I am not clear as to how they will "help."

7:00 AM. Since Rigsum has told me that he has done this *khora* in eight hours, I speculate that, considering the difference between our paces, I may be able to do it in twelve. I'm worried about my ability to walk at this altitude, an annoyingly useless emotion, even though the year before I trekked in the Himalayas climbing passes from 12,500 to 18,000 feet, in the Indian provinces of Ladakh and Zanskar, with a guide ashamed of leading a Western woman, a cook with an eye infection, and a novice pony man. As the cautionary warning on mutual funds reads, "past performance is no guarantee...." I'm obsessed by 20,000 feet and soft ice.

We are in the grisaille light of dawn. I look back to Kailash's neighbor mountain, Gurla Mandata, which I had seen an hour ago from the outhouse roof. We, beginning our path, are still in the dawn shadow of the ridges that surround us, but Gurla is brilliant in its rumpled sheet of snow under morning sun. I try to stride through my fear; I will be all right or not. I am not in control. I put my next foot forward. The mountain will decide.

Climbing, I measure my pace by my breath, admiring the rolling hills that wear nets of small yellow flowers. Plants on the Changtang plateau clutch the earth firmly against the wind's prying fingers. Rocks are splotched with orange lichens, a variety that thrives only where there is no pollution.

Rigsum, Jigme and the porters stroll ahead, stopping to let me catch up. We sit companionably before moving on. I appreciate this because often as soon as I, the slow one, catch up everyone rises as though my arrival were a signal to move on. It's restful to listen to a conversation I don't understand. Do they discuss what they plan to buy with their fees — or their spiritual goals, a scorecard for which every Tibetan has in his or her head? How much merit will they receive by doing the inner *khora*? But perhaps because they are paid to walk this *khora* there is no spiritual merit. Surely they relate anecdotes of other trips, funny or dangerous incidents.

Yellow flowers cast their net around a rock blotched with orange lichens that will only grow where there is no pollution.

One of my "helpers" happily perched in the midst of Kailash's detritus.

I would bet they discuss the pulchritudinous assets of their favorite waitresses in Darchen. Rigsum takes me to particular restaurants quite obviously because he likes the waitress. Any Darchen waitress worth her yak butter has a coterie of smoking, card-playing drivers and guide admirers. But I'm fine listening without comprehension. Tibetan sounds like water hurtling over stones, melodious with guttural punctuation.

The men are engrossed in their conversation; I start alone. I'm slow. They'll catch up easily.

This is even better. Voices fade, subsumed by the stream's chatter that comes and goes as the flower-webbed hills rise, a baffle against its babble. There's birdsong, trilling and chiming from invisible feathered bodies. I'm enveloped in the majesty of a spare, ascetic world. Light is lucidity itself; odors are pure wind alternating with a parched smell of dust; sounds are water over rock, dawn bird voices or silence immense as the landscape, profound as a sounding whale's dive. Silence expands about me. Solitude is my companion. I pretend I'm alone in this stark world with the tor-topped mountain before me, a world that in reality I can only visit, not just for political reasons, but because I cannot possibly, physically survive in it.

Hostile as this landscape may appear to others, it feels the opposite to me. The huge, deserted land makes me happy. It cocoons me in psychic comfort. Fear's weight lessens as though as I walk I'm emptying an imaginary 30-pound backpack of one unnecessary item after another—sequined sweater, can-opener, lint remover roller, high heels—discarded among yellow flowers and orange lichens. I feel strong. I feel the presence of the mountain I cannot yet see. We have a relationship.

Mount Kailash, a 22,028-foot mountain in southwestern Tibet, is sacred to Hindus, Jains, Bönpos (the religion preceding Buddhism in Tibet), and Buddhists of all varieties. At the moment of writing, I've walked the outer *khora*, a sacred path of pilgrimage, around Kailash seven times, in 1995, 1999, 2002, 2004, 2007, 2009 and 2011. What I am walking this time, however, is the inner *khora*, a different path.

Treasure-hoards of boulders are spilled about me, some halved by freeze and thaw like pumpernickel loaves whacked by a cleaver; some are rosy as Bermuda's sands inside, or speckled black and white. There are fist-sized hunks of white marble, black shiny stones fractured into small, coal cubes and great boulders of conglomerate, pebbles, in many shapes and colors, protruding from their matrix like encrustations of gems on a brooch.

Mount Kailash head on with the cleft of scar left by Naro Bönchong's drum as it bounced down her side.

When the men catch up with me, I remove my down-jacket, stuff it into the daypack the older porter carries. When I look up again, I realize that the sun has burned away the cloud-scarves around Kailash's dome. I walk toward her whiteness, trying to synchronize my lungs and my feet so as not to find myself having to stop and pant. Surrounded by sun beaten rocks, light splintering from cliffs, I'm warmed by sun and walking over mountain litter. Internally, I'm a helium bubble of happiness. Looking up I talk to the mountain, not as with a grandiose Goddess but as with an old friend, "Hi, Lady Bird, I'm coming to you. Please be nice to me. I'm old."

Kailash is unusual in that it is a relatively symmetrical, isolated mountain. It is formed of stratified, conglomerate rock that sits on a plinth thousands of feet high, capped by a snow dome. It is by Himalayan standards a medium-sized mountain, not at all in Everest's class of almost 30,000 feet and shorter than Gurla Mandata, its neighbor, which is the third highest mountain in the Himalayas at 25,350 feet.

The Himalayas are a result of a collision that started 45 million years ago when the super continent, Gondwana, crashed into the Eurasian tectonic plate. Since continents grind to a halt considerably slower than eighteen-wheelers or ocean liners, the crash is still going on at the rate of four centimeters, about an inch and a half, a year. But something has to give in a smash up of this magnitude; the eighteen-wheeler buckles between cab and trailer; the ocean liner crumples its bow as it tears up the pier, and the Indian plate, the remainder of Gondwana, has been making an accordion of the Eurasian plate, rumpling the earth up into the Himalayas, the highest mountains in the world, creating an area with the thickest crust on earth.

On average the globe's crust is 30 kilometers, 18 and a half miles, thick. In the Himalayas, it can be 70 kilometers, 43 and a half miles, thick. And, the Himalayas are still growing. Everest can increase in height a half inch in a year.

Since I consistently slept through my 9:00 AM Geology class in college, receiving a dishonorable D, I can't identify much of what I see in Tibet except conglomerate, shale, marble, and tuff. Scree I know from personal experience, having encountered it on two continents, on a hike in Colorado as well as a long trek in Bhutan. The spectacular up thrust of layers that obviously used to be well below the surface causes me to be remorseful over sleeping through that course. I would love to travel Tibet with a geologist in tow.

I call Kailash a "she" because that is what she is to me. However, many of those who write about her refer to her as "he." I think of her as female because she looks like a huge, ice cream scoop of breast with, when the wind blows, a shimmering ice cap for a nipple. I am tired of so many things being identified as priapic in the world. I want a little female representation in the landscape.

Kailash is the Hindu name for the mountain. To Tibetans it is Kang Rinpoche, the Precious Snow Mountain.

Kailash was revered and circumambulated long before the arrival of Buddhism, and possibly before the Bön faith, Buddhism's predecessor, perhaps because in its vicinity, four major rivers of Tibet, India and Nepal have their origins, the Indus, the Sutlej, the Karnali, and the Tsangpo, which becomes the Brahmaputra upon entering India. All rise in this area of Tibet and the Holy Ganges has its source not far away.

The path before me is becoming invisible since the hard earth takes no mark. Little cairns, heaps of stones that pilgrims have piled up, signal the way. Sometimes I lose the path, which is barely discernible being just scuffed, hard earth and the cairns multitudinous. I turn, shout a question back at the men, who point or come to lead me. All green and the nets of yellow flowers are behind us.

The meaning of time and, therefore, of life has expanded here far beyond the human sense of time, that is barely the length of a hyphen. The idea of rock-time stretches the little human hyphen making a millennium an inch. Here eons extend into a geologic vastness that is emotionally difficult to comprehend. This is time we can intellectually count but not internally understand, like the distance of light years disappearing into the dark between stars. The striations of the mountain's plinth, a stone deposition of eons, rise in terraces supporting her dome.

This is her work area where by wind and water she grinds earth. It's her place, not ready for habitation by any but the elemental. Few animals or plants intrude. No birds sing. Wind is its voice. This is her property. Trespass is not forbidden, but you approach at your peril, based on her grace.

The landmark before us with its tor top, like an altar, is called by Tibetans Arhat Yenlanglung. It has been interrupting our view of Kailash. We pass it and she is full before us now, immense and close in the thin air, unobscured by clouds, the black cleft made, according to the myth, by Naro Bönchung's falling drum, running down on the right. The stream is a trickle of glacial melt, a mercury gleam in gravel. Rigsum, Jigme and the porters sit beside it on

Grey green flowers used to cure headache or induce sleep.

boulders engrossed in conversation. I sit a while. Jigme pulls up a clump of round, gray-green flowers I've noticed, saying in English, "Medicine." "For what?" I ask. Rigsum says, "Sleep. Headache."

I rise, walk in the huge peace of her silence where time does not tick, where, with only sky, air, rock and water, world and thought dissolve to the emptiness of meditation. I think that perhaps in meditating one leaves human time and enters into geologic time. Between us, the mountain and me, lie many gravel, pebble, scree and boulder-covered rises. Slowly, keeping my pace so I don't have to stop to breathe, I move toward her in a walking meditation.

The climb is steep, unrelenting. I slow my pace. Footing is difficult on rolling pebbles and stones. We come to the top of a flat-topped hill. Rigsum tells me we are at the height of Drölma La, the pass one climbs to circumambulate Kailash in doing the outer *khora,* 18,600 feet, only 1,400 to go.

Kailash rises before us, an immense striated whiteness, ledges limed with snow alternating with dark shelves blown clear by wind. Near is a cairn of carefully balanced book-carton sized rectangular rocks, white *khatas,* scarves given as offerings to honor a holy place or a person, tied around them. They mark this dusty area of barrenness as sacred, although weather and dust have left them grey and tattered.

I stare at her blissfully, feeling blessed but conscious of being on her territory. Everything is hers, made from her elements. They say you don't climb a mountain; it "allows you to climb it." I am aware of being allowed this close; I am permitted.

Rigsum, the "helpers," and Jigme line up facing the mountain to do prostrations. There are only five of us on this inner *khora,* the two "helpers", Rigsum, Jigme, and me. I ask, "How many do you do?"

"Three," Rigsum responds.

I do prostrations, my form watched by Rigsum with a critical eye.

I position myself, do three to their amusement, trying to recall the formula: hands together at forehead, mouth, breast, bend knees, lower hands, go down flat. Then I remember, on the third, arms overhead with hands clasped in prayer at the end. Probably what amused them was my rump going up and down. But it is important to me to perform this act of physical humility, part of my sense of our relationship, that I honor her in the local manner.

Rigsum points out our path, up gravel, scree, boulder-strewn slopes, each higher than the previous; then up the pitch descending from her side, a fan of mountain detritus. Above, on a ledge there seems to my eye to be a one story, gaily-painted monastery. Rigsum says it is the ledge we will climb to, covered with *chörtens*, a pyramidal Buddhist commemorative structure, and ropes of prayer flags. It is, at 20,000 feet, the sacred goal. I don't notice that there is a gap between the top of the scarp on Kailash's side and the ledge. If I had, I might have worried about how we would get across that perpendicular, pathless hiatus.

PART II

1987, A Promise To Aunt Liz

One Sunday in 1987 I called my Aunt Liz as I did almost every weekend. She was 99, waiting for death in an assisted-living home in Fargo, North Dakota.

"How are you?" I asked.

"The way you are at 99," she responded with asperity.

"Okay, I understand, but if you go and die on me without letting me know I'll be furious at you."

She laughed. We went on to talk of other things. Ten minutes after we had hung up, she called back.

"You had better come out here. I think that is what is happening; I am dying."

I flew out to Fargo. She kept a shoebox in her dresser filled with jaggedly torn scraps of paper on which she'd scrawled, in her impossible handwriting, instructions for her funeral.

We went through the shoebox, and I did errands for her.

One afternoon, with the North Dakota heat shriveling the elm leaves outside her window, we sat with the air conditioning on, the oscillating fan turning its head, rippling our hems as we talked. Our conversation was comfortable, relaxed, about her friends, my teaching. We were curious about each other's lives. She wanted to know about my classes, having taught herself. I found her interactions in the home as well as at the St. Vincent de Paul secondhand store, where she volunteered, full of quirky interest and lessons for my own aging. Besides being the repository for my family's past, she was and is my role model for how to grow old and prepare for your death.

My Aunt Liz in her sixties.

Suddenly she said, "When your father died, you took some of the money and went somewhere; I can't remember where, but you had a very good time."

"Mongolia," I responded.

"Well, I'm going to die. There's going to be some money. Where will you go?"

My mind raced madly, a frantic, hyper-gerbil on its wheel. I had thirty to sixty seconds to find the perfect place to honor her, this woman who was closer to me than any of my other relatives had been. She had been my mother much more than my mother. My morality, my ethics, much of my thinking sprang from her, far more than from my parents.

"Tibet," I said.

"Good," she said.

I have no way of knowing if she would have said, "Good," if I had said, "France." Probably she would have. She just needed a place-name so that she could think about me going there after she died. By giving her a geographical location, I was giving her a kind of future at a time in life when the idea of the future has been foreshortened out of existence.

Many families have a generationally recurrent disease: cancer, asthma, arteriosclerosis. In my family our disease involves running away from life, emotions, whatever is causing us discomfort. My father was alcoholic, my mother cocooned her emotions in layers of Wonder Bread and marshmallows, my Aunt Liz, afflicted by insomnia, became addicted to sleeping pills. She was the only member of my family of that generation to recognize her addiction. In her seventies she detoxed herself on her own.

My parents, despite being aware of my father's alcoholism, had treated drinking casually in my childhood. When I had been in my early teens my mother ordered a beer for me when we were on a trip in Pennsylvania during my Easter vacation. The waitress had looked a bit scandalized, but my mother ignored her. I don't remember my reaction to this drink except that I thought it tasted peculiar but pretended to like it because I knew drinking was a sophisticated activity. I desperately wanted to be sophisticated.

My mother in, obviously, the 1950s.

. . .

However, at sixteen I was given a drink before some celebratory family dinner. There was something ceremonial in the way the drink was offered. It was clear that both my mother and father felt that this drink was a right of passage, yet we all three knew at this point that my father was an alcoholic. People tend to stay carefully unconscious of alcoholism in the family even when its presence is that of a blimp bouncing off the living room walls.

My father made me the drink, a Brandy Alexander, sweet enough to make your bridgework sing. The effect in this case was immediate. One thought detonated in every cell in my body, "MORE." I couldn't follow this mental directive because my parents were there, and I knew that I could only have the one that was given to me. It was decidedly painful, like being psychically rent in half, to not be able to have another and another. Considering this, I think I was an instantaneous, on contact, alcoholic. In my case, all my DNA bytes, all my genes, were standing at attention, waiting to move into action.

My father after the party.

There may also be another factor, which I am aware of in myself, and that is beginning to be noticed in the world of addiction. I have a similar but much less intense, more controllable, reaction to sugar. Sugar and alcohol are close relatives. My mother was certainly addicted to sugar, which resulted in her being overweight and dying of congestive heart failure. In my drinking days I thought myself much superior to her because I had no interest in sweets, just alcohol and cigarettes. It never occurred to me that I was often ingesting the equivalent of at least half a chocolate cake in liquid form a night. Sugar, candy and cookies are more socially acceptable, particularly for women, than an addiction to beer or gin. One substance may affect you more violently than the other, but each results in its own mental and physical problems.

During the first ten years of my drinking, once I was popping beer cans every night, I could, with a great deal of effort but not reliably, get control over the amount I drank but "MORE" was always there in my mind once I had my first drink. The outcome was just a matter of would I have the willpower to fight off my overwhelming craving or would I succumb.

I got drunk the first time when I was seventeen. I was working with some of my fellow high school students for a woman caterer at a wedding. When we were cleaning up in the gently sad morass of crepe paper streamers, trodden flowers, icing encrusted plastic plates and lipstick stained plastic champagne glasses, she said, "There's some champagne left. Why not finish it?"

I had a first glass, a second, a third, finding I liked the taste of champagne a lot. Suddenly the world was a warm place, full of lovely, charming people, of whom I was indubitably the most charming. The bubbles weren't just in the champagne; they were out in the world bouncing about in the air around me or perhaps I had entered the bottle; everything was golden and effervescent. I was no longer afraid of my fellow students. They had become delightful people to whom I wanted to talk for hours. I drank enough to get my feet caught in an oblong galvanized tub in which we had chilled the bottles. I couldn't seem to get them out. This was hilarious. I couldn't stop giggling. The son of the high school physics teacher "fell asleep" in the car on the way home. I've often wondered if he, too, developed an addiction problem. The remainder of my drinking career was an attempt to recapture that first, apparently carefree, Technicolor, "Umbrellas of Cherbourg" musical comedy ebullience. I never did.

My serious drinking started as soon as I got to college, away from parental supervision. Either I discovered on my own, with my bloodhound nose for booze, or someone had taken me to, the West

End Bar, redolent with the odor of sawdust and stale beer, on Broadway a few blocks south of Barnard where I went to college. Within a month, maybe only two weeks of the start of my freshman year, I had become a habitué. Many nights I took my books and went there after dinner to "study." As my father had drunk up money from his salary that his family needed, I drank up my allowance, but I was young, good looking, and men were always ready to buy me drinks.

I was a nicely brought up, middle class girl and this was toward the end of the conformist 1950s. If I had any sense that going into a bar alone as a woman was not the thing to do, or at least a decidedly odd thing to do, I either ignored it or rationalized it, deciding that I was just being a bit dangerous in a romantic way, a la George Sand who dressed as a man to go to the places men went.

In my freshman year, I got into trouble coming into my dorm, although on time for the curfew, very drunk, drunk enough so that the woman at the front desk turned me in. The school got in touch with my parents and my mother came to town to talk to me. I was terrified. We sat in the relative privacy of one of the rooms in the reception area of my dorm. She said in a kindly manner, "Don't you know when you should stop? Can't you tell when you have had enough? I can. The tip of my nose goes numb." She was speaking a different language, the language of people who drink socially. What she didn't understand was that I wanted to get drunk, that was my goal. Possibly I wanted to black out. I yearned to be in that dark place that felt safe of semi or total unconsciousness where there was no pain, no fear.

When I started drinking in college, I was very impressed with my ability to down whatever was available. I could consume more than six-foot men. I almost never slurred my words or staggered, although I certainly lost my inhibitions. But my promiscuity was pathetic, or perhaps bathetic, because it had nothing to do with sex and everything to do with my desperate need for affection and supportive love. Promiscuity is like sentimentality. If you are sentimental, you are attempting to enjoy the emotion without doing the suffering. Promiscuity is trying to get love without any investment, as a celebrity, such as Paris Hilton, may have fame without any accomplishments. These are all cheap substitutes.

My ability to drink large quantities without slur or stagger was, although I didn't realize it, a signal that I was an alcoholic. Within the first six months of my freshman year, I was having blackouts. At first I was frightened, and then I decided it was just a price attached to drinking the way I wanted. I developed an odd assortment of friends among those who hung out at the West End, people who sometimes fell off their chairs, came to, and picked up their glass of Pernod or scotch again.

I had friends at the bar who were not college students. Ken, courtly, white haired, tall and lean and crooked as a heron's neck, who always had a paperback with crimped pages in his pocket and measured out his life in carefully-spaced beers. He told me that at the dental clinic they had said that he could have his false teeth in any color he wanted. He asked my advice, flirting with the idea of flashing a robin's egg blue smile on Broadway.

I was, at this point, an alcoholic. People speak of crossing a line as one moves from social drinking to alcoholism. In my case there was little demarcation. I did retain for some time into my twenties, a slender, unreliable ability to stop after two or three drinks.

In the months after Liz's death, her absence caused me to search her out. I found in a box of photos my favorite picture of her at the age of perhaps six in a little-red-riding-hood cape with a boy whom she had picked up on the way out of town, when running away from home. Aunt Liz was, along with my mother (for years I refused to recognize her as an influence on me), a role model for my traveling. She looks quite cheerful and pleased with herself in the picture in contrast to the glum expression of the boy, who appears to be anticipating his parents' reaction. The picture gave me another perspective on her. There is mischief in her eye and a devil-may-care air in her stance. What parents may think does not impress her.

My Aunt Liz after her escapade of running away with a little boy she picked up on the road.

With such a large age gap it was difficult to imagine her as a girl. But this picture gave me a glimpse of the child I could never know. I admired her bravery and her intrepidness before both the open road and parental rebuke.

We tend to perceive our relatives from only one perspective, the one we formed in childhood. This is not a false angle of sight; but since it is singular rather than multifaceted, it is apt to flatten them to one dimension thus, unintentionally warping their image. It is difficult to overcome this. Therefore, pictures, stories or letters are an important aid to revealing the person from another perspective.

Although Aunt Liz didn't give up traveling outside the U.S. until at age 80 she got dysentery on a tour, of Egypt that frightened her into staying home, she worried about my traveling when I was driving back and forth across the country, for six years, to teaching jobs. She would send me anxious letters stuffed with articles scissored from newspapers about what to keep in my car in case I was stranded in a blizzard. Frightened by the Rocky Mountains in February, I followed those instructions—flares, a coffee can to pee into, granola bars. In those years, driving in snow and ice storms through mountain and plain I learned daring was unwise under dark clouds. Knowing that pitting myself against nature is arrant idiocy has helped in my trips to Kailash.

My mother engineered for herself a three-month stay in Tunis alone in 1930, but Aunt Liz always went on tours, not being in adulthood as adventurous a traveler as her sister. Although she was my mother's elder sister, outliving her by eleven years, she never married, leading the footloose, marginal life that many single women live.

Aunts are often a critical component in a child's existence, offering alternate possibilities for life. Without them there is only the role model of a mother and perhaps some partially glimpsed mothers of friends. There were not many varieties of female lives in 1950, suburban Westchester. I adored my Aunt Liz, at least in part I am sure, because she seemed to be the opposite of my mother. She was non-intrusive, unlike my mother; an intellectual of immense curiosity, unlike my mother; and politically a liberal, unlike my mother. Liz revealed this fact to me one midnight in the family kitchen in Fargo, when the two of us were wandering the hundred year old family house, creaking in the night under the impact of August heat, a pair of insomniac ghosts in white cotton nightgowns. She swore me to secrecy. Being the two closet Democrats in the family was a new bond between us.

Because Liz's manner of living was so dissimilar from my family's and our neighbors, it allowed me to realize there were other radically different ways in which I could live and think.

Liz had been a dancer in the Ziegfeld Follies, gone out with George Gershwin, heard him play "Rhapsody in Blue" before it was publicly performed, been a neighbor of Eugene O'Neill, acted in Schubert-financed productions, and been Al Jolson's dance partner in the musical, *Sinbad*.

I loved her stories of being in the theatre. They brought an aroma of romance and the slightly illicit to my safe, middle-class life. Possibly to our suburban neighbors she was a somewhat pathetic, single, older

Theatrical publicity photo of my Aunt Liz.

woman (this was in the 1950s); but to me she was a glamorously intriguing, "woman of the world" who went places and knew things. Which of our neighbors, secure in the perfect lawns of their lives, would have been able to tell me that if you get into a good show you should save up a hunk of money to buy an expensive ring because if you go on the road the show might close unexpectedly, stranding you in Buenos Aires. You could sell the ring to get passage home. She obviously enjoyed telling me these tales, but I treasured them as being full of important life-knowledge, a single woman's survival kit.

I didn't have much interest in my mother's survival strategy which seemed to exclusively involve attaching yourself to a man like a limpet to a rock and just hanging on no matter what catastrophes the tides brought in. Such was the wisdom of her time. I didn't think much either pro or con about marriage, but I did feel that it might be necessary to know how to live on your own.

One evening in the Lion's Den, the restaurant and bar in the basement of one of Columbia's buildings, I had looked across the room and seen a man of heart-stopping handsomeness, a dark-eyed, dark-haired Adonis, who had provoked in me a cyclone of desire. I had asked whomever I was with who he was. My companion had introduced me to my future husband, Michael, who was going to Columbia General Studies. It turned out he was a motorcyclist. I was enchanted. How daring and dangerous!

My husband age 18 when he entered the Navy.

That night we rode his Royal Enfield, the exhaust blatting into the cool spring night, to the West Side Highway, Robert Moses' elevated highway then in existence. It was chilly, so Michael gallantly lent me his duffel coat. I had never been on a motorcycle before. I was thrilled. The West Side Highway, which was paved with cobblestones, occasionally covered with asphalt, had lots of curves. We leaned into them with me romantically encircling Michael with my arms. However, his foot peg caught momentarily in a crack between two cobblestones and I went soaring over his helmetless head. I, of course, had no helmet either. As I flew I thought, "Keep your head up and remember to roll when you hit."

Luckily there were very few cars on the highway that night. When I hit I thought I immediately rolled; but when I came back to Michael, who was pulling the bike upright, we found the wooden toggle buttons on his duffel coat I was wearing were abraded almost half way through.

Both Michael and I, of course, had been drinking before we straddled his motorcycle. Later, as our relationship progressed, if I tried to talk him out of driving after we had been in a bar for hours, he would become furiously self-righteous about his ability to drive.

Our alcohol-soaked romance developed into a booze-sodden marriage, ending in an equally well-marinated divorce. The marriage was innocently urged on by my mother-in-law-to-be who largely engineered the enterprise and paid for it when my parents refused to contribute. Martha, my mother-in-law, a self-made woman, was a literary agent and a role model for me. She was generous, kind and supportive. It may be that she thought I could save her son. I couldn't. I couldn't save myself. But we had a bond. Many years after my divorce, years after her death, my son told me that she had once said to him, concerning my husband taking another woman, "He threw out the good one and kept the bad one." That she thought me "the good one" is a greater honor than an Academy Award to me.

My family contributed my grandmother's wedding dress, almost one hundred years old, her wedding ring and a hundred dollars with which I bought a dozen pairs of white cotton underpants and a black velvet "at-home" gown. My parents came to the wedding and reception, held in the apartment of my new in-laws. It takes a certain amount of gall to go to your daughter's reception that you are not paying for. When my parents and in-laws met, it was close to comic. My mother, while being very refined, polite and trying to retain her genteel, or was it gentile, superiority, was quite obviously intimidated by these sophisticated, culturally *en point* New Yorkers.

My parent's voiced intention in not paying for my wedding in my hometown of Chappaqua had been to coerce me into postponing the wedding. But the speed of my marriage was not their real objection; it was that my mother didn't want me wedding a Jew in my home parish for all to see. In the event we were married in a chapel of St. John the Divine, next door to Columbia University, after we had both asserted a belief in the Trinity neither of us had.

After two years, the marriage began to buckle and show signs not so much of splitting as shredding. Therefore, with consummate, cool logic and lucid intelligence we decided to have a baby. Not that for one instant I regret this decision. Somehow I intuited that you didn't drink while pregnant and I drank very little as we traveled around Europe. My son's birth, instead of mending the marriage, thinned the worn fabric further. Michael started going directly from work to a bar. He came home in the early hours, frequently with his trousers torn from falling up the subway stairs. Alchys seem to fall up stairs far more often than down. I sat at home with my baby waiting for my husband, drinking, of course.

A year or so later, he started not to come home at all. Sometimes it was only one night, sometimes more. If I asked where he had been, he told me he had worked the overnight or had stayed with a friend. I was either very stupid or too vain to face the ugly truth, or perhaps I just didn't want to know because once I knew I was going to have to take action. One morning our son, age eight, walked into the bedroom, looked at the empty side of the bed and said, in a voice redolent with accusation, "Oh, he didn't come home again last night." This declaration from my son, who was being taken to see my husband's woman friend while being sworn to silence, helped me realize what was going on. Once I acknowledged the situation I started to plan.

I was going to need a job; and the only jobs I had had were as a waitress in a diner before I went to college, as a clerk in a Doubleday bookstore, and in the Planetarium bookstore of the Museum of Natural History. I knew I couldn't support two of us on those jobs, and I did not trust my husband to support his son. I had been brought up to enter the profession of wife, to wear white gloves and pass silver trays of canapés. My fear of people made interviews excruciating. The thought of working in an office with other people around me, their proximity activating my fear, was like living in a nest of spiders not knowing which ones had the fatal bite. But I told everyone I knew that I was looking for work.

Part of my problem, although I didn't realize it, was that I had that bizarre double vision of myself that heavy drinkers tend to have. I was convinced that I was simultaneously intrinsically incompetent, that there was nothing I could do well enough to be paid for it, while being equally sure that my mental brilliance overshadowed everyone else. I bounced from earthworm to Einstein.

I found a job at The City College of the City of New York teaching in a new program the college had instituted, Open Enrollment, offering remedial courses to students who were not able to pass the usual entrance requirements. My credentials as a published poet got me the job. I had put together a book, which Martha's agency was sending around.

The finale of our marriage was operatic in its melodrama. I was cleaning out the maid's room in our Brooklyn apartment for a friend who was coming to stay. The little room had become a dumping ground for Michael's collection of motorcycle magazines, and motorcycle parts. As I moved one box of magazines I noticed that the top ones were humped up as though something was under them. I removed the top layer to discover a chrome-plated revolver gleaming at me. I picked it up as though it were a land mine to find it was loaded. For the next fifteen minutes my mind was so chaotic that I would not describe what was going on as thinking. I was aghast, terrified, sucked down into a maelstrom of questions. Why was it loaded? Why was it hidden? The maid's room was off of the kitchen where I, naturally, frequently was. Did he intend to shoot me? Was he planning on killing us all? Round and round the questions galloped, an out of control carousel. I got my brain out of its centrifugal spin enough to break the suction of the questions and consider what I should do.

I called a former student from City College and asked him if he knew anything about guns. He said, diffidently, that he did. I explained to him the situation and asked if he would come over to unload the revolver being careful to wipe off his fingerprints.

He was over immediately, unloaded the gun and dismantled it into pieces, carefully wiping all of them clean of his fingerprints. Now, what in heaven's name was I going to do with the pieces? I started by distributing them around the house in various hiding places. I knew that wasn't the ultimate solution but I could not think of anything else to do.

Michael came home after a number of days' absence the next afternoon. I knew I had to tell him I wanted a divorce and was trying to find the strength to do it when he went into the maid's room, coming out in a rage.

"What have you done with the gun?" he yelled.

"I have it and I am not giving it to you. What were you going to do with it?"

"Give me my gun."

"I want a divorce," I lobbed into this stew of shouting. Our son who was about nine was running between us asking what was the matter. Neither of us could respond to him. I could see the fear in his small face but had to keep at this argument.

"I am divorcing you," I said, so terrified that I thought of throwing myself out the kitchen window to escape the feelings I was having. I was gashed by emotions as though I were rolling over razor blades. I thought I might die from them.

"Take some clothes and get out of here. You aren't living here anyway. I'm going to change the lock. You can have your things after I've talked to a lawyer. You haven't needed them anyway for the last four days."

"Give me my gun."

I realized that if I didn't resolve the gun issue he wasn't going to leave. He was capable of saying that sentence endlessly. I had a moment of comically, Freudian inspiration.

"I'll give it to your mother. You can get it from her."

He left. I went to talk to my son who was in his room, distraught and weeping. Although I received 3:00 AM phone calls threatening me, saying he had people watching me all the time, he was gone.

I have, to this day, no idea what his intentions were around the gun. I have learned that alcohol causes us to have crazy thoughts and believe those thoughts. At one point, long after the divorce, he told our son he didn't think he was his father. Sensibly, our son got a DNA test and that finished that. Addiction is bad for your sanity. Perhaps he didn't know himself what he proposed to do with the gun. His intentions with the weapon, his twisting of his adultery into my having an adulterous child doesn't, sadly, matter anymore since, as Shakespeare's Shylock put it, "Anyway the wench is dead."

Aunt Liz, deciding that the number of five foot two inch dancers who made it big on Broadway were few, became a Drama and English teacher in private schools around the country.

While at the Knox School in Cooperstown, New York, she organized each year a medieval Christmas pageant with the girls of the school beautifully dressed as the real Lord and Lady of the castle, the Christmas Lord and Lady of Misrule. There were jugglers, jesters, the combatants, St. George and the Dragon, and the quack doctor who revived the wounded Saint. I was allowed to attend this fete one year when I was seven and was given the role of the page, who carried the mustard pot to the table for the enchantingly dressed guests of the Lord and Lady in their towering gauze draped pointed hats and heavy velvet trains. I felt I was in a wonderland composed of both the pantomimes the girls acted out, many farcical, and the graceful, brilliantly colored medieval costumes of the court which Aunt Liz had designed. I was enthralled by the magical world she seemed to have created largely out of crepe paper, colored gels and tulle.

In 1951 she combined travel and teaching, taking a position at the American School of Monterrey in Mexico. At that time my mother was told that she needed a hysterectomy. Since her recovery would be long, it was decided that I would travel with Liz to Mexico spending the year there.

Those months during which we lived together, my freshman year in high school, while my mother was recovering, are full of happy memories. We both read at dinner. I was, of course, never allowed to read at my mother's dining room table. We would saw our way through the Mexican chicken, tough and stringy as shredded rawhide and politely interrupt each other's concentration to read aloud some special tidbit from the book we were engrossed in or I would ask her a vocabulary or philosophical question.

"Why does Ernest Hemingway in *For Whom the Bell Tolls* have one of the communist/socialist men pray as he encounters the enemy? If he's a communist or socialist he wouldn't pray, would he?"

She explained, "People often revert to earlier behavior and thinking when they are under pressure or greatly frightened."

My mother would have either ignored my question or laughed at me for asking it.

Aunt Liz introduced me and my classmates at the American School of Monterrey to Chaucer, insisting we memorize the first twenty-seven lines of the *Canterbury Tales*. I can still recite them. She encouraged my interest in poetry, although her taste inclined toward Victoriana, Tennyson's "The Stag at Eve." On my own, I discovered Dorothy Parker, less mellifluous but more to the feminist point, becoming aware that there were few women poets and they seemed to be a subcategory of the men poets. Aunt Liz encouraged my reading in whatever direction it went racing off. My mother tended to worry about possible, nefarious sexual content.

I had always thought of myself as a shy introvert. Actually, the problem had been that I was extremely self-centered and had no social skills. This was no one's fault. Certainly my mother had made every effort to make me into a socially viable human, but part of what I had inherited with my father's alcoholism was a desperate fear of people. My mother always wanted to make a big event out of my birthday with dozens of children filling the house, playing games of all kinds. I hated this, feeling that they had usurped my birthday, that it was their celebration, or my mother's festivity, not mine. I wanted to go to New York alone with a grown friend of my mother's, the one she had gone to Europe with, and see a show. I could talk to adults but had no idea what to say to someone my own age.

This feeling of social inadequacy and fear of people seems to be a common trait of alcoholics whether they are a loud, good fellow buying everyone in the bar a round, or a solitary drinker hunched over a TV and a scotch. I wonder if there is some connection between autism in which people have difficulty initiating normal social relations and the problems alcoholics have interacting with people.

There were many attitudes and latitudes in my social inabilities. I was never equal with anyone but always either superior or inferior. Instinctively, I felt inadequate. I thought that drinking made me extraverted, that it helped me have fun, that it opened me up to be more adventurous. That wasn't true. It was yet another alcoholic delusion. As my addiction progressed, my behavior under its influence became more and more anti-social, aberrant, and dangerous, dangerous to me.

For one instance, I had dinner with a friend and her husband at their apartment on the Upper West Side getting very drunk and making a pass at the receptive husband in the elevator when he took me down to get me into a taxi. So drunk I could barely maneuver into the back seat, I gave the driver my Brooklyn address.

By the time we were in my area of Brooklyn, the driver was lost; and my speech, usually clear no matter how much I drank, had reached an articulated-through-a-mouthful-of-mashed-potatoes stage. The driver couldn't understand me. I felt myself wobbling on the verge of blackout oblivion, as though teetering at cliff edge above a deep, unfathomable abyss. Through the haze that was closing in on my brain, I heard the driver say, although his voice seemed to come from the wrong end of a telescope, "If you can't direct me to this damn address, I'm going to drop you right here."

Gazing into the night, I realized that we were near the Gowanus Canal, a slummy, certainly around midnight, dangerous neighborhood. I forced the encroaching cloud of inebriation back as though it were the enormous curtain of the Metropolitan Opera House. Looking out the taxi window at a street sign, I began directing the driver. But as we approached my house my bladder, like a water-filled balloon, reached bursting point. The pressure was irresistible and I peed in the back seat of the taxi, leaving a puddle behind for the driver to discover and deal with. As I lurched up the stairs of the stoop of my brownstone, hanging on grimly to the railing I could feel my sodden cotton trousers clamping and clinging to my legs so tightly that they hobbled my walk. The taxi sped away. I let myself into the house.

The next morning I rose to a dry-mouthed hangover in which light and sound were amplified to searing pain, dressed and sorted the books and other materials I would need for teaching before heading out to the subway.

My Aunt Liz was a passionate and imaginative teacher, having an intense yearning to transmit her love of literature to her students. This whirlpool of emotion around the written word took its toll on her physically. She would enter the class with her hair neatly pinned up, her skirt and jacket decorously trim, her stocking seams straight. By the end of the hour her hair was standing up in elf locks as though a cow had been licking her head, her blouse was wrenched from her chalk-streaked skirt and flapped its wrinkled tail below her jacket's hem, her stocking seams wriggled up her calves like frightened angle worms. That intensity has always been my ideal of teaching.

My drinking had affected my own teaching in two ways that I know of. I had been afraid of everyone, my students as well as my fellow instructors. This had resulted partially from a twisted and exaggerated sense of hierarchy. If I decided a person was above me in the hierarchy, I couldn't talk to them, or else my talk was stilted and artificial because I was terrified of them, as though they had the power of life and death over me. It didn't occur to me until I got sober that there was something decidedly odd about such thinking. I never knew what to say to people because I was totally focused on myself rather than on the person I wanted to speak to. From this situation came the unuseful presumption that they didn't like me. My competitiveness fueled this situation. Drinking helped to numb both these thoughts and their accompanying emotions.

Without being aware of it, I felt in danger; and as I discovered much later, when we feel afraid we go on the defensive, we get angry. Anger is empowering; it charges you with adrenalin. My defense was, "You don't like me. Well, I'll fix you. I will dislike you first." I was always trying to defend myself from imagined aggression. I certainly felt that my mother didn't like me; and if your mother doesn't like you, who is going to like you? Enveloped in attitudes of this sort, which formed an armor plating over me, an armadillo's shell, I spent my life curled up in a ball of fear and defensive rage.

I walked through life radiating anger. Students, understandably, are afraid of an angry teacher. One young man said to me, "Why are you so angry at us? The semester has just begun. We haven't done anything yet." I was startled by this statement since I had no idea I was angry.

I suspect that I also acted in a haughty manner towards my colleagues as if they had done me some injury and I was, out of my superior graciousness, being polite rather than cutting them. My attitudes and behavior were at the very least potentially alienating to both my students and my colleagues.

However, never, ever, did I call in sick for work because of a hangover. I knew that I could not be an alcoholic because I never missed a day of work. The fact that I showed up somehow erased my drinking from my mind, or perhaps the virtuousness of showing up for work vindicated me.

Fear tainted all my relationships. The more intimate they were, the more intense was my fear. Never, ever did I go to bed with anyone even half-sober. I had to numb my fear before I could make love. I always felt inauthentic, the plastic snakeskin wallet among the real ones. Perhaps I felt that if I were close to someone they would discover that I was a fake, a pasteboard Hollywood front of abilities, of maturity, behind which cowered a fearful child.

In 1976 I, along with others in the category of last-hired-first-fired, were let go from City College. For six years I taught as Poet-in-Residence at universities around the country. I drove back and forth across the United States ten times in six years.

Toward the end of this personal diaspora, I taught at Denver University. In my graduate class there was a young man, tall, raw-boned, who was a fine, dedicated poet. His fellow students talked with palpable relief about how he had recently given up drinking. I don't believe he and I ever talked about this at that time, but he had me in his sights and knew what was wrong with me.

During my semesters in Denver, I had terrible debilitating hangovers that sometimes lasted all day. One night I became aware as I sat at my typewriter trying to write a poem that my mind was not occupied with my writing but was off having a fantasy about success. I was horrified and frightened by this. It was, I think, the first time I realized my drinking was destroying my ability to write, eating into it with the corrosive bite of fantasy.

My father had moved in with me in Brooklyn after a failed attempt to live with his younger brother. That summer he drank downstairs; I drank upstairs. A long letter arrived from my Denver student. (I wish I had kept it.) Without ever suggesting that I had a problem, he told me what a change had come over him when he had stopped struggling to stay sober on his own and had gone to an AA meeting. He wrote of how the company of others with the same difficulty had relieved the daily tension of staying away from a drink, the sense of isolation and uniqueness. On coming into AA, his obsession to drink evaporated. He told me how the conversations he was having in AA were changing his perspectives on writing and life.

His letter touched me. At that point in my life, the thought that anyone cared about me made me go as soft as the center of a jelly doughnut. I answered, thanking him and saying that my father was an alcoholic, that I might try an intervention with him. I never did that since it would have exposed my own drinking. However, I long ago gave up feeling ashamed of transferring the focus to my father. That letter was, like my realization as I was writing that night in Denver, yet another white pebble on a path leading me in the right direction.

The next year I taught at Scripps College in southern California. I drove across country arriving ahead of the students to meet with the

Dean under whom I was to work. I was given a small apartment in the dorm where I was in charge of the students.

Again, I drank every night. I was frightened because, while in New York and in many other places I had taught, you could walk half a block to a store to buy your beer. In California, I would have to drive. I knew the two things I did very badly when drunk were cooking and driving. I, therefore, was always sure to be well stocked.

I would sit down to write in the evening after correcting papers (I never drank while correcting papers) to find that I just drank and stared at the page, my mind a blank, or when I tried to read what I had written in the morning, my hand writing was indecipherable. I didn't know what to do. I was scared. My life seemed to be collapsing in on me like a falling soufflé. It never occurred to me to stop drinking. It never, consciously, occurred to me that there was a connection between my drinking and my shame, my despair, my continual sense of humiliation. I woke up every morning feeling as though I had been dipped in pond scum. I felt trapped, doomed. Yet drinking was my solace not my *tsuris*, as one would say in Yiddish. There seemed to be no way out, no exit. Although somehow I had come to understand I was an alcoholic, there was no connection between that and my misery for me. They were two separate entities. This inability to comprehend the connection between my drinking and my despair was a territory of denial, like the white areas on 19th century maps of Africa and Asia indicating unexplored areas.

I flew back to Brooklyn for Christmas. After our Eve party, I said to my son, "I think I'll just take the bottle with me and have a drink before I go to sleep."

"You usually do, " he said.

With that reply I felt my son had branded me, "ALCOHOLIC," a scarlet A with blinking neon lights across my forehead. I am very grateful to him for having said that. It pushed me a little further along the road.

When I went out to California to teach that spring, I was, without knowing it, at a crux in my life. I think we are all given opportunities, crossroads in our lives, where we are tendered the possibility to change. At first I enjoyed my life as a vagabond teacher across the country, Poet-in-Residence at universities or, more humbly, a Poet-in-the-Schools, but slowly and subtly that gypsy life repositioned my awareness of my drinking. Living in isolation with my alcoholism made me aware of how much and consistently I was drinking but not how it was destroying me. I was in too much denial for that. It did thrust me into a state of incomprehensible despair and desperation. Something was terribly wrong but I couldn't understand what. To anyone standing outside my life, the answer would have been obvious.

It would have been apparent how insane I was in my drinking, as day after day for year after year I expected somehow, miraculously that this night would be different; I would not get drunk; I would only have two drinks; I would drink the way other people did; I would not do something embarrassing; I would not pick a fight or bring home someone who would be as shamefaced as I the next morning when we woke next to each other not knowing the others' name.

In the spring while I was teaching in California, my Denver student got in touch and asked if I was drinking. If I wasn't, he said he would come out to visit me. Oddly, by some grace, that undeserved and unrequested gift that suddenly appears in one's life, I was not drinking. I was doing one of my two-week stints of abstinence to prove I wasn't an alcoholic.

He came out to California and spent about five days with me, talking steadily about his own sobriety. He never mentioned my drinking. Before he left, I said tentatively, "If I go back to drinking, perhaps I will try AA."

"If I go back to drinking"? What incredible hypocrisy. In twenty-eight years, except for two-week breaks to prove I wasn't alcoholic, I had not gone a day without a drink except during my pregnancy.

He returned to Denver. The term resumed after spring break. I went to a faculty party of some sort and left with a half-bottle of Lancer's Rose, I was never a high-shelf drunk, under my arm. I woke the next morning to my usual self-loathing, plus a rock and roll percussion hangover that so preoccupied me that I forgot about a class that I was supposed to teach and missed it. This, when a student came in and told me that they had waited for me, appalled me so that my self-hate appreciated by one hundred percent. I had, by missing my class, dynamited my rationale for why I could not be an alcoholic. I always showed up for work. Well, this time I hadn't and it was because I had been drunk the night before.

A woman I knew slightly in the Art Department stopped by my office door at this point, looked at me and asked, "What's the matter? You look awful." I told her I had the hangover from Hell and that I had just missed a class.

"Do you want to go to an AA meeting?" she asked.

"Yes. Will you take me?"

Where did those words come from? That may have been the first time in my life that I had ever asked someone for help. Like my father, I believed everything had to be done solo with grit molars.

She drove me to a house that had a snack bar and a large bare room full of laughing, chattering people sitting at cafeteria tables. I was stunned and certainly not at all clear as to what was going on. Three people spoke, one after the other for about twenty minutes each. I cannot remember two but the other was a heavy woman in what I presumed was a nurse's uniform who spoke of how she had had an alcoholic seizure, awakened from it and gone straight out to buy another bottle. "After all, I'd just had a really bad experience. I needed a drink to get my head straight and think about it," she said to roars of laughter.

I couldn't laugh, but I understood the laughter had to do with the paradox of her behavior. I also totally identified, although I had never had a seizure, didn't know you could have seizures from alcohol, with her thought process and how drinking short-circuited any emotion or ability to confront her/my experience.

At the end of the meeting, the chairperson asked if there was anyone new to AA in the room. I stood up, although this was not necessary, and said, "I'm Karen. I'm an alcoholic." About one hundred tons of lead, pond scum and the first load of chips fell off my shoulder. I knew I would be back in that room because the people had spoken without reservations, with a crystalline honesty about their emotions and experiences. I had never heard anything like this.

In the town I had grown up in, as in towns anywhere in the world, many people were pretending most of the time, pretending to have more money than they had, more social status, more knowledge, and certainly no one had any family difficulties. Husbands were always faithful. Children always behaved. Once a Thai man, when I hesitated before answering his question about how much I earned said, "Why don't Americans like to answer that question? Do they lie about their income?" I felt there was very little lying going on in that room. The night after that meeting I did not drink.

Sitting with my aunt in the North Dakota heat, why did I choose Tibet when my mind dove into the ragbag of countries available in the world? I'm not sure, but I had been traveling by that time in Asia for about five years and it was the farthest, the most difficult, the most unknown place I wanted to go to, so I chose it for my beloved aunt.

Distance and difficulty are to me a way of expressing love. If you love a person you should, it seems to me, want to do what is hard and far, perhaps do something you fear, in order to demonstrate your love. "See, I love you so much I will go to the end of the earth for you, walk through my fear, spend days in the back of a Chinese truck covered with dust eating dried ramen noodles out of their cellophane wrapper. That's how much I love you."

My choice of Tibet may look like a snap decision, a coincidence; however, I think one of its origins had been in my trip in 1979 to Nepal with a group of anthropologists, the same trip on which I had discovered the *Lonely Planet* travel guide. While in Kathmandu, we had kept hoping to see the Himalayas, but every day the clouds had smothered them. We had been told that if we rose very early, 5:00 AM at the latest, we would be able to see them.

Groggily, a couple of us had climbed from bed in the Kathmandu Guest House to stumble onto the balcony. There they were. My breath caught at the long line of hunched white shapes defining the horizon with their bulk, a caravan of behemoths under white burdens, a silent procession of frosted mammoths: The Himalayas. I had to get to them.

Some years later, on a trip to Bhutan, I met a Scots woman who told me that once you see the Himalayas you will return. Whether you believe that, perhaps, sentimental superstition or not, certainly both mountains and sea draw people. There is no doubt that I am drawn by mountains.

I did, and do, however, believe something I read in Somerset Maugham, that each of us has another country, another place in the world that we belong to as much as we belong to our birth country. Our connection to our birth country is physical; but our link to the second country is instinctive, has an intimate aura of enigmatic imminence. How sad that so few people discover their other country that is there waiting for them, another self, an unrealized twin. I think we have, out there a place, each of us, another land of the spirit.

A second factor in my choosing Tibet may have been that there was no snap decision or coincidence because my subconscious or something outside of my conscious was already plotting to position me at the physical trail-head of my spiritual search. All countries have a characteristic that supposedly epitomizes them. America is the gun-toting cowboy; France the epicure of food and wine. Tibet is epitomized in this world as being a spiritual nexus. Certainly I was aware of that, and I had reason to be interested in a transcendent connection. Having, after 28 years of destructive drinking, joined AA where the idea of a God with a capital G, had become moot in my life.

When I told Aunt Liz that I would go to Tibet for her, I was grateful that we had no religious discussion. A large part of my difficulty in locating a Higher Power since joining AA had been due to my anger and resentment of the Catholic church in which I had been raised. She had tried, in the past, to get me to return to the Church. She cut out articles about how the Church was liberalizing its views on women and gays, but I had remained uninterested not only in Catholicism but all organized religions, particularly those with celibate, male clergy.

In one of her letters to me, Liz quite gleefully pointed out, and it was true, that she was a better Christian than my mother. Liz had whatever makes us capable of spiritual insight, something that my mother had been denied.

In my first month in AA, I had been mentally befogged but one night had peered through the smoke-laden atmosphere. Smoking was ubiquitous in meetings since most of us, having eschewed alcohol, proceeded to wallow in cigarettes and caffeine, to read "the window shades," long scrolls on which are printed the Twelve Steps and Twelve Traditions of AA. I saw with alarm that God was mentioned a number of times and thought, "Damn, maybe this isn't going to work. I don't believe in a God. I don't want to believe in one. But maybe I can just ignore the 'God' part." I had ignored my drinking for years so to ignore God might be easy. I didn't quite understand that AA had a spiritual base. It was obvious that it was neither a religious cult nor a bible-thumping organization.

The people around me gently insisted that I didn't have to do anything I didn't want to do, that the Steps were suggestions, that I could take the group as a Higher Power, since they were a group that didn't drink which was something I didn't seem to be able to do alone. At its most primitive, the AA definition of God is someone or something capable of not drinking. They said I should find my own god or whatever spiritual situation suited me. I found this very confusing because I was used to the idea of a rigid, rather unpleasant, concept of god. I thought of god as something given to you, or perhaps forced on you, something prescribed certainly, not a freely chosen entity. God and religion were welded together in my mind.

I didn't and don't like monotheistic religions since, first, in my view they all mistreat and malign women, and second, because they appear to be structured around the principle of "I'm right and you're wrong. My God's better than your god," automatically setting the stage for conflict. To me religion feeds into one of the most noxious needs of woman/mankind, our desire to be superior and right. Perhaps all humans are so innately insecure that we need an imprimatur stamping us superior and right.

I had been taught catechism every Sunday after mass by Mother St. Frederick, a French nun in her late sixties, who always had a drop of snot trembling on the end of her bony arched nose. The whole class of eight year olds waited in fascination for it to drop, partly because we were bored silly at reciting, year after year, the same answers to the same questions.

"Who made you?"

"God made me."

"Why did God make you?"

"God made me to know, love and serve him in this world."

I thought Mother St. Frederick was sweet, and I was willing to perform like a seal for her every Sunday; but I would not have trusted her to give me directions to the local diner much less a putative heaven. I was aware that Mother St. Frederick and her fellow nuns were limited in their experience of the world and were not particularly bright. My mother may have been a social snob, but I seem to have popped out of the womb a full-blown intellectual snob.

Despite my rebellion against religion, I had never consciously questioned the idea that the concept of god was a given entity. I knew

I didn't want the Catholic Church's god back in my life. But the way the people in my initial AA group talked it sounded as though there was a God Shoppe in LA where you could buy a "Build a God Kit." I was immensely suspicious of what I considered "California spirituality" where people in white robes at the edge of the Pacific shouted repeatedly at the sea, "I am God."

Following that thought of being god, I did begin to understand that I had to stop playing god by trying to be in constant control. This was difficult because I came from a family where we thought everything was our fault since we were in control of everything or certainly ought to be. A small example; Aunt Liz at 95 had terribly dry skin and told me, "It's my own fault. I should never have taken those long soakings in the tub when I was younger." She had caused her itchy condition because she had control; it wasn't because one's skin gets drier as you age.

I decided to ignore god until I had more information and replace that negatively loaded word with the bland, margarine locution, "Something." My god problem was ameliorated a bit by a friend who said, "The word god is just a capacious receptacle into which we deposit all we don't understand." Where I thought additional information would come from I don't know; but someone did say to me once when I was fretting over this, "Don't worry. You don't have to look for god. He, she or it isn't the one who is lost."

I didn't think, when I made my promise to Liz, about the fact that Tibet, invaded in 1950 and brought under strict Chinese control in 1959, had only opened a few years before to foreigners in 1984. In fact, for a number of years I conveniently forgot about my promise, either because I was procrastinating or because I was afraid. I wanted, if possible to go alone which raised all the fearful questions: "How will I get a visa? How will I travel around the country? Where will I stay?" I had no idea how to get there or how to get that visa. I tried once to apply for a Chinese visa in New York, putting down that I intended to go to Tibet. I was greeted with blatant suspicion and given such complex instructions that I could see the red tape disappearing like a railroad track into the distance across the plain of an infinite future. I decided applying for the visa in the U.S. was not the way to do it.

Luckily, I had a friend, who in 1992 when she received a Fulbright to Nepal, got in touch and urged me to visit. When she told me she'd been to Tibet, I knew I couldn't procrastinate any more; I had to fulfill my promise. My friend instructed me on which agency to go to, and I put down the money for my first trip.

My promise to Aunt Liz was a link in a chain, reaching back in time, each segment preparing me for the next. My first trip to Nepal made me realize I was in a part of the world that felt right to me. My first trek in Thailand awakened me to my need to exercise seriously if I wanted to do difficult, physical travel. There were psychological and emotional discoveries that also prepared me for the next link, such as the recognition of my fears while traveling in Thailand. The physical, psychological and spiritual were not separate elements but were twined, a strong rope leading me to Tibet where I would unwrap my emotions like sparkling presents.

All of this was a huge surprise because I assumed that as a Westerner I would be immune, indeed, inoculated by my Westernness, against any spiritual contact in the Eastern part of the world, that such occurrences in Tibet were only available to Tibetans, as though spiritual experiences were locale and nationality specific, as though being out of context I could have no contact. Wrong.

A journey is always a search, the object often more numinous than concrete.

PART III

1992, First Trip To Tibet

Bronwen, my friend on a Fulbright Fellowship with whom I was staying, took me to the agency she had used in Kathmandu headed by a Chinese man who spoke excellent English. His office, wall papered with travel posters, was across from the vividly pungent, emerald, scum-covered pool of Nagpokhari with its sinuous, gilded cobra on a pillar at its center. They offered weeklong bus tours to Tibet. Seven days, I thought, was probably too short a time but that was what was on offer. I also was not happy about being on a tour. Having by this time traveled alone in Thailand, Hong Kong, Burma and the islands of Indonesia, I wanted a solo trip; but the Chinese, always in control, were not, apparently, letting in solo travelers. I signed up but asked the tour operator, at Bronwen's suggestion, if he could arrange an extension of my visa so that I could stay on for another week alone in Lhasa. He had no difficulty with that. There was, obviously, some kind of ruptured logic here I should have wondered about. I could not enter Tibet alone, but I could stay on alone?

My traveling companions were amiable and frequently funny, the things I saw hard to comprehend, but I was focused on the future, straining on my Chinese leash, to when I would travel alone.

We gathered with our bags early in the morning in front of the agency office, trying not to size each other up too obviously. As each of us boarded the bus, a member of the office staff draped a silky white scarf around our neck. "What is this?" I asked. "A *khata* to honor you as you are leaving on your journey, to bring you luck," the woman told me. *Khatas*, usually white, are given as an offering to an image, a sacred place or person or to someone, as we were, leaving on a trip. We drove through the green terraced rice fields of Nepal to the Friendship Bridge.

In 1979 I had gone with the group of anthropologists I had traveled with to the foot of this bridge, which marks the border between Tibet and Nepal, but we could not cross it. We did not even get out of our van. On the other side was a monstrous black and white portrait of Mao, looking like a fat-faced teenager, which made it plain that the north bank of the river was Chinese territory. This time, there was no picture of Mao, just the towering walls of the chasm covered in drenched and dripping greenery that rises above the river, Sun Koshi (River of Gold) in Nepal, Bhote Kosi in Tibet. Looking up we could see the cliff edge road that would take us to the Nielamu Pass.

Just before the Friendship Bridge we were herded out of the bus we had driven in from Katmandu and loaded onto another with windows that had been painted black; its seats, walls and ceiling were covered with cut crimson, quilted, vinyl velour. Was it a retired, itinerant brothel-bus? A boy, standing guard at the door, tried to fend off interlopers who scrambled onboard as we lurched through potholes on the unpaved road that climbed the gorge. About half a dozen men pushed him aside as they swung up onto the bus. There was no acrimony; they joked pleasantly with him once they had secured their places. One could hardly blame them for cadging a ride considering the climb.

Zhangmu, the border town you climb to after crossing the Friendship Bridge into Tibet/China, which was built into the cliffs of the gorge.

As we started up the hairpin turns of the rutted, potholed, dirt road from the Friendship Bridge to the border town of Zhangmu, Alessandro, an Italian doctor, who wore a fresh Lacoste shirt in yet another vibrant color every day, peered through a place where the paint had been scratched off and commented, looking over the edge of the guard-rail-less-cliff-edge road, down into the abyss with its silver thread of river below, "I think the windows are black so that we won't die of heart attacks." It is a quip that returns to me every time I go up from the Friendship Bridge to the town of Zhangmu across the Chinese border. The road was composed of stones in a slurry of mud; streams frequently channeled across. At one point we slued so sharply toward the edge that I inadvertently clutched at the Nepali interloper sitting next to me. He was kind enough to understand the distinction between terror and a pass.

At the customs office, next door to the bleak and dreary Zhangmu Hotel, the interlopers went through with no trouble while we filled out endless forms, showed our cameras and concealed our pictures of the Dalai Lama. Our Chinese guide urged us through this process. Passport control was run by a young Chinese who didn't look thirteen and sported a fragile moth of a moustache.

A walk about Zhangmu seemed limited in its attractions, yet better than sitting in the chilly concrete block hotel. The only road in town is a series of switchbacks connected by small alleys often in the form of stairs. We saw lots of lean dogs and houses with pots of flowers on their windowsills and balconies. On one balcony two luxurious, seafoam white sheepskin coats were spread out to air. Looking down at the roofs of the houses in the switchbacks below I could see that the thick shingles were held in place by stones, suggesting that nails were a rare commodity.

We passed a handsome woman, smoking a long-stemmed pipe, her hair swept back into a tight, shining, black bun, her neck encircled by large, irregular chunks of amber, playing a board game somewhere between chess and checkers against a male opponent. Judging by the bantering of bystanders she was winning.

Zhangmu before the 2015 earthquake. It rose in disheveled terraces up the walls of the gorge.

We were picked up by a little boy who wanted to show us his town. With great glee, he led us through the alleys that connected the switchbacks. These gave us views of tiny backyards planted with flowers and more windowsills on which pots and tin cans held marigolds, nasturtiums and geraniums. We gave him pictures of the Dalai Lama when we left him but he stood for a long time outside the hotel looking forlornly after us. It did not occur to me then that perhaps he had been hoping for a cash tip or handful of candies or pens.

The traffic jam above Zhangmu caused by a landslide. A porch has been built over the road to keep the waterfall from washing it out.

The next morning we were loaded on yet another bus but with unpainted windows. We were full of enthusiasm for cresting the pass and entering the Tibetan plain. But a few kilometers outside of town we stopped. The road had been washed out in a landslide during the night. Getting out to investigate we found that a waterfall gushing down the side of the gorge, leaping and vaulting over the boulders of the slide, was pummeling the place where a narrow ledge had served as the road.

Our guide insisted we had to clear the slide, since the Chinese army had, ironically, Sunday off. He appointed me, to my great embarrassment, "leader" of the group, probably because I was the eldest, making it my duty to tell my companions to clear the slide.

The landslide outside of Zhangmu that our Chinese guide expected us to repair, although he had the money to pay local people to do the work.

In talking to our guide, I discovered he had money from the agency for emergencies such as this, but if he didn't use the money it reverted to him, a sort of built-in tip. He was immoveable in his belief that we should do the work rather than having him hire local people. So we hefted and rolled large slabs of rock. The army, young and very drunk, much apparent at the side of the road swigging beer, smugly watched us lug stones to the edge to hurl them down accompanied by their empty beer bottles.

The gorge with its waterfalls.

The narrow ledge-road of boulders we had rolled into place was deemed sufficient. A Land Rover, containing three Belgian widows, went first without any difficulty. Then the first bus attempted to cross. It stuck right in the middle of the repaired slide. The drivers tried pulling it out with the Land Rover, but that didn't work. The men then got behind it and pushed but it lurched at such an angle that we were all sure it was going to turn over on its side and slither down into the gorge with its driver. The Chinese Army watched with great interest through unfocused eyes.

Finally the first bus was successfully pushed and pulled across. Our bus followed with no trouble but we all walked across the slide rather than riding over our repaired road.

Driving up to the top of the pass, we looked into the depths of the amazing, frightening gorge clothed in dark trees garlanded with pale moss among which spill slender, white threads of plummeting falls. The trees lean out reaching for sun from the sheer cliffs on which they grow. Across the chasm we could see water shimmering down slabs of exposed rock while below the dirt and rock route turned hairpins, a gleaming gray snakeskin.

At one point there was a rude wooden canopy over the road to protect it from a waterfall that with liquid fists hammered at it and then spouted out beyond the road into space. A little further on we had to stop for a flock of sheep with horns twisted like wrung-out washcloths, their bells and bleats the only sound in the silence of the chasm.

The gorge. The road is a barely discernible line on the left.

The view from under the porch that protects the road from the waterfall.

At the top of the gorge, when we crested the pass, the world changed as though by the magic wave of a wand. This was another kind of border, a natural demarcation between the lushness, the green that the water in the gorge brings and the stark mineral theater of rock, ridge, and mountain that marks its absence. Ascetic and barren, it was heart-stoppingly magnificent. We looked down occasionally into valleys made green by rivers in gravel beds that twisted like yarn a cat has played with; but where we were, at about 7,500 feet and climbing, all was dry, bony and stark.

At the top of the pass above the green gorge you are in the rain shadow of the Himalayas.

I shared a room with an Australian girl, an easygoing, pretty blond, who was accused at a checkpoint (there were many of these testifying to Chinese uneasiness about their control of Tibet) of having taken a picture of it; one of many forbidden activities I was to find. The young soldier in charge of the post, a white-washed, mud-brick rectangle in the middle of nowhere, leapt into our bus, marched up and down the aisle in a fury, grimacing fiercely, shouting and waving his arms about. It was hard to take him seriously since he looked no older than fifteen. We sat silently, staring out the window at two Tibetans standing on either side of a wooden frame from which hung the skinned, bloody carcasses of two goats, a Tibetan roadside stand. As the soldier returned down the aisle still yelling, I whispered to my roommate to slip her film down her cleavage. She did.

Besides my Australian roommate, there were an English couple, soft spoken and loving toward each other, but beginning to feel sick because of the altitude, the Italian doctor, his voluble, charming wife, a Danish couple, and a German man. The Chinese soldier, having had his tantrum had to let us go since he couldn't imprison us in his mud-brick rectangle. I suppose the drama reassured him about his importance.

Later that afternoon, we sighted a procession of farming families heading up a mountain path carrying flags, including a Chinese flag, the Tibetan flag being forbidden, with flowers and food to celebrate their harvest with their elderly monk on a horse so small his stirruped feet were only inches from the ground.

The harvest procession. The Chinese flag is being carried to protect them from any accusations by local cadres or Chinese police/military of being anti-Chinese.

The Italian doctor, Alessandro, shot, a cork from a bottle of Asti Spumante, off the bus, camera at the ready, racing on his chubby, short legs to be the first and he was. No mean feat at that altitude and a more likely way of getting a heart attack than looking down into a gorge.

The harvest procession in their best clothes headed up the mountain to give thanks. They are carrying other flags beside the Chinese flag, but not the Tibetan flag which it is illegal to display or own.

Jumping off the bus I had a try at running but decided it was not something I could do at that altitude. Walking up the incline to the procession, which had stopped to wait for us and our cameras, caused me to pant.

Women in the harvest processions wearing handwoven aprons; this signals that they are married.

Being photographed seemed just another part of their celebration to the Tibetan farmers and their wives. When we were done, had thanked them, given them some candy we had in our pockets, they continued up the mountain; we climbed back on the bus, exhilarated by the meeting.

Some of the men in the procession with the village drum. The boots, by the way, are hand made.

I knew from the trek I had made the year before in Bhutan that it would be days before I would be able to walk up a modest flight of stairs without heaving for breath at the top. I was also waiting for THE HEADACHE to hit. It is the most common bodily reaction to altitude, and I had my Tylenol at the ready. It hit that night, a feeling that my brains were growing inside my skull, pushing against the bone, trying to squeeze out in a mashed potato mass from my eyes and ears. But a Tylenol or two took care of the problem.

I am lucky that I have never had any of the more serious effects of altitude sickness, throwing up and sleeplessness often accompanied by a fear that one will not be able to get the next breath.

A view down into a valley from our unpaved road.

My funny, enjoyable companions distracted me from thinking of Aunt Liz, or even from concentrating on being in Tibet. The other impediment was that what we saw, both in the natural world and the sites we visited, put me on sensory and intellectual overload. I need to be alone with the unintelligible to begin to probe my way toward either understanding or just acceptance. Companions, however charming, interpose themselves inevitably between the incomprehensible, which is my goal, and me. What I don't understand is what fascinates me.

Me by the side of the road somewhere between Zhangmu and Tashilumphu. I am hugging myself because I am cold to my marrow.

We stopped at three important monasteries with their temples, *gompas,* in Tibetan. The first, Sakya, I found disappointing from the outside since it resembled a fortress, factory or prison, forbidding with its 100-meter long, red and brown windowless walls. There are no windows in *gompas,* light comes from butter lamps or from a skylight high above. Inside, beyond the enormous, at least twelve foot by twelve foot, heavy drape of a coarse felt curtain of yak hair, which keeps the wind out, and a confusing set of vestibule-like rooms, we entered a large chamber with pillars, some made from single tree trunks that reached into the gloom high overhead. It was morning; sun struck down from the skylight above in broad shafts dancing with dust motes. There were rows of cushions, a monk's red robe neatly folded on each and sometimes a yellow hat shaped like a cock's comb with fringe along its crest.

The silence was deep. The altars shimmered with gold deities, flickered with dozens of brass, yak butter lamps, their dancing flames reflected in pools of their melted grease. All was gold and fire in the darkness.

I was overwhelmed by the foreign, the unfathomable. I had certainly achieved what I wanted, to be in a place so alien to me that I understood nothing.

When young I had had no money to travel, being strapped to a frugal budget, although I had spent almost my entire pregnancy in Europe with a husband who had not enjoyed travel and who, being fearful of foreign food, had eaten steak and French fries with ketchup from England to Italy. Once my son was born, I had time to reflect on my months in Europe. I found that time interesting, a trip to grandmother's house where all was older, grander, and more finely done but familiar. I enjoyed connecting the political, cultural and historical dots in England and France, the art history dots in Italy. Yet there was something I wanted that wasn't there, although I wasn't sure what that misty wraith of desire was.

Sixteen years later, divorced, in 1974, with said son in tow, having had a windfall of three thousand dollars from the sale of a piece of furniture I had inherited, I took off for Iran where a friend had a Fulbright to teach at the University of Teheran. I did this despite knowing that I was likely to lose my job in the next year or so and might need that money for bottles of milk. We spent twenty-eight days in Iran traveling, mainly by bus, to Isfahan, Shiraz, Yazd, Kerman and Bam.

Returning, I again reflected. This had been much more what I wanted from travel. The mosques in Isfahan, the shimmering, aquatic blues of their tiles, enthralled me. The pillars of Persepolis in the wind-stirred desert near Shiraz and the ruins of the citadel at Bam that culminated, after a steep climb, in a courtyard with a ruined fountain as its centerpiece and an unobstructed view across the desert to Afghanistan had awakened me to my ignorance about this part of the world, to the undiscovered histories of places that had been before my trip merely names on maps.

But there are places where the culture eases your passage and places where the culture sets up walls with broken glass on top. For most western women, certainly for me, the Moslem milieu is definitely a razor-wire experience. When my son and I waited in a bus station, the entire room would fix their eyes on me and never remove them. If I looked at a woman across the room and smiled, probably feebly, no answering smile appeared. I learned to immerse myself in a book while we waited for our bus, never looking up. I have rarely felt as dehumanized and objectified anywhere in the world.

However, Iran made me realize for the first time that what I wanted from travel was adventure, which meant, for me, being in an incomprehensible culture. I wanted to be an ignorant outsider. Adventure was finding my way in an alien milieu.

After Iran, again I had no money to travel. Then in 1979 I had saved up enough for another trip. I had intended to keep on going from Iran into Afghanistan, even though it was Moslem, but that year the Russians invaded Afghanistan. I was teaching at the University of Idaho, Moscow, prowling the campus in a huffy grumble about how I couldn't go to Afghanistan. Someone suggested I contact a professor of anthropology who was taking a group of mostly graduate students to Nepal. I located Nepal on a map, not being sure exactly where it was, over near India was my guess. I found it, a slice of meat between the bread of Tibet and India. I called the anthropology professor and went.

When I got out of the plane at what was more a mud-brick shed than an airport and saw the grinning faces of snotty-nosed children peering over a wall with a backdrop of terraces planted with potatoes and corn made greener by the rosy bricks piled around the chimney of a nearby kiln, and rising above all of these the gold tops of shrines shimmering among the trees on mountain sides, I thought, "I've found it. I bet I don't understand anything here."

Another encouraging gift from Nepal was my first copy of *The Lonely Planet Guide to Southeast Asia,* the only guide for backpackers at that time. I doubt that I knew what a backpacker was, although I was about to become one. I had never seen such a book. Like most

Americans I had assumed one was chained to the expense and the insipidness of middle-class hotels. What the *Lonely Planet* offered me was an incredible freedom that made me shivery with excitement. It didn't just expand my world; it blew it wide open, making available to me the back streets, indigenous restaurants and cheap guesthouses of Asia. I was like someone who having only traveled on super highways discovers the tree-edged blue highways of America. I came across this precious dog-eared, little, yellow book while wandering the street of Tamil in Kathmandu lying on a torn piece of fabric in the roadside dust. It was for sale with other paperbacks abandoned by travelers, mostly in English. I bought it and studied it with the intensity of a child memorizing the Koran. Although long since out dated that volume is still on my bookshelf.

My incomprehension was overwhelming as I stood in Sakya, but the irony was that the temple also had a whiff of familiarity. As in the Catholic churches of my childhood, there were a multiplicity of statues, an abundance of decoration, butter lamps instead of candles it is true, but a similar darkness with soaring pillars and ceilings. However, despite the slight familiarity, I could no more think of Aunt Liz in this strange locale than I could think of a pastrami sandwich.

I felt lost despite the notes of familiarity in the resemblance to a Catholic church. I was listening to a strange melody. The strength of the spiritual was as strong as my pulse in this place, but I was lost in its alien spirituality. I was standing in the midst of a void, isolated in a the quarantined circle of incomprehension I could not transcend. It was lonely.

Our Chinese guide was largely useless due to a combination of arrogance—nothing here could be of value because it was Tibetan not Chinese—and ignorance, although he told us he had graduated from college as a major in Minority Cultures, and finally his accent which made him difficult to understand. But if he had been immeasurably learned in Tibetan culture and had spoken English with perfect clarity, it wouldn't have made much difference. The shock of lack of recognition was so immense that I was not able to take information in, although the temple did remind me of the temples I had seen and also not understood in Mongolia. Our guide recited for us the names of various deities, but my brain seemed to have acquired a Teflon coating; the names, alien and exotic rather than penetrating, slipped right off. I took to jotting things down, spelling by ear, in hopes that this would help me retain some names. It seemed a good place to start.

It was apparent that our guide was uncomfortable and wanted to leave the temple. I could understand why. The atmosphere was as saturated with an intense human sensation of the spiritual as it was with the odor of yak butter. His patron saint was Karl Marx, rational, operating within a presumption of historical logic. Here the patron saints had fangs, bulbous eyes, and lolling tongues. Their job was to protect you from committing evil thoughts and deeds; rationality did not strike me as being a part of their creed.

What he was unable to supply in the way of information I acquired later by reading. The pillars that impressed me were forty in number, and four, formed from single trunks, were particularly noteworthy. One was a gift of Kublai Khan, an important supporter of the monastery. It had been hand delivered from China. Another, according to legend, had been carried by a tiger that died once it arrived with its burden. The tiger's skin is attached to its pillar. I didn't see this or saw it and it didn't register on my Tefloned brain. Another was transported on the horns of a black yak. The fourth came from a tree inhabited by a spirit which, when the tree was chopped down, bled black blood from the cut. In Buddhism, the natural world and the creed are not isolated from each other. There is a mutual dependency between them.

That night we ate at a local Tibetan restaurant, not that there was anything else available, where, since there was no menu, we went into the kitchen in order to point out what we wanted to eat. There was no refrigerator, the packed dirt floor was shiny and slippery with grease, but there was a huge, scarred and cracked chopping block, the base of a tree, with hunks of various kinds of meat lying beside a wicked looking cleaver, and wilted vegetables in heaps. On a shelf that ran along the wall were open bags of noodles and rice. We pointed to the meat and various vegetables, deciding one dish for all of us would be simpler. It was a stir-fry meal, not unlike a Chinese stir-fry but with chilies, making it hot. We asked for a bowl of rice and another of noodles to accompany it, a good choice since the latter turned out to be homemade.

The kitchen was as much a lesson in Tibetan hygiene as the dining room was a lesson in the weight of Chinese authority. The dining room walls were covered with signs in Tibetan that we asked our guide to translate. They said things like, "A friend of the police is a friend of the country." The myths of lumber-toting tigers are beautiful but the reality of tyranny spread a chill over dinner as we ate beneath these clichés of oppression.

Our next stop was Shigatze and the Tashilumphu monastery, home of the Panchen Lama, with its *gompas*, and a golden Buddha two stories high. I had to throw back my head to look up into his blue eyes. I wonder why Tibetan Buddhas have blue eyes? They also, sometimes, have blue hair. I have never received an answer to this. In another building there was a *chörten*, the tomb of a former Panchen Lama that looked like a baroque brooch in gold, set with turquoise and other gems.

Tashilhumpu Monastery once the home of the Panchen Lama.

The word *chörten*, according to Victor Chan's mammoth *Tibet Handbook*, the bible of all of us who are obsessed by Tibet, literally means, "receptacle for offerings." It is a tiered monument, an adaptation of the solid dome of the Indian stupa, a Buddhist structure that you circle to the left, clockwise. All holy things in Buddhism are circumambulated clockwise. This practice is so ingrained that horses will pass any object by circling to the left. In India it was customary to bury the remains of revered Buddhists in stupas. Tibetan *chörtens* frequently contain relics but they are also constructed as an offering, an expression of gratitude, or as a memorial of an event.

The turquoise swastika set into the floor of the entrance to one of Tashilumphu's temples. The swastika, whose arms go in the opposite direction from the Nazi emblem, is a symbol of spiritual strength.

I remembered the bejeweled *chörten,* the gold, blue-eyed Buddha and a swastika, perhaps two feet square, composed of black-veined slabs of turquoise set into the pavement before the entrance of one of the *gompas.* The swastika in Tibetan Buddhism is a symbol of spiritual strength. Its arms flow in the opposite direction to the Nazi symbol. All other objects and buildings evanesced into an alien blur.

The man with the coral and turquoise earring who gave me permission to take his picture at Tashilumphu Monastery.

As I walked around the monastery I saw a bucktoothed older man with a bead of turquoise and another of coral on a thread through one of his ears, a poor man's earring. We smiled shyly at each other. I pointed at my camera and then at him. He nodded his permission. I was thrilled since I am hesitant to photograph people. It feels intrusive, true, but it also feels to me as though a photographer is taking specimens the way a lepidopterist pins still living butterflies to a board.

Tashilumphu has a central court with hundreds of Buddhas painted on its walls. I watched a nomad woman, one of a party walking around it, in her *chuba,* the Tibetan wraparound dress, edged with snow leopard fur, a large heavily embossed silver and turquoise talisman box hanging from her neck, a massive belt of silver around her waist and her baby on her back in a sling. At each small Buddha on the court wall she touched first her head, from which her hair hung in 108 braids, the sacred number whether in braids or prayer beads. Then she reached back tenderly and bent her child's head in reverence to the image. The importance of 108 comes from the fact that the *Kanjur*, the teachings of the Buddha, which is found usually wrapped in brocade, in *gompas*, contains 108 volumes. The ends of all the braids were tied together so that they formed a moving black curtain. I decided I would have to hold her in my memory. I didn't have the nerve to ask her for a photograph.

I realized she was on pilgrimage, perhaps going on to Lhasa and that her clothes, which were so grand, and to my Western cultural eyes magnificently medieval, that I had difficulty not staring at them, had been bought or made with her own hands specifically in honor of the occasion. Even in the America of my childhood people dressed up to travel. My mother had a blue silk travel suit reserved for plane and train journeys.

A young man who also gave me permission to photograph him.

That night I had a nightmare in which I was tested on the names of deities we had seen during the day, but I was not able to recall any of them. I wanted to remember everything. I may not have thought of Aunt Liz all day as I tried to digest what I was seeing, but it didn't seem to me, logical or illogical as the thought may be, that I was doing a proper job of making her trip if I couldn't remember the names of the things I saw. I wanted desperately to do the trip for her perfectly since I thought it my one chance to make this gift to her.

Our last temple and monastery before arriving in Lhasa, where there awaited us an indigestible number of *gompas* and monasteries, was in

Gyantze. The drive from Shigatze to Gyantze was largely along tree-lined roads through cultivated land with whitewashed, mud brick houses dotted among the fields. These were embraced by walls on whose wide ledges were neatly stacked dried cowpats, cut brush and roots for burning. There are no trees in central Tibet except for occasional willows along the rivers; therefore, dried cowpats, actually yak pies, are used as fuel. Sometimes I could see over the walls and glimpse a south facing balcony, painted with flowers and the Buddhist symbols, a hand-woven rug hanging over its rail to air.

People harvested by hand with sickles, threshed on foot-pounded, dusty squares next to the fields, stacked sheaves and tied them into hayricks. Although the backdrop to this labor were forbidding lines of barren mountains, still I felt that here humans and soil were bound together, the land a living, unsubdued, unquenchable and vibrant creature.

As we came into town, people passed us in carts with wooden wheels pulled by prancing little horses, tassels and bells adorning their halters.

One woman, whose braids, wound around her head, had pink and blue fringe woven into them, smiled at us as she waved with a flourish of her whip. Her gay figure and her little horse's dainty prance were the embodiment of the town of Gyantze for me as I fell in love with it at first sight. The street to the monastery was paved with huge stones, lined with old Tibetan houses, their windows full of leggy geraniums, their roofs at each corner bristling with bare withes of willow branches wound with prayer flags and *khatas* going ragged in the wind.

The main street of Gyantze
leading to the monastery.

A girl in Gyantze with slivers of turquoise in her ears and bobby pins on her *chuba*. Her friend is using her as a shield from the camera.

The entrance to the Gyantze Monastery with a view of the walls that surround it. In the center of the wall, the object that looks like it might be an out door movie screen, is a wall on which huge tapestries are hung on festival days.

Prayer flags are small, usually dinner-napkin-sized, pieces of fabric in white, red, green, yellow and blue, printed with prayers which the wind's breath will send all over the world for every sentient being. The usual image on a prayer flag is of a wind horse since it was, or perhaps still is believed that, when the winds blow the flag, Buddha will deliver horses to needy travelers. Seeing a little string of prayer flags on a fire escape in New York or a balcony in Barcelona or London always makes me feel I have had a secret moment of sharing with a stranger.

We went to the main temple first, the Pulchor Chode, of which I later found that all I could recall was the protector chapel hung with masks of animals and demons, their bared fangs glinting in the gloom and a painting of a vulture pecking out a dead man's eye. Tibetans are not reticent about death, nor do they prettify it. A protector chapel houses the fierce spirits that guard the local area or all of Tibet. These are also the deities who protect people from the evils of this world. They are former Bön deities, Bön being the earlier religion of Tibet.

Later I read that Guru Rinpoche, also called Padmasambava, thereby confusing the Westerner, a holy practitioner of Buddhism's mystical arts, when he entered Tibet from Swat, now an area of Muslim Pakistan, encountered the demons who lived in the Tibetan earth. They wanted to force him back off their terrain because in Tibet they were the owners of the earth and had to be appeased since they threatened the villagers and their crops. The people had been making offerings to them and worshiping them. Every mountain pass in Tibet still has its resident demon whom it is wise to supplicate.

It is difficult to think of two more opposite religious creeds than the calm, intellectual Buddha and the tongue thrusting, fanged, bug-eyed Bön gods. Through his mystical and magical abilities Guru Rinpoche converted these gods to Buddhism, making them swear to protect the new faith. Getting the Bön deities to defend the Buddhists and Buddhism was a brilliant way of incorporating the old religion into the new so that there would not be strife between the two.

Changing religions tends to make people paranoid. This incorporation of the Bön gods into Buddhism is similar to a phenomenon I became aware of when I visited Norwegian stave churches, extraordinarily carved, wooden, Viking but Christian, churches. The old Norse gods were carved into the pillar heads at the top of the church so Odin, Riga, Loki and Thor could and can look down upon the altar of the new god. I don't know if they were expected to worship the new god but certainly they were put in a position where they had to acknowledge him.

It is thought that when the Danes transferred their belief from Odin to Christ they may have dug up their former chieftains, who had adhered to the old pagan faith, and pitched them into the sea. Certainly their skeletons are not in their barrows.

Humans are rather apt to hedge their bets when changing religions. Like toddlers learning to walk, they keep a hand on where they have been, as they move to where they are going.

The Gyantze Kumbum built in the shape of a *chörten* houses 64 temples filled with 15th century paintings and recent statues that are replacements for those smashed in the Cultural Revolution.

The Kumbum next door with its delicate, tiered, wedding cake exterior was even better than the monastery. Just within the entrance, the monk/caretaker's apartment had, on a windowsill, a buffet of dahlias, begonias, geraniums and zinnias potted in tin cans. A boy, a monklet in red robes, asked in his limited English, where I was from. I told him the United States and gave him a picture of the Dali Lama.

Flowers in pots and tin cans at the window of the monk's residence at the entry of the Kumbum.

Recognizing me as a source for Dali Lama pictures he urged me to give one to his teacher, a smiling elder monk, and then to each of the women pilgrims coming through the door. As I did, each touched the photo to her forehead reverently; even a toddler did this with no urging, as the woman at Tashilumphu touched her head and her baby's to the paintings of the Buddha.

Our guide didn't see me hand out the pictures or I might have been reprimanded, as my Australian roommate was when he caught her giving them to Tibetans. It was not at that time illegal to give pictures of the Dali Lama, as it is now, but it was much frowned upon as supporting the enemy of China. A few years later you were arrested if you gave a picture of the Dali Lama to a Tibetan. There were pictures of the Dali Lama available in Tibet then, but those that were brought in by visitors were considered more precious by the Tibetans because they came from the part of the world where he was living.

The Kumbum's interior consisting of sixty-four, small, cave-like temples, exquisitely painted in the sixteenth century with images of monks, abbots, fanged and fearsome deities, many armed and many-headed, or female spirits with wasp-waists and navel-orange sized breasts, enchanted me. The delicate structure of the Kumbum was a delight in itself. The female spirits dainty, with serene smiles, gesturing with slender fingers, I found magical. They could have flitted out of a Tolkien novel, relatives of Galadriel, denizens of Lothlórien. There were also airy scenes taking place in vividly green forests and meadows of the Buddha's previous lives. I wandered in and out of these chapels, stunned between old paintings and new statues. The old statues were smashed during the Cultural Revolution and have been replaced by gaudy, but not unhandsome, new ones.

A deity on the wall of the Gyantze Kumbum. This picture was taken without a flash.

A multi-headed deity on the wall of the Kumbum.

The Cultural Revolution, 1966 to 1976, occurred when Mao Zedong sent students, instituting them as Red Guards, into the streets, giving them the power, carte blanche, to attack signs of tradition, the elderly, teachers, intellectuals, craftsmen, anyone perceived as having "bourgeois" values. In China proper, his intent was to eradicate the traditional values of the Chinese people which respected the learned, the old, the skilled, the intelligent. Through all this destruction he hoped to create a time gap during which the old ways, thoughts and traditions would be forgotten and forever lost.

One of the replacement statues in the Kumbum. All statues here were destroyed during the Cultural Revolution, 1966 to 1976 when Mao died.

One deity in a tiny dark chapel held a pair of dentures between his hands. His iconographic symbolism was and is a mystery to me; although I later looked him up in various books, I have found no information on him. Is he the god of toothaches, as logic would suggest? In Kathmandu I had seen on a street in the district of Tamil a toothache god, now disintegrated beyond recognition through the attentions of its worshipers. It is a piece of wood which has become armored with coins nailed into what remains of the wood. The coins are offerings from toothache sufferers of whom, over the years, there have apparently been enough to destroy the god.

The walk back to our hotel was magical. I watched a man buy bells for his horse, a woman sitting with her child knitting, a man striding along in a fierce moustache and black Stetson-type hat, with cubes of yak cheese threaded on string swinging from his belt. Children called out as we passed. I noticed a young man bicycling ahead of me. There was something indefinable about his posture or perhaps his clothes, although they were as dust encrusted as everyone else's and were not noticeably Western, that made me think he was a Westerner. When he turned into a gate I saw his profile; he was a Westerner. So, somehow, it was possible to avoid being on a tour. It could be done. But how? Quite unconsciously, only a few days into my first trip, I was gathering information for my return.

Our hotel was a recently built but already dilapidated Chinese cement block structure whose rooms turned out to be carpeted with what looked like red felt embedded with cigarette butts and bobby pins. The next morning, perhaps in subconscious recognition that I was planning to return, I had *tsampa*, ground, roasted barley, a staple of the Tibetan diet, mixing it with yak cheese and yak butter tea as a sort of breakfast porridge. It tasted quite all right. I had not yet worked up the nerve to drink yak butter tea straight up. Maybe that culinary venture would signal my final commitment to returning and I was not quite there yet.

Getting back on our bus, which looked like an aged, retired school bus, I thought I had the beginnings of a cold. Not being knowledgeable yet about the effects of altitude, I didn't realize that this sensation was the classic symptom caused by altitude, aridity and dust, which combine to dry out your nose while inflaming your sinuses. This usually causes blood scabs in the nose.

En route to Lhasa we stopped at a glacier whose edge looked like the puckered poufs that are piped from a cake decorating tube. Nearby were black nomad tents around which yaks with long belly hair grazed. We stopped for a photo and a man, one of the yak herders, came up to watch us with his three children. He was sewing a boot made of yak felt. People were always working. A woman watching sheep kept her spindle revolving.

Sera Monastery, north of Lhasa, fits quietly into the mountain's creases and crevices.

We went over a pass, coming down to follow the river through sandy places with dunes followed by fertile villages until we saw ahead of us the red and white striped towers of the Potala.

In Lhasa we stayed at the Holiday Inn. I felt, as if I were spending my nights in Cincinnati and my days in Lhasa. The cultural split was discombobulating. We were taken on the usual tourist round—the Potala, Sera Monastery, the Jokhang, (the St. Peters of Tibetan Buddhism), and the Norbulingka, the Dalai Lama's summer residence.

Sera is famous for the debates held in its courtyard between young monks.

At Sera I walked through the courtyard paved with large, dark grey, river stones where the young monks, supervised by older ones, debated. The young monk who was presenting the doctrinal ideas would clap his hands sharply when he made a point and then draw his right hand back along his left arm. It was a graceful, yet emphatic gesture which all of us tourists tried to capture with our cameras.

The Sera monks debating. When a challenger makes his point he claps his hands with a graceful gesture that ends with a sharp report.

Alessandro's wife went off into a corner of the courtyard to practice the gesture, which obviously delighted her. The monks ignored us completely. The rest of the monastery faded into a jumble of buildings, and the Jokhang was a crowded, dark place full of indistinguishable statues, butter lamps and the odor of yak butter, which I was beginning to like.

A dragon finial on a roof of Sera.

The Buddhist wheel of dharma, the Dharmachakra, on a roof of Sera Monastery, with eight spokes symbolizing the eight-fold path. It is guarded by two deer from the Deer Park of Sarnath.

Roofs of Sera.

A monklet hurtling down the stairs of Sera Monastery.

The Norbulingka stood out only because one mural caught both my eye and imagination.

The Norbulingka is a group of summer residences of the Dalai Lamas. This was the summer home of the present Dalai Lama.

I stopped before it trying to imagine what this series of pictures, rather like a cartoon sequence, could be about. The central figure seemed to be a monkey, dressed as a monk, who was having dealings with an extremely large, ugly woman and a man who looked to me like an abbot because of his hat. I asked our Chinese guide who told me, his voice drenched in scorn, that the Tibetans believe they are the progeny of a monkey monk and an ogress who was infatuated with him. She threatened that if he didn't marry her and satisfy her lust she would go off with a fellow ogre and populate the world with little ogres. The monkey monk, in a bit of a fix, consulted his abbot who urged him to marry the ogress, which he did. They produced children who were half monkey, half ogre in both looks and behavior.

I was fascinated since as far as I know the Tibetans are the only people who figured out the monkey/human connection without the aid of Darwin, recognizing that convergence over two thousand years before his theory. It certainly suggests that the Tibetans have a far less romantic notion of the uniqueness of humans than we Westerners have. Of course, the legend also neatly accounts for the fact that humans paradoxically unite within themselves diametrically opposed abilities for good and evil.

A young monk at the entrance to the Norbulingka. In a society with cameras one learns how to arrange one's face for a picture. In a culture without cameras you just look at the device.

Whenever the group was given free time I snuck off to try to locate a guesthouse to stay in when I would be on my own. I couldn't afford to remain at the Holiday Inn and didn't want to. One of the problems with middle class hotels, or upper class for that matter anywhere in the world, is that none of your fellow guests will talk to you, except the staff who are paid to do so, because it isn't respectable to strike up a conversation with a single woman. This can make for acute loneliness.

I had read in the *Lonely Planet* about four backpacker hotels, the Banak Shol, the Kirey, the Yak and the Snowlands located somewhere near the Jokhang temple. I hailed a rickshaw, which had ruffles, striped in blue, red and yellow around its canopy, and asked for the Banak Shol. I was puzzled when the driver dropped me in front of the Jokhang but we were at a linguistic deadlock so I gave up and walked about the square before the temple saying, "Banak Shol" to anyone who would listen to me, hoping someone would give me directions. Most of the Tibetans just gave me an odd look and went on their way, but two thoughtful women motioned me up an alley where I found a public toilet, a good and kindly, if in this case incorrect, guess. It was also an education. There were trenches, which presumably were washed out occasionally, but at that moment they were full and very odiferous.

I found out later that the area around the Jokhang is locally known as Banak Shol. Therefore, it was as though I had stood in the middle of Times Square asking for Times Square.

Feeling discouraged, I started to pull out my *Lonely Planet* when a Nepali man, who told me he was in Tibet buying antiques, asked me in English if he could help. I explained that I was looking for a guesthouse or hotel called, the Banak Shol. He offered to take me there on his motorcycle. I had some years before, in Sukhothai, Thailand, accepted a motorcycle ride, after stranding myself in over 100-degree sun on a road among rice paddy fields with no water bottle. The driver was packing a revolver in a holster, not quite concealed by his decorously pulled down tee shirt, therefore, there seemed no reason to turn down this offer.

Along the way my driver pointed out other hotels. Standing in the courtyard of the Banak Shol, I could smell their toilets. The rooms were dreary and not very clean, although there was a pleasant looking restaurant. The Kirey was only slightly better. I walked on toward the Yak passing an elderly woman, sitting near some billiard tables on the street, knitting wool socks for sale. I was beginning to feel discouraged but the Yak cheered me up. I couldn't smell the bathroom until I was in it and it looked clean.

The Yak was built, as are all old Tibetan hotels, like a caravansary with rooms around a courtyard open to the sky. Caravansaries were the inns along the Silk Road, where caravans stopped, rectangular buildings with rooms around their perimeter and an open space in the middle for stabling animals and cooking over open fires.

At the Yak, the gate into the courtyard, barred at night with a huge wooden beam, was twenty feet high and wide enough for a truck to drive through. During the day it was kept under surveillance by a smiling elderly man who always said *tashi dilay* to me every time I went in or out. The hotel's rooms were painted with Tibetan scenes of hermitages and mountains and the eight auspicious Buddhist symbols: the conch symbolizing the melodious sound of the Buddha's teaching, the eternal knot representing interdependence, the parasol which protects from suffering, the fish symbolizing fearlessness, the vase full of inexhaustible prosperity and long life, the lotus for purity, the banner for victory over disharmony and the wheel of the Buddha's teachings. My room, crammed with brightly painted furniture, had gilded dragons dancing on the scarlet ceiling. Casement windows, their mullions painted sunshine yellow, looked out on the court that formed the center of the hotel physically and socially. There were large concrete basins for washing clothes and benches on which to sit and talk with fellow travelers. I told the manager, whom I couldn't bargain down from his price of eight dollars a day, that I'd return the next day.

That evening when I again had time on my own I went downstairs in the Holiday Inn to the CITS office, the official Chinese tourist bureau, filled with nice, polite people who have traveled very little, to arrange my flight out. I was nervous about this. What would happen to me if I didn't get this flight set up? What if there was some sort of confusion? I did not want to end up in a Chinese jail. I said to the head man, after arranging to bring him the payment for the flight the next day, "When my group leaves tomorrow I'm moving out of the Holiday Inn. It's too expensive for me."

"You can't do that," he said, horrified. "It's against the rules."

"Still, I'm moving out. I am being very honest with you. I would appreciate it if you would be honest with me."

"Well, he said reluctantly, "If the police ask whether you came in with a group or alone, say you are traveling alone."

This information caused me to ruminate caustically on the ethics of the tour operator who had given me the extension but no information.

I thought I would miss my group when they left, and I did until I left the Holiday Inn. I was also a bit frightened until I left, worried about the Chinese authorities. The Holiday Inn was so obviously their turf. I had lost my sunglasses. My Australian roommate lent me hers; I mailed them back to her from the U.S. Alessandro, the doctor kindly gave me some antibiotics because I was running a temperature of 101 with no other symptoms.

But the hard part of my entry into my new life was physically getting out of the hotel, which I had hoped to do unobtrusively. If you lug a thirty-pound backpack at 12,000 feet through the lobby of the Holiday Inn in Lhasa with your face the color of a bullfighter's cape you are not unobtrusive. It was obvious to me, and everyone in the lobby, that I was on the verge of a coronary explosion. I got to a rickshaw whose driver charged twice what I had paid previously. I was in no condition to argue, but I arrived at the Yak safe and sound.

Because of the fever, I decided to hang out at the Yak for a day and do nothing. It was an entertainment just to be in my room with its creamy yellow walls afloat with pink lotuses. If I lay on my back I could look up at the dragons on the ceiling their bulbous eyes full of joyous mischief, their pink tongues curling out of their mouths. I did take a short walk to a market for toilet paper. You have to provide your own at most guesthouses.

The walk, much of it along the Barkhor, the street that encircles the Jokhang temple, embodied all that had been missing from the tour. The area around the Yak had not been rebuilt in the Chinese concrete style that was replacing all of the original buildings. It was still full of old Tibetan houses, above whose windows, on the outside, red, yellow and blue ruffles whiffled in the breeze while below on window sills flowers bloomed in rusty tin cans. The effect was very cheerful on a bright,

The Barkhor as it used to be, bustling with stalls and shops.

wind-swept day. As I came to the square in front of the Jokhang temple I saw people prostrating themselves again and again as they approached the entrance, before which are several large urns where juniper is continually burned as incense.

The Jokhang, the St. Peter's of Tibetan Buddhism, encircled by the Barkhor, the sacred path around it.

The pilgrimage to Lhasa is a lifetime ambition for Tibetans and often they expend all of their money on the trip to the city. To earn funds to return home they sell their daggers, their jewelry or sit in a circle before the Jokhang playing flutes and strumming homemade mandolin-like instruments. I watched men with powerful shoulders and high cheekbones, their skin the color of a dried tobacco leaf, play an assortment of flutes. We passersby threw money into the center of their circle.

People playing music in the square before the Jokhang to earn money for their return trip to home after spending everything on the pilgrimage to Lhasa. The Jokhang would be the primary site of that pilgrimage. Notice the hefty young monk in his red robes.

But there were other beggars before the Jokhang. I eased my way into the center of one crowd to find a young woman in a basket, skeletal arms and legs twisted into contorted positions, although she was able to oscillate her head with a grimace to stare back at her starers with lively and intelligent eyes. Next to her on the ground was a white cloth on which was printed her story in Tibetan script with a brief translation in English. Her mother abandoned her and her siblings when she was sixteen. It was impossible to tell how old she was now.

A ragged old man twirling his prayer wheel took my arm, very gently, and examined my cheap watch with great care. Two men, obvious yokels from the way they were staring about them, passed me. One had a beautiful red fox pelt over his shoulder. The other was walking with a grotesquely, lumpily stuffed snow leopard slung around his shoulders like a boa. But I stared as much as the yokels, being a yokel from New York, at silk jackets lined with sheepskin, stalls where women and men sold carpets, Tibetan women's wraparound dresses, *chubas*, teapots, jewelry of every sort, religious articles, felt Stetsons, embroidered hats with ear flaps, prayer beads carved from yak bone, horse bells, prayer wheels, silver amulet boxes inlaid with turquoise, plastic shoes, great slabs of butchered yaks, haunches of goats and, outside one store, a tiger's skin nailed to a board. I felt transported to Marco Polo's time as I walked by Muslim teahouses selling noodles and lotus-seed tea or Nepali shops selling Indian snuff and biscuits. I was beginning to have the adventure I had hoped to have for both Aunt Liz and myself.

When not staring at shops and stalls I stared at people. Women wore earrings of twisted gold, or had turquoise beads braided into their hair or talisman boxes in silver and turquoise on handmade silver chains around their necks. They tied striped aprons over their *chubas*.

The *chuba* is a robe worn by both men and women. The female version is a wraparound sleeveless dress. Under it is worn a Chinese silk blouse. While the *chuba* is usually of a sober color in wool gabardine, the blouse may be either pastel or a vehement shade. The word "*chuba*" comes from the Arabic "juba" which is also the root of the French word "jupe." A striped apron, once handwoven from wool, is worn over the *chuba*; its colors denote what part of Tibet the wearer is from and that she is married. Now the apron, usually shiny rayon, is store bought.

Women also wore hats that designated their area of origin but those, magnificent affairs hand embroidered or of fur and brocade shot with gold, are now rarely seen. The one I ache to own is a cartwheel of crimson and gold brocade with curly, black sheep fur on its underside.

Then there were the men, equally striking, with faces the color of polished teak who threaded their long, shiny, black hair through a bone ring and knotted it up with a length of scarlet fringe or fastened it with a silver barrette studded with coral and turquoise. They carried themselves like princes. They also wore *chubas*, but theirs were short jackets worn off one shoulder. The off-the-shoulder style is due to the fact that Tibetans, in the old days, were archers, and needed more freedom of movement than a sleeve would allow.

Back at the Yak I forced myself to rest until evening. I was very excited to be on my own and a little frightened. A group gives one a sense of being protected. I was feeling a bit naked being solo.

I went down the street to eat at the Tashi restaurant, which I had also read about in my *Lonely Planet*. There I met my fellow backpackers over yak burgers and listened to them talk–they were the knowledgeable ones and I the one in need of instruction. Over those international backpacker specials–banana pancakes, spaghetti, and fried chicken–I become acquainted with the matrix of foreigners in Lhasa. Many had done a variation on what I had done, coming in on a tour from Kathmandu and then applying for an extension for their visa. Others had come in from Chengdu, the capital of Szechwan province in China, with a group that they left; others entered by bus from a town named Golmud, also in Szechwan. A very few had managed to come in solo through the luck of a lax border guard.

I met a young German woman, Annalisa, who was also living at the Yak. She kindly took me under her wing and the next day we walked the Barkhor, the street that circles the Jokhang temple in a sacred path. This was exceptionally nice of her since often, young women really don't want to have anything to do with older women travelers. It seems to me that this is particularly true of young American women who often look as though they are going to bolt if you so much as ask them for directions. I suppose it is a mother thing that they are terrified you will transform into their mother and start bossing them.

Annalisa explained to me that the Tibetans had their own version of what in the West would be called a "sacred way," named in Tibetan a *khora*. It may be around a *gompa*, a temple, as the Barkhor runs around the Jokhang temple, or it might encircle a *chörten* or it might be the trail around a sacred mountain. But it is always a path, a way, encircling something holy that you walk with spiritual intentions. It is different from the pilgrimage of, for instance, Santiago Compostela, in that it is circular, going around the object of veneration.

As we strolled around the Jokhang on the Barkhor, doing the *khora*, I noticed surveillance cameras positioned on lampposts around the square before the temple. The thought that some poor Chinese was sitting, duty bound, before a monitor somewhere in a room in the city watching, made it hard not to make a face into the camera. That night at the Tashi One Restaurant I commented on the cameras to a young

American who said blandly, "They must be there to track criminals, pickpockets." I was amazed at his innocence and naiveté.

In the morning I bought, under Annalisa's guidance, yogurt from an elderly woman who brought her yak yogurt to the hotel for sale. I gave her tourist money. The Chinese at that time had a dual monetary system, notes specifically for tourists, Foreign Exchange Certificates, and regular money for everyone else. She had never seen tourist money. I had never seen the regular Chinese money. Annalisa rescued us from our confusion. Yak yogurt is a little stronger in flavor than cow and very creamy.

Since my temperature was now normal, I decided to revisit some of the places I had already been to but hadn't been able to grasp. I took off for the Jokhang with Annalisa. This time, going at my own pace, rather than that enforced by a tour, I was able to get a much better sense of the temple from its dark corridors filled with brass prayer wheels and bright murals rippling across its uneven walls, to the roofs with their shinning gables of gilded copper from where we looked down on people prostrating before the temple in leather mitts and aprons that protected their hands and clothes.

People performing prostrations in front of the Jokhang, the St. Peter's of Tibetan Buddhism.

In one courtyard monks were playing the long, long, metal horns, their coppery mouths propped up on big wooden blocks.

I was able to concentrate on the blue-eyed Jowo in his arch of silver plated dragons. He is the image of Buddha that people come on pilgrimage from all over Tibet to see. I spent time in the main chanting chamber with its huge statue of Chenresi in gilded copper, whom I now knew was the god of compassion with eleven heads and a thousand arms with which to reach out to help humanity. The Dalai Lama is his living presence. Near by is Jampa, whom I realized five years later is the Buddha of the future.

The urns in which juniper is burned before the Jokhang. Inside the wall are two stone monuments. One erected in 823 commemorates a treaty between China and Tibet. The other, now illegible, gives instructions for the city in case of an outbreak of small pox.

Women washing sheets, towels, and household items during the Bathing Festival. Some young women are taking a tea break on the right.

Blankets and carpets laid out to dry in the Bathing Festival in Lhasa. People also bathe in the river but what one sees mostly is blankets, sheets, carpets and all kinds of coverlets washed and laid out to dry.

It was the day of a festival when people take things out of their homes and wash them in the river. A group of us from the Yak went to the island in the middle of the river and watched people with their children, bathing, washing rugs, washing robes and then laying them out on the sand or draping them on bushes to dry before settling down to picnic lunches.

That night I returned with Annalisa to the Jokhang to listen to the monks, sitting in their red robes in long rows to chant, accompanied by cymbals and drums. Some of them did deep throat chanting, also called over-tone singing, in which the voice is lowered to that of a Western *basso profundo*, or perhaps lower, a wonderful, growly sort of sound. Again, there was that echo of Catholicism, as the monks' canticles reminded me of Gregorian chants. I fantasized that Aunt Liz was leaning over the bar of Heaven listening to them. But I seemed to fall spiritually between my old, rejected Catholicism and the deep, tidal voices of these monks.

Returning to the Yak after dinner I was reading a guidebook in an attempt to get some of the names and postures of deities to stick in my brain—Chenresi has eleven heads and a thousand arms; Manjushri has a sword, Palden Lhamo wears an opera length strand of severed heads and rides a donkey—when there was a knock on my door.

"Madame, may I enter your room?" It was not really a question.

I opened the door to find two ever-so-polite policemen in crisply ironed green uniforms.

"May I see your passport," asked one.

I rummaged in my pack and handed it over silently, although my heart was making a noise like the percussion section of the New York Philharmonic playing the 1812 Overture.

"Did you come to Lhasa with a group or alone?" he asked.

"Alone," I replied with a cold spot at the base of my spine, the "zero at the bone" that Emily Dickinson felt upon unexpectedly seeing a snake.

"Thank you, Madame," he said returning my passport.

And that was that.

The next day I returned to the Potala where I saw nomad women whose *chubas* have large, bright patches of primary colors on them performing a foot stomping dance, a circle of brilliantly colored swaying skirts, in one of the chapels before the images. The odor of yak butter was overwhelming and the bannisters slick from hands greasy with yak butter.

The Potala that housed government offices, a university, the treasury, an enormous library, temples and the Dalai Lama's home in Lhasa.

Out of town monks on the path to the Dragla Lugug cave temples playing for contributions to support their monastery. Since many monasteries are rural they do not have enough support for their population.

Even Tibetans pause for breath on the stairs to the cave temples of Dragla Lugug.

I went on to climb up to the Dragla Lugug temple walking along a lane fluttering with prayer flags and lined with women beggars and *mani* stone carvers displaying their wares. Above them were brightly painted Buddhas cut into the rock. The temple was created from caves on the hill. In one of the cave-chapels, among the more usual images was, under a fringed hat, a nasty grin with uneven teeth. I bent down to see what was up under the hat and found myself staring into a pair of fierce round eyes. He was hung with necklaces, offerings from women. But what would you request from this deity with angry eyes and ripsaw teeth?

The Potala seen from a terrace of Dragla Lugug.

From the terraces of these chapels I looked out to the Potala, a white and red composition of towers and terraces.

I took a bus to Drepung Monastery with a young Englishman I had met at dinner the night before. The walk from the main road was a chest heaver since it was up hill all the way. My companion argued about the entrance price and, to my astonishment, got us in for half price. The huge complex with fifty to sixty houses built from the 17th to the 18th century was just as confusing to me as it had been the first time, full of bookcases stuffed with brocade wrapped volumes of the *Kanjur*, the Buddhist scriptures, and a room painted black with fierce images of various deities outlined in gold. We stood for a while on the terrace in front of one of the *lhakhangs*, an assembly hall, which overlooks Lhasa and its green river valley.

One of the many buildings of Drepung Monastery.

Boulders painted with important Tibetan Buddhist personalities. I think the near one is Tsong Khapa (1357-1419), founder of the Gelugpa order to which the Dalai Lama belongs.

Stairs and court at Drepung Monastery.

A monk carrying water to the kitchen at Drepung.

Golden finials on the roofs of Drepung looking out to the Himalayas.

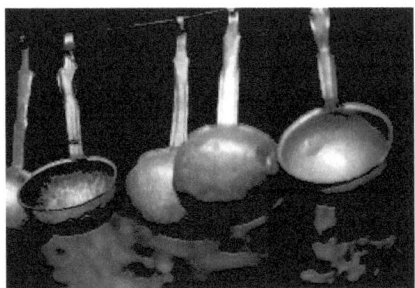

Ladles hanging in the kitchen of Drepung Monastery.

The thought of walking to the main road to find a bus back to Lhasa felt like more than I could cope with. I noticed an elderly American man with a Chinese guide who had a hired car and asked him if he would take us back to Lhasa. He was not very willing but it is hard to turn down an older woman from your culture. I knew I was taking advantage of him. He, of course, was staying at the Holiday Inn. He looked at the Yak when he dropped us off with a combination of curiosity and contempt.

I thought I was finding my stride, beginning to get a feel for Tibet. I found that Tibetans, like Americans, tend to automatically smile if your eyes meet while the Chinese who seem more earnest and a bit grim, seldom smile.

In the next few days I began to make friends with some of the chambermaids at the Yak. One day I was chatting with them in the courtyard when a small, older, Tibetan woman came up to me to ask, in perfect English, if I would help her. Although taken aback at being addressed in such sterling British English, I immediately said, "Yes."

She reached into her *chuba,* the front of which forms a capacious pocket, and brought out papers.

"I have been guiding an Italian group but they are unhappy with the rooms I found for them. They want Western bathrooms but such rooms are more expensive. Could you write a contract for me?"

"I'm not a lawyer but I can write out something simple saying what you will get for them at what price. Is that good enough? And where did you learn your excellent English?"

"That will be fine, thank you. I learned English when I was a girl at an Episcopalian convent in Darjeeling."

With a start, which I hoped was not visible, I realized I must be talking to a member of the Tibetan aristocracy. Who else would have been sent to India for an education?

"I never thought, when I learned English back then, that I would ever use it. But now with travelers and tourists coming to Tibet it is very useful. My name is Sonam."

"I'm Karen."

I took her up to my room to talk about the contract which I wrote up for her. As I handed it to her I asked, "Would you like some lipsticks?"

Somehow I had intuited that the cosmetics available in Tibet would be bad. It turned out that they were either really awful, dangerous-to-your-health, Chinese or not very good Indian products. I gave her some lipsticks for herself and her friends.

"My family and I have a shop where we make *chubas* and other clothes down the street. Come visit us," she offered.

I visited her store and began a friendship that gave me an opportunity to understand something of another world. My approach to the friendship was, ironically, through my mother. Because of my unhappiness with her, I have always had substitute mothers. While I thought Sonam was probably about my age, she seemed wise in ways that I was not. This made me feel she was a little older than I. She was also kind and sympathetic. I could feel that she was going to be a substitute mother for me, a Tibetan substitute mother. How lucky can you get?

Mothers are, like the poor, always with us. Never do we manage to slough off a mother's influence, good and/or bad, no matter how old we are, no matter how many times the cells in our bodies change. As mine used anything I told her to attack me, I learned not to tell her things by the time I was in third grade.

I had come home having pulled off a coupe in trading cards, a late 1940's female recess pastime in which playing cards with pretty pictures on their backs, that had been obtained from bridge and canasta playing parents, were exchanged on the basis of personal taste and arcane peer criteria. I had acquired a much-desired card picturing a highly polished dining room of Chippendale furniture under a crystal chandelier in exchange for one card of a kitten in a pink ribbon and another of a basket of puppies. I was brimming with this triumph when my mother asked, "What happened in school today?"

Frantically fending off my need for the praise I was unlikely to receive, saying to myself, "If you tell her this she will find some way to use it against you, say you cheated or you take advantage of people," I said, "Nothing," and quietly closed the door to my room.

For the rest of her life, I kept to that answer as much as possible. I remember this because it took all the will power in my eight-year-old body to deny myself the false hope of praise. I felt I had achieved a major triumph. I had. It was the right thing to do at that time, but that triumph forty, fifty, years later translated into trouble since not only didn't I tell people about my successes and failures but also, by keeping them wrapped in silence, I didn't feel them within myself. What is not shared is not fully realized.

Years later, in the late 1960's, when I told her I was getting a divorce I had an unguarded moment when she said, "And I'll bet he's been using you sexually." I took a stone out of my wall and replied, "No, because he has another woman, there's not been much sex."

"Oh," my mother shot back with a sneer, "you have hot pants." Contempt was her forte; the lash of her contempt was even worse than the sting of the dog leash she beat me with.

If I had turned on her at that point and said, "Do you think a mother should talk to a daughter that way? You have no respect for my boundaries. You need to apologize to me." If I'd been able to say that, we would have had a very different relationship. But I didn't have the courage. I was terrified of her as you are inevitably terrified of a person who has beaten you.

Coming from an Austrian Catholic background, in which children were considered innately bad, if not evil, because of Original Sin, she believed beating a child would lead to goodness; the duty of a parent was to pull the child from the clutch of Satan's quick sand through corporal punishment. Rather than rebelling against the beatings she had received from her father at her mother's instruction, she accepted implicitly that this was the way to raise a child.

When I was in Vienna years later, I witnessed a man, walking with his wife and children, focus on his eldest. I could hear rage rising in his voice. Although I could not understand his words, I had a moment's flashback to my childhood. Looking over my shoulder, I saw the boy shrink into himself, an ineffectual cringe, as his father's hand lashed out striking him across the face. I knew both the hand and motion well. It once broke my nose.

Physical punishment allows a parent to take out, unconsciously, on the child whatever frustrations she or he may be suffering from. I knew instinctively that punishing me was an emotional outlet for her. Fear and conflicts raged in my mother because my father was an alcoholic, although she didn't realize that for a long time and when she did, she still didn't understand how his drinking affected both his behavior and her own.

But violent corporal punishment of children was just the way it was in my time. What my mother did was not all that unusual, although even then there would have been a few who would have frowned on such behavior.

The last time she beat me–the instrument was always the dog's leather leash–it was for forgetting a dental appointment. I was twelve and had learned that if I sobbed hysterically, even without tears, she never seemed to notice, the noise I made would cause her to stop as though she were coming out of a seizure. She was in effect in an emotional seizure. As I sobbed dryly, "I'm sorry. I'm sorry." I was thinking, "I want to kill you. I want to kill you." For many years I hated her, was obsessed by my hatred for her, right down to the marrow in my bones.

But both of us suffered in our different ways from my silence that ostracized her. She tried many years later to make a bridge by humbling herself, telling me things she had done to me before my memory. She told me how when I was an infant, a friend of hers, a single woman who claimed to know all about babies, and was up on all the latest ways of treating them, came to visit.

I started to howl in the bedroom and Mother, knowing that according to the experts of the 1930's you did not pick up your child if it cried, sat talking to the woman, through my screaming, until she left. When she came to my crib she found I had thrown up and, because she had forgotten to close the window, my vomit was frozen into my cheeks and hair. Learning of this incident didn't build a bridge between us; it reinforced my belief that she was so narcissistic that she would always sacrifice me to her ego needs, as in this case her image in her friend's eyes had preempted my crying.

I did not try to build any bridges, mutually condemning us to separate silences. Among her letters that I inherited at her death I found one in which she laments my lack of openness. "I get little pleasure out of her conversation because she tells me nothing. She meets my friends, converses gaily with them and they tell me about it but she never tells me anything." It is interesting that she never used the information about me that she learned from her friends to humiliate or criticize me. In all probability she was never aware that she used my confidences as ammunition with which to abuse me.

I had learned my lesson and tried never to confide in her, knowing that anything I treasured, anything important or beautiful to me, she would destroy if I told her about it. Had I had the courage, as an adult, to confront her, tell her what she was doing and why it made me mute in her presence, we might have emerged from the mummy wrappings of our isolated silences but I was much too afraid of her, even as an adult, to do that, although I did confront her once. The scene was as terrible as I had anticipated.

I left the Catholic Church in my freshman year of college, although in truth I had been slowly withdrawing since grade school when I decided that the nuns who taught catechism, although sweet, had no sense of the real world or any ability to live in it.

In high school I was sent to Friday religious education released-time classes where we were, in our self-centered, acned adolescence, taught by a young man training to be a missionary. We were certainly training for him, being a frequently sniggering, always pimply audience from hell. We had that peculiar brittle cynicism that teenagers seem to acquire. He had developed a little parable about virginity, which he told us.

"My sister was asked to a formal party. She and my mother went to the store to pick out a dress. There was one she really liked but it was too expensive so my mother suggested she wait for a few weeks for the sale. When they went to the sale they found the dress but it had been tried on so many times that it was bedraggled and stained. She decided she didn't want it."

My hand shot up. "Maybe, but well worn shoes are more comfortable than new ones," I said. Why didn't throw he me out of the class?

Somehow I was able to talk my mother into letting me out of the released time classes. I felt it was my first step out of jail.

The anti-female aspect of the church infuriated me with its institutionalized vision of women as inferior as well as intrinsically bad and corrupting. It seemed to me that women were made into scapegoats to blame for everything. What I was taught about religion was superficial, didactic and resembled an anthology of fairy tales to me.

I realized I was going to have to tell my mother I'd left the Church and I was scared silly. I diddled around, trying to avoid the confrontation, but finally forced myself to face her. I told her one night in the kitchen in Chappaqua.

She went immediately into her contemptuous mode. "You just can't do anything difficult. You don't have a spine."

In a seething volcanic rage I turned on her spewing out, "I've done lots of hard things. I just haven't told you about them. Because of the way you dressed me in those long cotton stockings the boys at school threw me in a ditch and pulled up my skirts to see what held them up. That's just one instance."

"But why didn't you tell me?"

"What could you have done?" I responded with the contempt I'd learned from her.

" I would have gone to the principal."

"That would have been a big help," I sneered. "You would have made me into a social leper. Don't ever tell me I can't do difficult things. I just don't want to be part of the Catholic Church. I'm out and I don't want to talk about it." I marched off to bed with my heart doing a drum roll, feeling amazed that I was still alive. It had taken determination to not tell her about my triumph when I was in third grade but this was like walking on nails through fire. It felt as though I had barely escaped dying. I was physically shaking when I reached my bedroom. She was all-powerful and yet I hadn't died but this incident did not lead to further confrontations. I didn't want to go through fear like that again. I was very afraid of fear. This is ironic because many years later, long after her death, when I stopped drinking and began to rediscover my emotions, the first to raise its head was fear.

Walling myself in, I buried my feelings, sunk them down a well, until I didn't know what I felt. In not sharing my emotions with anyone, I denied their existence to myself. The first time a therapist asked me "How does that make you feel?" I thought, "What an odd question.

Why would she be interested in what I feel?" I drank my feelings out of existence. However, noticing that other people had feelings and talked about them, I began to pretend to feel things. Having no idea what I felt, I opted for an emotion hoping it would be appropriate. I swung, a pendulum, between numbness, melodrama and hysteria since I had no idea what sizes feelings came in.

Once I sobered up and began to be able to feel my emotions they appeared, and occasionally still do, false because they are so unfamiliar to me. I think, "That's not true. You're just feeling sorry for yourself," or "You made that up. That isn't real."

I had an affair with a wonderful man; only after he died was I able to admit to myself, too late to tell him, that I loved him. The walls were firm, the well deep and dark; I could not get inside myself; the way was locked and closed but to the outside world I was, "Fine." However, when I discovered that spectrum of magical elixirs called scotch, gin, bourbon, and beer my fear of people was eradicated. They acted as a solvent for my pain and the emotions I dreaded, making it possible to talk to people with relative ease.

As I feared my mother, so I feared other people. Wouldn't they also sneer at me? It took me years and years to realize I had these fears because I had obliterated them by drinking. Even today I, on occasion, hastily leave a party because I am claustrophobic in my fear of people, my emotions becoming so warped I want to sprint over the horizon. My child-emotions have returned me to childhood and my mother's influence. After all if my mother hadn't like me, how could anyone else like me?

But Sonam, my new Tibetan substitute mother, did seem to like me. She was kind and full of plain, practical sagacity, invariably telling me, when I got my knickers in a knot, not to worry, to relax. I had to go to the Holiday Inn to pick up my ticket for Kathmandu. The Chinese don't believe in issuing these until a day or two before the flight. I was trying to get them to issue it a whole four days before the flight. Out of nervousness I asked Sonam, whose daughter worked for CITS, the Chinese government travel agency, if she would go with me, although the people in the office spoke English well enough. We had to wait, causing knots in my underwear, but I received my ticket. We walked back to the *chuba* shop to have a celebratory cup of jasmine tea.

Over the years of our friendship her realistic wisdom helped me to examine ideas I had acquired through my family and culture and had taken for granted without examining them. Travel offers us the opportunity to learn other ways of encountering life than those we have grown up with. Suddenly there are alternatives that would not have occurred to us if we had not moved out of our own culture. When you change the way you think, you change the way you act. However change can also occur in the opposite direction. If you change the way you act, your thinking will slowly change. I visited Sonam at her store between sight seeing and spending time with my fellow backpackers.

The road to Tsurphu Monastery.

Two days before I left, Annalisa asked if I would like to go to a monastery called Tsurphu that is out side of Lhasa. She had a ride. We would share the expense with a couple who were going there. The couple turned out to be an American ex-drug addict and his German girlfriend. I watched fascinated as he turned a vivid shade of scarlet after popping vitamins the way he once, perhaps, popped less legal mood-changers.

We left in grey curtains of rain passing the polluting cement factory. But the sun came out as we turned off onto a dirt road with a neck-breaking surface that took us past tawny barley fields in terraces, a clear rushing river, alpine flowers and glimpses of snow hooded mountains. We were in an old Land Rover which seemed to smell of something smoldering all the time. We were bone chilled, Annalisa and I, since we had not understood that we would be going a thousand feet above Lhasa. If Annalisa had not lent me her scarf I would have been frozen.

The car in which we drove to Tsurphu Monastery.

Monks young and older on the stair at Tsurphu Monastery.

The American man, rescued from his addiction by his devotion to the *Karmapa* of Tsurphu, was now involved in running an American branch of the monastery. A *Karmapa* is a reincarnated llama who, when he dies, returns again to continue his lineage in his order of monks. The monks of the order, once the old *Karma* is dead, go out to find his reincarnation. This is achieved by having selected children identify objects — a pair of glasses, a butter lamp that belonged to the previous *Karmapa* — which are mixed in with things owned by the examining monks.

When we arrived at his quarters the monks came in with food for them but it took the pair ten minutes to offer us anything to eat.

A door at Tsurphu Monastery.

They told us that the new *Karmapa*, who was now five or six years old, was to be recognized the next day.

Inside Tsurphu Monastery.

We had a private audience with the youngster on the roof of the *gompa*. One of the monks, who was in charge of the boy, said to us in very good English, "It would be nice if you would prostrate before him."

I gave this request serious thought, knowing what a prostration was. I had seen people doing them in front of the Jokhang but despite watching I wasn't confident that I knew how it was done. I decided I wasn´t going to attempt a prostration, partly out of insecurity about the motions but mostly because I was much too Western in my thinking to get down on my belly in front of a 5 year old. Probably I am still too Western to do that. I have learned to do prostrations but I do them only before a mountain, one specific mountain.

I did give the *Karmapa* balloons. He accepted them politely but a little disdainfully, having, after all, just received a walky-talky from the man from one of the American divisions of his order. A young incarnation is given pretty much whatever he wants in the way of things, and gets to order grown ups about to some extent, which must be a stunning experience if you are from a poor Tibetan family, but this is very definitely a reciprocal situation, although the child may not realize that fact at first. I observed the older monks who were in charge of this youngster and was deeply impressed by their gentleness and humor around him.

I saw the *Karmapa* again, a few years later, age 11 or 12. He had totally changed. He was leading his monks in a chant, erect, serious and dignified. The bond, his sense of responsibility toward these men, even though he was a boy and they adults, was obviously intense, deep and vibrant. The monks responsible for his up bringing had done a superb job. A few years later, at the age of, I believe, 18, he walked with some of his monks out of Tibet because the Chinese were exerting pressure on him to endorse their regime. He is now in a monastery in Sikkim, in northern India. But whenever I go to a *gompa* of his order, I think of him and of that astonishing transformation from a slightly bratty five year old to a religious leader of twelve.

Houses along the road from Tsurphu. The mound dead center in the photo is a pile of yak pies which will be used as fuel during the winter. They exude a sweet grassy odor.

Bringing in the harvest along the road from Tsurphu to Lhasa.

Returning from Tsurphu we ran into a roadblock manned by Chinese police. Our driver stopped; he, and the boys hitching back to Lhasa with us, raised the hood, pretending to fix the engine until the police were too busy to notice us. While we two foreigners scrunched down in the back, afraid we might get the boys and our driver in trouble, I whispered to Annalisa, " Explain *Karmapa*, please. I don't really know what it is. I understand he's an incarnation of some sort."

She whispered back, "He's an incarnate lama. His order is the Kagyüpa sect whose main seat is Tsurphu, although they have other monasteries big and little all over Tibet. It is an order that allows marriage. A man named Marpa who taught Milarepa founded it. Do you know about Milarepa?"

"No."

"He's the most important saint and religious poet in Tibetan Buddhism. You can recognize him in paintings in *gompas* because he always has his hand behind his ear. He is listening to his teacher Marpa. "

"Oh yes," I said. "I have seen him but I didn't know who he was. He's wearing a sort of Roman tunic with no sleeves?"

"Yes, that's him. It is a very light cotton tunic, which he wore even in terrible cold because he could do a practice that would keep him warm. I think we are past the check point."

We peered cautiously out the side windows. Finding we were clear of the police we hoisted ourselves back up onto the back seat.

"He had a magical battle with the head of the Tsönpos. Do you know who the Böns are?"

"Yes, they are the religious group that preceded Buddhism. Their religion included a lot of shamanism and demons who were converted to protect Buddhists and Buddhism by Padmasambava in the 8th century."

"Right. Milarepa won Mount Kailash away from the Bönpos for the Buddhists but he was pretty tolerant. He gave them their own mountain. I can't remember what it is called."

On my last day, Annalisa said to me, " This is your day because it is your last day. What do you want to do?"

I was touched by her generosity in giving her time to me.

"Let's go to the *ani gompa*, the nunnery you mentioned."

"Oh, the Ani Sangkhung. I hope I can find it again. It's on the other side of the Jokhang near the mosques."

It took us a long time and a lot of walking as Annalisa tacked her course through the small lanes in the Tibetan quarter.

Modern Chinese architecture on display in the facade of a disco in Lhasa in 1992.

Tibetan timber on its way to China.

Along the way we saw a depot of some sort where trucks with huge logs stopped. Obviously some part of Tibet, where there were trees, was being deforested for China's profit.

As we walked I asked Annalisa if she planned to return to Tibet.

"Oh, I would love to but it takes so much money to come here. I would like to go to Western Tibet."

"Yes, it is expensive to come here and the profits go to the Chinese not the Tibetans. What's in Western Tibet?"

"There is a mountain there, a sacred mountain, named Kailash, the one Milarepa won for the Buddhists. I would love to go there and circumambulate it. It is an important pilgrimage for Tibetans. But Indians do a pilgrimage there too. Then there is an old fort, a citadel called Tsaparang, I want to get to and nearby an old temple, Tholing."

I made a mental note of the names, Kailash, Tsaparang and Tholing.

The outside of the Ani *gompa*, the nunnery. Nunneries are always painted yellow. I've no idea why.

The inside court of the nunnery, the Ani *gompa*, full of nuns and flowers.

The steps up to the temple of the Ani Tshamkhung, the nunnery.

We walked through the gate of the nunnery, to be welcomed by two nuns, one official looking and older, who motioned us to walk wherever we wished. The *ani gompa* is a small nunnery with a chapel, cells for the nuns, a secret room where the first historical Tibetan king, Songtsen Gampo, prayed, and a place where they handprint Buddhist texts from woodblocks.

Annalisa spoke a little Tibetan so we are able to exchange names, nationalities and the fact that I was not Annalisa's mother but her friend, not that I would have minded being her mother. We also whispered that the Chinese were no good. This is the phrase every Tibetan seems to know in English, "Chinese bad. Tibetans good." Annalisa asked if she could stay in the nunnery as a paying guest and was elated to find she could.

Young nuns were printing sacred texts by rubbing carved wooden tablets with ink, then pressing paper onto the wood. We handed them paper and stacked the finished pages for a while. Then we wandered down a dark narrow corridor into the secret room where Songtsen Gampo prayed. There was an image of him with a lamp before it, its flame licking the walls with its light, in the hollow where he had meditated. We visited the chanting hall where there were Polaroid pictures of monks who advise the nunnery tucked in among the images.

Descending the temple's steps behind an American couple, we heard the older nun, and her companion ask, through the couple's guide, if they would like some yak butter tea, a welcoming, hospitable gesture. Both Americans made faces of disgust. What is the matter with us that we behave this way? Did they think the abbess was struck blind and could not see the repugnance they so clearly expressed?

I was disgusted with my own fellow Americans, so when the nun and her companion turned to ask us the same question I immediately, and rather loudly said, "Yes." That yes was to far more than tea.

I found that yak butter tea was not repulsive, nor made with rancid butter, although it might be if you had the misfortune to encounter a slovenly, miserly cook. It may take effort to get used to, it is an acquired taste, but it is worth the effort since, at altitude, animal fat helps your engine run better than candy, which Westerners tend to depend on. The other alternative is lots and lots of carbohydrates, leading to the dismal all-white dinners of rice, pasta, mashed potatoes and bread I have had set before me by more than one well-meaning trekking cook. The other big plus of yak butter tea is it obviates the need for lipstick or Chap Stick. Your lips stay well greased if you drink butter tea. It also keeps your skin from drying out in a climate that parches you.

Because of altitude, the Tibetan diet is the reverse of the Western low-fat diet. It may help to think of butter tea as soup, rather than tea. It is very difficult to describe the flavor, but if you were to add salt and butter to a strong cup of Lipton you might get a faint idea of the taste. Yak butter has a stronger, deeper, flavor than cow butter, just as buffalo meat tastes stronger than beef. The stronger flavor may be why people think the butter is rancid. Butter tea is a subject on which Tibetans are a bit sensitive.

The older, more official nun, whom I later discovered was the abbess, the head of the nunnery, gazed at me thoughtfully as I entered the kitchen. Around her neck hung a rosary of 108 prayer beads carved from yak bone into small skulls. After looking at me thoughtfully for a moment, she lifted it off of her neck and lowered it over my head. I couldn't believe that I had received such an extraordinary gift. Why?

My brain kept asking, "Why? Why me? I have done nothing to deserve this."

While we drank tea I wracked my brains for something to give in return. I pulled out my guidebook for them to look at the pictures. They delightedly vied with each other to identify the various monasteries and *gompas*. When I saw that the abbess was holding the book at arm's length, I took my American drugstore reading glasses off my head and gave them to her, motioning that they were hers.

It made me happy to give back, a practical gift for a spiritual gift. This trip's purpose had been to fulfill my death promise to my Aunt Liz and here, with the exchange of prayer beads and glasses, I felt that the completion of my promise had been acknowledged, not by Aunt Liz specifically but by something which eludes my understanding and which I could not and cannot name.

I was silent on our walk back to the Yak Hotel, fingering my new beads, thinking as I rubbed each skull between thumb and forefinger, "*Om mani padme hum*" but not really saying it. My throat was tight and aching with tears. I do not come from a family that give and to be given to makes me feel vulnerable. It seemed as though Tibet had extended an open hand to me with the prayer beads, with Sonam's offer of friendship. An ineffable connection I felt was being presented to me. I was humbled and awed to have people I did not know, whose way of life I only very superficially understood, open themselves to me. But it was not only people. A door had swung on its hinges. Perhaps what I mean is that the abbess and Sonam were a Tibetan door swinging open before me. I could either walk through it or turn my back on it and plan my next trip to India or Pakistan. But with that cup of yak butter tea I had accepted that although this trip was ending, I would return to Tibet.

Annalisa opened another door to me by telling me about Kailash, Tsaparang and Tholing. Not only do the people you meet become a part of you and your trip but also the trip is not a direct line, not as the crow flies—Lhasa to Kailash. The journey is a sum of the places visited, an addition of place to place, a multiplication of individuals met, of stories heard, a spiritual coral reef of people, incidents and places. But I didn't know that yet.

Later, after I returned home, I wrote to Annalisa at the address she gave me but never received an answer. However, that doesn't matter because she is part of every trip I make. I hope she has been able to return to Tibet many times, that she has done the *khora* around Mount Kailash more than once, has climbed the citadel of Tsaparang and stood looking up at the smiling deities in the old murals in the Tholing *gompa*.

I consulted Sonam about how to get to the airport since I had been told I would have to be at the Holiday Inn at 5 am and might have to bribe the driver to get onto the bus, which was reportedly reserved for tours. I had at that point in my traveling career never bribed anyone and the thought of doing it made my palms sweat. Sonam connected me with a Canadian who was going to the airport with a Tibetan family who had been visiting relatives. They were headed back to Switzerland where they were living in exile, and had hired a private car to go to the airport.

The Tibetan mother and I, in the dawn light of the Yak courtyard at 5 am, as we waited for the car, which was late, expressed our despairing and desperate anxiety by wringing our hands at each other and then bursting into laughter at our wordlessness. When the car arrived, with its abashed driver, it was a jolly ride, and a fast one to the airport, a mud brick house with a couple of rooms through which we pushed and pulled our luggage. It was not very different from the old airport in Kathmandu. Last on line for weighing, we boarded the plane with the uncle taking his butter churn with him. It resided between his knees throughout the flight causing difficulty when we flew over Everest and everyone rushed to his side of the plane to take a photo. The plunger of the butter churn bifurcated the window and Everest neatly.

China Southwest Airlines at that time was not strict about hand luggage. Besides the churn other impedimenta bulged into the aisle so that the food cart had difficulty on its journey to deliver our odd lunch of, a large bag of cashews, a Kit Kat bar, and a hundred-year-old-egg, which you could wash down with either a beer or an orange drink.

Looking down on the Himalayas. Everest may be there somewhere. Since it is almost 30,000 feet we are flying well above that.

As I craned my neck to look down on Everest, I thought about the mountain Annalisa had told me about, Kailash, about the path, the *khora*, that circled it. Arriving in Kathmandu I went to the Pilgrim Bookstore, a wonderful musty smelling emporium full of new, used, rare, and leather bound books. Books, for me, are like chocolates; I can't have just one. The Pilgrims Bookstore is the kind of shop in which I can spend $500 in an hour, no problem. I went to the Tibet section and bought and bought and bought. Some of the books were by the publishers I would expect, Vintage, Oxford University Press, and were current. But others were reprints of English titles long out of print like Sir Charles Bell's *The Religion of Tibet* and *Lhasa* by Perceval Landon, first printed in 1905, reissued by Pilgrims Publishing, the Indian central office of the book store in Varanasi. These reprints with blurry photos attest to the continuing interest in Tibet among Westerners and Indians.

In the next year the image of Kailash, the sacred mountain, began to form in my mind. I vaguely knew there were other sacred mountains but there was never a contest; there was never even a choice. Everest, also sacred, didn't interest me largely because it is associated with climbing, and the idea of conquest, an attitude I find hubristic in its assumption that humans can, and perhaps should, triumph over nature, that we need to be in command of, in charge of, and somehow superior to the world we live in.

What did appeal was the idea of pilgrimage, as I segued my way through such esoterica as *The Way of the White Clouds*, by Lama Govinda, *Lhasa and its Mysteries*, by L. Austine Waddell, *Seven Years in*

Tibet, by Heinrich Harrer as well as books by Tibetan art expert Giuseppe Tucci. However, the decisive volumes were *The Sacred Mountain*, by John Snelling and Charles Allen's *A Mountain in Tibet*.

I began to understand that the Kailash pilgrimage along the *khora*, the sacred path around the mountain, is not exclusively Buddhist, that its origins recede into the deep distance of other ages, other ways of believing, like rank after rank of curling breakers coming into shore. The fact that its sacredness is not attached to one religion appealed to me, as did the object of the pilgrimage: to change. I knew I both wanted and needed change to dismantle the barriers I had erected as a child against my mother, which were now fortifications against the world, against people, against love. I stumbled across a sentence by Rumi, a thirteenth century, Persian, Sufi mystic, that seemed apposite to me: "Your task is not to seek for love, but merely to seek and find all the barriers within yourself that you have built against it." I needed to find, or perhaps reclaim, my vulnerability. I was not thinking specifically of my walls against emotion and people, but the promise of change was, even if frightening, also appealing.

For Tibetans the point of any pilgrimage, according to Dorje Yudon Yuthok in *House of the Turquoise Roof*, is "to achieve two essential aims: to increase the pilgrim's store of merit and to purify his negative tendencies." The beauty of the journey, the meeting of other people, the physical adventure is also of importance to Tibetans.

Merit comes from generosity of any kind, material, emotional or spiritual or may come from the difficulties of the journey. If you ride a horse on your pilgrimage, the horse receives part of the merit that you on your two feet would otherwise gain. "Negative tendencies" means in Tibetan Buddhism our attachment to *samsara*, to the self we imagine to be real, the things of this world, as well as negative emotions such as hate, fear, anger, and envy.

I read only a little about Buddhism, instead, concentrating on the mountain itself and the people who have been to her or been close. I read Alexandra David-Neel, a French woman Buddhist who in 1924 was the first Western person to reach Lhasa and a Tibetan biography of

Milarepa. These two, Easterner and Westerner, shared the ability to make themselves warm, raise their body temperature, through meditation.

David-Neel who walked to Lhasa, disguised as a Tibetan woman, was the diametric opposite of Nina Mazuchelli who almost 50 years earlier in 1876 was the first Western woman to see Everest. She, accompanying her English husband, was carried to that view in a sort of chair called a Bareilly Dandy. The seventy porters she, her husband and a friend employed, took turns hefting her in it up to and down from passes not because she was crippled or weak but because she felt it necessary to be dressed and shod as she would have been at home, as a lady.

However, being a lady cripples you. It isn't just that you can't climb the Himalayas in a corset, although that is probably true, but that those superficial accouterments of your culture whether they be clothing, customs or ideas need to be examined for their utility, their truthfulness in life and discarded when they are found wanting.

I realize that my attitude toward travel is to many decidedly odd. Most sensible people travel for relaxation, for a change of scene, going to resorts, or out of curiosity to see the Grand Canyon, or to learn more about Baroque architecture in Mexico or the history of the German States or Italian Renaissance painting, or just to enjoy lovely meals in Provence.

However, travel for me is a life course for which I registered late. How am I ever going to catch up with what I should have done when I was twenty-five? My attitude toward travel is rather academic. I, therefore, feel compelled to pile on the courses, carrying a heavy schedule. In retrospect I can see that my journeys to Indonesia, Burma, Vietnam, Cambodia and Laos were my undergraduate courses. With Tibet I entered graduate school. I now have a Ph.D. and am embarking on postdoctoral studies.

Therefore I felt, reading book after book on Tibet, Lhasa, Kailash, as I had after my first trip to Thailand, that I had not done a good enough job in traveling in Tibet and needed to do it again and do it right for

Aunt Liz. I didn't feel I had failed my travel course but perhaps received a B when I wanted an A or perhaps this trip was an introductory course, Tibet 101. What better way to commemorate Aunt Liz, and get that coveted A, than by enrolling in a pilgrimage to a sacred mountain? Kailash was next.

PART IV

1995, My First Trip To Kailash: Pilgrimage and Altitude.

My intent was to walk the *khora*, the sacred path, around Kailash thereby doing one circuit of the Buddhist wheel of life from birth to death to rebirth. Death would be, I presume, the pass, Drölma La. Very appropriate considering the way you feel laboring up its last slope. By authority of custom, one *khora* erases the sins of one life, twelve eradicate the sins of one *kalpa*, an era consisting of a thousand cycles of twelve-thousand years each, and 108 circumambulations will get you to *nirvana* at the end of this lifetime. The more *khoras* you do, the purer you become and, therefore, you are allowed closer to the mountain. This is all dependent on your attitude, of course.

I was not approaching my first circumambulation from the point of view of sin eradication. My goal was to walk *in memorium* around Kailash remembering Aunt Liz. I didn't yet know what happens to your brain when altitude and physical effort combine. I was interested in the idea of dedicating one's self to the idea of change but I was not considering my proposed circumambulation as a spiritual act, purely as a memorial walk.

The Kailash *khora* is about 33 miles in circumference. Its highest point is at Drölma La, 18,600 feet, about 6,000 meters. Buddhists circumambulate clockwise, Böns counter-clockwise. Some people, whether Buddhist or Bön, circumambulate by doing prostrations, a feat that requires great physical strength and endurance. It can take a month to circumambulate by prostration. But the prostrators I have seen on the path are relaxed, moving along usually with a small tent and making themselves tea from time to time. A prostration is similar to the yoga Salutation to the Sun. All of this, of course, must be done with the necessary reverent attitude or it does not count. The Tibetan bandit, who wanted to be absolved of his future robberies as well as those already committed, received according to the legend, nothing from the mountain.

Haystacks in the fields beside the road into Lhasa.

My Tibetan guide, Rigsum, who has guided me around both the inner and the outer *khora*, questioned whether guiding people around Kailash counts as a reverent circumambulation since it is work for which he gets paid and, therefore, is attached to the material world of *samsara*. We have discussed this problem but reached no conclusion.

I came into Lhasa this time from Chengdu in China's Sichuan province on a one-person tour. The drive into town from the new airport was beautiful. Out of the car window I serenely watched the farmers harvesting by hand, binding hayricks and leaning them against their houses. In the fields, the livestock, lean cows, fat tailed sheep, an occasional yak and wobbly, bulging, black pigs were cleaning up any dropped grain and munching on stubble. I would hate to lead an agricultural life. It is such hard, physical work, but I do love watching it. This hypocritical paradox reminds me of Graham Greene's comment on the excitement felt by a traveler in a country in upheaval who has a return ticket in his pocket.

Since my guide, a Tibetan woman this time, had a child and, therefore, was happy not to drag me around all the time, I had a lot of freedom. I did have to stay at the hotel they sent me to, the Ximalaya Hotel. But I knew Lhasa well enough now so that I could find my way about. I was worried that the Chinese might have flattened everything Tibetan in Lhasa, but they hadn't. I realized that I was somewhere near the nunnery.

I set out feeling happy and exhilarated to be back in Lhasa. I stopped a plump, middle-aged, Tibetan matron, neat as a pin in her *chuba* and apron, wearing a little straw hat with a couple of daisies on it. Hats were very in that year. Every woman in Lhasa seemed to be wearing above her sober *chuba* a frothy, flowery, or veiled creation suitable for an English garden party. After we exchanged greetings I asked, "*Tsankhung?*" That is a variation on the longer *anisangkhung*. We said this word back and forth to each other a number of times. Then she motioned me to follow her; like a duckling after its mother I trotted behind her along the irregular sidewalk until I recognized the mustard yellow walls and red roof of the nunnery building. I waved goodbye to her as I passed through the gate.

The nunnery hadn't changed. It was as spotless and burgeoning with all kinds of flowers as ever. The only new things were a framed history of the *tsankhung* in English and a big collection box with a lock on it. But the chapel, the grounds, and the underground cavern were all happily inhabited by my memories of Annalisa.

I walked on toward the Yak and stopped to see Tashi, who did not know who I was at first; but when I said, "I brought lipsticks last time and have some with me this time, too," she knew me immediately. I asked if she could negotiate a good price for me at the Kirey, which she promised to do. I also told her about my Kailash plans. She was delighted and supportive since she had done the pilgrimage only a few years before.

I knew from my first trip that there were bulletin boards in all guesthouses in the Tibetan section of Lhasa on which people posted notes in an astonishing variety of languages and alphabets asking if anyone wanted to go to the Nepali border, the airport, Namtso Lake or Kailash. There was no note in any Western language I could read about going to Kailash on the Kirey bulletin board so I posted one giving my room number.

Nomads packing up in the courtyard of the Kirey.

One of the *khata* sellers who used to be on the Barkhor before the Jokhang. A *khata* is a ceremonial scarf given to sacred images or objects as well as to travelers beginning their journey.

At the Yak, I was amazed when the old man who watched the big gate greeted me. I was touched to have stayed in his memory. I found on their board a note posted by two American men, Ben and Arthur, who were looking for companions to share the expense of a trip to Kailash. So excited that I could hardly breathe, I appended my name and my room number at the Kirey with the suggestion that we meet that evening at the Tashi One restaurant.

There were little incidents as I walked back to the hotel that filled me with effervescent delight. A Tibetan man gave me, for no apparent reason, a military salute with a grin as he passed me. A woman as she came along side me took my hand and we walked together, in the best Asian manner as women friends do, holding hands until she had to turn off. Arriving back home at the Ximalaya, I watched a bus disgorge people of all nationalities with bicycles who would pedal back to Kathmandu. The very thought made me short of breath.

Over dinner that night at the Tashi One, I became aware that Arthur, tall, sinewy, good looking, was very much in charge, which was fine since I certainly didn't feel capable of leading the group. He looked boyishly American with his brown-blond hair cropped short. Half way through our meal, I also began to realize that he didn't like me. Since we had only just met and I'd done nothing to offend, I put this down to a general dislike of older women. Maybe he had a nasty grandmother or had been bitten in the calf in the supermarket by a grey-haired woman prejudicing him against my age group. I decided to handle him with kid gloves and sugar tongs.

Ben, however, equally handsome but with a strongly muscled build and reddish, slightly curly hair, was well disposed toward me. I learned that they had not settled yet on an agent but had done enough basic research to know that we needed ten people in order to make hiring a big Chinese truck fiscally feasible for our slender backpacking budgets.

It turned out that they already had seven or eight people who were interested. The next night all of us met at the Banak Shol's restaurant which was full of travelers and much more cheery than the rooms I had seen there on my first trip. Over dinner, a disagreement developed about payment and the length of time people would stay with the group. People wanted to break off at various points after the circumambulation of Kailash and felt that the amount they would pay should reflect the amount of time they would stay with the group. The problem was that there seemed to be no equitable way to decide how much someone only going to Kailash should pay as opposed to someone who would leave the group at Tsaparang or someone who intended to go to the Nepali border.

This was complicated by the fact that Ben and Arthur wanted to do an illegal climb of Gurla Mandata, Kailash's neighbor mountain. It was illegal because they were going to do it without the necessary papers and guide from the Chinese government, both of which were prohibitively expensive. Their idea was to circumambulate Kailash in one day, before heading off to Gurla while the rest of us finished our circumambulation in two more days followed by a rest day. I had, at this point, no understanding of what a feat of physical endurance that one-day circumambulation would be. They would hitch back on our rest day, rejoining us for the next segment of our trip, which was going to be the citadel of Tsaparang and the temple at Tholing farther west in Tibet. I was the one urging for these sites, the others not having heard of them, although they were immediately interested. I breathed a little thank you sigh to Annalisa.

By the end of the evening it was apparent that we had a group of three, me, Arthur and Ben. I was discouraged but Arthur felt sure that in a few days we would be able to assemble another group. He was right. I posted notes in the Kirey, the Snowlands, the Banak Shol, and a new one at the Yak.

The next day I moved out of the Ximalaya and into the Kirey, first because it was cheaper than the Yak, but more importantly because there were nomads in spectacular outfits and hats that denoted which tribe they came from, totally different from the frothy tea party hats the Lhasa women were wearing, staying in the building in the center of the courtyard. They and their men all wore their best jewelry. Earrings, chandeliers of coral or pearls stroked women's shoulders. Men wore only one earring, usually a large turquoise set in silver with coral accents.

I went to the Jokhang with my female Tibetan guide whose English was so heavily accented that I only understood about thirty percent of what she said. The temple was packed with pilgrims. I almost tripped over a man who was prostrating; gently he clasped my ankle to warn me. In the central court where the copper and gold statues of the thousand armed Chenresi, the god of compassion, and Padmasambava towered under dust streaked sun beams, a Chinese man was having his picture taken, hands on hips, the pose of a conqueror. He must have been an important Communist official, for generally only monks and lay people who are performing ceremonies are allowed within this fenced off area. Never before or since have I seen someone having their picture taken within this enclosure. Tibetans waiting on line with their butter lamps and bags of *tsampa* to see images in the many chapels that surround the central court glared at him and muttered among themselves. One sidled over to me and whispered angrily, "Chinese bad."

Afterward, we climbed to the Potala, the enormous fort, temple complex, mausoleum, university, government compound where the

Dalai Lama had lived, I saw in his meditation room a spectacular skull cup, used in tantric ceremonies, with bulging silver eyeballs and a set of silver teeth. But everything was amazing, not just big things but little details such as hinges with serpentine designs on them, door rings with dragon faces, screens in brass or bronze lattice work with faces where the pieces crossed. It was endless and overwhelmingly strange, exciting and beautiful. Since this was the second, or in some cases the third, time I was seeing these places, I was able to concentrate on details rather than being overwhelmed by a tidal wave of the unfamiliar. I was beginning to feel less separated from Tibetan spirituality. It wasn't mine but it was no longer estrangingly alien.

A side view of the Potala.

I broke away from my guide and went to the Post Office, an offensive building covered in white bathroom tile. I stood on line behind a Western man who turned out to be a soft-spoken ex-New Yorker working for a rug company, a joint venture between the Chinese government and an overseas Tibetan. He had been living in Lhasa for two years and told me there were around twenty resident Westerners.

I asked, "Are you followed and spied on?"

He answered diffidently, "Well yes, at first I was; but I don't think they pay much attention to me any more."

People of all nationalities began leaving notes at the Yak and the Kirey —one Australian, one Dane, two Germans, three Israelis, and two Spaniards. It looked as though we were going to have a group. We decided to wait another day or two to see if anyone else wanted to join because it seemed likely that some people would drop out once they knew the price, which was going to be around $1,000 each.

The next morning I decided to have a hot shower. The Kirey provided rooms but they also had a bakery division on the first floor in the back. In the dark before dawn they made hundreds of steamed buns to be sold around the city. At first light you could see them being rolled and carried out through the courtyard past the building where the nomads stayed. The side benefit of this was that steaming the buns gave them a reservoir of hot water. You paid for your shower, giving the Kirey management a double profit out of heating the water, a good business. The showers were also on the first floor in the back, a series of booths. You wanted to get there early because, of course, the water cooled down over the day.

I arrived at 9:00 a.m. with towel and soap. The water was so hot one was likely to be scalded. It came out in pulses and didn't seem to mix with the cold very well. However, I found that if I stood at the far end of my cubicle and let the steam and scalding water heat the room I could then move in and try to get the hot and cold to mix. But if I stood too close to the door, my feet froze from the cold air coming in under the door. You had to judge your distances carefully. There was also the hazard of nomad men trying to see into your cubical. There was nothing sneaky about their intent. They were quite loud and jovial about wanting to see you naked. When I left, the rusty old shower head was still puffing and wheezing steam convulsively rather like an aging dragon.

Janet, a pert and pretty blonde, and I, having met at a dinner conclave of our group, went shopping since we were now quite sure that the trip to Kailash was on. She sensibly bought herself a padded jacket. She seemed to be traveling around the world with a wardrobe that consisted solely of black tights and black tee shirts, with matching black sneakers. We found a wool cardigan and a cotton shirt to layer with it and a pair of heavy hand-knit woolen tights, but we couldn't find any socks that weren't acrylic. We did well with gloves. I bought two pairs, one of thin acrylic knit like the socks, the other a pair of padded Thinsulate gloves, in lavender and pink. We also bought strings of prayer flags.

She had come to Tibet on a whim and was wandering the world visiting places she felt "drawn to." A Western-style Buddhist, to my amusement, she disapproved of magpies because she said they were violent and carrion eaters. It hadn't occurred to her that we each have our job in the ecosystem, and it's a good thing someone likes dead bodies for dinner. By Western style Buddhist, I mean those who have a superficial knowledge of Tibetan Buddhism which they apply to the world in eccentric and frequently judgmental ways, such as Janet's disapproval of magpies.

However, she did something so beautiful when we stopped for lunch in the midst of our shopping, that I didn't care how she felt about magpies. We went into a hole-in-the-wall place on the square in front of the Jokhang and ordered by pointing at what people around us were having. Janet ordered noodle soup. I had steamed buns filled with greens. They may have been from the Kirey bakery.

There were lots of beggars of all ages about, from children to a toothless old lady. When Janet had eaten as much of the soup as she wanted she offered it to two young men who had been hungrily watching us eat. What a good thing to do I thought and added some of my buns.

Back at the Kirey, I ran into a woman from Holland, a little older than I, with short curly, crisp white hair, whom I had talked to a week before over dinner at the Tashi II restaurant, which was within the courtyard of the Kirey. She had left about four days earlier to hitchhike to Chengdu from where she intended to take a plane to Hong Kong to meet a friend. I was a bit awed that she was hitchhiking. Surprised to see her back at the Kirey I asked, "What happened?"

"Oh, I was stopped by the police at a truck stop in Amdo where I was trying to get a lift that would take me on to Chengdu. They sent me back to Lhasa in a truck and told me I have to fly out, not go by road. Foreigners aren't allowed on the roads around there, too dangerous. There are lots of landslides and the roads are not much more than tracks. The policeman said to me, 'I should fine you. It's a big fine, but

I am just going to send you back. Why are you doing this? My mother would never do this?'"

We both laughed at that. No, the young policeman's mother would never travel as we did.

Our hopeful group met a few nights later at the Banak Shol. Arthur, having learned from our last attempt, announced that anyone could leave the group at any time, but everyone would pay the same amount. This was accepted. Sadly, because the truck would only hold ten people, we had to slough off the last two people, an Israeli couple who had wanted to join. We also agreed on the amount each of us would put in to buy provisions for the trip. We decided on a vegetarian diet because of the problems of spoilage.

Heinrich, one of the two Germans in the group, was a short, brown haired, muscle-cube, the perfect physique for trekking. Obviously tough and knowledgeable, he immediately began to dominate our decisions about food. I suggested that we also buy a large quantity of ramen instant noodle packets, as well. People decided how many cases of packets they wanted and gave me the money to buy them at a neighborhood market I had found near the Kirey, full of bloody yak haunches, dried fruit, bulging bags of rice and dented Chinese canned goods.

Going home that night, excited and happy at the thought of the coming adventure, I floated along the potholed sidewalks of Lhasa like a lady bug on a breeze-driven autumn leaf. I passed, as I glided in the evening light, a couple of dashingly dressed Tibetan women. One, in a red suit with a short boxy jacket trimmed in red fur, high heeled black ankle boots and short black leather gloves, peddled a bicycle. Her intensely black hair was slicked back from her face into a knot at the nape of her neck. I wondered where she was going. The other woman was striding along in an ankle length, tan, belted leather coat, very smart.

The next day we walked down Chongsakang Lane to pick out the agent who would supply us with a more or less English-speaking guide, a driver, and a big, baby-blue Chinese truck. One agent was a bit better in price and we agreed with him on that and the dates of the trip. Then Arthur, Ben, robust Heinrich, others who were interested, and I went to the Lhasa main market, a huge open-air affair, to buy provisions. Heinrich knew what he was doing since living on a cooperative farm he had a sense of what quantities to buy for a group. I felt immensely lucky to have such knowledgeable companions since I had never provisioned a trek before and had only done overnight trekking twice, once in the hills of Thailand and once in Bhutan.

In the big Lhasa market, we finished our shopping among open bags of spices, the brilliant yellow of turmeric, the crimson of paprika, the hard maroon kernels of Szechwan peppers, the various shadings of yellow, red and brown curries whose aromas enveloped us. Chiam, the handsome Israeli, was particularly taken with these, bending over them as if they were bunches of roses to inhale their perfume. We loaded our supplies into a taxi, taking them to be stored at the Yak before shopping some more.

The fragrant heaps of spices in the Lhasa market.

Yak meat displayed for sale in the market.

Arthur suggested that we buy foam mattresses to line the back of the truck, a brilliant idea considering that once out of Lhasa none of the roads would be paved. However, what we needed was foot thick foam rubber not the inch thick available. He also suggested we buy some of the cotton quilts that hung outside shops. In buying these we also spent time in Chinese army surplus stores where Janet had bought her jacket the day before. They had lots of green padded jackets and trousers for sale. I bought a pair of trousers, which by the end of the trip were so splotched with stains and filth that just looking at them made me queasy. I threw them out, but they had kept me warm.

Miguel, distinguished looking but reserved, or perhaps he just seemed reserved because he spoke little English, and Amelia, the prettiest designer of barns and stables on the Iberian peninsula, were from the bull-running town of Pamplona in Spain. They enjoyed investigating the oddities of army surplus with their German friend Alex but didn't find anything to buy in these shops full of clothing, bedrolls, gas masks and large tins of Chinese army pork that we looked at contemptuously.

Not buying some of those tins was a big mistake as they would have supplied us with a stock of unspoilable protein to put in our vegetable stews. I remember longing, mid-trip, to lick the fat from a can of pork that our guide and driver had opened. With Gunar, the Dane, quiet and closest to me in age, I did buy packages of tasteless biscuits, some sort of rations with incredibly high fat content, intended obviously for the Chinese army in Tibet. They were a good source of energy despite their lack of flavor.

We also bought a pressure cooker but being inexperienced didn't realize it was missing its valve. When we cooked, we had to wait patiently for our driver and Dawa, our guide, to finish with their pressure cooker so we could borrow their valve. Heinrich delivered a didactic lecture on testing before buying. Too late for that.

Janet and I went to the market near the Kirey to buy the noodles, also stocking up on peanuts in the shell, dates, raisins and apricots. The dates turned out to be dry and tasteless, but the raisins and apricots were excellent. I was interested to find that if I soaked the apricots, grimy, hard, little orange rocks, the night before putting them into my morning *tsampa*, they turned the water Mississippi-mud brown. Dust in various forms was inescapable. I thought of the American expression, "You gotta eat a peck of dirt before you die," hoping I wasn't exceeding the peck limit.

I was lucky to have experienced companions but also lucky to know Sonam. When we discussed my plans, she suggested I buy a monk's winter cape, which had been what she had worn when she did the same journey, also in the back of a truck. Her shop only made *chubas*, but she knew where to find me a cape.

I thought the cape a good idea, but told her, "I can't possibly take it home, although I would love to, because it will make me overweight on all my flights."

"I can sell it for you when you come back to Lhasa. I know a nun who will be interested. That way it will only cost you about $35."

She instructed me in the gastronomic ingredients for a Tibetan pilgrimage—yak cheese, sugar, powdered milk, *tsampa*. Cheese, milk and sugar are mixed into the *tsampa* with butter tea that any restaurant, home, or tea tent could supply. However, I was not yet used to eating this mixture day after day and didn't. Therefore, there was a great deal left over.

But she also touched directly on some of the spiritual ingredients. When I voiced my uncertainty and my growing fear of traveling for a month in the back of a truck with a group of strangers, Sonam gave me a direct look with her brown eyes the color of oiled chestnuts that illumined her intelligent, lined face and said bluntly, "You lead a luxurious life. Temporary hardship will be good for you." I couldn't deny the former and the latter seemed likely. It did not occur to me then that there is a long tradition, East and West, of the alignment of hardship and spiritual growth. One must earn, whether through emotional trials or psychological discipline or physical endurance, a path to the spirit. I did not think of all those saints out in the desert.

Only later did it occur to me that Sonam spoke from experience. She had grown up in an aristocratic Tibetan family with servants and had been sent to school in India; but with the invasion of the Chinese followed by the Cultural Revolution, she had had to learn how to survive at a lower economic and social level. I was impressed by her practical sense of the spiritual as manifested in her treatment of people. She never raised her voice or lost her temper. She, controlling her emotions while not denying them, was always generous. Sonam exemplified how I might, in circumambulating the mountain, want to change.

I was afraid of traveling with strangers, as well as simply being with strangers over a long period of time, but also afraid of whether I would be capable, physically, of what the trip would require of me. I knew that fear was at the corrosive core of my difficulties in interactions with other people.

While drinking and through my first year in AA, I had no idea that I had an emotion named fear or other emotions for that matter. I would have told you I was not afraid of anyone or thing. Yes, my mother, but only her. I had anesthetized myself so what emotions I had palpitated deep within an alcohol cocoon. My fear was revealed to me on my first trip to Thailand. In Nepal, discovering the right guidebook and my delight in my incomprehension of its culture, I decided next I should travel alone into my incomprehension, as though it were another country. The actual country I chose was Thailand. I was not conscious of being fearful around this decision.

I had nurtured much resentment against my mother; but I knew she was never, ever, wrong when it came to traveling. In her sixties she took a trip around the world, going to the Far East for the first time. When she returned, I asked which country she liked best. Without a butterfly wing's flicker of hesitation she said, "Thailand. The river in Bangkok vibrates with life, and in canals off of it women paddle in peapod boats from landing to landing of houses up on stilts selling fruits and vegetables."

This trip was a big adventure since it was my first trip alone in sobriety as I had joined AA about a year and a half before. I went to meetings in Bangkok, there were not many, at the parish house of the Church of the Holy Redeemer.

My primary feeling for much of my life had been numb. Believe me, numb is a feeling; but as I wandered around Bangkok, I became aware of something different, although I wasn't sure what. It was like groping for an object in a grab-bag full of a miscellany of unidentified shapes. It took me a day or two to decide that the shape my mental fingers were feeling was called fear.

I complained to my fellow AA members in the parish house that I had an eggbeater of fear in my gut all the time, and I had no idea what I was afraid of. They were sympathetic and assured me that I would figure it out. Slowly, I became aware that what I feared was mostly amorphous—not rape, not being robbed, not even being killed by a Bangkok bus charging like a bee-stung bull down Rachadamri Road, all its rusty fenders juddering. I was *just* afraid. It was the fundamental fear of a child losing her mother's hand in Macy's, of finding one's self powerless, lost in a primal way like an astronaut tumbling in dark space with no way home. I was afraid of everything—getting on a bus, getting on a train, getting off a bus, going to a guesthouse, a restaurant, everything and anything. I walked through the city inside a self-insulating balloon of fear all day. What came into sharp focus was the fact that I was afraid of people, all people, whether they spoke Thai, French, or English. This was a huge revelation. The only people I trusted were those in the meetings, and not all of those. On this trip to Thailand, however, my fears seemed to be arranging themselves around my inability to get out of my hotel and into a guesthouse.

Before leaving the U.S., I had chosen from my precious guidebook, the original one I'd found in Kathmandu, a guesthouse in the Banglampoo district of Bangkok, the Suneeporn. However, when I walked out of the airport into the hot, damp, smothery night of the city, raucous with taxi drivers competing for my custom, all my courage evaporated like cheap perfume in an uncorked bottle. After bargaining with a driver to get a reasonable price to Banglampoo, I asked him to take me to an American-style hotel, the Viengtai, rather than to the Suneeporn Guesthouse. Ashamed of my lack of courage, I was stricken that night as I went to bed by the thought that perhaps in the morning I would not be brave enough to even leave the hotel. Fear, like alcoholism, it occurred to me, is a progressive disease and, as with alcoholism, one has to admit to its power before one can overcome it.

The Viengtai was across the street from the alley where the Suneeporn Guesthouse was located. Each day I would look yearningly up the alley but could not get myself to switch. I traveled north to Chaingmai and yet again my courage failed; I stayed in a hotel. However, once I started taking buses, coming down from Chiang Mai in stages back to Bangkok, there were no hotels in the small towns I would be staying in, just guesthouses. I was trapped.

Among the passengers on the bus driving south from Chaingmai was woman with a small, fractious child, a mother's nightmare of whimper and squirm, uninterested in food or anything pointed out to her from her window. I found the balloons I had bought before leaving the U. S. in the bottom of my daypack and blew one up. (Balloons are perfect presents for children since they don't decay their teeth, are very light to carry and unlike giving money, don't teach children to beg. I learned this from a fellow traveler on my trip to Mongolia.) I blew it up and offered it to the little girl who immediately stopped crying.

The mother burst into broken English, "I ashamed. I not speak English. Father send me learn but I lazy." I pointed out that I didn't know any Thai, but she went on excoriating herself. The man sitting next to me, amused by our dialogue, offered to translate; but by that time we had exhausted the topic of our mutual linguistic inabilities.

He turned to me and asked, "Would it tire you if I spoke English to you. I rarely have a chance to practice my English. We don't have to speak all the time, of course."

I was delighted by his typically Thai thoughtfulness, remembering a young Iranian who questioned me non-stop on a bus from Tehran to Isfahan for four or five hours. Perhaps that consideration broke through my usual fear of people. We had an excellent time. He got to use words he had been, I realized, hoarding and savoring for years. "Charisma" was one he pulled out of his secret cache with a flourish, saying to me, "You have charisma." I doubted it but was happy that he got to use the word.

I confessed, feeling a bit idiotic, that I was afraid of guesthouses, having no idea how to chose one. He suggested I ask the price and look at the room before deciding.

"When we come into town, I will point out some of the ones I know."

He did and I followed his instructions finding a room with a clean squat toilet and a cold shower in the form of a pipe coming out of the wall for two dollars a night. The mattress was lumpy and I was a bit anxious that night, but nothing untoward happened.

When I returned to Bangkok, I triumphantly moved from the Viengtai to the Suneeporn Guesthouse. I was still afraid of people; but I had recognized my first emotion, fear, and learned to differentiate between two kinds of fear: the kind that is rational—fear of treading a six-inch path across a recent landslide—and irrational fear. The latter fear is the enemy, insinuating itself between you and the potential of experience, cutting you off from what you want most, reducing your world, never, ever expanding it, a wet, rawhide noose slowly constricting, choking as it dries.

To this day I find I cannot always parse the difference between fear and excitement. But fear was the first emotion I unwrapped, a many-carat canary diamond. Travel was working for me. By turning outward to the world, doing what I feared, I was cracking myself open using other cultures and climes as a mallet is used on a walnut. Now, with this journey with companions I was taking myself to a new level of familiarity which would challenge my fear.

The morning after our food shopping spree, I went to Ganden Monastery with my guide, her mother with a gold tooth in her smile, and her two-year-old in split pants. Tibetans don't use diapers. Split pants are the their solution to the diaper/landfill problem. Their babies' little trousers are split along the crotch so a mother can hold a child away from her to pee or poop and then wash her/him off. Older children can wander off to squat without having to deal with a lot of zippers, buckles, buttons or elastic. Of course, at the beginning you have to be in sync with your child's bladder and intestines; but once at the toddler stage, they allow a child to go wandering off to relieve him or herself at will. The child does, however, have to develop a sense of discretion and decorum. Once in the Jokhang in Lhasa, the St. Peter's of Tibetan Buddhism, in a dark corridor, I came across a little boy squatting shame-faced behind his puddle as a tall, voluminously-robed monk towered sternly over him.

Ganden Monastery cupped by mountains.

Ganden was, before the Cultural Revolution, one of the six great monasteries of the Gelugpa monks, the sect the Dali Lama belongs to. Around 2,000 monks lived here. When I visited, about 300 monks were allowed to be in residence by the Chinese. Because, from a distance, it is set so high into a magnificent curving hollow at the top of a mountain you don't realize that you are looking at two things: roofless rooms with blasted walls and empty windows now blooming with green leaves of shrubs and trees where the old buildings were dynamited during the Cultural Revolution and the new buildings which look raw and unfinished. The same contrast can be seen between the new *thangkas* of Chinese design made with harsh chemical colors and the occasional old *thangka* with its graceful figures in vegetable and mineral paints.

After the devastation, individual Tibetans sought with great patience to rebuild it; but the Chinese regularly either arrested them or punished those involved by raising their rents and taxes. Within a decade, Beijing began to ignore the Tibetan's restoration efforts and, in fact, eventually took credit for them. The change of heart sprang from a realization that the renovation would attract large numbers of Western tourists and their cash.

Trees have grown up in the interiors of the temples dynamited during the Cultural Revolution at Ganden Monastery.

My guide, her mother and, hidden between them, their son / grandson, as they walk up to the temples of Ganden.

In one chapel, the Serdhung Lhakhang I asked to see a small *chörten*—in this case a multi-tiered silver vessel containing a relic—that I had read held the tooth of Tsong Khapa, founder of the Gelugpa order, the Dali Lama's order known as the Yellow Hats. My guide translated my request to a monk, who carefully removed a small, exquisitely delicate, silver and gold *chörten* from a cabinet. Shaped like a tiered pyramid, it was intricately contrived and decorated with small turquoise stones. To my surprise the monk, without asking, raised the reliquary above first my head and then my companion's, blessing us both by touching it to our bowed backs. I was amused that I was caught unawares in this blessing, which if it had been from a tooth of Saint Claire I probably would have objected to.

I was less interested in the blessing than in seeing that the reliquary was totally caved in on one side. Apparently it had been smashed by something, perhaps a rifle butt, another casualty of the Cultural Revolution.

We saw some other chapels where both my guide and her mother offered dribbles of fat from their small butter lamps into the large basins of the monastery lamps. Then my guide stayed behind with the baby while the grandmother and I started up toward the ridge to do the *khora*, the sacred pathway around Ganden.

The mountains from a roof at Ganden Monastery.

My companion, probably younger than I, picked an herb, which she explained through motions and sounds, was excellent for coughs. I sat on a stone and looked out, while I waited for her, over the valley below which is cut by the skein of a river's many passages. There was a small village with a new white *chörten* and on the opposite bank of the river what I presumed was a Chinese industrial enclave with its own little cloud of pollution hanging over it. As we continued on, we picked up an elderly monk with no front teeth, a wisp of whiskers, and a cane. He pointed things out to my companion, small holy places that were usually a polished place on a rock. She would stop and burn a few sprigs of juniper at these halts.

The picnickers, with their dog, who gave me a bottle of water at Ganden.

Coming around a corner ahead of them I found a complete Tibetan family, including dog, having a picnic on a promontory overlooking the river valley which is surrounded by a phalanx of green mountains and above it another of higher snow-speckled mountains. They offered me a drink from a bottle of water. I was most grateful since I had foolishly forgotten to bring a bottle. When I moved on, one of the women ran after me to offer the whole bottle. I took it.

We rambled on with the Tibetan family catching up with us and were joined by another monk. This one wore a yellow, shovel shaped hat of yak felt. He volubly explained the various sacred places to his attentive Tibetan audience while I admired the slopes of the ridge daintily tapestried with the trumpets of blue and purple gentians. It was as though a part of the sky had fallen.

Mountains and prayer flags at Ganden.

A young woman with her child. She, the mother, is very young but look at her hands.

The easy acceptance of the sacredness of everything from hollows in stones to a silver reliquary no longer gave me the sensation of being alien; while I did feel myself outside the circle of belief, it was not in a alienated or lonely way.

Looking back at Ganden.

When I got back that afternoon, I stopped by Sonam's. She had two cloaks for me to choose between. One was brown and had an outer shell of silky brocade. The other was enormous, very regal being of a double thickness of maroon wool on the outside and tufted on the inside with pompoms of yarn, making it look as though it were lined with red sea anemones. It was warm but incredibly heavy; it seemed about the weight of an old-fashioned diver's suit. I decided the back of a truck was not a place to wear brocade and chose the one lined with red sea anemones.

Early the next morning the baby blue Chinese truck growled in through the portal of the Yak. We were leaving Lhasa. The truck was a sort of modern prairie schooner with steel ribs over its bed covered with a skin of heavy blue tarpaulin. Already there were three huge drums of gasoline in the back since at that time there were no gas stations after, as I remember, Tashilumphu. We had to carry gasoline with us for more than half the trip. The remaining area of the truck we lined with the inch-thick foam mattresses we had bought, hoisting into the cavernous interior 20 kilos of onions, 30 kilos of potatoes, a half dozen cabbages like monster green marbles, a sack of rice, a blimp

Our truck on the road.

of zucchini-type squash striated with green and white markings, bags of garlic cloves, carrots as thick as a child's wrist, turnips, various spices, and eight cardboard cases of instant noodles which was mostly what we ate. When desperate with hunger, which was often, we consumed a packet as though it were potato chips, crunchy, dry and pre-boiled.

But we were in high spirits as we turned out of the Yak's gate. Ben, in imitation of bus boys all over Asia, who call out their bus's destination as it wends its way through town, leaned out the back of the truck and yelled, "Kailash, Kailash, Kailash." At the edge of Lhasa, where we could look up at the mountains like carious teeth that edge the city, the truck stopped. Our guide, Dawa, came back and started, with the driver's help, putting three broad boards over the opening above the tailgate. We protested against this since it meant that if we were sitting down we could see nothing but the sky and would be in relative darkness surrounded by our packs, our food, our sleeping paraphernalia, and the large steel drums of gasoline. But they insisted that the boards had to be up for at least a while. They were obviously afraid of the Chinese at checkpoints, so we grudgingly gave in. I stood up gazing over the boards as we thumped along the dirt road outside of Lhasa at the ruins of destroyed monasteries on the sides of mountains near villages that still existed. I did see one new white *chörten* with a golden spire sitting half way up a mountainside.

Yamdrok Lake, where the Chinese blasted a dam into one end.

We slowly climbed the hairpin turns twisting up the grass-covered mountain to the pass which looks down on Yamdrok Lake, stopping at the top to gaze on its huge polished turquoise surrounded by white-peaked mountains. Here we took down the barrier boards. Then the next problem immediately became apparent. Coming down from the pass above the lake on the dirt road, dust boiled up from our rear wheels in a great beige spume and poured into the back of the truck engulfing us. We put on masks that we had bought in Lhasa; but behind the cotton layers, I could chew on the dust, taste it, smell it. We couldn't see clearly since the dust coated the surfaces of our sunglasses both inside and out. I tucked my long braid into my jacket hoping to keep some of it out of my hair. Later I tied a plastic bag around my braid. Nothing helped.

Suddenly, on a particularly bad pothole jounce, one of the five-gallon water jugs, a plastic one, burst. With incredible presence of mind Heinrich grabbed it and hurled it over the tailgate.

A little later, we all smelled gasoline. The odor became stronger and stronger. When we stopped at a restaurant in the middle of nowhere for *momos*, dumplings with yak meat or vegetable filling, the driver and Dawa, our guide went into the back with Ben and Arthur to heft things about and find the leaks in the gasoline drums. They were able to stop them up but Chaim's tent cover was saturated. When we hung it up to air, the fumes gave us all headaches. Luckily the leaking gas didn't get to our food.

Back in the truck after lunch, the vile dust continued to pour in endlessly covering our faces and hands. We were miserable. Hats on heads or scarves wrapped over nose and mouth, some of us with face masks over noses and mouths as we passed through utterly barren country where slabs of rock glowed in soft yellow or striations of red under the sun which, in the thin air, was more intense than at lower altitudes. In this whole trip I saw one cloud, a small lenticular powder puff. We passed both glaciers I had seen on my previous trip. This time they looked like frozen surf. There was next an area with a multitude of snowy crests appearing and disappearing behind barren heights. I watched a herd of yak running down one, fluid as a dark stream. I knew we were approaching Gyantze when willows began to appear, leafy sentinels along the road and around stout walled farms.

Some of us found the truck worked well as a gym. We had stopped to take out all the gasoline barrels and Chaim's tent which stank of gas.

The roadside restaurant where we stopped for *momos*.

Karo La glacier. It is within walking distance of the road. Now, the Chinese have gussied it up with *chörtens* they have built and shops. It was, years ago, populated by extremely poor nomad women and their children selling crystals and other rocks. The men were with the flocks.

Horse carts with merry bells passed us on their way back from town or as they came from the fields, the carts so heaped with great, untidy poufs of hay that not only were they invisible but the little horses pulling them were just dainty legs and hooves prancing along without bodies or heads. Chiam, sitting by the tailgate, shouted that he could see the Gyantze's fort on its hilltop.

We arrived in Gyantze looking like breaded veal cutlets. If we slapped our thighs, great clouds of dust rose out of our trousers. We walked into the Hotel of the Nationality Clothing Factory just as the sky turned lavender. This was where I had seen the man on the bicycle, whom I had recognized as a Westerner, turn in on my trip with the tour from Kathmandu. I was conscious of a feeling of triumph at now being an independent traveler on this spot where I had seen my first Western independent traveler in 1992.

We ate at a Chinese restaurant feeling disloyal to the Tibetans but were too exhausted to walk around town to find a Tibetan one. Dawa, our guide, walked me home from dinner, possibly because he felt it was his duty to see that the eldest got home safely. He told me he had been taught English by an American woman.

"She have your name, Karen. She live in New York City. You know her?" he asked.

"Do you know her last name?" I queried. "There are more than eight million people in New York."

"Well," he said a bit sullenly, "I just asked." Then abruptly he queried, "How old you?"

"I'm 59," I said, neither startled nor offended, being used to people's curiosity about my age, what I did for a living, where was my husband, or how many children I had.

"Too old. Too old," he responded.

Every time I go around Kailash I think of that pronouncement of his. It is going to be true soon but in the meantime I've had twenty years of trips to Kailash.

The next morning I walked up to the fort even though I knew it was a reconstruction since it had been destroyed by both the British in 1904 and then again by the Chinese during the Cultural Revolution because I'd never been there, but it was closed. I came down, went to the Pulchor Chode, revisited the masks with their bared teeth as well as the man having his eye pecked out by a vulture in the protector chapel on the first floor. Discovering that the second floor, which I had not seen on my last trip, was open, I went up and ran into Gunar, our Danish member, staring at a huge bronze mandala. It is a piece of extremely complicated open work with layer on layer of small figures; gesticulating monkeys prance around the sides of one tier.

The Pulchor Chode, the main temple of the Gyantze Monastery.

A mandala is a plan, a sort of blueprint, of the spiritual universe that Buddhists and Hindus use in their meditation practice. There is a circle inside a square with a deity at the gates at each of the four sides.

In meditating, you enter the mandala mentally at one of the portals on one of the four sides and move toward the center.

The Kumbum in Gyantze.

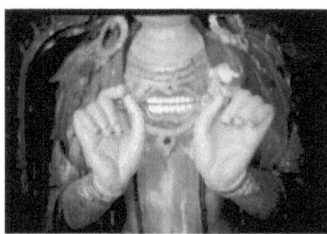

The Tooth God?

We continued on to the Kumbum together, which was as wonderful as the first time. The same little monklet was there but he didn't, of course, remember me. I showed Gunar the deity holding a set of teeth which he'd seen on a previous trip but he also had no idea what the significance of the statue was. This was Gunar's fifth trip to Tibet I discovered; that definitely made him the old hand of the group.

We sat outside the gates of the Pulchor Chode on some logs waiting for the driver to return so we could go on to Shigatze. I fed a horse my pear core. Ben, to the leaping, giggling delight of some little boys, juggled three balls.

I got to ride in the cab of the truck to Shigatze, out of the dust but in the Bollywood music that Dawa and our driver loved to sing along with. They knew most of the words having listened to the tapes endlessly; but since they didn't know Hindi, they had no idea what the words meant. We took turns riding in the cab of the truck. Since there were ten of us, it was a rare treat that got us out of the dusty thumping we had in the back.

There were a number of tourist buses when we arrived at Tashilumphu in Shigatze. I was aghast to see Westerners with their cameras standing over nomad pilgrims who were prostrating. They went at one group of nomads who were waiting for a temple to open, pinning them against the wall, cameras clicking. The nomads tried to hide their faces from the cameras but did not otherwise protest. When Chiam also took a picture, Heinrich said quietly to him, "It is not all right just because others are doing it."

I was happy to see Tashilumphu again, although this time the nomad pilgrims were not beautifully dressed and bejeweled. I paused for a moment to look at the mosaic, which I remembered, of rectangular turquoise that formed a swastika before the door of one of the temples, brilliant blues against the background stone.

Gunar, scrambling into the back of the truck as we left the parking lot by the temple, greeted us triumphantly with the news that he had seen a sky burial by following a group of Tibetans he saw going in a different direction from the pilgrims. I was pistachio green with jealousy since I wanted to see one and to this day never have.

Sky burial is a method of disposing of the dead that Tibetans have come up with since they live in a land where the ground is often frozen and always hard and rocky. They believe that since we use up more of the earth than other animals, we owe the earth a debt at our death. The corpse is taken to a flat place, always the same place, and a person, whose job it is to do this, butchers the body, cutting it into hunks, opening the skull, shattering the bones. This is so that the birds can get at the marrow. Since this occurs frequently at the same place, the birds learn to keep watch. They come down, vultures, ravens, eagles to eat the body and clean the bones. When they have cleaned the bones, which does not take long, the butcher pounds them until they are as close to powder as he is able to make them.

I asked Gunar what it was like.

"I didn't go very close or take pictures because I didn't want to disturb the family. I would say that it was both disgusting and fascinating."

That seemed as good a summary as one could get.

On either side of the road, there was continuous rock and scrub with beyond that the bare, angular bones of mountains. Amelia and I saw a marmot scurrying toward his burrow and a herd of either antelope or blue sheep running up a crevice in a mountain crag. They were too far away and we too inexperienced as wild life sighters to know which.

There were lots of hawks. These often positioned themselves on top of electricity poles, as they do in Nebraska, in order to see anything running across the flat earth.

We came to where a sort of raft-ferry pulled us across a river by a hand-cranked cable. Just up the slope from the riverbank was a whitewashed, walled house where a family rented out rooms. There was a central court, two rooms for rent, the family's room, a store selling batteries, household items, pens and, oddly, tall, clear, glass jars of mandarin oranges, built around a central court. In the court

The cable-operated ferry that took us and our truck across the river to the house where we spent the night, except for Heinrich who slept outside.

was a stove for cooking, strips of yak meat hanging on the wall to dry, a thin dog, a wary cat, a number of dusty chickens scratching about and everything that was broken but which the family wasn't quite ready to throw out yet. It reminded me of the front yard of many doublewides in Vermont.

The court of the house we slept in. The truck is parked outside.

Alex, Amelia, Miguel and I shared a room. There was a stove with a crooked pipe that exited through the roof in the center and hard benches, our beds, around the perimeter of the room covered with hand-woven rugs, brightly colored as a spring flowerbed.

After a day of being hurled about the back of the truck, inhaling huge clouds of brown or red dust, our gourmet cuisine urge was muted. Heinrich bullied us into cooking a curried vegetable stew in the pressure cooker which we poured over our beautiful handmade noodles. It tasted wonderful as we savored it sitting on various

Eating dinner made in the pressure cooker whose valve we had to borrow.

available rocks giving a view down to the river, spooning up cabbage, carrots and hunks of the big green squash we had bought in the market in Lhasa. We were glad to have made the effort, but we really did need Heinrich to bully us into cooking.

Arthur and Janet decided to sleep in the truck. Alex, Amelia, Miguel and I went into our room and slept unmoving as so many river stones until dawn when the family started stirring up the fire in the courtyard to begin their day. As we sorted ourselves out, repacking sleeping bags and toiletries, someone suddenly said, "Where's Heinrich?" None of us could remember seeing him after we had done our dinner wash up. Alarmed, we looked through the house, went outside and called, but there was no response. Ben went wandering around the area shouting, "Heinrich," and found him, still profoundly asleep, in the bottom of a ditch wrapped up in his sleeping bag over which he had pulled a woven plastic bag for warmth and to keep the morning dew out. We scolded him thoroughly for giving us a fright. He said he wanted to see how his body dealt with the cold. I had no such desire.

The thought that trekking on this trip might include sleeping in a ditch did not make me happy. I knew how inexperienced I was as a trekker. On my first trip to Thailand, because of my fears, there had been things I had not done. I had felt I had not performed well enough, and with my academic attitude toward travel gave myself a low grade. Therefore, in 1984 I had returned to Chiang Mai joining a group hiking the hills above Chiang Sen and Chiang Rai to visit tribal villages. It had been my first overnight hiking experience, not really a trek and not, in retrospect, very difficult.

There were five of us—an American couple, a British girl and her French boy friend. We were still on a dirt road, not even on a path, when the American man said to me, "Do you realize you're the color of a plum?" I did know that I was having great difficulty walking up the hill in the mid-day sun. I was winded and sweaty. That I was also the color of a plum was not a total surprise. That five-day trip was my wake up alarm. I realized I was out of shape and needed to start working out, which I did on my return.

That hike also made plain that there were dangers in this kind of travel and that they should not be ignored. Only three of us, all Americans, finished the hike. The British girl became sick, possibly from malaria, and on the second day her French boyfriend walked her to a road to find transport back to a hospital in Chiang Mai.

My shoes were stolen at the first village we slept in overnight. Our guide, an opium addict, had no authority to force the thief to return them. The shoes, attractive but not suitable for hiking for five days, had soft soles. I had shown little sense in choosing them for the trip. The villagers ignored our appeals and I started out barefoot.

After four hours on narrow paths I announced that I couldn't do it much longer even though the path was not rough or rocky. It was just hard packed earth. The soles of my feet were beginning to roughen as I worked my way through the one layer of tough skin I had. The British girl with her French boyfriend had left by this time. The Americans dug into their packs and gave me all their spare socks; neither one had spare shoes. I walked on in several layers of spare socks until we got to an abandoned village where our guide rummaged through house after house until he found a pair of men's rubber boots which he cut down to below ankle height. I wore them for the rest of the hike.

This journey, where each village we stayed in provided us with food and a roof to sleep under for a fee, and the trek in Bhutan, where our breakfasts, lunches and dinners were laid out for us on a folding table carried by a yak, was what I knew of trekking. The latter had been a luxurious trek with mostly Brits, who, because polite conversation must always be impersonal, ended up discussing twice how they stole complimentary bottles of shampoo and soap from hotels to stock their guest bathrooms. There were also one Frenchman and a Scots woman doctor. They and I were very lucky that I tore all the muscles on the inside of my right thigh tripping over a buried tent peg and had to finish the trip on horseback. I would always have been lagging behind, not being on a physical par with my companions, which would have, quite reasonably, have irritated them. This was even though I was by this time a maniacal exercise freak.

Someone else's truck
traveling to Mount Kailash.

As the days passed in the back of our baby blue truck, I would have worried about my trekking future if I hadn't been living in a miasma of exhaustion as though swimming in an aquarium filled with glycerin. At first I had little in the way of coherent thoughts that didn't have to do with my physical situation, or food. My daydreams were deprivation-specific, plans for a dustless, warm room and a hot shower in Kathmandu or what I would chose to eat in Bangkok—green chicken curry with little eggplants—but then one day my fantasies switched tracks. I started to have a romance with a widowed, wealthy Thai, a business man. When we moved in together, I decorated our apartment in Bangkok with Thai and Chinese antiques. I worked out strategies to get his children to accept me. We bought a second small apartment in Hong Kong. At first, this fantasy was a warm nest I returned to after each stop to pee or eat, feathering it with the minutiae of kitchen arrangements, antiques for the living room, and details about my step-children's occupations—the boy an architect, the girl a lawyer. The quantity of detail seemed to block, like furniture piled up against a door, my real world but finally my phantasmagoria collapsed one afternoon like a punctured blimp. The psychic distance was too great, too tenuous to sustain against the tan surf of dust boiling up from the wheels into the back of the truck veiling and revealing astonishing visions of snow-etched mountains.

Amelia and I compared bruises on our calves, deciding they were caused by other people resting their legs on top of ours. We were a little cramped for space. She and I concluded this bruising was connected to the altitude; the women suffered from it more than the men, but we had no idea what the link was between altitude and bruises.

By the second day out of Shigatze, we all had runny noses, coughs, sneezes, our sinuses producing huge, at first disgusting and then commonplace if annoying, outpourings of gallons of mucus as they became irritated and then infected by the dust. We could not bend to tie a shoe without something repellant descending from our noses, a portion of mucus capellini or fettuccini or, occasionally, lasagna. But we also suffered from the opposite problem—our noses were clogged with dusty blood scabs. It was like having constipation and diarrhea simultaneously. We reached a consensus that public nose picking was acceptable. I would wake with tiny mud puddles in the corners of my eyes since my sinuses spent all night trying to expel the day's dust.

Dawa one night told us that he had heard from a fellow guide about a group that had started out ahead of us from Lhasa but had had to turn back because the members were arguing, and fighting over everything to the point of coming to blows. Dawa's report made us feel pleased with ourselves; we decided we were doing very well despite our physical misery.

In my red cape, my back against one of the three huge steel drums sloshing with gasoline, I was not thinking about change, or Aunt Liz or spiritual goals. I was just hanging on.

We were a salmagundi of ages and nationalities, I the eldest at 59. Our solace, while being thrown around the back of the truck on potholed, dirt roads, or fording rivers while praying the engine wouldn't be inundated as we rocked back and forth over stones, or while eating instant noodles boiled or unboiled or a vegetable stew, which at this altitude took two hours to cook, was to tell each other stories. Listening to these helped to calm my apprehensions of others and their reactions to me. I love travel stories. They also helped me to feel related to my companions, rather than separate and afraid. Story by story I connected to them, as each presented me with a thread with which to darn the hole in my spiritual fabric.

Heinrich, like other German men I have met traveling, was built like a cube, all muscle, no fat, apparently impervious to cold and altitude with a vigorous sense of daring. He had lively eyes and the temperament of a mythic trickster, perhaps the Coyote of Native American legend or the Raven of the Pacific Northwest. Putting one over on officialdom was more fun than bungee jumping to Heinrich. I admired his courage, how the flint of his wit sparked solutions in difficult circumstances, and I certainly envied his physical endurance.

He lived on a cooperative farm he had helped to found and suffered from carpal tunnel syndrome, not from computing, but from milking, another repetitive syndrome.

He had, after graduating from gymnasium where his final paper had been on a particular Afghan tribe, driven a Mercedes to Iran for a man who paid him a thousand U.S. on delivery. In the 1970s Iranian customs had a specific stamp for your passport that noted you were entering the country with a Mercedes; and if you left without it, you had to pay a monster tax, more than the price of the car, unless you were given a document exempting you. The new owner of the Mercedes put Heinrich off for months, finally becoming unavailable on the phone.

I knew Iran in the 1970s, having gone there with my teenaged son in 1974 on the pretense of visiting a friend who was there on a Fulbright. We crossed the country by bus and the occasional airplane. I had heard about Germans and other Europeans driving Mercedes into Iran, but Heinrich was the first one I had met.

Meanwhile, Heinrich worked in a carpet store so as not to use up the thousand he had earned from the delivery of the Mercedes. During the Shah's time, there were many tourists and Americans living in Iran eager to buy carpets. Developing affection for a small one, Heinrich bought it. His employer gave him a rococo certificate attesting to its authenticity with a big blob of red sealing wax, a signature replete with curlicues and flourishes, and, of course, a red ribbon.

Heinrich, never idle in a difficult situation told us how he tracked the Mercedes owner by going to the post office to talk to the postmen. One recognized the name of the Mercedes importer as someone on his route.

"The postman was very nice to me. Everyone in the post office was sympathetic," Heinrich said. "I went to the address and rang the doorbell. Just speaking English got me past the maid. I found the man who had bought the Mercedes in his courtyard reading the newspaper. I told him who I was; we had not met before, and sat down. Of course, he had to be polite so he ordered some tea for me. Over tea, sitting under a bougainvillea vine I told him, 'I called my father, who is assistant to the Foreign Minister, last night. I will have dinner with him next week when he comes to meet with the head of your secret police.'"

All lies, but Heinrich received the necessary paper.

Heinrich's ingenuity was entrancing. Telling his tale, he beat his broad hand on his thigh, partly in emphasis, partly to pound the ubiquitous dust from his jeans in little clouds as he chuckled, eyes dancing, delighting in his cleverness. A smooth trip would have been as boring to him as flat terrain to a mountain biker. The obstacles make the journey.

He took off with rug and certificate for Afghanistan, on the second leg of his adventure. Buying a horse and having a saddle made at a fair, he headed into the mountains to find the tribe he had researched. An official stopped him for being in the area without a permit.

"So," said Heinrich, "I whipped out my carpet certificate, a scroll with a seal and a red ribbon at the bottom. 'Here's my permit from the Interior Department allowing me in this area.' I pointed to the seal and the signature."

The man, semi-literate, most impressed by the red seal and signature, waved him on his way. We howled with delight in the back of the baby-blue truck, rooting for Heinrich.

Shortly after this encounter, Afghan horsemen surrounded him, waving rifles and shooting, mostly in the air. I was awed by his traveling skills. He explained that in this situation it was imperative not to show fear. I noted this fact particularly when he added that if you did, you might be shot.

It was his tribe, the one he had studied. He stayed with them until an official, the superior of the previous one, very literate, speaking perfect English, arrived asking to see the permit. Heinrich, however, rather than being jailed, spent the duration of his stay, as a guest of the official, who found him, I am sure, considerably more interesting than any other company locally available.

I tried to absorb Heinrich's ability to ad-lib in and out of situations. I wanted his canniness. Perhaps I acquired some since, when I hitched back to Lhasa on another truck, I was not fazed getting to a checkpoint for which I had no permit. I folded a twenty-dollar bill into my passport, adjusted my face to innocence and received my passport back sans the twenty. While this was going on, I talked to a young American who was being driven to the border because he had tried to enter Lhasa without the necessary permits.

After our circumambulation of Kailash, Heinrich left us at Tholing, in far western Tibet. His parting present, which it later turned out he should not have given us, were some *tsatsas* he found in a cave in Tsaparang. A *tsatsa* is a little image, an inch or so high, made by pressing mud into a mold. Sometimes they are of Buddha or Manjushri or are just a miniature *chörten*. Despite being of friable mud, they are often quite complex images with lotuses, jewelry and other ornaments difficult to reproduce. They are offerings that people leave in sacred places and he should not have touched them, but he, and we, didn't know that.

He intended to go from Tholing illegally, since there was no way to get the necessary permit, to Kashgar in far western China. But I am sure he was heading back to his tribe in Afghanistan. For someone like Heinrich it is just a pleasant stroll from Kashgar to Afghanistan. I hope he found his way there.

This was, for him, a physical adventure as it was for Ben and Arthur. His land of spiritual attachment was Afghanistan, not Tibet. At first, I thought none of my fellow travelers had a family association or a sense of being on pilgrimage in Tibet, that they had not brought their dead along with them. That proved not to be true, but amongst us yearnings for, or bemusements about, the sacred were not apparent to me.

A dog guarding his house in Raga.

The morning after we stayed with the family near the ferry, we rode through light snow which skirled and whipped its whiteness like a low mist over the frozen dirt road as it fell out of a clear blue sky. We stopped in Raga for a lunch break where the main store was filled with ragged children, snot dripping from their noses saying, "Tashidelek. Hello. Tashidelek. Hello." I gave them raisins and peanuts and made myself some *tsampa* laced with cheese and moistened by yak butter tea bought from the storeowner. A hefty teenager came into the store and grabbed peanuts from the hands of the two children. A woman with a baby, who had come in behind him to beg from us, went into a fury, screaming at him, hitting him over and over again with her fists, tears in her eyes. I gave the two children more peanuts and raisins.

In 1995 hunger was still endemic in Tibet because the Chinese had destroyed the local economy when they destroyed the monasteries that had acted as banks, lending both money and grain. There are, of course, no statistics because the Chinese deny the problem's existence, but there was anecdotal proof everywhere as I traveled through Tibet. People, particularly children, were often hungry.

As we were preparing to leave Raga, the driver and Dawa came to us to ask if we would let three Tibetan girls travel with us in the back of the truck for a few days. Since there was disagreement, I suggested we put it to a vote; we took them. They sat near the tailgate where the dust and the jouncing were worst, trying to make themselves into small bundles so as not to take up too much room. They hid under their coats, ate candy and dried fruit we gave them, comparing the condition of their dusty hair and laughing. I had given up on mine. I combed it out gingerly every night appalled at how it broke from the dryness and dust before re-braiding it.

That night we came into a town with a Chinese government guesthouse which Miguel got out to look at, reporting back that it was a pigsty. We drove on, finding a pleasant place with a fairly clean john.

I was assigned to sleep with the three Tibetan girls. I went to bed early in my usual state of bone-aching tiredness. Just as I fell asleep Dawa and the truck driver banged through the door—locks are rare in Tibet—towing the three girls with them, turning on the light, leaving the door open so that an Antarctic breeze, unaccompanied by penguins, came hustling in after them. The two men stood in the middle of the room yelling at each other.

I rose, a gritty pillar of offended, Western, middle-aged womanhood and told them they were rude and should not turn on the light, leave the door open or enter without knocking—rarely do Tibetans knock, although they are incredibly polite and sensitive in other ways—and that the men should leave and the girls go to bed. Dawa explained that he had been looking for a guide for the girls who were escaping from Tibet the next morning, planning to walk out as Dawa had through the mountains to Nepal so that they could go on to Dharmsala in India, see the Dali Lama, and go to school. In Tibet they could only get an education in Chinese, not in their own language. As part of their effort to kill off Tibetan culture, the Chinese are also intent on eradicating the language or at least making it a language of the ignorant.

I don't think Dawa or the driver gave a thought to whether or not I or any of us, would go along with the girls' escape. I would guess he just assumed that as a Westerner I would, of course, be in favor of this flight as, indeed, I was.

Closing the door firmly, twisting wire around a nail to, at least, keep the wind out, I talked in sign language to the three pretty faces bundled to their ears in scarves, hats, layers of sweaters and jackets with flimsy Chinese sneakers on their feet. I contributed a bag of raisins and dates bought in Lhasa to the girls' food cache. We four went to sleep, or I did, since surely they couldn't, considering what they were facing in the morning.

At 4:00 a.m. there was a knock on the door. I sat up sleepily in bed to see the girls packing by the light of a pair of candles attached to a table by their own wax. I waved goodbye from the shadows and warmth of my bed. They offered my raisins and dates back to me, since it is polite in Tibet to refuse a gift a number of times. I refused the return. I whispered, "Kaliy pay (Go slowly)" to them and they responded "Kaliy shu (Stay slowly)" as they slipped out into the cold to start their escape. There was no halo of bravery around them. They were doing what they needed to do. What was impressive to me was their quiet faith that they would find their way over the mountains.

Dawa learned English at a Tibetan school in India. He walked with eleven others over the mountains to Nepal with one blanket between them and insufficient food. They were continually afraid of encountering Chinese soldiers or a police patrol. The cold at night was so intense that, as Dawa charmingly put it, "It was dangerous to the fingers." In the morning they couldn't buckle their belts because the leather had frozen.

But he was rewarded on arriving in Dharmsala, India, by meeting the Dalai Lama who arranged for him to learn English so that he would be able to become a guide on his return to Tibet. Speaking of that meeting, his face softened and his voice trembled with reverence for the Dalai Lama.

I learned more about Dawa while we stayed, after doing the Kailash *khora,* in rooms he found for us at a house in a town on Lake Manasarovar's shore. The lake, right next door, is the spiritual companion to Mount Kailash. People also do pilgrimages to the lake and circumambulate it as they do the mountain. He arranged for me to sleep in a home that included a shrine for a man who had been a revered teacher. The teacher's son, Dawa's friend, a guide for a Nepali trekking company, was short and cheery with better English than Dawa. He seemed to have no difficulty going back and forth across the border.

As I was around these two, I began to wonder if they were a gay pair. The complexity of gayness in Tibet became evident when Dawa's friend told me he loved Dawa but they had never consummated their relationship because "it would mean making a girl" out of Dawa and "that would be shameful." As Hamlet noted, "There is nothing either good or bad, but thinking makes it so."

I also realized that Dawa definitely had a drinking problem. We all understood after one night when we watched his personality change totally as he drank.

We were in a Tibetan house that Amelia and Miguel were staying in. It was a revelation. The floor was paved with large, smooth river stones, the roof held up by carved and brilliantly painted pillars, the walls decorated with *thangkas*, scroll paintings of various deities in either their fierce or their beautiful form. I remember one of Palden Llamo, not as her usual fanged self wearing an opera length strand of severed heads but as a beautiful, dark-eyed woman with a lotus in her palm. There were also rugs patterned with Buddhist symbols hanging on the walls. Our hostess served us delicious butter tea. Dawa came in to join us. He started out as his usual, slightly sullen, but not unpleasant self, but after a number of slugs of some kind of white-lightning he had on him, changed to a physically aggressive, abusive person who attacked Miguel for no reason. It took Gunnar, Heinrich, Ben, and Chiam together to control him and get him out the door. Our hostess was exceedingly alarmed because if they had bumped into one of the pillars a part of the house would have caved in.

I would guess that Dawa misinterpreted Miguel's reserve as contempt, and the moonshine exacerbated his feelings of being despised until they broke out into violence, a case of alcoholic hierarchy.

I, along with the other women, withdrew to the far side of the room. I hate being around excessive drinkers. My father was one; my husband was one; I was one. Being around them provokes my fear, and in that mirror my self-hatred rises like acid reflux.

My mother had discovered my father was an alcoholic one day in 1952, when going up to the coop where we had kept chickens during World War II, she had opened the door to be greeted by a cascade of his cache of brown whiskey bottles. She wrote her aunts in North Dakota, "I may divorce him. How can I trust him? He used money his family badly needed to buy liquor. He is selfish and weak. Only weak people drink like that, people without willpower."

Her belief that his drinking and his inability to stop were the result of weakness of character and willpower was standard thinking for the 1950s when alcoholism and all addictions were viewed as a problem of willpower, not as mental illness. My mother was definitely a standard thinker, her head a hive of received opinions.

Besides believing that his drinking was due to weakness of character, rather than the disease of addiction, I have realized as I have read her letters that she didn't recognize the link between his addiction and one of the ingredients of his personality, fear of all people in authority. Certain personality traits are associated with drinking—inability to earn at the level of your abilities, fear of people, an exaggerated sense of hierarchy, to name a few. It is not that these characteristics are exclusive to the addict. Many people suffer from these problems; but the alcoholic, rather than attempting to find a solution to his problematic personality trait "solves" it or, perhaps, tries to "dis-solve" it, by drinking. This leads to shame, avoidance, magical thinking, and other unuseful behaviors.

I can think of a dozen people who are/were drinkers of magnificent proportions who suffered from none of the aforementioned flaws, achieved huge successes, were totally, easily gregarious, and apparently ignored hierarchy; but at the other end of the balance scale, I see a friend who panicked if he was in a room with more than six people, another who became a resentful doormat before all she decided were "above" her, and my father who could not ask for a raise and, therefore, was invariably underpaid.

His ability and talent were undercut by his fears. We were always on the brink of losing the house he had designed, a barn reworked into an elegant home. (Recreating barns as homes was the 1940s smart move as in the 1970s renovating dilapidated brownstones in dubious neighborhoods in Brooklyn was the chic life for young couples.) All through my childhood, I lived with the worry that we might have to sell the house because my father didn't earn enough for us to pay the taxes. My great aunts in Fargo did come to the rescue.

But the constant fear and worry made my mother tight-fisted. She also had grown up in a family with a haphazard earner and her mother returned to her family to cook and housekeep in order to pay the way for her two daughters and herself. My mother's miserliness expanded to a lack of compassion. She rarely gave money or sympathy unless forced to by society's judgment so that she was both fiscally and emotionally mean-spirited. I learned, growing up, not to expect generosity and not to give it. Sonam's generosity and that of people I traveled with, as well as Tibetans I met was, therefore, a source of inspiration for me.

I woke, it seemed, every morning to my mother bashing pots and pans about in the stove drawer. That meant my parents were having yet another fight about money. He, trapped between the rock of his fear of his boss and the hard place of his wife's fury, would eventually ask for a raise, in terror that he would be fired. The raise, always given, would see us through to the next crisis. Although she found his cache of bottles, she did not understand that living inside those bottles bloated his feelings of inferiority.

Living with an addict in constant need of reassurance and support, however, skewed her thinking about men. She was bound by the limitations of her perceptions of the world, and like most of us, she assumed that her world-view, which had been formed by her particular circumstances, was the only reality.

Some years after my divorce, driving me to the station to return to New York, she asked, "Do you think you will marry again?"

"I can't answer that question. Maybe when I'm fifty I will be lonely and marry again, but as of now, no," I said emphatically.

"Don't," she responded in an anguished voice. "Don't. Men rob you of your life. They take everything away from you."

Well, yes, if your spouse is alcoholic his dependency and passivity will drain you.

I am grateful that I have many of the letters she wrote to friends, aunts, and her mother which have allowed me to see her from alternative perspectives from the one-dimensional view a daughter gets of her mother. They have given me a chance to see her as someone other than "my mother," as the photo of my Aunt Liz, happy at the end of her childhood adventure of running away from home, has expanded my vision of her. After all, in her life she was more than my aunt as my mother had a life before my birth. The letters and photos also enrich their stories for me, give them depth and resonance.

Slowly the rest of my companions rose, and we breakfasted on dehydrated noodles mixed with the vegetable stew left over from the night before. We climbed into the back of the truck that morning without the girls, but we were all thinking about them as we set out. Huge clouds of reddish dust billowed up and were sucked into the back of the truck. We dodged under our Chinese surplus quilts, but nothing, not even my monk's winter robe, protected us. When we smiled, our teeth were streaked with dust. When we sneezed, we sneezed clots of dust. Our sunglasses wore a patina of shimmering dust. Cold enveloped us. What sustained us through our travails was each other's company, though we were not without stresses and strains. Since Arthur did not like me, I stayed clear of him. Chiam had bouts of acute rudeness. After getting down from the cab of the truck once I asked him if it was Gunar's turn next in the cab and he snarled at me, "Ask Gunar."

But we were company for each other in a way that companions on a tour bus are not. The shared misery created an intimacy in which we were more willing to reveal ourselves. Possibly our communal misery caused us to be more compassionate with each other. My close proximity to my companions, their incessant, unrelieved company, put me in a situation where I was constantly aware of my fear of people. I worked hard to control my reactions, to separate and eject from my mind thoughts that came to me shaped by fear.

I knew intellectually there was nothing I could do to change Arthur's attitude toward me, that it had absolutely nothing to do with me or with my actions; but emotionally I wanted desperately to ingratiate myself with him, to get him to like me. This, of course, was pure ego. I wanted him to like me since I would feel better about myself if I felt I had his approval. I managed to always be pleasant to him. As days and difficulties increased, it was harder being civil. We were always tired, stretched to our physical and psychological limits by altitude, climate, and physical difficulties. It helped that with ten people you can avoid anyone you feel tension with. But there were times, as when Chiam was rude, that I desperately wanted to do a verbal dismembering but somehow I didn't. However, I don't think I was very thoughtful of my companions, being too self-absorbed with my own physical distress, the leitmotif of each day's song, as I huddled in my monk's winter robe. We tended to each live in our individual dystopian trance in the back of the truck.

The night after the girls left us Dawa, since as evening fell we were not close to any village, took us off the road to a house that was sitting, a solitary rectangle, near some dry fields. It was an un-windowed cave, one room lit by their cooking fire and a glimmering butter lamp, the walls slick with soot and grease. Living in such a place you would have difficulty keeping clean. But everything was neat—utensils and herbs hung from the ceiling, clothes on pegs—but since the smoke went out through a hole in the ceiling with no pipe to guide it, everything was sooty. The couple told us we could sleep in their house. Certainly it would be warm, but I didn't think I would be able to breathe. We did cram in to cook since they kindly lent us their yak dung fire that smelled sweetly of grass. My eyes quickly began to tear from the smoke, and I had to go outside every few minutes.

We offered to share our food in an attempt to pay for the fire they had lent us which was the result of many hours of walking and picking up yak pies. They took a little, but we and our vegetable stew were too strange for them. They offered to sell us a beautiful, small, burled wood bowl decorated with designs in silver around the edge, an heirloom. It was the kind of bowl that Tibetans carry to make their *tsampa* in. I, idiotically, tried to tell them through Dawa that they should keep the bowl because it was part of their past. You cannot eat an heirloom, nor can you use it as medicine.

There were two women, the wife and her older sister who was going blind, possibly from living in a constantly smoke-filled house. I wish I had bought the bowl.

I wanted Arthur to give them more money but he was firm and, within the traveler/local inhabitant economy where inflation is always a problem, he was right. But I was haunted by the kindness of these people, their generosity when they had so little and frustrated at my inability to make a difference in their lives. I was constantly aware of how powerless I was to help; a few peanuts, some raisins were all I seemed to have to give. I was desperately conscious that it was not enough, that it was like placing one drop of water in the Sahara.

We watched the sun go down, bloodying the vast empty plain, and then the stars, millions of brilliants against the black velvet sky looking so close that I expected the fog of my breath to cloud them. That night I slept in the truck with the driver, Dawa and a few other people who also were unable to coexist with the smoke. The driver put his sleeping bag, a home-made affair, huge as a mummy case, right where I would have to step to get out of the truck if I needed to climb down to pee. So I didn't leave the truck all night which turned out to be a good thing. My feet, although cocooned in layers of socks, didn't get warm until dawn when Dawa stepped over the driver onto the hitch below the tailgate of the truck to descend. There was a hellish uproar of growling, snarling and barking. Dawa leapt back into the truck, pale with fear. All the local dogs had gathered to sleep under the truck. He was very lucky not to have been bitten a number of times. The man came out of the house to scatter the dogs, throwing stones at them.

We started out again, after a depressing breakfast of instant noodles, into blue sky and infinite dust. Miguel and Amelia told us that after seeing a friend's slides of Dharmsala, India they decided to travel there. Once there, they had met Tibetans whom they had liked so much they decided to go to Tibet, despite the fact that Amelia, while in a monastery in Dharmsala, had had her bottom bitten by a large mastiff. She told us that she had made eye contact with the dog, which had been two rooms away from her in a temple. As if this visual contact were a signal, he came loping straight at her and bit.

An elderly monk sought her out the next day to tell her the bite was part of her *karma* and that it would purify her. She said that, oddly, in a few days she did feel different, that she'd had an attitudinal shift. For them, too, the journey was more for the physical experience than for a pilgrimage. Thomas, their close friend, had joined them, thinking Tibet sounded like a good adventure.

For others, however, there was a family connection. Chiam stated that he'd come to Tibet because it was the one place his father hadn't been, suggesting a little Oedipal rivalry. Gunar had, I suspect, come to Tibet for a different Oedipal reason, to fulfill a promise similar to mine to Aunt Liz, spoken or silent. For him, the trip to Kailash was a pilgrimage. In Gunar, I sensed a quiet, tensile relationship to Tibet's landscape, an intuitive link.

Gunar was closest to me in age being in his early fifties.

He told us, "My father was a housepainter. He supported us during the Great Depression by wandering around Europe painting houses. He loved to read and somehow in his travels picked up a copy of Sven Hedin's *Transhimalaya*. When he came home, I remember he would talk about how he wanted to go to Tibet, to see what Hedin had seen. It was his big dream which used to make my mother smile because she knew it would not happen. When he died, I decided to go to Tibet. I have now come here five times. I think next year I will go to northern India. I want to look up at the Himalayas instead of being in the middle of them."

What he did not mention, but I knew from my reading about Kailash, was that Sven Hedin had been the first Westerner to circumambulate the mountain.

Gunar had, like Sonam, an aura of peace. I wanted that peace as much as I aspired to Heinrich's canniness.

Over a lunch of cooked noodles, peanuts and a Snickers bar—Tibet is the only place I've ever been where you can eat a Snickers bar a day and not gain weight since, because of the altitude, just the effort of breathing causes one to burn as much as 2,000 calories a day—Gunar told his tale. Pale, with thinning blond hair, he had the requisite Danish blue eyes and a build more stringy than strong. But that he was strong became apparent. He had a wry Scandinavian sense of the ridiculousness of life and self. The apparent blandness of his exterior belied a character layered like a *pousse-café*.

"I traveled two years ago to Kailash with my friend, Peter. We came in the back of a truck which meant we didn't have to carry our packs. Foolishly, we brought too much. We each had two packs. That was alright until we left Darchen and had to start carrying things. The next day we walked carrying a pack a hundred yards, then put it down to go back and carry the one we had left behind. It was very slow going. But we crossed paths with some men from Dolpo, the Tibetan area of Nepal. They were willing to be our porters for a day or two until we reached the Nepali border. I thought there we would have no difficulty finding nomads who would either be willing to be porters or would rent us a horse or a yak to go over the pass to Nepal.

"But arriving at the camp we found that the nomads, who are always independent, weren't interested in being porters. They explained to us as though we were small children that they didn't need money; they had their sheep, yaks, and horses. The nomad chief pointed out the pass to us, saying it would take half a day to go over into Nepal."

Listening, I cracked peanuts, which hurt my fingers. My skin had become so dry that the pressure applied to break a peanut shell was painful.

They went over the pass carrying their packs a hundred yards, then going back for the second pack, a desperately tedious process. They had no visas for Nepal and spent their time as they climbed the pass discussing what story they should concoct to explain their unauthorized presence.

This discussion continued after they reached the pass as they made their way to Simikot where they knew there were both a hospital and airfield. Peter, having pain in one leg, convinced Gunar that should be their excuse for coming into Nepal without visas.

Gunar, rubbing his unshaven chin told us, chuckling, how, when they arrived at the Simikot bridge, Peter announced to anyone who was interested, which was no one, that he couldn't walk. Gunar went into town to find a horse and horseman to carry Peter to the clinic where they examined his leg, setting it in plaster as a precaution. They had no x-ray equipment which meant they couldn't diagnose Peter and, therefore, suggested he go to Kathmandu to be x-rayed. Still without visas or stamps in their passports they flew to Kathmandu.

They now had two choices: to go to the Danish embassy and tell their tale or go to the black market to buy a visa. I'm sure Heinrich would have headed for the black market; but Gunar, while amused by their predicament and later their escape from it, did not exude a Heinrichian sense of triumph at hoodwinking the authorities. Peter went to the hospital; Gunar went to the Danish embassy.

"There," Gunar said, "I was very lucky to find a sympathetic woman. I told her, 'My friend and I have had a terrible time coming from Tibet. I had to help him walk as well as deal with our backpacks because he injured his leg. We are here illegally, no doubt about it, but we couldn't get any medical help in Tibet. I am now afraid to go to the police. What will happen if they don't believe us? And how are we going to leave the country?'"

She wrote an explanatory letter on embassy letterhead for Gunar to show to the police. Next he went to the police station where they didn't believe a word of his story but were stymied because of the letter the woman at the embassy had written. Reluctantly, they gave him the visas and stamped both passports. Again fiction, apparently, triumphed over fact.

Gunar then went to the x-ray clinic with the good news, expecting Peter to be dancing. But the doctors, discovering a hairline fracture in Peter's shin, had re-plastered him. There was a happy ending, however. Gunar called their insurance company and two days later they flew out business class sharing a bottle of Chateau Margaux with dinner.

I tried to absorb Gunar's travel virtues, not getting your knickers in a knot over events, taking difficulties as they appear, quietly.

In the afternoon we passed through country with big sloping sand dunes. We took a break near two bridges, one an old span, a graceful suspension bridge. The other, its replacement, was a new cast concrete job. Bridges in Tibet, particularly suspension bridges, have an aura of romance about them since the first suspension bridges were built here in the 15th century by one of Tibet's most eccentric, multifaceted characters, Tangton Gyalpo, aka "The Madman of the Empty Land." Tangton is a Tibetan historical personality who alters and shimmers between myth and history like a holograph in which the image and its colors shift as you move it about.

The two bridges over a ravine. The suspension is no longer used.

Besides creating the first suspension bridges from hand-forged iron links that have not rusted in the 600 years since they came glowing out from under the smith's hammer, he also invented Tibetan opera. To raise the funds necessary to build his bridges, there were once 58 of them in Tibet, he arranged performances of his musical dramas, charging entrance fees.

In an alternate story, he traveled around Tibet with a song and dance troupe of seven sisters, the Andrew Sisters, doubled plus one, and collected money for his bridges from their performances. Many of his *chakam*, his bridges, were destroyed during the Cultural Revolution, but two or, perhaps, three still exist. I have seen one in the town of Riwoche. Despite 600 years of being above the Tsangpo River, despite centuries of rain, snow, sleet, and hail, there is no sign of rust.

I stood on the river bank, pushing aside the prayer flags wound around the rectangular links. I felt the iron and ran my fingers over the roughness of its surface formed by hammer blows 600 years ago. Underneath, the turbulent, grey-brown Tsangpo River hurled itself over huge boulders. I did not cross it since it had no floor. I would have had to cross by hanging on to the top row of iron links while fitting my feet into the bottom row. But I think of "The Mad Man of the Empty Land" now when I see the Brooklyn Bridge, the George Washington, the Golden Gate.

We stood in the wide valley looking past the bridges at the amazing horizon-long line of mountains. They reach as far as the eye can see from one side of the horizon to the other, a continuous, uninterrupted, waving and cresting line of white. There appeared to be nothing between us and them, not a tree, not a house. Not even a little rise of land was apparent. Gunar pointed saying, "I think that's the Annapurna massif. If you start walking from here, you can be there in a week." That dream of walking, mesmerized by a mountain, I understood.

Mountains from horizon to horizon.

The horsemen gathered in a small town. Notice the carpets on the horses and the handmade stirrups. The man in blue in the foreground has dangling from his belt a container that holds his flint and small tinder with which to start a fire.

Further on we stopped at a tiny town, neat, white washed mud brick, reminiscent of the towns in American westerns. We had butter tea that was served by an exceptionally pretty woman fastidiously dressed in her wrap-around dress, blouse, and Tibetan apron of many colors. When we came outside, there was a group of horsemen in the middle of the road exchanging gossip in their dashing, broad-brimmed hats. Their horses were small but beautifully cared for with handsome carpets under their saddles and shiny new stirrups with Buddhist designs pounded into their metal. They stared at us; we stared at them. We asked permission to take pictures of them posed proudly beside their horses whose foreheads were adorned with pieces of embroidery or designs worked in many colors on leather. I am sure if they had had cameras they would have taken our pictures standing proudly beside our baby-blue truck.

Kailash from afar.

We were now a day away from the town of Darchen, the starting point of the Kailash *khora*. It was four days since we had left Shigatze, six since we had left Lhasa, but it seemed an eternity. All sense of the world as it appears in *The New York Times* or *The Economist* had shriveled and blown away from my dust-addled brain. Dust and wind were my only reality.

The most washing we had been able to do was a little warm water in a basin splashing our faces with cupped hands. But our hands were so dirty that they just muddied our faces more. We wore the same clothes day after day since there was no way we could wash or dry anything. We were miserable in our grime as only those used to daily cleanliness can be under such circumstances. But we complained very little and generally were able to laugh about our physical miseries.

At our lunch stop, Chiam, the magnificently handsome Israeli with his mop of wavy jet-black hair, took me aside to tell me his story privately, away from the others. "If you ever tell this story," he insisted, "don't make me the hero. We all did what we could. It was terrible." He spoke in a rush, a river cracking a dam. At times his face tautened with anguish; he would grimace at a memory, as he relived the pain of his adventure.

He, with eight other Israelis, started from Darcha, in the Himalayas of northern India, to go to Kargil. They had horses to carry their backpacks, a ponyman, and a cook. It took them three days to reach Sengge La, Lion Pass—also spelled Singi, Senge, Singay, Singila and Singe—a sixteen thousand foot plus pass with a reputation for treacherous snow storms late into spring. It is often not the height of the pass that causes difficulties but the steepness of its ascent and its weather.

Years later, on the same route, I had an interchange with Sengge La of my own which upheld its bad reputation. My ponyman refused to take the horses over the pass because there was still snow, although nuns in red robes were tripping down with their donkeys. When my guide demanded I turn back, because the ponyman had never taken his horses on snow before, I refused saying I would meet them at the monastery where we were scheduled to stay the night or I would continue on my own if they turned back. Since that meant shame for abandoning me, and no pay, they made it over the pass.

Somehow the horses got up; maybe the guide and ponyman carried them. I was a long way ahead, reveling in my mountain solitude. I'm sure Heinrich, Gunar and Chiam parented my adamantine stance.

But Chiam's situation was more harrowing. His group camped at the base of the mountain waking to snow and cold. They stayed in their camp thinking, since it was June, the sun would appear and melt the snow, but each day the cold and clouds continued. Bored, they stalked round and round their tents, entertaining themselves with snowball fights. I could imagine, with no difficulty, Chiam's tall, nervous figure winding between the tents or packing snowballs. The ponyman said he would lead them over the pass the night after the first sunny day.

The fifth day was sunny and that evening the ponyman tied everything to the horses. But getting over Sengge La was only the beginning. They carried their packs since the horses, weakened by short rations during the wait, could only carry tents and cooking equipment. On the other side of the pass one woman, as she crossed a stream on ice veneered stones, fell in. They made a shelter for her from what they could find in their packs and she changed into whatever extra clothing people could give her. It was viciously cold. Then they lost their way.

Because they were wearing their backpacks, they sank into the snow. Chiam and the other men stamped a path for their companions. The horses floundered in snowdrifts, neighing, crying in fear. Chiam's face tautened as he remembered the horses. The woman who had fallen into the river shivered with fear and cold. Others shed tears of exhaustion as they continued to walk. Chiam found a flat place where they could camp.

"When I took off my gloves to put up the first tent, my hands stiffened with the cold. The horses shivered, whinnying in the freezing wind. It was terrible to watch them, poor things. You knew they thought they were going to die. We all thought we might die.

"The woman went into the tent with a sleeping bag shaking with cold. Someone had a thermometer that read -15 F. We couldn't find some of our backpacks because it was now dark."

Morning brought sun and good weather, making them optimistic. They felt they could make it to Kargil. They continued carrying their packs. Since the horses were too weak to keep up, the ponyman said he would follow at whatever pace the horses could manage. They had nothing left to eat but chocolate and biscuits.

The weather was beautiful; the sun pooled starbursts of light in above-the-knee snow, but they were walking at altitude with heavy packs. Chiam had no sunglasses. When they arrived in Kargil, exhausted and hungry, Chiam rushed into the first guesthouse. With no language the people who ran the guesthouse understood what had happened. Chaim's group abandoned their packs outside the house. Fully clothed they fell into all the available beds.

"I woke two hours later to find I could not see anything. I didn't understand in those first few minutes what had happened, and I was terrified by the idea that I was permanently blind. Then I realized that I had snow blindness. I was unable to see for three days."

When he told me this, his face contracted in pain at the memory of his fear. The next day when they went out to retrieve their packs, they found no one in the poor, largely Moslem community of Kargil, where there were and still are pictures of Ayatollah Khomeini in many of the restaurants, had touched them.

The stories of your fellow travelers while being entertainment, cautionary tales, or models for future behavior when otherwise you might be overwhelmed, unable to function, or examples of how you would like to act or, in some cases, not act, are also integral to your experience. Fellow travelers form a temporary family, sometimes dysfunctional, but frequently as warm as a blood family can be. Chiam, Heinrich, Gunar, Amelia are part of my relationship to Tibet, inextricably intertwined with my attachment to that far place.

My relations with my temporary siblings helped me to look at and face my fears about people and to behave in ways I might not have without the examples of their tales. Stories form a web. I live in a net, as do we all, of family stories, friends' stories and, if we are travelers, the tales of those we have met along the road giving us glimpses of other lives, other ways of living and of seeing or experiencing the world. The web is a psychological, intellectual, but also a spiritual net.

We drove into Darchen, the garbage-strewn town from which one starts to circumambulate Kailash. Until this century, most things Tibetans owned and used were biodegradable; but they are a people who have never had a rep for cleanliness.

Between the World Wars, Robert Byron, traveling from Sikkim to Gyantze with friends, noted of a town they passed through, "The streets, seven feet wide, were runnels of filth and strewn with bones and pieces of bloody hide. Enormous ravens, croaking and disgusting, crouched on the house-tops or flapped a few feet above our heads, as though in appetite for ourselves."

Tibetans, whether in Tibet or India, continue to litter; but now what they discard is not biodegradable. The Dalai Lama has urged them to pick up in their communities in India to no apparent effect. However, they think it admirable when foreigners pick up. Collecting trash in Dharmsala I was told by passing Tibetans that I was good person. However, I don't think of dirt when I think of Tibetan towns. I think of barley bending to a breeze, yak dung pats adhering to walls, painted doorways and gnarled roots stacked for winter fires on top of walls. Darchen, however, is different story.

My experience is that towns near sacred sites tend to be trash heaps, perhaps because much of the population is transient. I have a memory of Guadalupe in Mexico also being a garbage bin. However, Tibetans are personally clean which is, I think, incredibly admirable since I cringed every time I had to take off my clothes in a drafty room, where the temperature was more or less above freezing, to wash with cold or tepid water.

Darchen, while not in the league of Byron's town, has, beside the river, the only local water source, a fungal growth of trash along its banks—beer cans, broken bottles, abandoned clothing, plastic bits of broken pails and basins, rusting enamel basins, rusting Chinese army pork tins, paper, cardboard boxes, decomposing Chinese sneakers. Tibetans, not understanding batteries are poisonous, throw them in the river. This is scary. On every trip I fish them from the river, the water used for drinking, cooking and washing, put them in my backpack and pack them out.

We stayed in a guesthouse, a row of icy, cement block rooms off a central corridor. The outhouse, a mud brick affair no worse than usual, was a stroll through dogs who fought all night but which, if you bent to pick up a stone, immediately left, tail between legs. The rooms were clean, except for the ubiquitous dust, neat, painted with Buddhist symbols and tromp-l'oeil ruffles in a cornice below the ceiling, but were Frigidaires with four beds, each supplied with a comforter that was as heavy as cement paving. The rooms had no locks and were very un-private.

Tibetans barged in to look at us and satisfy themselves about what Westerners are like and what they own. One monk bustled in, picked up my postcards and looked through them. I signaled him to the window for better light. At each picture of Kailash he stopped, touching it reverently to his forehead.

We didn't get to bed the night we arrived until after 1:00 a.m. because, at 16,000 feet, it took three hours to cook dinner. The next day we slept, did laundry, particularly socks, which immediately fluttered off the line on the first rollicking wind to roll about like kittens in the dust. The wind on the Changtang plain is fairly constant but, after 5:00 p.m., due to the difference in temperature between air and earth, it becomes a *force majeure* punching at obstacles like a maddened boxer.

We tried to get the dirt off ourselves, not easy when you have to wash area by area in a freezing room using a small basin with only the hot water from a large thermos, which is all the hot water you are going to get to drink as well as wash. The technique is to start with your face, working downward, as quickly as possible, clothing each part as it is cleansed. The used water, now a grey-brown shade, we learned to throw out the window.

We tried to get a second thermos, but the ladies who were in charge turned us down firmly. When we had used up all the water in the big bin in the hallway, Arthur and Ben took it down to the river to refill it. It was arduous labor hauling it back up the slight rise to the guesthouse.

My hands were swollen from altitude, sunburned, and encrusted with dust. But Gunar's hands were frightening, so blackened and scarred by sunburn in the soft space between his thumb and first finger that the skin was cracking. It looked like the dried, broken patches of sunbaked mud.

The next day we found an excellent restaurant run by a woman who cooked in a wok over a roaring, probably dangerous, petrol, or perhaps kerosene fire housed in a steel barrel. We pointed to what the Tibetans were eating, which got us lamb with potatoes and rice, heavenly tasting because we hadn't cooked it and there was meat which we hadn't had for almost a week. She had various kinds of tea, jasmine, milk or yak butter. We listened to the Tibetan men solemnly and politely sucking it in.

One man opened a sack and started passing around bowls of burled wood he was selling, like the one we were offered in the house we had stayed in but without any silver decoration around their rims. The men inspected these minutely for scratches, dents, and any flaws, deciding if the grain was good or to their liking.

Although the restaurant was in a mud brick house, everything was temporary. The woman, at the end of pilgrimage season, packed up. Returning from our circumambulation, we found her gone. We mourned her loss sorely.

Ben, like Chiam, took me aside to tell his story as we wandered the trash-strewn streets of Darchen. In college he took drugs, paying for his habit by the logical step of becoming a dealer. While in Canada on a buying trip, friends called to tell him the police would arrest him when he got off the plane on his return. Not surprisingly, being in his late teens or early twenties, he was paralyzed by this news.

"I thought I should stay in Canada, try to disappear. I was gripped by doom and panic.

I could see that in memory the fear was still alive, forming two perpendicular lines between his eyebrows, as I watched him gazing at the desiccated landscape beyond the crumbling mud brick of Darchen walled on one side by dark ridges over which the white peak of Kailash peered.

"I should tell you," I interrupted, "that I've been in AA more than ten years now."

He smiled, acknowledging the connection my admission had made between us.

"I called Arthur who talked me into coming home, making me realize that the only way forward in my life was to face what had to be faced and go on from there."

"Do you know the Robert Frost line, 'The best way out is always through'?" I asked.

"No, but it's the truth. I went to jail but not for very long since it was my first offense, although it certainly felt damn long. Arthur visited me every week, my lifeline to the hope I might someday have a real life."

This made the bond between the two men completely understandable and also made me admire Arthur. Friendship exudes angelic qualities.

I heard from Ben a few months after I returned to the States while the adventure of Kailash was still misting about me. They left the truck at Dingeri, before the border. After all, how could two mountain climbers resist a look at Everest from her south face. Walking to Base Camp One, they hiked to Two, deciding to attempt Three. To move quickly, they abandoned all extras, including a water bottle. A snowstorm enveloped them. Retreating, they found passing nomads had taken what they had left at Camp Two, including the water bottle, which they now needed.

I could see, as he talked, the terrible loneliness of those two dark figures struggling in the unmarked expanse of whiteness, the snow's blank a sort of physical oblivion, with merciless outcroppings of rock, they the only things moving in the dense whiteness.

Coming down from Camp Two to One, an avalanche buried Ben when a snow ridge he was walking on collapsed. He remembered to cross his arms before his face, giving himself, literally, breathing space. He said that for a moment he came to in his arm space under the snow; panicking, he hyperventilated and fainted. Arthur dug him out with his hands.

Laboring though knee-deep drifts weakened Arthur so that Ben had to help him walk. They lurched and dragged themselves to the dark shelter of Rongphu Monastery. There, in rooms where firelight leapt on the stonewalls, the monks took care of them as they have cared for others before and after them.

Ben and Arthur planned to walk the *khora* in one day. Gunar, and Heinrich, expected a two-day circumambulation. Chiam and Janet, carrying their packs, thought to do it in three. I would have needed a month to do it with a pack.

The other German, Thomas; the Spanish couple, Amelia and Miguel; and I finished in three mind-and-body-numbing days. Porters carried our packs. I was grateful for our group. To have done it alone might have cracked me physically and psychologically.

We hired four porters, since a porter cost 50 yuan for the three-day trip, about $4.25, while yaks, and you had to hire a minimum of three, were 85 yuan each. We had three men and a woman whom I suspected was following her man, a handsome fellow who looked so like a Native American I expected him to speak Apache. He said his name repeatedly, but I could never decipher the sounds.

Jemi, the woman, wore an old nun's robe, had very short hair, and was burned dark by the sun. Not a bit pretty and certainly not feminine looking, she exuded warmth and goodness like a lily of the valley pouring its scent out on a spring day and was so obviously in love that it was painful to watch her. I wondered if she had left the nunnery to follow him but the robes could have been cast offs; she could have shaved her head because of lice. Not my business anyway, although I was aching with curiosity.

Alone, I started the *khora*, following the packed dirt path out of Darchen. There was nothing to distinguish it as being the path, the right path. It was just a narrow, dusty trail that meandered up and down little hills with barren ridges on my right, a view across the plateau to Gurla Mandata and its company of white peaks on my left. It could have been a dusty track in high country anywhere in the world. I only knew it was the right one because I could see ahead of me our three porters. We had started late, ten rather than eight, ahead of Amelia, Miguel and Thomas, who were doing something in the guesthouse kitchen. I had followed the porters thinking it unwise for them to be left alone with our packs.

My fears in these difficult circumstances made me suspicious. I was inexperienced. By the end of the trip, I had become a devotee of Tibetan porters. Anyway, I was ridiculous in thinking I could possibly keep up with them. They walked with our packs, their packs and sleeping bags, which were much bulkier than our sleeping bags, with the briskness of someone worried about missing a train at Grand Central Station.

Chaktsal Gang marks the first view of Kailash on the *khora*. Prayer flags and *khatas* have been wound around an imported stick. There are no trees for many miles. Besides *khatas* and prayer flags there are *mani* stones, and Böns offer steer skulls often with prayers carved into the forehead.

The trail, a little wider than my foot, scrawled up and down low, brown, grass tufted hills. I had to stop at every rise to pant. The porters kindly paused to let me catch up. The initial catch-up spot was a heap of rocks, some carved with mantras—mantras are written as well as vocal prayers —and a long, curving willow stick, brought from heaven knows where, since we had not seen a tree in days. This heap is Chaktsal Gang, in a direct sight line with Kailash's white-layered dome, the black scar from Naro Bönchung's drum down her right side. People wind prayer flags and *khatas* around the stick draping them over the stones as well.

A *mani* stone is a stone with prayers carved into it. I had a porter on one of my Kailash trips who earned his living as a *mani* stone carver.

In Chaktsal Gang's heap there were also yak skulls with mantras carved into the bone of the forehead between the horns. These may be Bon—the pre-Buddhist religion of Tibet—offerings, which often involve animals. I put up my first string of prayer flags here to the porters' obvious pleasure and approval since it showed I had reverence for the mountain. It would also give me merit. Once you leave this spot, Kailash disappears again behind barren ridges.

It reappears further along the path, rising beyond the *tarbouche*, visible in the distance, at the end of a long line of black ridges raising its snowy head against the sky. It is dome shaped, a breast or, if you wish a less sensual simile, an upside down turnip.

If you look *tarbouche* or its variant spellings up in a dictionary, you will be told that it is a Middle Eastern hat, a fez. In Tibet a *tarbouche* is a pole, about one and a half telephone poles in length, which is raised in a sacred area, the forecourt of a monastery or temple. Yearly, on the anniversary of the Buddha's Enlightenment, Saga Dawa, the full moon of the fourth lunar month, all *tarbouches* are taken down, the grey, weather-tattered old flags and *khatas* stripped from them and new ones, donated by those who come to the festival, attached. Giving prayer flags to the *tarbouche* is a way of acquiring merit. At Kailash people from all over Tibet gather to watch the new pole, cocooned in fresh wrappings, be raised by two big trucks until it stands upright. Lines of prayer flags reach out from the pole making it the center of a web of fluttering, wind-rippled, joyous, flags in primary colors which are a startling contrast to the stark, ascetic landscape of treeless ridges behind it. The *tarbouche* at Chaktsal Gang is the most important one in Tibet.

Near the *tarbouche* we passed through the large white, "two-legged *chörten*," topped by a sun and a crescent moon, called Chörten Kangnyi. Tibetan villages often have *kangnyis*, gates, which, according to Tsewang Lama in his book, *Kailash Mandala,* signify a spiritual wall "within which the villagers hope to achieve peace, harmony and prosperity." *Chörten* Kangnyi denotes the spiritual wall of Kailash. If you walk through this gate with the proper attitude, your sins from this life will be erased.

When you walk through Chörten Kangnyi, the two-legged *chörten*, it erases the sins of this life time.

To confirm their willingness to change through circumambulating Mount Kailash people slough off clothing as they hope to slough off bad habits, or leave a hank of hair or a tooth. The horse's head is probably a Bön offering.

The hill rises across the river from the *tarbouche*. The dots beside the river are yaks.

Surrounding this special *chörten* at the beginning of the Kailash pilgrimage were heaps of cast-off clothing, long hanks of hair, bracelets, earrings, necklaces, socks and the head of a black horse. I'm not sure of the significance of the latter, although it was probably a Bön offering, but the former are gifts symbolizing the pilgrims' willingness to change. To walk the pilgrimage around Kailash is to commit to sloughing off the snakeskin of your old self, in order to become a different person.

Some distance away, on the other side of the La Chu River a great red-grey hill/mountain rose up, its face traced with what looked like narrow paths. (When one mountain is almost 30,000 feet, it is hard to think of something that is a mere smear of 17,000 feet as also being a mountain.) I had a sense of its hugeness only because yaks grazing along the river in front of it looked like a swarm of black ants.

Committed to doing the *khora* in three days, we had to keep moving and, therefore, on this trip I saw only a few of the sights along the way. We skipped the sky burial site, and Chuku, the first monastery on the *khora*. We didn't know about the sky burial site, and I'm not sure that we even noticed Chuku up above the river. Built of the local rock and mud brick, it disappears into the hillside completely, becoming just another pile of stones.

The stone pinnacles that look to me like the habitations and fortresses of unseen watchers on the *khora*.

All monasteries on the *khora* in 1995 had been recently rebuilt since Red Guards, some of them Tibetan, leveled them during the Cultural Revolution, a time when devout Tibetans did the *khora* at night so Chinese soldiers and police would not see them. That contradiction of some Tibetans assisting the Chinese to destroy their own religious monuments while others risked their lives to venerate them is the paradox caused by how different people reacted to the oppressive terror of the Chinese.

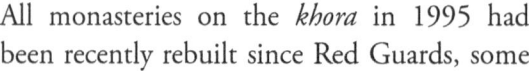

Drira Phuk Monastery, one of three on the *khora*, in the 1990s when it had recently been rebuilt after being leveled in the Cultural Revolution.

Having passed the *tarbouche* and *Chörten* Kangnyi, again Kailash disappeared behind stark ridges of rock weathered into architectural formations suggesting graceful villas, pavilions, castles, and cathedrals with fantastical roofs. Beside the river we followed a rising path with these defiles of wind and snow-carved rock marching along on either side of us. I found it eerie walking with only the sound of the river and the occasional birdcall, while above us towered these grandiloquent, wind-carved fantasy habitations. I imagined them filled with otherworld inhabitants, demons, and dainty, wasp-waisted deities, Taras and Dakinis, who if they looked down on our progress along the stone-strewn path, were invisible to us.

These mountain ridges are known to Tibetans as the sixteen Arhats, the men who became the first monks to attain enlightenment.

We crossed the river, which like most Tibetan rivers had a gravelly bed of many channels, by leaping from stone to stone. Jemi was unbalanced by her companions' sleeping bags, always given to the weakest member of the porter team since they are bulky, not heavy. She was afraid of the last leap. Although he made fun of her for being fearful, her man jumped over to the rock she was on and relieved her of the sleeping bags so she could make the leap safely. Why we did this crossing I don't know; there was a perfectly fine bridge a half a mile away.

The south face of Kailash as seen from Drira Phuk Monastery. She towers over you.

Just before arriving at the guesthouse of the Drira Phuk monastery where we stayed the night, we reached the point where the lower ridges around Kailash part and fall away revealing a full frontal, magnificent view of her from the north. She rose above us in the clear evening air, seeming an arm's reach away, her white snow-crown glowing pink from the reflected sunset, pristine, serene, a goddess, an object of awe. Staring at her she seemed to me to be simultaneously the epitome of both what she literally is, a mountain in Tibet, while radiating an aura of the intangible, the ineffable, the perfect union of the material and the spiritual.

Amelia, Miguel, Thomas, and I, having no tents, stayed in the monastery guesthouses. Janet and Chiam, although carrying their packs, had arrived there before us. This first guesthouse, below Drira

Phuk Monastery, was identical to the second at Zutrul Phuk. All surfaces were crusted with mud; I spread my poncho as a ground sheet for my sleeping bag. The beds were rows of muddy, rough-hewn boards, some with bark still adhering, covered with mud-smeared pieces of cotton-covered foam.

The previous is not meant as criticism since, considering the surroundings, it would have taken Lewis Carroll's "seven maids with seven brooms" several weeks to institute cleanliness. There were four beds in a room so that Amelia, Miguel, Thomas and I fitted in neatly as sardines lined up in a tin.

My mother had given me Thailand, but she had also prepared me to travel beyond the nice hotel with dinner on a white, cloth-covered table and to accept physical discomfort on the road. I thought of her with gratitude as I arranged my sleeping bag.

Before I entered this mud-crusted room, I had known that if I wanted to travel off the beaten track I was going to have to be willing to put up with physical discomfort on a spectrum from slight, a hard bed in a cold room, cabbage soup night after night, to severely, smelly squat toilets littered with used Chinese menstrual pads and a room with two beds in its center surrounded by pails under leaks in the roof, my sleep interrupted by the occasional scurrying rat.

Mother told me once about her trip with her friend to Tunis in 1929. They bought second-class tickets on the boat from Sicily for $10. The cabin, full of three tiered berths that were over run with bed bugs, was below the water line so they could not open the windows in the suffocating, humid heat. She spent the night moving from berth to berth attempting to discover one without bugs. Finally she woke Anne, her friend, who had been sleeping soundly, and forced her to move so that she could try that berth. She continued to be bitten, while Anne continued to sleep unmolested.

I cannot remember the names of the towns and cities from Rome to Kathmandu where I have woken blotched with bedbug bites. She also had run-ins with fleas, which delights me since I've had encounters with the little buggers getting into my sleeping bag from the yak it was traveling on. How wonderful, if odd, and funny to have bed bugs and fleas as part of your bond with your mother.

Fleas, bed bugs, dirt are just part of the deal for adventure. You pay for adventure. As in everything else in life, once you dare beyond what most people do, or what is accepted as the norm, there is a price to be paid. That is one reason why people don't travel adventurously. On the other hand, the rewards of going beyond the usual level of experience is often enormous, opening one to possibilities far beyond one's expectations both in the outside and inside world of the self.

Another interesting factor is how our personalities split, how humans bond together within themselves diametrically opposite psychological traits. My mother was a conformist who accepted her culture's declarations on most issues, never questioning what others told her: "Don't pick up your crying child," or "Alcoholics are weak people without will power or character," or "Don't associate with Jews and Blacks." I married a Jewish man; she would not send my wedding pictures to my great aunts in Fargo because "Everyone will know you married a Jew."

This shifted in her sixties. After the massacre in Munich of the Israeli Olympic team she called me sobbing. "Why did they do that? What is the matter with people?"

After sixty my mother began to notice that received opinion was not always right. Perhaps this was due to the fact that at that age, as one begins to realize that the full moon of death is rising on the horizon, not a rich husband, or a better job, or a bigger house, the impact of society's demand for conformity begins to wane.

An amazing characteristics of all humans is our ability for unrecognized self-contradiction. What interests and confounds me about her is that a woman so rigidly conventional spent three months on her own in Tunis and accepted bed bugs and fleas as part of her choice without having hysterics or feeling that she was a martyr.

If the rooms in our Darchen guesthouse had been Frigidaires then this was the freezer. Reluctantly, as though supplying us with some ineffable liqueur, the man in charge of the rooms handed a thermos of hot water to each of us and a blanket which, amazingly, was clean. His reluctance with the thermoses of hot water was understandable since the water had to be carried up from the river and then heated over a yak dung fire for which he, or someone, had spent hours collecting the dung.

Amelia cooked a packet of Knorr dehydrated tomato soup on their Primus stove. If she hadn't I would have munched a packet of dry noodles, too exhausted to cook. I still remember Amelia's soup as exquisitely delicious and was amazed years later when I took the same soup on another circuit of Kailash to discover it tasted like dehydrated soup. They also had cheese and sausage, heavenly Spanish sausage, a *fuet*, from home. I was grateful down to the chilly soles of my feet for their generosity. It was a feast from which I learned to always bring sausage, if Chinese customs will let me bring it in, and, if possible, cheeses of various sorts. These are a huge comfort on a circumambulation or any trip across Tibet.

We had no difficulty sleeping that night, even though we were well over 16,000 feet. If anyone snored and, considering the condition of our noses, it seems likely, we slept through it.

In the morning, after a breakfast of hot noodles and a slice of sausage, we started the climb to Drölma La, the pass that would bring us around the mountain.

The horse will gain merit by his circumambulation of Kailash, leading to a better incarnation in his next life. If his owner rides him on the *khora* the horse receives half the merit of its master's circumambulation as well.

We did not even go into the monastery of Drira Phuk, since all our energies were focused on climbing to the sacred pass where the first circumambulator, Götshangpa, was led by twenty-one Drölmas, to the rock of Drölma Neri. Before the great block of stone their elegant, dancing female forms metamorphosed into twenty-one wolves which vanished as though sucked into the rock. Drölma is a goddess of salvation who is considered a bodhisattva of compassion. She is the feminine aspect of enlightenment.

Even a horse should wear his best on the *khora* to show respect.

According to Victor Chan, whose authoritative volume, *Tibet Handbook,* a number of us lugged about the *khora,* this day's trek is seven hours. It took me ten. What I remember was my feet among rolling pebbles, which destabilized my steps. I became fascinated by the colors of these stones, some white marble, others flat pieces of slate or shale, almost plum colored.

Bringing a small piece of a Tibetan slice of slate, a lush shade of purple in the light around Kailash, to New York, I found it lost that lovely purple, retaining only a faint remembrance of its old color. The light in the thin air of altitude imbued it with that rich plummy hue. Similarly, shells, lustrous in the sea, lose sheen once dry. Objects in their environment have a resonance, as do travel experiences. Intensity is related to place and fades on removal. Retaining the vibrancy of emotions or sensations experienced in an alien environment is difficult, and the intensity decreases with time and distance like a dying note.

I tried to keep my balance as I leapt in terror from rock to rock across a field of boulders beneath which I could hear icy water chuckling, imagining the scenario if I broke a leg. I had never thought to get traveler's insurance. I slipped once smashing the lens filter on my camera. I was passed not only by Tibetans, walking with the stride of New Yorkers late to the office, but also by all the members of my own group.

My solace were the porters, particularly Jemi whom I would find sitting on a rock in her red nun's robe as I came around a corner. I had given up any pretense that I could carry my daypack; she carried it for me and, when I rounded a corner, had it on her lap ready to reach in for my water bottle or camera.

At one stop with Jemi and the other porters, her man pointed to my prayer beads that I wore around my neck and, through an intricate series of gestures, it is amazing how much can be said without words, asked if I was wearing them as jewelry or if knew their purpose. I recited for him, Buddhism's best known mantra, "*Ohm, mane padme hum,*" while fingering the skull carved beads, between thumb and forefinger, totally frustrated that I was not able tell him how I acquired them. But he was obviously gratified that I recognized their sacred purpose. Apparently, in his thinking, the fact that I came from the other side of the world was not important if I knew how to pray with the beads. They were mine because I knew how to use them. Their origins and mine were not in conflict. This was a confirmation that I needed.

Jemi and her man were two of our porters.

I got a sense of Tibetan priorities when I saw that while he had a large, ornate, silver prayer box strapped to his belt with a picture of the Dalai Lama smiling in its window, a smile not yet forbidden by the Chinese, he had to eat his noodles out of the cellophane bag they came in because he owned no bowl. To my amazement, he could hold a bag of noodles with boiling water in it cupped in his hand.

Jemi and her man vanished round a bend ahead. As I walked, time stopped or, perhaps, became endless. I concentrated on my feet and the path to Drölma La's 18,600 feet, oblivious to much of the scenery. All that existed was the path. But earlier in the day, when I was not quite so absorbed in my breathing, I noticed plump marmots popping in and out of their holes, whistling news to each other and, ravens gliding, steady and smooth, on dark out-stretched wings on wind currents in the sky's hard cloudless turquoise. I thought that if the wind were to have a shadow it would be these wings.

The path was marked by little and big cairns, heaps of stones that people piled up and balanced as they passed. These have a practical purpose marking the path, and, if tall enough, they are useful when it snows. But their spiritual purpose is to build communal stupas, an act of worship, along your path. I found myself bending over to add to the piles, looking for pure white stones, for the occasional heap of white marble rocks.

Sheep walking the *khora*. They will not be slaughtered as the sacred path is a no kill zone.

Vaguely I knew, while trying to get oxygen into my lungs, that Tibetan pilgrims walked with me, because in the last stages of the climb, in an area where the Tibetans have built a rough stair up a particularly steep slope, I found myself, when pausing to pant, standing beside Tibetan women who smiled in commiseration, but they always started walking before I had enough breath to engage my feet again. I was not thinking of Aunt Liz, or how to change, or how to be a better person because the physical effort was so intense that I had no discernable thoughts. I was walking in an expanse of mental emptiness that I have rarely achieved in meditation.

Then there was the trickster slope. On any pass, there is usually a trickster slope. I looked up and could see the top of the pass with its gay confusion of prayer flags in the sun apparently straight ahead, not at all far. I thought, because of the angle, "Ah, this is the last rise before the top of the pass." But the angle concealed the fact that there was part of the path I could not see but was going to have to walk. When you get to the top of the rise you have been looking at, you see that there is a dip in the path and then yet another steep rise between you and the pass. A friend suggests this is an echo of what happens in Buddhist practice. After you have worked to achieve a certain level of proficiency in meditation your teacher explains that now you are ready for a yet further level to which you must rise.

Small flocks of fawn-colored birds made a sweet noise in the silence, as dense as a block of granite. At the top, in a wild festival of fluttering, brilliant prayer flags, *khatas,* and abandoned clothing, I noticed a long hank of grey hair laid carefully, as an offering should be, on a flat rock. I attached my prayer flags to those already up. Jemi and two of the men sat down taking food from their packs, hard nuggets of yak cheese, and a little dried meat in strands. It is customary to stop at the top of the pass to share food.

Part of the prayer flag display at Drölma La, the sacred pass that leads around Kailash, and the high point of the *khora* at 18,600 feet literally as well as spiritually.

These women's faces are shaded by their superb sheepskin hats.

This is a variation on the shovel hat I saw a monk wearing at Garden. But this one has side curtains to protect further against the sun.

A hatless woman with the snowy wall of Kailash behind her.

A man with a superb barrette set with turquoise and coral. He is wearing his hair in the Kham style adding to his own hair a length of fringe, which is pulled through a bone ring and then wrapped around his head. The Kham are admired for having fought fiercely against the Chinese invasion.

An intense look from a hatless pilgrim.

As we were snacking at 18,600 feet, along came an interestingly, if a bit erratically, outfitted group of Tibetan pilgrims in a fabulous assortment of hats. One of red serge, a twill fabric, had the same shovel shape I had seen on the monk at Ganden. It worked well to shade the front of the face. Another was high and round, rather Russian looking, trimmed with gray, curly sheep's wool, yet another had a tall brocade crown with fur ear flaps.

I took out a bag of dried, yak cheese cubes I had with me and offered it around, a calculated bribe for photos. I was fairly sure that having innocently taken from me, the owners of these fascinating hats would feel they had to pose for me when I asked. Otherwise, without the bribe, I was quite sure they would say no. In the event, only one or two women refused to be photographed. They may have believed the camera would capture their spirits or they just may have not wanted to be pinned eternally as Tibetan specimens by a foreigner.

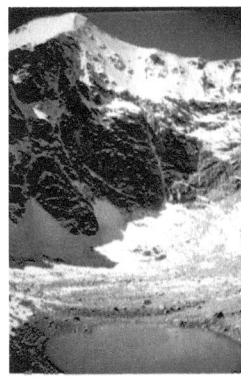

Lake Gaurlkunda which you see from a path high above. Usually it is frozen. Often Hindu pilgrims break the ice and bathe in it.

The path down was narrow, strewn with small pebbles rolling underfoot at cliff edge. There was a drop I couldn't estimate to a small, sacred pond of frozen, gleaming blue-green ice, Lake Gaurlkunda. We crossed a field of glacial boulders under which a stream gurgled, then there was another long, narrow, steep, switch-backed path with rolling, treacherous pebbles which cut through rocky places alternating with tufts of spiky grass which ended in springy tundra beside the Zhong Chu River. There was a tea tent here that the Tibetans piled into. The altitude was lower, the path mostly level. I could walk at a normal pace for the first time in two days.

But, most strikingly, things were green beside the river, although on either side stark, grey mountains rose, their tops mist-swirled, some cradling snow in their hollows.

At our tea stop with other pilgrims there is no conversation but much laughter.

More hats. I never saw another high hat like this again.

A straw hat with a sizeable hole.

Now I walked with the porters; I seemed to have become their mascot. They stopped to make tea with salt but had no butter, gathering dried grass for the fire that Jemi's man started with the flint attached to his belt. Some passing men joined us out of curiosity. I handed out more hard cubes of yak cheese before asking if I could take pictures; again hats of different varieties were prominent.

One young man was wearing a straw hat, more holes than hat. Another looked into the lens grimly. I pulled my mouth up at the corners into a smile; the rest broke into laughter at us both. The last young man, smiling and handsome with a delicate but snotty nose he didn't bother to blow when I focused on him, whipped from his pack a huge, handsome, red, fox fur hat and adjusted it proudly for his portrait.

We walked by the river. A group of nomads with exquisitely caparisoned yaks and horses caught up with us. The head yak and horses had leis of brass bells glinting gold in the sun around their necks, making a sweet, mellow sound as they walked. Red tassels were tied through holes in their ears and their reins were decorated with ribbons fluttering as they walked.

Loaded yaks beside the river.

On one yak, a boy of five was perched, "high and disposedly," as someone once described Queen Elizabeth I. He looked comfortable and princely on top of the family's quilts, magnificent in his yellow brocade jacket and hat with fur flaps. His father, who carried another child on his back, led the yak.

A pretty little girl, from the same family, swathed in layers of sweaters, scarves and jackets, walked beside me companionably for a while, but tiring of my slow pace she rejoined her troupe. Suddenly, coming to a considered decision, she turned and walked back to me. She stopped, pointed into the lens of my camera, before poking her chest with the same small finger. Stunned I took her picture. I said from the depth of my mystification, "Tujeychey," "Thank you," my new word, feeling humbled by her. What thoughts led to her decision?

The girl who decided she wanted her picture taken.

Turning a corner we came upon a young couple. At first I thought they were caring for a pilgrim covered with a sheepskin coat, but then realized it was someone, a relative probably, who had died on the *khora*, a good death, like dying in the midst of a prayer. The woman, silent in a heavy wool *chuba*, the pink silk of her blouse surrounding her throat like a corolla of peony petals, had tears in her eyes. The man, in a greasy, worn sheepskin coat, looked stunned.

As we passed, nomads, porters, and me, we dug into our packs, pockets, pulling out what we found. Heaped in front of the couple and the body were silver coins, a few bills, candy, dried apricots, a little juniper to burn for incense, a packet of dried noodles, offerings for dead and living. Death, though startling, seemed natural, in its element, here.

We stayed in the monastery guesthouse at Zutrul Phuk, just as muddy as the previous one at Drira Phuk, but instead of Kailash, we had a view of green meadows along the river sparkling with the shards of hundreds and hundreds of broken beer bottles.

Sloughing off my sleeping bag the next morning, I noticed the muscles that enclosed my ribs were sore; each inhale was accompanied by an ache. The path the day before over Drölma La caused me to work those muscles far beyond their normal capacity to get enough oxygen in and out of my lungs.

As we packed up, a porter caught a raven, spinning it in a great wheel at arms length, to be safe from its razor beak. He had a delighted grin on his face, it's not easy to catch a raven, while the bird in distress made piteous noises. Self-righteously horrified I begged him to free it before he hurt it. As carrion eaters, perhaps ravens aren't respected as other animals are around Kailash where killing of any kind is forbidden.

Walking around the *gompa*, searching for Milarepa's cave, I startled a herd of delicate-legged antelope on the cliff above and many large rabbits out having breakfast, which somehow escaped the hawk that skimmed just above my head startling me.

It didn't occur to me that the cave was, of course, inside the *gompa*, that the temple, indeed, had been built around it. When I came back and asked for Milarepa, the elderly monk took a flashlight and led me to the cave chamber. At the end was the shrine; you can see nothing without a flashlight and even then Milarepa, carved out of alabaster, is so swaddled in *khatas* it is hard to discern him. I looked at the other images and then up at the indentations Milarepa made with his hand and head when he decided that the ceiling was too low and pushed it up.

Before the trip, reading my multitude of books about Mount Kailash, I had learned of the cave's legendary past. Originally sacred to the Bön religion, the shamanistic, animistic precursor of Buddhism, Kailash was called Yungdrung Gu Tse, the Nine-Story Swastika Mountain. The swastika is, in Tibet, a symbol of spiritual strength. The Bön founder, Tönpa Shenrab, descended from heaven, landing on top of Kailash, thereby making the mountain an important location for the religion. This method of arrival is quite common in Tibetan tales. The first legendary king of Tibet also descended from heaven but he came down a rope.

In the 11th century, Milarepa, who became a black sorcerer because of his mother's insistence on revenge, killed many of his relatives. They had stolen his inheritance, enslaved him, his mother, and sister. Repenting his murderous actions, he sought a guru to teach him the Buddhist path.

He found Marpa, a famous translator and head of the Kagyüpa order, who, for many years had him build and tear down temples, as penance for his murders, never stating that these building projects were acts of atonement. Finally, when Marpa's wife interceded for Milarepa, he took him as his student, teaching him meditation and other Buddhist practices.

Milarepa is always portrayed with his hand behind his ear listening for the voice of his teacher, Marpa.

Milarepa spent his life as a meditative hermit with nettle soup as his primary sustenance, causing him to turn green, rather as a vegetarian friend of mine, binging on bib lettuce when it comes into season, similarly turns green from over indulgence. Milarepa, a saint and poet, became the patriarch of the Kagyüpa order after Marpa's death.

He competed with his archrival, Naro Bönchung, the Bön priest, in magical contests to decide whether Kailash would be a Bön or a Buddhist mountain. Milarepa agreed to build the ceiling and Naro Bönchung the walls of a shelter. Milarepa selected a huge rock and with his bare hand, sliced it in two, suspending one half in the air as the ceiling of the room. Naro Bönchung, awe-struck by this performance, could not produce the necessary walls and Milarepa finished the structure. However, going inside, he found the ceiling too low and pushed up on it with his hand and head. Pilgrims to Zutrul Phuk put their hand and their head into these impressions in the ceiling.

The final bout in these contests, a race to the top of Kailash, between the Buddhist and the Bön occurred early one morning. As the sun was just breaching the horizon Naro, in a green cloak, threw his leg over his shaman's drum on which he tapped furiously, slowly rising toward Kailash's dome.

Milarepa's disciples were distraught. Their master hadn't even risen from his tent. As the first sunbeam slanted down toward the top of Kailash, Milarepa, emerging from his tent, threw his leg over the beam and with his cloak flaring in the wind, soared instantly to the crown of Kailash, as it was touched by the morning sun. Naro Bönchung fell head over heels down Kailash, his drum bouncing and crashing after him, creating the deep cleft in her side, the black scar in the white snow of her dome.

Michael Moorcock has proposed that, "By means of our myths and legends, we maintain a sense of what we are worth and who we are. Without them we should undoubtedly go mad." But it is also through myth and legend that we establish our relationship with the landscape we live in. We bind the part of the earth on which we dwell to us by the weavings of our stories. We imprint ourselves on *our* landscape through *our* legends, making it ours, creating a mysterious liaison between us and it. Scholars can go on proving that King Arthur never existed; but the facts they assemble, neatly crafted as a child's Lego building, will never erase Arthur and cannot extinguish his knights or adulterous queen from England.

Böns still circumambulate Kailash counter-clockwise honoring the descent of the founder of their religion from heaven even though many old Bön deities became protectors of Buddhism through the offices of Padmasambhava, Guru Rinpoche, with whose small, battered, silver *chörten* I had been blessed when I went to Ganden monastery earlier in the trip. These fierce, tongue thrusting, white fanged spirits distinguish Tibetan Buddhism from other forms of Buddhism.

I fitted my hand into Milarepa's print on the ceiling with the help of the monk's flashlight. Returning to the main chapel I reached into my pocket for a contribution and felt my Alcoholics Anonymous 14-year coin. I rubbed my thumb over the familiar symbolic triangle and raised lettering once and then left it with my contribution in a plate put out for that purpose. It seemed right to leave it there as an affirmation of my sobriety but even more of my desire to change.

My attachment to Tibet means I am always reading yet another book about it, not as a purposeful, goal-oriented activity but as a form of information gathering and cozy armchair travel allowing me to retrace my journeys in dustless, day dreaming, comfort.

In 2014 reading *Circling the Sacred Mountain* by Robert Thurman and Tad Wise, which recounts their pilgrimage to Kailash in 1995, the same year as my first pilgrimage, but later in that year, I happily followed them around the *khora* comparing experiences. However, I sat up in astonishment when I read this conversation between two of the men at Zutrul Phuk, the last monastery on the circumambulation:

> *"Will you just look at that!"* he repeats, picking up a coin from the altar plate. It's about the size of a silver dollar but bronzed, with an English-

printed prayer on one side. On the flip: "To thine own self be true" around the edge and a large XIV stamped in the center.

"But what exactly does it mean—this coin?"

"It means—dear boy—that whoever left it here hadn't had a drink in upwards of fourteen years. And yet they left it here. All that time and here it sits on the altar plate of Milarepa's miracle rock gompa. Incredible!"

Reading that passage, many years after having done my first Kailash *khora*, I was astonished. It was my coin they were talking about. I felt an instant, visceral connection with both the speakers, whom I have never met, and with the mountain. I was there with them and they were both with me in the room I was reading in. I felt as if I could turn my head and see them. Both the men speaking were having difficulties with alcohol. I hope that they both have been long, safely sober.

I walked out of the temple to find everyone gone, but the path was before me so I followed it. It was companionable to walk with Jemi but exhilarating to walk alone, solo in this stone landscape that gave no quarter, knowing that just behind those ridges on my right the mountain was wound in her white snows. Though brief, my solo walk seemed to infuse the word "independence" with a new perfume of meaning.

My mother had accepted the opinions of others and not done much thinking of her own, but in one area she had not only believed in her own ideas but her thinking was different from that of all other mothers of my childhood.

My Aunt Liz, since I was her only child too, had paid for my music and ballet lessons in New York. At first Mother took me into town and back, reading while I had my lessons. But when I was nine she spent the summer teaching me how to navigate the New York City subway system starting from Grand Central Station. In the fall when my music and ballet lessons began, I was sent off on my own, by train, to then transfer to the subway, with perhaps the best instructions I have ever heard for a woman in any city. 1) Walk purposefully, never stroll. 2) If a man talks to you say, "I'm meeting my father at the end of the block." 3) Never yell, "Help." Yell "Rape. Murder." They will at least be interested. 4) If you see a crowd gathered around something, don't go look. You'll be sorry you did. 5) If you need help, go to a policeman or a middle-aged woman.

However, she sent a friend of hers to track me on my first trip when classes began. I caught the woman coming through the turnstile behind me at the Grand Central subway stop at the beginning of my journey and was livid both with her and my mother. I came home a fireworks display of recriminations, resentment and flaming righteous indignation. "I thought you trusted me," I accused in a fury.

She completely and immediately understood my outrage. To my amazement, she apologized. This was one of the few places where we were at one with each other, where each understood the root of the other's emotions. She did trust me, just not the first time.

I was immensely proud to be going into New York on the train alone, to know how to take the subway. No one else in my age group or, indeed, older, in high school, that I knew in Chappaqua was allowed to go to New York alone. I felt I was superior to my classmates, more sophisticated. What she gave me was confidence that I could be independent. She was also teaching me, whether she was aware of it or not, that the world was not a terribly dangerous place. Surely, part of my ability, to say nothing of my delight in traveling solo starts here in learning how to go from Grand Central to the Lexington Avenue Y for ballet lessons.

That independence, that need to know that one is capable of managing alone in an alien environment, must have been very important to her, otherwise, I don't think that she would have spent three months in

Tunis at the age of 30 in 1930. My story comes from her story. Our stories branch off from each other but are rooted in each other. Her stay in Tunis is part of my trip to Nepal, Thailand, and finally Tibet. Without her trip to Tunis, it is probable I would never have gone to those places. Perhaps women acquire courage generation by generation. We are a lineage not isolated events.

My mother, a vivacious and pretty blond from Fargo, North Dakota, at 29, in 1929, took all her money out of the bank, the then rather large sum of three hundred dollars, quit her job, which was about to become a budget cut, as a buyer of fancy lingerie at Macy's, gathered up a homely friend, Anne, and boarded a ship to Europe. Her reasoning was that since the world was in crisis she might as well take a vacation from it until it either returned to normal or she ran out of money. If a bank were likely to make your money disappear, wouldn't it be better to do the job yourself and enjoy the process? Both my mother and my Aunt Liz thought like this. I have a letter from Liz saying, "I think there's going to be another crash. Why don't we all go to Portugal," and I have inherited their thinking.

I have many of my mother's letters and postcards from her 1929-30 trip. She and homely Anne took a freighter with twelve other passengers from New York to Antwerp for $140 round trip. They did the usual things. In Paris she worried about expenses, noting that the hotel cost them a dollar a day each, and then went on to tell with delight, "A dollar ten for filet mignon steak with the most marvelous French fried potatoes, a large bowl of *salade*, and some kind of cooked celery."

They moved on through southern France to Italy where she talked Anne onto a boat sailing for Sicily. Two single women in 1930, which it now was, in Sicily, a blond and a red head? Sicily was not considered a safe place for single women at the time. Something odd was at work. I suspect it was my mother.

She bought reams of postcards, sending them to Fargo in numbered batches, her narrative on their backs. In Taormina, her postcard odyssey started with a picture of Porta Messina and her commentary: "The street seen thru the gateway is the most enchanting street in the world at night with the light streaming from shop windows and gleaming on the narrow way, lighting and transforming everything— not that anything needs transforming. It is like fairyland come true— the shops lying just within the gate have everything exquisite one's heart desires. From house furnishings to personal attire. Nothing cheap, however."

In Taormina she bought and sent home wonderfully gaudy tassels and blinkers embellished with embroidery and mirrors, which donkeys then wore on feast days in Sicily. Years later when she and my father moved to a retirement community, we went through the attic, coming upon the donkey adornments nested in the tissue paper where they had lived for forty or more years. Even at this late stage it was difficult for her to give them up. I wish now that I had taken them, but I was still too angry with her to be kind.

Someday I too will have to part with objects that are the locus of treasured memories, but to someone else they will just be foolish trash, such as my Tibetan amulet box, bent and battered, missing its original turquoise stones and set with chipped glass.

In Palermo, their next stop, due to linguistic confusion, she and Anne, enquiring for a hotel, were directed to the catacombs. "I would never willingly have gone to the place, but when I entered this chamber suddenly looking for bed and board and finding skeletons—the sudden shock and ludicrousness of the situation completely overcame my aversion and Anne and I walked among the poor old things, giggling and making wise cracks at their expense."

Then she talked Anne onto another boat, Palermo to Tunis. Its imminent sailing was enlivened by a woman who "was losing her mind over the departure of her son on the same boat. It was a circus to watch her. She fainted three times—screamed—moaned— called on

God—took off her hat and pulled her hair. The boat nearly capsized because everyone stood on one side watching her."

Why Tunis? I've no idea. There my mother talked Anne into returning home. I suspect she was bored with her company. In a letter she says, "Well Anne left yesterday and I feel as if I should give myself a party. She would be dreadfully hurt if she knew how happy I am to be alone after five months of never being alone, hardly long enough to go to the bathroom. It is strange that I am so constituted. She cannot bear to be alone so she doesn't consider that while she might be uncomfortable to tell me to take an afternoon off occasionally, she would be cementing our friendship. It was not unbearable to be with her so steadily, only I am so happy to be alone." But I'd bet this was an adventure she didn't want to share.

She spent three months in Tunis first in a hotel catering to down at the heel French counts and princes who, after the First World War, leased their villas and chateaux to rich Americans. Later she transferred to a boarding house run by an untitled French woman trying to make ends meet.

Her mother and sister, my aunt Liz to be, then in New York, and her bevy of aunts in North Dakota were all worried sick. Since I have letters written to friends as well as family, I know the reassurances she gave, such as the following, were totally false. "Don't worry about my walks, Mother, I never leave the roads that are the main arteries of traffic. These are paved and there are so many people on them in cars, trucks, carriages and walking that I couldn't be touched at all without many people seeing it." The little liar was up and down every back alley in Tunis.

There was also in New York a man, Jim, to whom she was engaged; in Tunis there was an Italian, Luigi, whom she saw every day and whom she kissed at least once.

I know this because of a letter he sent, in the most elegant hand, before he lost hope. It reads, in rapturously ruptured English,

"After two weeks I received yesterday news from you, a letter from the delicious blond girl! And a nice letter, not so dry as the others. I'm very happy to see, that you don't forget me, that perhaps I have a small, small place in your little heart, that you think a little at me. My darling (can I say to you 'my darling' now)? I think also always at you, especially in the evenings, then I take all the letters you wrote me and I read them. First those you wrote me from Kairouam and Gabés. Your first letters! They are so splendide, so full of love. When I read them, all the things of this time comes before my eyes: The first time I meet you one evening in the small restaurant. Our walking through the arab town. And then the first kiss from your wonderfull mouth. And when I was sick, you was so good, so sweet, so, delicious to me. I think this time you loved me really. And then the delicious, delicious time I had with you. Hours so wonderfull, that it could not be for long time. And the day you leave Tunis. I see you standing on the train and saying good bye with your little hand raised. 'Surely, Luigi, I come back, surely, surely.' I Hear still those words 'Surely, surely' And then you disappear from my eyes, but not from my heart. Oh my Dorry, it was the last time I have seen you? Will I never see you?"

But she never did return except in memory. I asked her once why she didn't marry Luigi. She said he was too jealous but I wonder if it wasn't the idea of crossing the bar into another culture, and one with more rigid attitudes toward women, that killed the relationship for her.

Luigi should have given lessons in writing love letters. I admit I am a bit envious of my mother. No one has ever written me a letter like that.

When her sister, Liz, told her that Jim, her American suitor, was anxious about her, she responded, "I am amused at Jim's worrying over me. He should worry and get wrinkles. My ambition is my own business." Perhaps this attitude on his part, or her part is what parted them, bringing my father into her life.

And her ambition was a grand one: willing to be alien, she wanted to be independent, to experience another culture, to see, feel, taste, hear and smell another part of the world, to attempt to get some insight into that world's ways. Out of a night during Ramadan in Tunis came this letter exuding delight.

> "Monday night was a gala night for the Rhamdon (sic)—it was the night—the one night in the year when the Bey walks thru the souks before his people. Of course I would lose a limb to see it.
>
> "The souks were lighted by a million tapers. Some were hung from the ceiling in the shape of the African water jug. Others were strung in festoons. These latter were only of white tapers and they were lovely. The tapers that formed the water jug were in colors—one color to a circle. My old familiar souks that I know almost as well as the insides of my suitcases were transformed into a real fairyland. We stood on the steps of the mosque crowded back among a thousand dirty Arabs. (I didn't pick up one flea that night but last night I picked up seven tho' my only dissapation (sic) was a ride home on the street car after dinner.)
>
> "The bey was preceeded (sic) by his ministers and the royal princes—one of whom is the most beautiful young man I have ever laid eyes on. His prime minister in a light French blue uniform walked directly in front of him. The Bey is a large well built man—not young...It was a cold night and the Bey wore a winter overcoat with fur collar and cuffs which covered the brilliant uniform with many orders pinned on his chest. As he passed, fezes were torn off and loud cries in Arabic passed from mouth to mouth preceeding (sic) him, and dying out behind him. In the street of the perfume shops, which we could just see, the crowd pressed so closely to him that his nobles and attendants drew their sabers to preserve the space. It was very romantic to see the flash of the steel in the candlelight.
>
> "After the Bey passed we fell in with the mob that trailed him and visited several coffee houses in an effort to find amusement in the form of dancing or music. We visited all the coffee houses in the souks without success, when a Holland man suggested that we go to the place de la Kasbah and see what was there. The fort, the Bey's palace, several government buildings and a small coffee house flank a small green park. Upon bresting (sic) a small hill the park suddenly is before one, but this night it literally burst on us because it was a mass of glowing colored lanterns—strung here and there like mellow moons among the trees, they

merged into a design in the middle of the park. You can imagine the picture with globes of colored lights against the blackness of night, dimly lighting the sauntering white robed figures that seemed to glide under them."

I inflate with pride reading her letters. She's my improved Isabella Archer, a wonderful risk taker and a vivid writer. I should also say that my spelling is just as erratic as hers.

There is no doubt she received a *frisson* from being a pale, bosomy, blond among shrouded women. My mother was, as a rule, conventional, traditional, duteous, respectable, and conforming, but part of her longed to break the rules. In Tunis she could, as a visiting American, do that. She was an exception and the rules did not apply. I understand that *frisson* of power in being alien and free. Women don't have a lot of power in this world. I also have stood beyond the boundary of the rules and taken a deep breath of the contraband air of outsider's liberty.

However, duteously she returned from her adventure, met my father, and married him. An unmarried life was unimaginable. That was, largely, the end of her travels, although she and my father went to Europe a number of times and she did get to go around the world.

By unfair coincidence or inheritance, I acquired the life she wanted. She never urged me to go to North Africa but recounted her experiences with such joy I knew that time had been a precious oasis, which over the years must have come to seem a shimmering mirage.

However, there was a huge difference between this traveling woman I admire and the woman who was my mother. What links them is that she unconsciously—as unconsciously as she abused my confiding in her—urged me toward a life of adventure. When I had mumps and measles, she read to me for hours as I sat in bed with my white mouse for company climbing the Himalayas of my knees down to toe-valley or moleing under the blanket. She read to me, from a time before my memory, poetry. Not just the heavily rhymed thumpity-thump kind for children, but bits of Frost, Dickenson and Hopkins among others.

I didn't always understand these poems but what I received from them was a permanent fascination with words, the interweaving of sound and sense that undoubtedly led to my becoming a poet.

We each have a number of mothers. It has taken me years to accept that I have mothers I like and mothers I don't. I have an adventurous mother, a conformist mother, a bigot mother, a family-loving mother, a tightwad mother, a mean mother, and a social climbing mother. On it goes.

One day I thought to myself, "Suppose you could have the mother you think you want, but you would have to give up everything you received from your original mother. You cannot take any of her gifts with you and your new mother will not give you any of those things. Would you do it?" I considered that. She gifted me with whatever writing skill I have. She endowed me with my love of risk and travel, my disinterest in the hardships on the road. No, I would not trade her for the warmest, kindest most supportive mother because what she gave me is what is most precious to me. I'll keep what I have, thank you.

My final conversation with her strikes me as sad, ironically funny, and very human. She had gone into hospital for a check-up because she was short of breath when she walked any distance. Calling, I was greeted by her anger, "Don't call me. You're wasting money. I'll be home tomorrow." She was dead at 10:00 a.m. on that morrow of a heart attack.

I crossed a wooden bridge sounding hollow and loud under my solitary boots. I snuggled into my aloneness on the unwinding cursive script of the path under the barren ridges to my right. Later I read that the little stream I crossed is considered to be the urine of Kailash, suggesting that the mountain is thought of as a sentient being. I walked on wrapping the silence around me, recalling a poem of Kipling's in which silence is equated with the presence of the Old Gods. When "Very Many People" come they "string a clamorous

Magic/ to fence their souls from thought", a people who "comfort themselves with neighbours. / They cannot bide alone," causing the Old Gods to leave. I had seen, not often, but occasionally, Westerners laboring up to the pass their ears plugged into devices that supplied them with their own music from their own culture rather than the mountain's chords of wind, birds and silence. The Chinese in small villages in Tibet set up huge speakers to keep the silence of the Changtang Plain at bay as though it were a dangerous animal.

Often I forget sound is as much a part of recognizing a place as is sight. I would immediately know where I was if I heard a European ambulance klaxon rather than the shrill scream of an American ambulance siren. Part of the sound-scape of Hong Kong is the fast tick-tick-tick of the imperious, green Walk signs on corners that become flooded with people. When the light changes the sound becomes the slow tick–tick-of the red Don't Walk sign.

After a few bends there was Jemi sitting on a boulder, waiting for me with a smile and my bottle of water. My short interval of independence was over.

Jemi, her man, and another porter taking a rest. Jemi's man is praying on his beads.

I trailed behind her for the next three and a half hours, of what, according to Victor Chan, is a two and a half hour walk. I watched her do little rituals as we visited all the legendary places—the hoof print of Gesar's horse that flew from place to place, the print of the Soul Yak's hoof. It is the blood of the Soul Yak which gives the gorge's cliffs their red color. I had read about them in Chan's very complete coverage of all the legendary places on the Kailash *khora*. Gesar is a pre-Buddhist, mythical, indeed mystical, king, the Beowulf of Tibet, a hero who saves all from disaster. Beowulf is a pagan with Christian overtones. Gesar is halfway between Bön and Buddhist. In both epics, magic rules.

There was a hollow in a rock darkened by pilgrims' applications of yak butter. Jemi took up another rock banging it a number of times in the stone hollow, a mortar and pestle; then urged me to do the same. I did, although I had no idea what the significance of my action was. Again and again there were places I recognized as sacred because there were small hollows in rocks that were dark with yak butter. At one stop a group of women had little funnels with markings on them. They filled these up with seeds and threw them repeatedly over their left shoulders. Seeing me watching them, they motioned me over and lent me one of the little funnels, instructing me on the right motions. Again I had no idea what my action was supposed to accomplish but was grateful for being included. As when Jemi's man had inquired if I knew what my prayer beads were for and then accepted me when I recited the mantra, my willingness to perform the ritual meant that being a stranger did not mean being excluded. If you were willing and open to participating then you were part of.

The gorge with its red walls.

Throwing the seeds over my shoulder I thought of how, when I was about nine, I had asked a friend, not a Catholic, to go to church with me. We had gone up to the altar rail to receive communion together when there was a great bustle and she was gently removed. I had not realized that communion was only for Catholics. I felt shamed by my religion's inability to include my friend.

In another place people were digging by the side of the trail for *sana*, a medicinal earth that people take home with them. Further on people were doing more digging but this time it was for pebbles. I couldn't understand what made some pebbles the "right" pebbles and others worthless. If you find a pebble that is "right" you drill a hole in it and wear it as a necklace or you keep it in the family treasure box. These stones are considered prophylactics against strokes and epilepsy.

I was fascinated by the eclectic, flea market of sacred sites around the mountain that are attached to the Bön, the Buddhist and just the folk beliefs of Tibet. I had originally thought that there would be a continuity, connections between these tales attached to sacred sites but instead there were endless unconnected stories like the swatches of a patchwork quilt. There is stratum upon stratum of tales, footprints, hoof prints, mysterious maidens, medicinal locales along the path, intermingling, jostling against each other in this place of sacredness. The crowd of bumping, shoulder shoving beliefs reminded me of the web of stories that surrounded my travels, the interconnections of people's lives—my mother's story, Annalisa's story, Chaim's, Gunar's, Dawa's, Heinrich's, Amelia's, Ben's, Sonam's. We were a netting of tales knotted to each other by the places where our lives have touched.

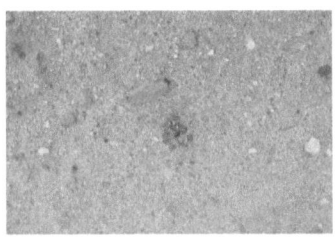

A determined flower by the side of the path.

I walked behind Jemi, like a child following her mother, beside the gorge of the Zhong Chu River, with gold, green, and blood-red cliffs. We stopped to gaze out above the river gorge where there was a breath stopping panorama across the spread of the Barga Plain in front of the huge, but peaceful, rumpled snow mass of Mt. Gurla Mandata. I felt, although the technical end of the *khora* is Darchen Monastery, that this was for me the finish of the sacred path.

My throat tightened painfully. It was so constricted I could not swallow. This is what I do instead of crying. If I cried my mother accused me of wanting sympathy. I did want sympathy, but what I usually received was a slap and, "I'll give you something to cry about." I lost my tears. Will I get them back before I die? I thought Jemi's kindness and my gratitude toward her might have caused my constricted throat. Those dry tears were, I have come to believe, the first sign of my bond with the mountain.

Did walking the *khora* change me? How do you gauge change in yourself, although it can be easy to see in others? But I do believe there was change. Certainly I became more aware of change as a choice, as an option available to me, and of the necessity of working to make it happen. Change was not going to be given to me free of charge.

I could look back and summarize what I had learned. From Heinrich, Gunar, and Chiam what I acquired from their attitudes toward their difficulties, crises, and challenges helped me adjust my behavior under stress. Considering the kindness and generosity of Sonam, Amelia, Miguel, and Thomas, I felt ashamed of my lack of generosity, realizing that it was not money generosity that was important, indeed, money generosity is a cheap version of the virtue, but what I lacked was generosity of spirit. I came from a household where meanness, monetary, emotional or spiritual was acceptable.

Through Jemi and the porters, through my time with my companion travelers I recognized the foolishness of my suspicious, fearful attitude toward people. I needed to be conscious of it. Fear breeds anger instantaneously, since anger makes us feel powerful.

Tibetans, when they behave well, behave exceptionally well. Of course, some don't. But when they do, they actually fulfill the dictates of their religion. They are generous; they show compassion. Jemi and her man became role models for me, as did Sonam. I was aware that I had choices of behavior.

We traveled on after the circumambulation to Tholing and Tsaparang, places Annalisa mentioned when she told me of Kailash. They were as wonderful as she thought they would be. I hope she has gone there.

After leaving Darchen we drove toward the Nepali border, stopping at a pass before the town of Nyalam. I asked Dawa to talk to some truck drivers traveling in a caravan in the opposite direction in two trucks one of which had a winch. They said they were not going to Lhasa but would take me as far as Shigatze for 200 yuan, twenty-five dollars. Once there I would be able to catch a bus to Lhasa. I am sure the Dutch woman's hitchhiking attempt enabled my decision to hitchhike by truck back to Lhasa. Recognizing that my stab at bargaining with the truck driver was ineffectual, I accepted his price, pulled my bags out of my old baby-blue truck and put them in my new baby-blue truck, climbed into the seat next to the driver, who was most disappointed to learn I couldn't speak Tibetan. Sitting next to him, watching herds of antelope, seeing how careful he was not to run over the big jackrabbits that leapt like furry-rumped Nijinskies across the road in panic, seemingly intent on suicide beneath our wheels, I contemplated my fears.

Lang La where I left my companions and started hitching my way back to Lhasa.

I realized that I had/have very little physical fear. I had just a wisp of it changing from my old truck to my new unknown truck. I was not worried about how my truck driver would treat me, although I was sorry that I didn't speak Tibetan. In my own culture, I was afraid partly because of my exaggerated sense of competition with others, partly because of my hyperbolic sense of hierarchy, partly because of my fear of my mother's contempt and rage, and my anxiety as I walked on the fragile ice-crystals of my father's needs, fears and alcohol inspired rages. Amongst my own I ranked everyone automatically into a hierarchy and feared those above me. I don't know if hierarchy exists among reptiles but certainly all mammals are hardwired for it. Anyone who has owned more than one cat knows that out of three cats there is only one that gets to be first to use the cleaned pan. Humans are just the same.

I knew I didn't want to be a sixty-year-old woman still blaming my mother, still tied to negative emotions originating in my relationship with her. Although Freud certainly helped to free up our sexual thinking, he unfortunately also created a scaffolding of thought in which the parents are the originators of their children's malfunctions. Parents are blamed for everything and anything and it is, therefore, quite all right to hate your parents. This is an admittedly simplified version of what Freud proposed but what most people understand is that simplified version. In Thailand children are taught to be grateful to their parents since the parents have, by creating them, enabled their children to have a new incarnation in which they can increase their good *karma*, moving closer to nirvana.

I wanted to take responsibility for my life. Knowing my mother, through her letters, as she was before she was my mother helped me to identify her as her self, a human being separate from me, some one who was not my mother. Someone whose spirit I admired. As we bounced and jounced along the road I began to see that my fear of people while it had roots in my mother also was firmly planted in ideas my culture had given me about high and low on the societal totem pole.

We pulled into a truckers' motel that night where my fellow guests as well as the staff were also disappointed in my lack of Tibetan. I found that the door of my room had no lock. I pushed my backpack against it and climbed under the leaden duvet. At 5:00 a.m. when the truckers started revving their engines, I awoke.

I found lying there, not knowing where I was—somewhere west of Lhasa and north of Kathmandu—combined with the inability to communicate with the people around me, gave me a surreal, floating sensation of intense happiness. I felt joyously free, like Pinocchio singing "I Have No Strings on Me." I have had this sensation only twice that I can recall in my life. I find it wildly intoxicating, beyond my ability to express it, to be alone in the middle of what to me is nowhere, although it is home to others, with none of the cultural structures I am used to about me. I also experienced this sensation in northern Thailand once on a bus, sharing a seat with two other people with whom I could not converse headed toward a small town I knew only as a name on a map. It is like riding the wind naked. Nothing intervenes between me and the life I am experiencing with total exhilaration. I think an outrageously anthropomorphic thought, that gulls I see surfing air currents on steady wings must be feeling this kind of freedom.

Nomad tents along the way.

We started off at eight and soon arrived in Old Dingeri, a Tibetan town (New Dingeri is a Chinese town) occupying terraces on the side of a hill. This is the town that Arthur and Ben started from when they made their unfortunate climb to Everest Camp Three. The area around the bottom of the hill was a mix of Tibetan houses and the dusty black tents of nomads. We stopped among the tents. The three drivers in my two-truck caravan were intent on buying some sort of meat. I could see thin sheets of it hung over clotheslines between the black tents. It was a monochrome scene, the color of whole-wheat flour—black tents powdered with dust, pale houses, pale smoke rising from them all while hundreds of ravens lifted and settled among black dogs, donkeys and horses.

We drove out of town crunching through the frozen meanders of the Phung Chu River, which is just a shrunken stream in the fall when there is less melt from the glaciers. The drivers were trying to locate a road but were unsuccessful. Instead we found Land Cruisers full of people going to Everest Base Camp. The road we ended up on was hellish.

As we drove out of town, we passed Chinese soldiers in green uniforms straggling back into town from some work assignment. They did not look pleased to see my Western face up in the truck's cab. I couldn't blame them. It must seem the worst possible duty if you come from the green riverine landscapes of southern China to end up in this cold, parched landscape suitable only for saints and other ascetics.

Following the road through mountains that appeared to be totally devoid of vegetation, we arrived around noon at a place that I believe is called Baila, a dreary checkpoint of broken, green beer bottles and discarded plastic noodle bowls that, given the dryness of Tibet, will remain there for posterity's posterity. There was a store and a restaurant with a billiard table, all owned and run by a Chinese man who charged me four times what he charged Tshu, my Tibetan driver, for the same lunch.

A desperate Tibetan family with four children begged before the door of the restaurant. The man played a sort of mandolin; the children put out their palms; the mother comforted them. I gave them handfuls of raisins, which I heaped up on the dusty billiard table.

It was at this checkpoint that Tshu realized I had no travel permit to reenter Lhasa. His alarm sprouted paranoia in me which leafed out when I talked to an exceedingly tall, young, bearded American who was headed toward the border in one of the trucks lined up at the checkpoint. He had tried to get to Lhasa but had been turned back at the Lhatze checkpoint because he didn't have a permit. It hadn't occurred to him to smile innocently and ask if he could buy such a permit there at the checkpoint.

Through the medium of my phrase book I told Tshu about this. He looked thoughtful but assured me that we weren't going to Lhatze. I folded a twenty-dollar bill into my passport, receiving it back without any folding money.

The land we traversed in the afternoon was alternately jagged and level. The level parts were covered with farms where people were winnowing, threshing and shooing cows and donkeys away from their grain. It looked like an excellent harvest, but when I got to Lhasa Sonam told me the Chinese were forcing the Tibetans to sell so much of their grain at such low prices that there was a possibility of famine during the winter. In each little town there was a fancy building put up by the Chinese that was the local co-op headquarters.

Around 5:00 p.m. we stopped at a farm beside the road. This was a scheduled stop; I could tell because the farmer's wife, when she saw us, went hurrying off to the house and returned with a kettle of *chang*, homemade beer with a low alcohol content. The drivers took from one of their packs a wicker box wrapped and tied neatly in a woman's kerchief. It contained what Tibetans call "old meat." This is a correct description. The meat is not cured or smoked. It is just hung up on a clothesline to parch in the dry air of Tibet. This was what they had bought from nomads in Dingeri.

We all sat on the tundra. I was handed a few ribs to try. It was very good but terribly difficult to get off the bone. While I was wrenching and pulling at the meat, the children in the family were slowly closing their circle around me. With snotty noses and hands black from handling pots that sat in the fire, they were a grotty lot. The eldest, a boy, was the first to get close. His goal was my daypack, not for what was in it but for the fascination of the buckles that fastened it around my waist. These he quickly learned to manipulate so that they gave their satisfying click as they closed. I fed his brothers and sisters dried dates, raisins and apricots from my food sack. He moved on from my daypack to my Reeboks that had Velcro fasteners. The others watched him gravely.

My drivers who were bantering with the farm wife, urged her to take some of the "old meat" many times, and finally as we left she did. I was very flattered that the little boy waved, smiled and even stuck out his tongue at me as I climbed back up into the cab. Sticking out your tongue is the old-fashioned way of showing respect in Tibet.

Night was coming on as Tshu avoided the leaping rabbits in the road, sheep frantically trying to run up the road, down the road, across the road all at once, cows standing still and stolid. At some point after dark we stopped at a monastery. I thought perhaps we were going to stay the night there, but, no, we were visiting a monk to whom we delivered a package. The two men talked as I drank my butter tea and ate yak cheese and sweets that had been set out for me. Tshu took a package from the lama and off we went again.

The truck started to make an odd noise, *chick-i-kung, chick-i-kung*, and there was a smell of burning rubber. Tshu stopped a number of times, borrowing my flashlight to illumine the under side of the truck. But he saw nothing untoward, so we continued on. Somewhere along the way we had lost the winch truck from the caravan. The next thing I knew I was being deposited at a tatty hotel opposite a disco in some town. After ten minutes and much work with my phrase book, Tshu looked at me with bemused exasperation. Pointing firmly at the ground before his feet he said, "Shigatze, Shigatze." "Oh," I said, finally comprehending. Then pointing his finger back and forth along the street, "Bus Lhasa," he said.

I paid him his 200-yuan and lugged my stuff upstairs to a room that looked out to the disco's flashing lights and resonating bass. I managed to get the management to put a bulb in the fixture in the tiny hall before my door, which locked with a twist of wire over a nail. At 7:00 a.m. I dragged everything downstairs again. I gave my dried fruit and a couple of pounds of *tsampa* that I was still lugging about with me to the exceedingly hung-over doorkeeper who stank of stale *chang*. I took up my place by the curb with my monk's winter robe in a sack and my pack on my back to wait for the Lhasa bus.

Arriving in Lhasa, I dumped everything out of my backpack and rammed the monk's robe in. At the *chuba* shop, I unzipped my pack and gave the robe to Pema asking, "Where's Sonam?"

She replied, taking the heavy, dusty robe from me, "Doing her evening *khora* around the Barkhor." The Barkhor is the street that circles the Jokhang temple. Every evening Sonam would walk that sacred route reciting mantras and whirling her prayer wheel or slipping her prayer beads through her fingers. She practiced her faith in its ceremonies and occasions quietly.

Waiting for her, I thought how she also practiced it in her relationships, being patient, generous and open with people. She did not have the feeling that had been present in my family that by giving one was taking away from one's self. Her generosity was rooted in the belief that there was enough for all, that giving never deprived the giver.

The ruffled rickshaws that used to take women and their packages home from market in Lhasa.

While I waited I looked at the postcards Pema had taped to a pillar in the shop. Most were from Israel. Israeli women coming to Lhasa had *chubas* made in Sonam's shop. Her name and the shop's location were handed on from group to group. I was impressed that Israelis, known for their prickliness as much as for their hardiness, adored her. She never lost patience with people. The only place I could see her struggling to be tolerant was with the Chinese.

There are a number of different varieties of Chinese. I once asked a Tibetan guide what he thought of the Chinese.

"Bad and stupid," he answered. "But also very cunning."

"What do you think of people from Hong Kong? They are Chinese," I asked.

"Nice, smart. They okay, not like Mainland."

"And Taiwanese?"

"Okay. Not as good as people from Hong Kong."

When in Tibet I tend to see the dark side of the Chinese because usually all the Chinese I meet are from the Mainland and subscribe whole heartedly to their government's attitudes toward Tibetans as a barbaric, dangerous people whom they have liberated and whom they are trying to civilize. It is not an attitude at all different from that of the English in the nineteenth century toward Indians, or Malaysians, or indeed, Chinese. Nor is it very different from the attitude of Americans toward Native Americans in the nineteenth century or the Vietnamese in the last century. Many Hong Kong Chinese don't believe in the inferiority of Tibetans or in the Chinese annexation of Tibet. Some Taiwanese see Tibet as a separate country.

An interesting phenomenon is beginning to occur. Chinese from all of these groups are returning to the practice of Buddhism and either going to Tibet to acquire spiritual instruction or seeking Tibetan Buddhist monks in provinces bordering Tibet, Yunnan or Szechwan. For hundreds of years before Mao, Tibet was the official source of China's Buddhist knowledge.

As I travel more in China, and as the Chinese have with the years become more affluent and, therefore, more interested in the outside world, more individualistic and committed to ideas of personal freedom I have seen them change and my attitude toward them has changed, as well. I see they have a hard struggle now and difficult choices ahead of them. Alterations in attitude can be seen in conversations I have had.

In 2007 traveling from Lhasa to Shanghai on the new fast train, the highest train trip in the world, I met a young woman who made me cognizant of how growing up in an environment of propaganda one naturally becomes an imitator of that kind of speech. It isn't government hype; it is a way of speaking one is proud to imitate when the opportunity arises. Being able to establish one's national superiority with a foreigner is an important way to score points.

Trying to find my bunk in the second-class car, I heard a voice behind me saying in precise English. "Could I help you?" I turned to see a thin, teenaged Chinese girl.

"Yes, would you please? I can't figure out where my berth is. Your English is excellent."

We found that my berth was in the midst of her family.

Later as we were sitting by the window talking, she said, with a smug little smile, "This railway across China and through the mountains proves the greatness of the Chinese people." The words popped from her mouth, a perfect, preformed piece of propaganda establishing China's preeminence. She was obviously pleased with it.

I couldn't resist so I responded. "Since the tracks were laid with the assistance of the Russians who have experience in building railroads at high altitude on frozen ground, and the cars were made by Canada, I think we could call this railway an example of a great international effort."

Chastened, she agreed.

In 2012, in Xi'an I had a startling conversation that abruptly made me aware of the tentacles of fear slithering out from a despotic government to make a citizen aware of her state bondage as well as her state of bondage. At breakfast at my youth hostel I sat next to a muscular Chinese woman in her mid-twenties.

"What has brought you to Xi'an?" I asked.

"I was in a bad mood, so I decided to come here," she said.

This struck me as unlikely, so I questioned further. "Why were you in a bad mood?"

"I come from," she named a town on the coast. "I had planned to go sailing but the weather was too foggy and I couldn't go."

This still seemed an unlikely reason for bad temper to me. We kept talking and slowly the truth came out, a terrifying truth.

"I applied for an exit visa. I wanted to go to England or to the U.S."

"They turned you down?" I asked. I know that is what usually happens.

"Yes, but they stamped in my passport that I had been refused an exit visa."

Now I understood her bad mood. With that stamp she had been branded with the mark of Cain. Any official looking at her passport would know she was not trusted; she was a suspect person whose freedom of movement could be questioned.

"Did you ask why they put that stamp in your passport?" I asked, horrified for her.

"They sent me a letter saying that they had put in that stamp because they thought I wanted to emigrate."

"I am so sorry," I inadequately sympathized. "Well, if you didn't want to emigrate before, you do now," I finished.

We would not have had that conversation in 2007. It made me aware of the despair that accompanies living in fear, your government leaning over your shoulder, rattling its manacles.

However, in Tibet I don't see the Chinese struggling for their freedom. I see their oppression of the Tibetans, their arrogance as when I saw on this trip, the Chinese man having his picture taken before the Chenresi statue in the Jokhang, legs apart, chest out, hands on hips, the pose of a victor.

Pema brought me some jasmine tea and in a little while Sonam arrived, untying from under her chin her little straw Uigher hat that looked like an Amish farmer's hat. In Tibet it is worn by Uigher Muslims. Its yellow straw made a halo around her head.

I told her about the trip and about hitchhiking back from Lang La to Shigatze, laughing over the twenty dollar bill I had slipped into my passport at the checkpoint and how I had not understood where I was when the driver unloaded my bag onto the sidewalk outside the hotel in Shigatze.

"I went to India last year," she told me, "to go to Dharmsala because I have an elderly aunt there in a nunnery. I wanted to see her before she died. I applied for a passport."

I can't remember now what the problem was with her passport; I do remember she had to apply to four or five different agencies for approval, first the local police station, then her neighborhood committee of cadres had to approve, then the government of Lhasa and on up the bureaucratic ladder. Either she never got all the approvals or she couldn't get an Indian visa.

I do know that crossing the border into Nepal and getting to Kathmandu was, for some reason, not a problem but she had to slip into India illegally because part of her documentation was missing.

"At the Indian border, I mixed with a crowd of people, Indian, Nepali, who were crossing and I was not noticed. But coming back it was more difficult because there weren't a lot of people around, no crowd I could mix with at the border checkpoint. I had to wait for the guard to turn his back; then I slipped across."

My belly goes cold at the chances she was taking. Indian prisons are more than grim, nor would you want to be returned to the Chinese border as an illegal alien. But she did it. She had time to sit and talk with her aunt whom she hadn't seen for forty years. It was odd but interesting that we shared this relationship with a beloved aunt.

I have seen, going to Tibet ten times, how economically things have improved for Tibetans. The Chinese are puzzled that this increase in prosperity does not cause the Tibetans to love them. It also has not caused the Tibetans, in most cases, to become materialistic. This also puzzles the Chinese who thought that they could kill Buddhism through making Tibetans materialistic. When Tibetans make money they spend it on temples.

Tibetans are watched, are under surveillance, constantly in danger. They are urged to spy upon each other. In monasteries and nunneries, monks and nuns are closely monitored. Often monks are required to take part in sessions in which they criticize themselves and each other or they are lectured on Communist principals being told that religion is evil.

"Sonam," I said. "You are so brave you take my breath away. What you have done is amazing and very frightening."

"Yes, a little, but really I just do what needs to be done. If I had not gone to see my aunt, I would not like myself. That was a thing I needed to do."

"You know, Sonam, I think we are the same age."

"No, that can not be true."

"I was born in 1936," I said.

"Oh," she said in anguish, looking, with her deep brown eyes, at me, at my Western face, so much younger than hers. "We Tibetans must have done something very, very terrible in the past."

Karma is the belief, in both Buddhism and Hinduism, that your actions, particularly your intentional actions, committed in previous lives, create the situation of your present life. She was, therefore, saying that by evil actions in the past Tibetans had brought upon themselves the Chinese invasion, the resulting poverty, and cultural attacks. By evil actions in the past they had created their present bad *karma*. *Karma* is based on cause and effect. Your actions in previous lives create your present life.

I said, not believing in reincarnation and *karma*, "No. I've had an easy life, you a hard one."

That we were born in the same year made a bond between us, since although we lived on opposite sides of the world, we had known that world through the same time span of World War II, the tension of the Cold War between Russia and the US, the tension between Russia and China. We shared a sense of our time.

I learned from Sonam. Her interactions with people taught me about my own deficiencies. She was my role model, generous, patient, and open with people. When I left Lhasa I took her with me as my standard for behavior. If you are afraid of people it is difficult to be generous and patient. I worked to lose my fear. I worked to lose my family's habit of clutching at things. We were so afraid we were going to lose what we had or not get what we wanted. To give to someone else meant depriving yourself. I tried to cultivate a feeling that I was being taken care of, that I had enough.

I didn't set out with the conscious intent of changing and regaining my feelings by traveling; it just happened, not suddenly, except once, but slowly over the years.

PART V

1999, My Second Trip To Kailash, Learning To Walk At Altitude

I went to Kailash the second time with a thirty-something English friend, Rachael. We met originally in Irian Jaya, Indonesia, the left-hand side of the island of New Guinea, when I, to her great annoyance, stumbled with my American vowels into her video recording of a pig feast she had arranged and paid for in a Dani village of houses that looked like hay stacks near Wamena. While I could hardly blame her for being upset, I'd had no way of knowing that she was recording. She apologized for her annoyance at me and apologized again over dinner when she asked if I wanted to join her on a trek she was preparing to do with a man who was reputed to be the best local guide. I was tempted but also leery because I didn't know her and had no idea what a trek of this sort would involve physically or what kind of terrain we were going to be dealing with. Being around twenty years older than she, I feared I wouldn't be able to do things that would come to her with medium difficulty.

When she returned, she told me she'd had to climb trembling, hand-tied bamboo ladders up otherwise unscalable cliffs, twenty, thirty feet high. At night she had picked lice from her shirt seams while holding her flashlight in her mouth. I was lucky to have refused. I don't think I could have done it. Trekking in jungle and heat puts one under different stresses from trekking in cold, dry mountains.

But we kept in touch. I learned that she was a software consultant who had assisted institutions in Britain's shift from being government run to being private. This is an area about which I know and understand little. She talked, bragging a little, about how she made a huge amount of money doing it, so much that her accountant would call her periodically to say, "Rachael, you need to stop working. You are making so much money that most of it is going to taxes rather than to you. Take one of your trips."

I was decidedly impressed both by her profession skills, which I didn't understand, her ability to make so much money, and her adventurousness. When I am impressed, I tend to assume that the other person suffers from no difficulties in life and has smooth psychological and social surfaces. This is a bad, not to say idiotic and sometimes disastrous assumption to make. A New York friend once told me that when she was young she thought that "suits" knew everything and, therefore, all she needed to do was to acquire a "suit," marry him, and then all would be well. I am afraid that I have a similar attitude toward people, male or female, who make lots of money. They seem so different from me that I don't expect them to have emotions or reactions similar to mine. Certainly, I expect them to be impervious to fear.

I wrote to Rachael about my first trip to Kailash. She responded with interest, asking if I would want to do a circular trip around Tibet going from Lhasa to Kailash, to Ali and then back to Lhasa by the northern route. We would start by heading west on the southern route on roads I had already traveled to Kailash, Tholing and Tsaparang but continuing beyond those two sites to Ali in far western Tibet, the town Heinrich had been heading to when he left us at Tholing. There we would take the northern route back, driving east to Lhasa through

Gerze and other minuscule towns in an area of Tibet populated more by nomads than by settled townspeople. I was elated and excited to find someone wanting to do a trip I had thought was probably impossible.

Emailing back and forth, we decided she would bring the tents and we would each buy food of the instant meal or dehydrated variety. I had never eaten or tried to cook such meals, nor had Rachael as far as I knew. We would get a guide, four-wheel drive truck, and drivers in Lhasa through some agency that would also arrange for the permits. I had an inkling of how difficult this trip was going to be on the physical side, but I am not sure that Rachael had much grasp of what lay ahead. This, it turned out, did not mean she underestimated our future travails. Instead, it may have caused her to exaggerate the dangers ahead. Certainly, in retrospect, in deciding to do this trip we vastly overestimated my abilities in cooking at altitude and underestimated the exhaustion—mental, emotional, and physical—that results from traveling at altitude. That is just taking into account the practical difficulties. The psychological/emotional hardships I didn't focus on until I was in the midst of them and then, of course, it was too late.

Rachael and I met at the Hong Kong Y on Salisbury Road, a favorite of mine because the rooms have the same view of Hong Kong Harbor as the luxurious Peninsula next door, with its colonial ambience, but at less than a fifth of the price. I can indulge my favorite travel aphorism, "Sleep cheap. Eat expensive," eating the excellent food at the famous Peninsula. They also have a good chocolate shop in the basement—the last one, in those days, you would see if you were going into China.

We immediately got everything necessary to a travel agency to speed our China visas; we would get our Tibet visas in Chengdu. We bought plane tickets and, at Rachael's insistence, silk socks to wear under our cotton and wool socks. I moved from the dorm at the Y to share a nice, but much more expensive than I was used to, room with Rachael the night before we flew into Chengdu. It had a superb view of the Hong Kong harbor, the light display of the skyscrapers across the water and the Star Ferry, a plump green-and-white duck, chugging dutifully back and forth between Kowloon and Hong Kong. I found that when she could go upmarket, Rachael did.

Arriving at any airport or railway station in the world late at night is almost always a terrible experience; Chengdu was no exception. In the poorly-lit, rutted, packed-earth parking lot we got into a taxi believing the driver would do the trip on the meter, since when I pointed at the meter he nodded "yes." As soon as we left the police at the airport, he stopped under an elevated highway and yelled at us mostly in Chinese but with just enough English so we understood we were no longer on the meter. We, meaning me, wouldn't budge from forty yuan, five dollars, the price given in our guidebook; but he was still yelling, in Chinese, for fifty. Finally I started yelling back.

He took off, flooring the accelerator. He would have won a race against all the bats in hell. I was in the death seat and terrified. It was an Indy 500 drive, but he was young with excellent reflexes. I comforted myself with the thought that he had no more interest in dying than I had. He wove through traffic. He braked violently. When he turned, he slewed the car in front of oncoming traffic and stopped. In town, he hit a trishaw's wheel, but we survived. He played his music at an all-the-devils-in-hell level. Arriving at the hotel, he stopped but wouldn't drive in through the gates. He turned off the motor and, while we looked longingly at the hotel, started yelling again. We had enough baggage so that hauling it a hundred yards or so was not enticing.

Rachael went into the hotel to ascertain the right price for a taxi from the airport while he continued screaming at me. On the advice of the hotel's front desk, we paid him fifty and he drove us through the gate with much swerving, making the brakes squeal like a pig being butchered. This was not a good introduction to China for Rachael who had been tense even in Hong Kong. Our hotel, next door to the bus station, had (and I believe still has) the unfortunate name of The Traffic.

The next morning we started the process of finding a tour to Lhasa, since one could only enter Tibet on a tour. There were three or four agencies with offices in The Traffic's first floor. We went from one to the next comparing prices and durations of tours. This uncertainty and our protracted negotiations stressed Rachael emotionally more. Perhaps she was used to having everything arranged before she left England. She had not slept the night before in Hong Kong. In the middle of talking with a woman at an agency about the cost of a flight to Lhasa, Rachael suddenly burst into tears. The woman was upset and embarrassed thinking she had caused Rachael's tears.

I finally realized that I had a real emotional problem on my hands but didn't know what to do and could not understand why Rachael was upset. The fact that I didn't comprehend (as I should have) that Rachael was scared silly and feeling paranoid, as would not be surprising, about the trip made things worse. It seemed to me impossible that Rachael would be afraid since she had done that Irian Jaya trek and she made lots of money. I can't imagine why I thought there was a link between making money and being fearless. I found the whole situation incomprehensible and anomalous. That incomprehension was caused by my not really paying attention in a concerned way to Rachael. I wasn't at that point capable of such an understanding or action. That I was failing in a spiritual situation never occurred to me.

We had a shot at arranging our circular tour of Tibet, both the southern and northern route, with one of the agencies at the hotel; but it became obvious that they didn't have a clue as to what they were doing. Then they jumped the price on me when I went back to talk to them. At that point I said a flat no; we would arrange things in Lhasa.

Needing a break, I left Rachael to take a nap while I went to find a better restaurant than the one available in the hotel. I found a place with an English menu, but they were out of food. In another they just stared and giggled at me. I gave up and went back to The Traffic where I found Rachael had been unable to sleep. I decided I had to do something besides making vague noises, hoping they sounded comforting. She had worked herself into a state of hysteria where she could not sleep, function or do anything except go in and out of tears. I have to say that I was not particularly compassionate. My attitude was that of someone trying to deal with a dripping faucet. Rather than thinking of her as a human being, I thought of her as something that needed to be fixed. But I could not seem to come up with anything to say that would be helpful. I was going blank and I was not able to connect to the fact that she was in a frantic state of insomniac fear.

That night Rachael stayed in the hotel to try to sleep while I went with some other people to a restaurant whose name I had acquired by asking one of the travel agents what his favorite restaurant was. I knew it wouldn't be expensive. He wrote the name and address in Chinese on a slip of paper. I, joined by others seeking better food than that available in the neighborhood, handed it to a taxi driver who did drive on the meter. As we were the only Caucasians, we were stared at; but everyone was pleasant and helpful. We had bamboo shoots in chili oil, potatoes with garlic, chicken with peanuts and chicken with three kinds of mushrooms, all heavenly, for $2.50 each.

When I returned to the room, Rachael, sleepless, was in an emotional maelstrom. I had no sleeping pills, no melatonin, to give her. I offered Tylenol and was inspired to say, "If you don't sleep tonight, you'd better go home rather than go on to Tibet. You're going to end up seriously ill if you go on like this." That was certainly true.

Something worked, Tylenol, words, or just exhaustion, because when we rose at 4:30 a.m. for the plane to Lhasa, Rachael was better having slept. I shuddered a sigh of relief.

The food on the flight to Lhasa was less peculiar than on the last trip, but heavy on sweets—two chicken wings, vegetables apparently cooked in a washing machine they were so soggy and wan, a sweet roll, a piece of cake and a cookie. First we had intermittent views of dark, green mountains with scarves of fraying white mist between their ridges, but soon we flew over a thick cloud quilt pierced by white peaks as though someone were holding vanilla ice cream cones just below the cloud surface.

On our tour, we were booked at the Banok Shol, which horrified Rachael. I couldn't blame her. It was pretty grim, four to six of us in a dorm room and a smelly, communal bathroom. I took her to the Kirey where they showed her a Western-style room with its own toilet and bath. I was surprised, as I hadn't realized they had Western rooms. I had a reunion with the chambermaids I had given lipsticks to. Since I had to economize, I did not join Rachael but returned to the grotty Banok Shol to share a room with two pretty, slim, blond, classic American girls, looking like Ralph Lauren mannequins, with the unlikely but charming names of Peach and Periwinkle.

I had a yak burger for dinner that didn't agree with me and was trying to sleep off my indigestion when Peach and Periwinkle came in. Peach was pale, sick, and shivering with cold. As she trembled, she told me, as if it were a badge of honor, about ending up in the hospital in some obscure town in China when her temperature descended to 86 degrees. Periwinkle fed her vitamins alternately giving her oxygen from a sort of tin can while I suggested she go to the hospital now. Two other Western women from a room on the floor above, who were nurses, having heard of Peach's illness through the travelers' grapevine, arrived in our room and started hurling questions at her like pitchers practicing spitballs in a bullpen. It turned out that she had not been drinking water, and was, therefore, seriously dehydrated and hadn't eaten anything all day. I was furious at her for her innocent, wide-eyed self-destructive stupidity but shut my mouth, put in my earplugs and managed to sleep. I woke the next morning to the sound of her vomiting into the wastebasket.

Early morning in Lhasa on what used to be called
Happiness Street. Now it is Beijing Street.

The day before, Rachael and I had located two agents offering reasonable prices for our trip and guides who seemed alright. One agent finally confessed that he could not get us an extension on our Tibet visas on such short notice. This was all done in a harum-scarum fashion because Rachael was going off on the tours that came as part of our tour package from Chengdu. We would meet between her visit to the Jokhang and her trip out to Norbulingka, her visit to Sera and then Drepung. I introduced her to Sonam and when I wasn't talking to agents with or without Rachael, I went to Sonam's shop.

When I first walked into the shop, she clapped her hands with excitement at seeing me, gave me a big hug, laughing and saying, "Soon you will come to Lhasa twice a year."

We hid among bolts of cloth in the back of the store where the sewing machine was kept behind a curtain, our chairs pulled back out of sight of the front of the shop. She whispered to me about her life in the old Tibet. Her marriage had been arranged, a polyandrous marriage, meaning she was married to a man and his brothers. This was not uncommon among Tibetans at the time. It wasn't, of course, about sex but about property. The reason marriages are arranged is to preserve and unite properties so that they become more powerful. A polyandrous marriage is often made when a family has only daughters and needs a son. The incoming husband takes his wife's family name and becomes, in effect, a son. The eldest brother is the primary husband and all children are presumed to be his. The other brothers frequently become traveling merchants for the two families. But if the first husband, the eldest brother, dies, the second eldest becomes the wife's new husband, and the family continues. There is no second ceremony as far as I know. This happened to Sonam.

Just before the Chinese army took over Tibet in 1959, her husband drowned in the Lhasa River. Most Tibetans cannot swim and they consider water to be a substance that should be avoided. The Chinese sent her new husband to a labor camp because he was an aristocrat. Hidden among the fabric bolts, we started, tense as rabbits on a lawn, at the thought of having been overheard when someone came through the curtain to the back room. This was usually Pema, a young woman with a delicate, tawny, cameo profile, who worked for Sonam. She brought us steaming, fragrant cups of jasmine tea and looked at Sonam with anxious eyes. She knew what we were talking about.

Fretfully, Sonam said, as I had heard other women of her generation in other cultures say, "I don't understand why women today are unfaithful to their husbands. All over Lhasa the children of my friends are getting divorced. I never wanted anyone but my husband. I never looked at anyone but my husband."

But I thought about the autobiography of a woman who was a relative of Sonam's, now living in the West. Her husband had been repeatedly unfaithful to her, although she obviously loved him. Finally, she had separated from him with great anguish because the pain of staying with him was even greater. I thought about myself with a drinking husband who spent all his time in bars and took our son, saying they were going to the park to spend time with his girlfriend. He then swore our eight year old to silence. I came out of my reverie to find that Sonam had moved on with her story.

"When the Chinese invaded in 1950, they allowed religious practices. But in 1959, before the Dalai Lama fled, they began showing contempt for our ceremonies. After he left, they abandoned all pretense of tolerating our religion and occupied Tibet. We are now a Chinese colony.

"After the Dalai Lama left in 1959 I was ordered to appear before a cadre who was in charge of our neighborhood."

"What does 'cadre' mean? I know it has something to do with the Communist Party but I've never understood what," I asked.

"It's anyone who holds a Party office, a government position, a military rank of any kind under the Communist system.

"I was still innocent and foolish at that time," she continued. "I went into her office all dressed up in my good *chuba* and the pearls my husband had given me. A big mistake. She immediately reached out and yanked the pearls so hard the string broke. They scattered all over the floor; I heard them, rolling and bouncing as she screamed at me that I was an enemy of the people. I couldn't have possibly bent down to pick them up, but I knew she would as soon as I left the room.

"She asked me what kind of work I could do. I could read as well as write in English and Tibetan and do math, but the Chinese were not interested in those things. I said I could sew and knit. I was sent to a sort of knitting factory, a room where women sat and knitted all day long. We were not allowed to talk to each other. There was a supervisor in the room to see we didn't and to see we never stopped knitting for one minute. We were not allowed to have our children with us. My son, who was about six years old, roamed all day eating what he could find in the garbage in the street. It was a time when we were all hungry. My husband was in the labor camp far from Lhasa. The woman who had been my servant had her own troubles surviving. She couldn't help my son.

"It must have been during this time that he got the disease that crippled him. For a long time we didn't know what was making him sick, but we kept going back to the doctors month after month. Finally, one of them in the new hospital in Lhasa did tests and told us what it was. I think it is in English," she paused and looked at me questioningly, "bone TB?"

"Yes," I said. "That certainly sounds very likely."

"I think Mao must have come from a small village with no doctor," she continued thoughtfully. "The one good thing that came out of that time was that the Chinese set up a hospital in Lhasa and brought in doctors. It is odd how the big events, the history outside of your personal life, alter your life, how someone whom you never meet changes your life. Because of Mao my son was infected by this disease which crippled him; but because of Mao there were doctors sent to Lhasa who could stop the disease which was killing him."

It is not often that one hears from a Tibetan praise of Mao. What he is blamed for most is the Cultural Revolution, which lasted ten years, a cyclone of violence causing devastation, personal, political, cultural and communal from 1966 to 1976. Mao Zedong became supreme commander of the nation and army, a euphemism for dictator, closing schools and universities to send students, organized as Red Guards, into the streets to attack signs of tradition, the elderly, teachers, intellectuals, anyone with "bourgeois" values.

In China proper, his intent was to eradicate the culture's respect for knowledge, intelligence, skill, and age, to kill the past and pride in it or any sense of beauty as admirable. A telling fact, the Chinese taunted

Tibetans, calling them childish because they grew flowers. Mao was intent on killing people's love of beauty, and in both Tibet and China admiration for beauty is strong.

I have also read that he instituted the Cultural Revolution because he was afraid that his countrymen would forget him. In other words, in order to remain in their memory he was willing to kill, maim, do all kinds of physical and psychological damage to his countrymen. If this is true, then Mao was a sort of IMAX edition of the child who is so desperate for attention that he willingly accepts and welcomes negative attention. Any kind of attention is preferable to none.

Sonam continued thoughtfully, "During the Cultural Revolution, Tibetan Maoists avenged old quarrels through the neighborhood committees that were created in Lhasa. People were spiteful over old injuries. A family downstairs from us committed suicide together rather than be arrested on the basis of what another neighbor said about them. Whole families committed suicide because neighbors were urged, or forced by being beaten or threatened with prison, to inform. Others, through a desire to retaliate, went to the neighborhood cadre with a story they had thought up. We were at each other's mercy. When I could, I would go to visit my husband at the labor camp. It was, depending on luck, a one- or two-day trip."

Where did you stay if it was overnight? There weren't, surely, any hotels?

"You stayed in peoples' houses along the road. It was not legal, but you could do it. When winter came, I went to see him taking a very good wool *chuba* of mine. It didn't matter that it was a woman's. He had no winter clothes and he was starving. They were given thin rice soup with a few vegetables in it and never any meat. They were made to plant and raise their own food. If they found, while gardening, a lizard, a snake, a bug, they ate it immediately. If they were caught, they were beaten. Most of the men who were my husband's companions in prison starved or died of the cold because they were given neither clothes nor blankets.

"On one trip, at a house that you could sleep in, there was just a big room with many beds, a man said to me, a Tibetan man, 'I am going to rape you.' We were alone in the big room. I pleaded with him, begged him, 'No, don't rape me. We are brother and sister. We are the same. We are Tibetans.' He didn't."

I could see the relief pour into her face as she came to the end of the story.

"My husband was imprisoned for eighteen years. When Mao died in 1976, at the end of the Cultural Revolution, he was released. Lhasa had been, in the years before his death, in chaos. Rival Red Guard gangs fought against each other to rule the city. Their competition ended in public executions by Chinese officials sent from Beijing to eradicate the gangs in 1969 and 1970."

While she told me all of this, she rocked back and forth in her chair like a child trying to comfort herself. From time to time, she would burst into laughter as she talked. Maybe I should say she would break down into laughter. At first I was puzzled by this laughter but then, horrified, I realized that the laughter was not laughter but her form of weeping. I felt totally helpless. I had never experienced anything approaching what she had been through. I had no words. I wanted desperately to comfort her but my knowledge of life seemed puny next to her recitation of events. I put out my hand and gently stroked her arm. She took my hand and held it against her arm, close, strong, and continued to breathe out her terrible laughter from time to time. As I watched that mirthless laughter, I knew she was my tearless sister. We both lived in the vale where there are no tears.

"When they closed the knitting factory. I was sent with other people, men and women, to work as a roof pounder. We pounded *arka* into the roofs of new buildings. Do you know what *arka* is?"

"No."

"It is a kind of clay which keeps water from seeping into the roof."

"Oh, it waterproofs them?" I asked.

"Yes," she said. "We sang songs and pounded a stick with a weight or a brick on the end of it to the rhythm of the song. Once a song was finished, the leader would say quickly and sharply, 'One, two three…' in English and then she or he would begin the next song, although I was probably the only one in the team who knew English. I liked doing this because we could talk to each other, exchange news. As long as there was singing the Chinese supervisor didn't think we were talking. I enjoyed the work, but I don't think I was very good at it."

I wondered if the use of English numbers went back to the British invasion of Tibet in 1904 under Colonel Younghusand when British sergeant majors bellowed the numbers at soldiers as they marched on their temporary parade grounds outside Lhasa. Later in the trip in Shigatze, I saw some people pounding a roof and could hear the leader saying, "One, two, three…." It is the only time I had heard of Tibetans using English numbers.

I had told Sonam that I wrote travel articles for the *New York Times* and the *Wall Street Journal*, asking her to spell Tibetan words that I had scribbled down in phonetic form. I always had a notebook in my pocket or purse. However, I never took notes about these conversations in case my journal was confiscated.

This never happened, but I knew of a young French woman who had intended to take a nun's letter to her sister who was living outside Tibet, meaning to mail it in France. She foolishly bragged in a restaurant about how she was taking the letter out with her; there was, as there often is, a spy. She was strip-searched at the airport, the letter taken from her. What happened to the nun no one knows, but it is nightmare fodder. Therefore, this has been written from memory, vivid even after many years.

When Rachael came back from her tour, we went out to shop for our trip.

A tent factory on a side street in Lhasa.

Over lunch at the Snowlands, we met a homeward-bound girl from Vienna who had an elegant, collapsible, little traveling stove that worked on kerosene, a fuel available in the tiniest of villages in Tibet, which she was trying to sell to keep her luggage from being overweight. Rachael looked at it, had the girl set it up and show her how to start it. I didn't think I could operate it, but Rachael thought she could and decided to buy it. The stove became the fountainhead of frustration at our evening meals, a worthy successor to the pressure cooker with its missing valve from the first trip. Halfway through the journey, we would both have cheerfully jumped up and down on the elegant little thing until we had pounded it flat, except then we would have had only the stove Rachael had brought from England which worked just as fitfully. It is the lack of oxygen that makes it difficult to light a stove and keep it burning.

Rambo outside a movie house in Lhasa.

At the Snowlands, we discovered that they also sold candy and trekking supplies. We bought Snickers and Mars bars, Mentos, canned tuna, peanut butter, muesli, toilet paper, powdered milk, and in a moment of sensible eccentricity, liver pate and canned duck. Walking down the street, we popped in and out of shops purchasing necessities such as basins for washing self and laundry, a storage bin for food, utensils, detergent, and a saucepan with a lid.

We went back to the agency to double check what they were supplying us with. The Chinese authorities required us to have a truck as well as a four-wheel drive, the theory being that the truck would rescue the four-wheel drive from sand traps and rivers, although often the reverse occurred and the four-wheel drive rescued the truck from a sand trap or river.

The tour we had been on was now over so I moved out of the Banok Shul, delighted to escape from Peach's vomiting, and into the imitation Western room Rachael was in at the Kirey. The bathroom was a brave but unsuccessful reproduction. The water drooled out of the shower head in a slack, lukewarm stream because of a dearth of pressure and slowly accumulated to ankle depth because the drain was blocked. Even though everything was still so new that the stickers hadn't worn off the toilet and bathtub, Tibetans do not remove stickers on toilets or sunglasses, all the fixtures had a dingy look of neglect. A sort of curse envelops bathrooms in locales where people don't usually have Western bathrooms that cause them to take on an aura of decay, an air of abandonment, early in their life.

The next morning Tashi sent Pema out to buy us homemade noodles, *tsampa*, ground, roasted barley, cheese, and honey. Pema had shaved her head preparatory to entering a nunnery. But she was giving up hope of this happening. The Chinese control the number of nuns and monks in the monasteries and nunneries. Pema had been waiting for a number of years now for an opening with no luck. She told us she was thinking of letting her hair grow back. She was a huge help, telling us where we could find supplies we needed or running out to find things for us at the last minute.

That evening Rachael said to me, "Would it be appropriate to buy Pema a necklace of some sort? I saw some nice looking pearl ones on the Barkhor today."

I was ashamed and guilt stricken that I hadn't thought of this act of generosity and gratitude myself. I had been thinking how open handed Pema was, how I would like to be like that. "Yes, let's do that," I responded, annoyed at myself, although I am not sure I understood my lack of generosity was due to self-centeredness.

That afternoon we went with Sonam to a compound on the edge of Lhasa, which housed a project for making paper and a school for those excluded from the Chinese free school system. If your parents were considered enemies of the Chinese government, you could not go to school, a clever way of marginalizing the children of the opposition. Some years before, the original project from which the school had grown, the making of paper, had been started by a group of Americans whose aim had been to get the project on its feet and then hand it over to the Tibetans to run.

Materials, recycled paper and rags, for making paper at the Paper Factory.

One of the people involved, a man who made handmade paper in the States, had discovered that at one time Tibet had been famous as the source of the best, the strongest, most long-lasting paper in the East. He and those working with him, including a woman artist from Seattle, found an old man who knew the ancient formula for making this paper.

The old man who knew the formula for making Tibetan paper.

This old man found me intriguing. Everyone he had known in his lifetime had black hair. Therefore, he wasn't sure what I had on my head was really hair. My companions caught him on camera testing me.

When everyone you have ever known has had black hair you want to test to see if hair of a different color is really hair. I was totally unconscious of the fact that he was touching my braid.

They started a small factory. The paper was made from discarded paper, fabric scraps and the special, secret ingredient, the root of a weed that farmers were delighted to be paid for bringing to the little factory. It is peeled and pulped before being spread on screens to dry.

The weed makes particularly fine paper because it is slightly poisonous and, therefore, repels vermin and insects. It is also resistant to mildew. Chinese monasteries in past centuries ordered large quantities of it, preferring it to other papers available, as the surface on which to write the holy *sutras*.

A young woman stirring paper soup in brilliant sun.

The shredded weed used to make paper.

On the roof of one of the buildings, as we stood peacefully contemplating the view across the city to the Potala's red and white terraces and towers rising out of the green of its surrounding trees, someone said, with a caustic edge in her or his voice, "Do you think the Chinese know where we are at this very moment?"

The answer, of course, was "Yes."

The next morning, walking down Beijing Street (ironically before the Chinese invasion it was called Happiness Street) as I was headed to the market to find nuts and dried fruits and then to the Barkhor for a pearl necklace for Pema, I noticed police shoving rickshaws with their red, yellow and blue ruffled canopies off into alleys. Tibetans had mysteriously disappeared from the street. The road was almost empty. With a sense of a trap door opening inside me, I understood what was about to happen. I had witnessed this a year before when I had come to Lhasa but not gone on to Kailash. Rachael didn't know. I only had a moment to say to her urgently, "Don't touch your camera," as we heard a siren wailing in the distance.

First there was a white police car, a man in military uniform with much gold braid looped on his shoulder seated squarely in the center of the back seat; next a squad of motorcycles with sidecars, in each an officer also with a shoulder looped in gold braid; last a blue Chinese truck containing half a dozen Tibetan men, each guarded by a soldier with a gun. Some forced their prisoner to bow, pushing their gun hard against his back. One raised his prisoner's manacled hands until pain made him bow. It was a calculated performance in humiliation.

One prisoner gazed at the mountains; face exultant with his last vision of the severe beauty of Lhasa's canine crags. Another stared with blank eyes, perhaps tortured to insanity or imbecility. They were, I had learned this the year before when I had witnessed the same ceremony, being driven to the ruins of a destroyed monastery at the edge of town to be executed. No charges. No trial. I wondered if there is comfort in dying among the broken walls of a monastery you knew as a child. First the Chinese have tried to erase your culture; now they erase you, a natural progression. These parades of power were a regular occurrence in Lhasa and may still be.

Most Tibetans had withdrawn indoors with their private sorrow and fury. Rachael was, of course, distraught. Our powerlessness made us feel hollow. We went to eat lunch ashamed of being hungry; ashamed of eating, ashamed that there was nothing we could do.

That afternoon we went to visit some buildings that were being rescued by the Tibet Heritage Fund, a two-person effort directed by a Portuguese woman and a German man who were trying to preserve both Tibetan buildings and crafts.

A street in the Tibetan section of Lhasa where the Tibet Heritage Fund was renovating homes.

Men reconstructing an old house for the Heritage Fund.

I had met them the year before at the Snowlands Hotel. They were working on the Meru Nyingpa Monastery, a branch of the Nechung Monastery where the main Tibetan oracle used to live. He is now in Dharmsala in India, having escaped with the Dalai Lama.

The courtyard was full of bundles of *pempa*, reddish-brown twigs, which I had never seen up close before. They are bundled together and used as a frieze on the outside of religious buildings. I could tell where new twigs had been inserted in a frieze because they were lighter in color. I asked where they came from and was told, "far away."

Next we were taken to an old house where an apartment was being redone in traditional Tibetan style, carvings over windows and doors, pillars with carvings and all this painted in rich, bright colors.

Men were stenciling flowers and Buddhist symbols on the ceiling beams. The woman who was to live in the apartment danced through the rooms thrilled, excitedly planning where to put her furniture, pointing out her daughter's bedroom, her son's, the windowless room that would be the family chapel hung with their *thangkas* and displaying their religious images.

Newly painted windows at the project.

New windows in the old style.

We were told that men were coming to ask to be trained to do carpentry, to carve, and paint. This would help to keep the traditional skills functioning. The problem was that one week the Chinese encouraged this kind of thing and the following week forbid it, producing scathing propaganda about how primitive the Tibetans are for wanting to live in apartments with this kind of decoration. Some years later the German and the Portuguese who had worked long and hard on this project were banished from Lhasa, their projects terminated.

A hand-carved window.

Men painting pillars in the new house.

Roof pounders preparing to stamp *arka*, a water proofing clay, into the roof of a renovated house.

The next morning our four-wheel drive rolled in through the Kirey's gate. I noticed that it had bald tires. I should have checked them but had forgotten. I hoped this wouldn't interfere with its ability to pull the truck out of trouble if necessary. But there was no truck accompanying the four-wheel drive. As was true on my first trip to Kailash, we had been told that we would carry gasoline in huge steel drums because of the paucity of gas stations in western Tibet. All our baggage, that of our guide, driver and truck driver would go into the back of the truck to be overwhelmed by dust. I was smug with delight knowing that I would not be chewing grit in the back of the truck huddled against the gasoline drums but sitting in the four-wheel drive with the windows rolled up, perhaps not dust free but certainly not enveloped in huge clouds of dirt. We stood about looking expectantly down the street for the truck.

The man from the agency arrived with white *khatas* which he draped around our necks and the news that we had a permit to go to Kyunglung, an area of badlands that houses the ruins of what once had been a huge troglodyte monastery. This was something that Rachael had read about and was very eager to see. We were less delighted when we were told that our truck would meet us in Lhatze. But there was nothing we could do about it. Sonam came running down the street to drape *khatas* around our necks.

We were hardly out of town when we were caught up in a convoy of Chinese army trucks. Not only wouldn't they let us pass, but it was also against the law to pass them. We crawled behind them for miles and miles until they turned near the airport. There were khaki tarpaulins over the beds so we could not tell what they were transporting. We also crawled behind cows and sheep but they got off the road more quickly.

The normal hazard of cows on the road.

The Buddha at the side of the road. It was believed that these images appeared out of the rock, that they were "self-manifesting." They are painted, always, in brilliant colors.

On the road to Gyantze, Tenzin, the driver, stopped by the Buddhas carved into a cliff side where some nomads, who had discovered that a living, of a sort, could be made by bringing their handsomest yaks to the road, magnificently saddled and adorned, stood hoping for tourists to ride or photograph them for a fee.

A yak dressed up for the tourist trade. You can ride him or take a picture of him for a fee.

Their children, ragged with snotty noses, came up to our window and made hunger motions hand to mouth. When I unrolled the window to give them some of the Tibetan bread Sonam had given us as a parting present, Rachael became very upset and ordered me to close the window. Again, I didn't understand that she was frightened. I also couldn't understand why she was afraid of children, particularly Tibetan children who even with their frequently snotty noses have an extra scoop of charm.

When I asked her why she didn't want me to feed the children, she explained that when she had traveled in Africa children had reached through the window and stolen whatever they could grab. I assured her that I had never known such a thing to happen in Tibet. The children inhaled the bread and motioned for more. They were really hungry, not just trying to get a little something from the foreigners as a game. But even with my explanation, she still didn't want me to open the window. I found myself becoming irritated with her insistence on considering the problems of one continent as transferable to another.

Driving on, we came to a halt at the end of a line of cars and trucks. Somewhere ahead we were told there was a recent landslide and the vehicles could not make their way over it. We would have to wait for a bulldozer, which was on its way. Children appeared out of the dust as though by spontaneous generation, but I didn't dare give to them because they would have surrounded us. When we didn't respond they wandered off. I caught up on my journal, always a task I am behind on. Rachael got out and walked down the line of cars to see the landslide and see if there was anyone to talk to. She found an Indian couple who were living in America. They were also headed to Kailash.

When she returned to our car to tell me about them, I got out, walked down with her past the line of dusty, mud-splashed cars ,and stood leaning into the window of Hema and Jay's car. Hema, with whom I am still in touch, and Jay, her handsome, kindly husband, were the most well-equipped travelers I have ever met. She had packets of Baby Wipes, all kinds of tea bags and flavored instant coffees in her bag. It was amazing. They were planning to do the Hindu *khora*.

For Hindus, Kailash is the home of Shiva, The Destroyer, and his wife, Paravati. They, therefore, refer to the mountain as he. When Gandhi was cremated some of his ashes were taken and, on August 8 1948, scattered on the shores of Lake Manasarovar, the holy lake next door to Kailash, which may be more important to Hindus than the mountain. However, like the Buddhists, they walk around Kailash clockwise as part of their pilgrimage.

Kailash is also sacred to the Jains, a Hindu sect established around the same time as Buddhism, the sixth century B.C., who compassionately spare life by sweeping before them as they walk and wearing masks so as not to inhale insects by accident. They believe their founder, Rishabha, attained *moksha*, enlightenment, on Kailash, which they call Astapada. They also perform the Kailash pilgrimage clockwise.

Until recently many Hindus died while circumambulating the mountain, since in Indian culture exercise is still something done by the lower castes and being fat proves you are prosperous. But the Tibetan guides, realizing the Chinese didn't care about the Indian death rate and were only interested in the fees they were collecting, decided they would have to take the responsibility of dividing groups into the able and those too much at risk. There is a place near Selung monastery, the starting point of the inner *khora*, where one can see Kailash. Many go there to do puja rather than circumambulating. Some are allowed to hike the *khora* for a day or two but are turned back before the climb to Drölma La, the pass, begins. Even then I have seen Tibetans literally dragging Hindus by the arms up to the pass.

When Hindus die on the *khora*, they must be cremated. This is a problem where there are no trees and only yak and sheep dung are available as fuel. The Tibetan guides have made environmentally-unfriendly cremation fires by burning the bodies with bald tires and straw.

I noticed that we passed many more military installations than had existed on my last trip to Kailash in 1996. Tibet was being turned into an armed camp.

Looking back at the turns taking us up to Yamdruk Lake.

We went over the pass looking down on the intense blue sprawl of Yamdrok Lake, Scorpion Lake, in its fortress of mountains.

Yamdrok Lake, Scorpion Lake, surrounded by mountains.

On a ridge above the lake there is the monastery/nunnery of Samding, dynamited during the Cultural Revolution but reconstructed and still in existence. It is home to the highest female incarnation Samding Dorje Phagmo, "The Thunderbolt Sow of Soaring Meditation." She is number three in the Tibetan hierarchy of incarnations. First is the Dalai Lama, second is the Panchen Lama whose residence is Tashilunpo in Shigatze, and third is Dorje Phagmo.

These rather baroque epithets, often featuring animals, by which people and places are named are always startling to the Western ear and mind, often making us a bit uneasy. Should we laugh or take this seriously? I have known Westerners to be insulted to find they were born in the Year of the Snake. But in the East these animals are viewed differently.

I was born in the Year of the Rat. This does not mean that I am slimy, sneaky and vicious. It means I am industrious, clever, adaptable, curious and thoughtful, although I am also stubborn and selfish.

Dorje Phagmo is the Thunderbolt Sow because she saved herself and her nuns by turning them and herself into pigs when the monastery once was invaded by the Mongols. The characteristics of pigs are honesty, frankness, tolerance, good heartedness, but they also have quick tempers.

On our way down from the pass I saw a dam at the end of the lake. I asked Dorje about this. He said that the Chinese had created this dam at the edge of Yamdrok, blasting a hole into the side of the lake. The dam did provide energy but then they discovered they were, unintentionally, draining the lake. They installed big pumps to pump the water back up to the lake at night. Yamdrok is a lake with no known entrance or exit. We passed other large Chinese industrial complexes, most were unidentifiable but one was a cement plant polluting the air.

Coming into the Gyantze valley, the mountains receded; the land opened into fields of barley, wheat, which was, to my astonishment blooming with pink flowers, and cheerful plots of yellow mustard seed from which oil is made. The pink, green, and yellow swatches made a patchwork around the walled houses. The richness of the fields contrasted strongly with the barren mountains of red and tan that preceded it.

Our entrance into town was a shock to me. On my first two trips to Gyantze, the town had been a rudimentary yet charming, dusty Tibetan village. What we entered this time was a flashy, glitzy, Chinese honky-tonk town. There were new buildings in what was becoming the modern Chinese traditional style—white bathroom tile and blue glass—as well as imitation Tibetan buildings with gaudy decorations and paintings. The streets were flooded with Chinese pop music from huge loudspeakers.

However, the street to the Pulchor Chöde monastery and the Kumbum's dazzling little, white, wedding-cake building, with its many chapels from the 15th century, was still lined with serene, old Tibetan houses whose spindly, red geraniums leaned out blooming into the sun from their window sills.

Flowers in the window of a house on a street in Gyantze that leads to the Pulchor Chöde and the Kumbum.

But there was a new feature; tables had been set up before the entrance to the Pulchor Chöde by local women who were selling relics of Tibet's past, probably from their own houses.

Our guide, Dorje, had claimed that we would have to go to the police in each town to find out where we were allowed to stay. This was a ruse to get us into more expensive hotels where he could get a commission. He took us to a high-priced hotel with reeking Chinese bathrooms, filthy and malodorous. We refused, ignoring his protestations that we would get into trouble or he would get into trouble with the police, we were not sure which, and took a 40 yuan room in a Tibetan guesthouse instead of the 150 yuan room in the Chinese hotel. Chinese johns are in a category of their own. Only a john at an Iranian bus stop, in the middle of a desert, still equals them in my memory for reek and filth.

Up a stairlike a ladder, the Tibetan guesthouse was charming with designs painted on its ceiling beams and around the casement windows that looked down on the roofs of nearby houses and the street. We spread our sleeping bags out on top of the woolen, many colored, hand-woven rugs in Buddhist designs, the eternal knot, the conch, that covered the sleeping benches. There was a clean, if odiferous, outhouse next to the cold water tap.

Dorje was an excellent guide, although because of his accent, sometimes difficult to understand. The next morning he took us through the Pulchor Chöde explaining things very well. When I paused at the entrance by a painting of a snow lion, a white, slightly bug-eyed, cheery, mythical creature with thick, green eyebrows and mane, he told me that the seventh Dalai Lama's mother nursed him on snow lion's milk and, therefore, they appear in the decoration of the temples.

Snow lions on the entrance gate of the Pulchor Chöde.

Other snow lions romping in mountains at the Pulchor Chöde.

The entrance court to the temple was full of dogs of all sizes sleeping in the sun. When I asked Dorje about them, he explained that the reincarnation closest to that of being human is to be a dog. Therefore, the monks in monasteries feed stray dogs as an act of charity to those who didn't quite make it.

Dogs are considered to be one step below humans on the ladder of reincarnation. Therefore, they used to be fed in the forecourts of monasteries. The Chinese have put an end to that.

In the protector chapel, I gazed up at the snarling animal heads, visited the man with the vulture pecking his eye and looked up under the drape covering one of the protectors to discover it was hiding Palden Llamo, the protectress of Tibet. She has not done a good job recently. In the gloom under the drape, I could see the legs of her donkey and the flayed human skin that serves as her saddle blanket, as well as her opera-length strand of skulls.

The Kumbum.

In the Kumbum, Dorje took us up all the way to the roof. At the foot of the ladder, Rachael and I stood and panted. A group of Chinese children was on the roof above, too many, and others were not allowed to come up. I, through gestures, indicated that they should come down so that others could have their turn. Reluctantly, they did descend and we mounted. It was scary on the roof as it trembled under our feet, but the swatches of yellow, pink and green fields spread like a magic coverlet between the walled, isolated houses. There were also in the distance small, white villages with clustered houses on whose roofs prayer flags flashed their primary colors in the wind.

The upper storey of the Kumbum.

On the drive to Shigatze the next morning, as we went over tongue-biting bumps and slammed into potholes, I became aware as I watched Dorje nod in and out of sleep how much and how consistently he was drinking. This realization caused an emotional pretzel in my gut, although there was nothing I could do about it. Dawa, our previous guide, had, I assumed, the same drinking habits; but I had not been in constant contact with him as I was with Dorje who was obviously leaving Gyantze with a hangover.

You might expect that someone who has sobered up would be sympathetic and understanding to the person still trapped in the thrall of excessive drinking, but the opposite is true. Many sober alcoholics hate being around anyone whose drinking is out of control, although we are always ready to help someone who wants to stop. Generally, we hastily distance ourselves from any active drinker in our vicinity. Perhaps we would like to disassociate ourselves from the inebriate we once were and the active drinker is creating a mirror, causing lingering shame. We want, desperately, not to be that person anymore and the active drinker brings that former self, whom we would like to freeze into a suitably sized ice cube and send to Antarctica, very clearly before us. We know we were like that, exactly like that. Watching Dorje going through the pain of his hangovers he was my doppelganger, and I was his "—Hypocrite lecteur,—mon semblable,—mon frère!" a la Baudelaire. Even now, although I have been sober for over 30 years, I don't like to write about "her," the person I was.

Contemplating Dorje as he pretended that he was alright, that all was normal, made my old self rise up and shimmer like a will o' the wisp in a vaporous swamp. It was a familiar and repugnant phantom.

One of the potholes we banged into and then out of cracked our plastic kerosene jug, flooding the back of the four-wheel drive. Dorje and Tenzin, our driver, took care of cleaning out the back in a cursory manner while we went through our packs assessing damage. What remained of the kerosene we gave to a little boy who turned up. A Tibetan man also strolled over from a field to watch us pull things out of our packs and bags. He tentatively pointed at our canned goods to ask if he could have some. We said no, but his need was puzzling since the fields appeared bountiful although the people looked poor. Perhaps the Chinese were again taking so much of the harvest to support their occupying army that not enough was left for the farmers and their families.

As we repacked the back of the car, a Land Rover pulled up full of boisterous, American, teenage students. They asked if we needed help, but we were fine. An hour later we came across them stopped at the side of the road. They had run out of gas, we had no extra since we had not yet met up with our truck, and they had to be towed into Shigatze, rather ignominiously, on a long blue leash to the gas station. It reminded me of driving in the winter in Wyoming when someone would stop to help me out of a drift and thirty miles later I would stop to help them or someone else who had skidded off the road.

Flying over the fields were flocks of pigeons, exactly like those in Times or St. Mark's Square but their slate blue and white wings were clean. With their bright pink, twiggy legs, they looked as though they were wearing stockings as they sought for food along the side of the road and in fields. Yet, because they were clean, instead of pollution and soot stained, they seemed to be a different species.

Coming into Shigatze, I didn't recognize it but thought some new Chinese town had sprung up between Gyantze and Shigatze. It was not as garish and trashy as Gyantze because it has tree-lined streets with wide sidewalks, but it was full of Chinese glitz and the constant noise that seems to be necessary to Chinese life.

Looking for a hotel, we ran into a distraught Australian, Sean, who was traveling with a group of Hong Kong Chinese. Because he couldn't distinguish between dust, earth dirt, and human dirt, he saw everything and everyone as filthy. He was terrified he was going to contract something that would lead to a terminal illness. He seemed to make no attempt to make friends among his companions, some of whom spoke English well. He was quite pathetic, ranting on to us about how selfish the Chinese were. I pointed out that extending yourself to others in a subsistence economy, whether urban or agricultural, might mean death for you and your family. He admitted that he hadn't thought of that.

On one trip to Tibet I had entered with a Chinese tour, so I had had a variation on his experience.

I had been stymied one year in Chengdu because without warning the Chinese had closed the border to individual Western travelers. I finally had been able to enter by joining a Mainland Chinese tour. It was not the most companionable group in the world since they were eager to attack me on the subject of the Dalai Lama. I told them we would just have to agree to disagree, that I had no interest in arguing with them.

They were not pleased with the food we were served, which was Chinese, telling me how it should have been prepared. They reprimanded the waiters and waitresses, consistently sullen young Tibetans, who did not present the dishes but slung them in any old order on the table, sometimes on top of each other.

But the person who most interested me in the group was a man who had escaped China at the time of the Cultural Revolution. He was a physicist who now lived in the United States. He challenged the guide in the Jokhang about the Cultural Revolution and his own persecution, also pointing out that the central part of the temple, where the Chenresi statue gleams, had been used as a pigsty and its chapels had been converted to offices for cadres. To my bemusement, however, despite having been a victim of the Cultural Revolution, he believed all the Chinese propaganda about the Dalai Lama and was convinced that Tibet should be part of China.

Thinking of Mao also brought up for me something that no one seems to talk about or recognize which is that humans consistently in different parts of the world have flung themselves full of wild belief into the arms of leaders who are definitely insane—Hitler, Stalin, Mao —men who should have been shut away to quietly sew wallets or paint watercolors. Yet people eagerly did their bidding and as a result suffered horrible consequences—defeat, hunger, poverty in Germany; hunger, poverty, massacres in Russia; famine, poverty, institutionalized persecution in China. What magic do the insane have that makes them our Pied Piper again and again?

This American-Chinese man suffered from one kind of inability to see, but the entire group was afflicted by another form of blindness. We were "attacked," not too strong a word, each time we left our bus by gangs of Tibetans selling silk purses, jewelry, phony daggers. They did this with big smiles but lots of aggression. However, once I said "No" in whatever language, I was left alone while they continued to badger the Chinese. One day when we returned to the bus one of the group, noticing, asked why I was treated differently. I decided I would try the truth. "They hate you and this is the only way they can get back at you," I said.

"No, no," they chorused. "That is not true."

I found myself wondering if people traveling to Navajo reservations, now and in the past, also refuse to see the rage and hate behind the commercial stance.

Sean's blindness was an inability to imagine how other people survive. He was obviously frightened, although I'm not sure he knew what he was afraid of, perhaps of anything that didn't fit his ideas of what the world should be like. The last time we spoke he said, rather frantically, "I don't want these people in my country. They're selfish and dirty. I can't wait to get home."

We decided to stay at the Tibet Fan Gyan Fruit Orchard Hotel, which was, indeed, in an orchard. Our room was spare, shabby, but clean with the usual heavy duvets, colorful rayon covered pillows and the strange, red, felt-like stuff that at that time was used for a rug in Chinese hotels. Leaning out the window we could see apples, small, but turning rosy among the dust-coated leaves of the trees. The toilets down the hall were cleanish but stinky, the female toilet being an airless Black Hole of Calcutta closet with no window. We both felt compelled to take a flashlight with us when nature called for fear that we might accidentally step into the hole. The men, I went in to investigate, had a window and two squat johns. There was plenty of water so we tried washing the kerosene out of our bags and the pieces of clothing that had been soaked. It helped but did not eradicate the persistent, headache-inducing odor.

A sign on our room's wall proclaimed:

OUE HONORABLE GUESTE WT WOWO LIKE PROVIDE YOU A COMFORT ABLE ACCOMODATION PLEASE CALLABORATE OUR WORK FOR TAKING CARE KF FURNNISHINGS IN THE ROOM IF ANY ARTICLE IS DAMAGED OR LOST YOU WILL HAVE TO COMPENSATE ACCORDING TO ORIGINAL COST IN FOLLOWING MENTIONED....

A price list followed.

Leaving the hotel to go to the monastery, we saw a little, tailless mouse, plump and well fed, running back and forth on the dirt path between the street and the hotel. A small boy with a stick was directing his movements. If he tried to go too far down the path the boy would stop him with the stick and send him back in the opposite direction. It would have been easy for the mouse to dodge around or jump over the stick, but he didn't. They both seemed to be enjoying the game.

Tashilhunpo, once a monastic city with a population of 8,000 monks, is a maze of buildings with images dating to the 12th century.

We were across the street from the entrance gate of Tashilhunpo in a part of the town that was less Chinese. The monastery was once a city of 8,000 monks and home of the 10th Panchen Lama who died in

1989. Now there were about 100 monks in the buildings, which were being renovated. I kept an eye open to see if the Tibetans who entered with us were going off in another direction. I did not intend to miss seeing a sky burial, if by chance there was one going on, since Gunar had had the luck to see one here on my last trip.

We climbed up the hill, panting, any incline brought on shortness of breath, to see the handsome two-story Buddha in gilded bronze, the silver *chörten*-tomb of the Fourth Panchen Lama and the tomb of the 10th Panchen Lama who died mysteriously. Unlike the Dalai Lama, the 10th Panchen Lama had hopes that he would be able to get along with and negotiate with the Chinese for his people. Therefore, he did not leave Tibet. However, when he realized after seeing with his own eyes what the Chinese were doing—the impoverishment of the people, the destruction of temples and monasteries—he became a vocal critic of the regime. Then he died.

At the front of each chapel we visited there were pictures of a little boy. I recognized him as the candidate that the Chinese had chosen to be the next Panchen Lama. The candidate chosen by the Dalai Lama, along with his entire family, has disappeared.

Going from chapel to chapel at about the same time as we were was a Chinese woman, a lone traveler, which was surprising. Chinese, particularly Chinese women, do not usually travel alone. I decided to try to get her to smile at me and by the time we got to the *chörten*-tomb of the Fourth Panchen Lama I received my first smile.

However, at that point an American couple appeared. They were trying to ask their guide about the child in the picture at the entrance to the chapel, but he either didn't understand them or couldn't figure out a politically correct answer to their question. I explained to them that the boy was the new Panchen Lama, the one the Chinese had picked, and that no one knows where the Dalai Lama's choice, with his family, is.

The Chinese woman stopped smiling. I received a mean satisfaction out of this. It was my petty revenge for the men in the back of the truck in Lhasa who were being taken to be shot at the ruined monastery.

Hollyhocks outside a monk's cell at Tashilhunpo.

A belled and tasseled sheep at Tashilhunpo. I presume because of his tassels that he's a pet.

That night we ate at a little Tibetan restaurant across from our hotel which, although we picked it at random, was a good choice. The proprietor was very solicitous; the waitress was his slim, dimpled daughter with big black eyes. We had an excellent soup in which bobbed delicate, round momos with a delicious spiced-meat filling secreted at their center. We were so happy with this soup that we would have had it again for breakfast the next day if we could have.

The drive from Shigatze to Lhatze was much better than it had been the last time. The road had been paved in almost all of the towns and occasionally it was even paved between towns.

I had been trying hard to ignore the tension between Rachael and me. I didn't want to come to grips with the fact that we were not very well matched as traveling companions. But there were two incidents between Shigatze and Lhatze that killed my pretense.

As we were driving past mountains in shades of copper-green, red, and the blue-green of old turquoise, Rachael said, "You're taking up more than half of the seat. Move over to your side." I did, with bristling resentment, and, thereafter, tried to be very careful about how much space I took up. It occurred to me that Rachael was the middle child in her family and that this insistence on what she felt belonged to her, was her right, might be a result of competition with the older and the younger girl on either side of her in the family.

One of my pens, which often happens at altitude, began to leak glutinous ballpoint ink all over me and the inside of my daypack. I wrapped it up in a Kleenex and asked Dorje if we could stop at a store in the next town. There are always small general stores in every town selling "sundries," everything from socks to batteries. When we pulled into a town, I hopped out saying to Rachael, "It'll just take me a minute to get a pen." I didn't want to hold us up. I went into the store which had all the usual bits and pieces for sale. As I was picking out a pen from a selection of two varieties, Rachael came swinging through the door in a fury and spat at me, "Don't leave me alone in the car while you go off to have an adventure." It didn't seem to me that buying the pen was much of an adventure, but I kept begrudgingly mum. I was making frequent deposits into my grievance bank account.

Again it seemed to me that she was being unnecessarily competitive or perhaps controlling, but I couldn't think of anything to say that would be helpful. I, of course, thought I was the perfect traveling companion, sensitive and thoughtful. It never occurred to me to just say, "I'm sorry there is so much tension between us." Just pulling a problem out of its hiding place and looking at it often helps. Coming from an alcoholic household where the important things that were happening between family members were never mentioned, I didn't know how to mention the obvious because it was always the obvious that was unmentionable. I was also lacking in any sense of compassion toward Rachael as someone who was suffering.

However, I did realize that on a journey so physically and psychologically challenging, it would be foolish to cavil about my companion. I was lucky to have a companion. There are not a lot of people who want to spend their leisure time being dirty, exhausted, cold, and uncomfortable while panting for breath or being cramped in a car slamming over lumpy, dusty roads and eating half-cooked dehydrated meals. I wasn't really aware at this time, but have learned since, that being deprived of your usual levels of oxygen causes not just shortness of breath but of temper as well and a mindset in which one is poised at the edge of umbrage at every moment, sure your companion or companions have taken advantage of you in some way or are about to.

Another result of the altitude was that as we grew less able to concentrate, we had more and more difficulty making our way through the thicket of Dorje's accent to understand his explanations. Not only were Rachael and I a source of irritation for each other, but also I, each day, as Dorje climbed into the four-wheel drive, obviously hung over with that pathetic, bewildered but determined look that drunks (I use that term fondly not censoriously) have, recalled my old self. I felt as though he was loading into the car the shrouded cadaver of my former self. While not an unbearable situation, this was an uncomfortable one.

Dorje may have been hung over every morning, but Tenzin was always cheery and bright. They were contrasting personalities. Tenzin was a delight, an irrepressible flirt of infinite charm in his well-padded fifties. He told me, with Dorje acting as translator, that he had been the first person to drive across Tibet in 1971. For some reason, he did it with a bus. Perhaps that was the only vehicle available. I never learned why he made the trip—language barriers mean you only get a part of the story. Many years and drivers later, he is still the most skilled I've ever had and I remember him fondly.

Going through towns, we passed carts and donkeys carrying everything from firewood to broken bicycles, plastic pails, and heaps of yak dung. There were maroon outcroppings of rock both before and after we went over Tso La strung with both grey rags of old, wind-battered prayer flags and brilliant new ones dancing in gusts of wind. As we went over each *la*, a *la* is a pass, Dorje and Tenzin chanted, "*So, so, so, so, so, so, so. La, la, la, la, la, la, la,*" followed by a mantra I couldn't decipher. It was not, however, the usual *Ohm, mani padme. So* means victory and *la* means pass. Therefore, I believe they were celebrating the victory of going over the pass. This was not done solemnly or softly but shouted with happiness, laughter, and a spirit of celebration. It seemed to me that there was also a little irony, a little self-deprecation, since our triumph in a car was quite different from what someone walking would have at cresting a pass.

A pass, a *la*, is always marked by prayer flags and white *khatas*, scarves, that float on a breeze or whip on a gust but disintegrate with weather into a laundry heap.

Brilliant, primary colored flags in an arid, barren landscape.

I asked Dorje about the road workers we saw all along the way. He said they were paid by the Chinese but very little. In one area, they were digging a trench beside the road which we were told would hold some sort of communications cable. Some villages looked prosperous, others didn't. In one, we passed several houses where the walls around the house had been topped off with beer bottles cemented in lying down position to raise the wall another foot in height. Some houses had red and blue stripes on their walls that extended a foot or so down from the top of the wall. Dorje told us this was the sign of a family that belonged to the Gelugpa sect, the yellow hats, the order the Dalai Lama belongs to.

This house has on its walls the red, white and blue stripes of the Gelugpa sect, the Dalai Lama's order of Tibetan Buddhism.

For a while after the pass, the landscape was more barren, a beige monochrome of large and small mountains.

In the late afternoon we pulled into Lhatze, a pit of screaming video shops, honking trucks, dust and ugly buildings of white bathroom tile and blue glass, Chinese modern architecture. We were in the same hotel, The Meteorological, as the Indian couple, Jay and Hema, whom we had met in backed-up traffic at the landslide site outside of Gyantze. It was a comfort to run into them again, although they were quite unhappy with their accommodations; but there was nothing more upscale in Lhatze, only lodgings much more down scale. They would have liked ensuite bathrooms, but all that was available was the squat john shared by everyone on the corridor. Its smell became stronger and stronger as you approached it along the hall. They were almost across from it and, therefore, constantly in the vicinity of its perfume. Rachael and I were further away and less conscious of its odor.

The Meteorological Hotel alien and intrusive in this landscape with its Chinese white tile architecture.

Rachael had a screaming altitude headache, the kind that feels as though a technical expert from the Spanish Inquisition has inserted your head in a vice and is slowly cracking your skull open like a hazelnut. She couldn't find her tea bags which caused mounting hysteria as she scrabbled and searched. I went down the hall to get one from Hema and Jay, but this made Rachael more hysterical as she thought I was abandoning her. Another deposit in my grievance account.

Hema and Jay had hired a truck, porters, and a cook from Nepal and were now worrying over the negotiations between their Tibetan guide and their Nepali people. By the time we had dinner that night, an entente cordiale had been achieved between their two groups.

Our room at the Meteorological was clean and plain, with a TV, desk, and two armchairs. There was the usual red felt carpet, pillows in ruffled cases in violent pink, which were then wrapped in towels of the sort you know you are not actually supposed to use, embroidered in eye-searing pink. The headboards, covered in shiny, hot-pink rayon, were stitched with scarlet cabbage roses. The effect was not simply gaudy but like staring into a barrage of neon. If you closed your eyes, you found the towels and headboard were shining and pulsing on the inside of your eyelids. A single bare bulb dangled on a shaggy, shredding wire from the ceiling.

One of the differences between Chinese hotels and Tibetan hotels is the amount of management-provided reading material. In Tibetan hotels, if there is any reading material at all, it is a notice on the back of the door informing you of the checkout time. However, in Chinese hotels there are pages and pages of warnings, price lists of the furnishings, and other information.

At the Meteorological a notice tucked into a plastic portfolio stated:

> "DIRECTOR MAKE A SPEECH. Drar passengers: I welcome to you out meteorological hotel and thank you is care for us and suported. You are have keen to Lazi hotel, we wish you good Lack and healty for the time."

There were, as well, warnings about personal habits:

> "Foor you want to smoke, must make five off," and the more comprehensible good advice, "Foor make agood rest, please don't drink much in your room."

I found these notices interesting as they suggested the expectations of Chinese hotel owners. They must have a hard time with people stealing furniture and TV sets or, and I'm sure this happens all the time since both Chinese and Tibetans are hard drinkers, people getting drunk and smoking—burning holes in the carpet, setting a pillow on fire—in rooms which have been made as attractive as possible by local standards. The Meteorological was, I thought, considering it is in a town in the middle of Tibet, pretty high on the luxury scale. This view was reinforced by the notes on the dresser that said:

> "Lazi Meteorological Hotel is a synthical business building in Lazi county. It is higher in puality and standard than other.

Wandering through the hotel lobby that night, I ran into Dawa, tall, lanky, and as good-looking as ever, who had been our guide on my previous Kailash trip. He was arguing at the top of his lungs in English about room prices, surrounded by yelling, outraged clients. They were threatening to take their sleeping bags out to the back of the hotel to spend the night among the beer bottle shards that littered the ground of the parking lot. To my surprise they managed, perhaps through vocal stamina, to get the price down 15 yuan.

I waved hello at him but we didn't get a chance to talk since the tempestuous argument was at full volume and velocity. Later, in the dining room, he stopped by our table, Rachael and I were eating with Hema and Jay, to tell me how useful he found the Victor Chan guidebook we had given him as part of our tip. But the conversation was uncomfortable because he knew, that I probably knew, that he and our previous driver had abandoned the remnant of our group who had foolishly paid them the rest of their fee in Nyalam before reaching the border. The remnant had had to hitchhike and walk the remaining distance to the Friendship Bridge and the border. I was glad, however, that he appreciated the Victor Chan book because it had been my copy and it had been a real sacrifice to give it to him.

The night was hideous. The DVD shops across the street had monstrous, shoulder-high speakers outside their doors that blasted us hopeful sleepers with car crashes, bomb detonations, grenades, building demolitions, rockets, and the relative quiet of machine gun fire until past 10:00 p.m. when the karaoke bars took over with off-key, excruciatingly syrupy lullabies, sung with a drunken slur until

3:00 a.m. That left an hour before people began drifting into town for the market. Earplugs were useless as was the pillow-over-the-head technique, and the two combined did little to muffle the continuous roar of explosions.

The next morning I wondered if Dorje had spent the night in one of those karaoke bars, he was so baggy-eyed and gray with his hangover. But, since our truck had not yet arrived, he took us to a very small monastery, quite new, at the edge of town. I noted that Dorje, no matter how hung-over, always did his job. I am sure he used this as an excuse to himself; he didn't have a drinking problem because he always showed up for work. I, too, had known that I could not be an alcoholic because I never missed a day of work.

Having shown us the little temple, Dorje went off, probably to grab a nap in the car. We wandered across the dusty but paved road and into the Tibetan village at the edge of Lhatze accumulating children as we went. There were cows, tilled fields and, delightfully, a hoopoe by an irrigation ditch.

I was thrilled. I had read about these birds but never seen one. I presume this one was in migratory transit, although I've no idea from where to where. His breast was orangey-red, rufous, his wings smartly striped with black and white; but the wondrous thing about him was his crest which he opened and shut the way a Spanish dancer snaps her fan while he stared at us with bright, shoe-button eyes above a long, delicate scimitar beak. His gaze struck me as very judgmental with the opening and shutting of his crest being somehow related to his verdict.

We found a mill at the side of a creek with two wheels grinding barley. The miller and his assistant, two powdery, gray figures coated from hair to shoe soles with the flour, motioned us in to watch as they poured the grain from huge sacks.

A sudden rattle of thunder sent us scurrying back into town where we had a lunch of noodles, green vegetables, and yak meat in a place that

Rachael had found. At the table next to us, three men were playing mahjong while on the floor another group was gathered cross-legged around the cushion on which they were engaged in the Asian dice game that I have seen from Bangkok to Shanghai but have never been able to find someone to explain to me.

Our truck arrived driven by a cheerful young man who looked as though he was in his teens. He had packed some of his relatives into the back of the truck to do the Kailash *khora* with us—his sister, a pretty woman in a rolled-brim straw hat with pink flowers on it, who, Dorje told us, was ill; her husband, definitely older than she, in a Western suit; and their two children, an older girl and younger boy. Dorje made it plain to us that this hitching of a ride *en famille* with foreigners was against the rules; but since they were already in the back of the truck where they were not impinging on us in any real way and since we both felt it would be horridly mean to send the family back to Lhasa on a technicality, we let them stay.

The son of the hitch hiking family our truck driver installed in the back of his and our truck.

The daughter of the family who hitched with us to Mount Kailash.

The mother and father of the hitching family. She is wearing a conservative version of the Lhasa Lady's hat.

Rachael immediately started teaching the children to count in English. The wife was neat in her sober *chuba* and a pale pink, silk blouse that miraculously seemed to stay clean although she was sitting in the back of the truck being engulfed by dust. She had topped off this dignified outfit with her Lhasa Lady's hat with its pink flowers, looking ready for a garden party, perhaps a tea with cucumber sandwiches rather than days of being thumped about in the back of a truck.

These hats deserve particular mention. They were very popular in Lhasa in the years I did the Kailash *khora* among those fortunate enough to live in town or be able to get to the city to buy one. Shops up and down Beijing Street offered them in a variety of colors and complexities. One year I bought a plain black one and wore it in New York all summer, frequently receiving compliments on it. Often, however, they were shady, big brimmed hats in pastel colors with matching veils. Could it be that these were a throwback to those worn by the few English ladies who came to Lhasa in the early twentieth century, wives of diplomats? Was it another cryptic British influence like the "one, two, three…" of the roof stampers?

Rachael and I thought the wife was quite mad to travel in the back of a truck over dirt roads while sick, to say nothing of walking thirty-three miles around Kailash at a final altitude of 18,600 feet. But their hope was that Kailash herself would heal her or some monk along the way would have the right medicine for her. We lost track of them for a few days after the *khora* but later ran into them at a monastery. She had been going to temples and monasteries along their route being diagnosed by various monks. They had all prescribed different herbal potions as well as patches. As a result, her face was covered with large and small pieces of sticking plaster. We never did learn what her illness was since her symptoms were not obvious, another language barrier loss.

We left Lhatze with Dorje in the front seat, still very hungover. Grasping the handle above the door in his sleep he leaned, periodically, into Tenzin's lap, jerking suddenly upright but not waking. Since his duty was to talk to Tenzin to keep him alert and us safe, this dereliction of duty irritated Tenzin until he barked at Dorje. Tenzin obviously disapproved of Dorje's drinking habits and was not hesitant to tell him what he thought. We didn't need any knowledge of Tibetan to know that.

We drove through mountains and fertile valleys dappled with villages and their fields. We passed a lake of transcendent blue where I saw circles made by surfacing fish expanding serenely on the water, but always there were military vehicles passing us. From this placid setting, we lurched suddenly into heavy rain through a river, up it, across it, testing Tenzin's considerable talent at the wheel. We accomplished one ford in pelting rain passing a military vehicle, its wheels locked between rocks, with a young Chinese soldier beside it, pants rolled and up to his knees in rushing water. His driver, soaked to the skin, was attempting to heave some of the rocks away from their rear wheel. We splashed by, smugly pleased at the soldier's predicament, definitely a case of *schadenfreude*.

Fording one of the swift rivers of Tibet.

The rain stopped and we came into ridges of, what I believe, was metamorphic rock, which had been thrust up at a terrific tilt.

Ridges that have been thrust up by the earth.

Toward nightfall we entered a vast valley with a lone conical mountain at the end of it topped by a monastery and a hermitage. It was a spiritual aerie, a lone eagle's nest. This was followed by the ascent of Pang La, which is very narrow at the top, the width of a truck with an inch or two extra on each side. The two high walls of dark rock look as though they have been shattered by the blow of a gigantic hammer to make the road. Between those two walls, we came to a halt behind a stuck truck, the driver's torso hidden under the hood, so that he looked as though the engine had consumed his upper half. Rachael got out and had the children recite their English numbers. I sidled crabwise past the truck to see the view from the pass while the driver, with Tenzin and Dorje's assistance, finished the repairs.

Unwilling to test my culinary skill until necessity forced us to, we ate in truck stops. The one we pulled into after Pang La was bursting with truckers and their wives with children in tow. There was a wall of windows looking out at dark mountains whose crevices were brilliant with snow.

Rachael and I sat at a table adorned with a rigor mortis rag, stiff with yak grease and road dust, and a large yak vertebra that, having been picked clean, looked like a Henry Moore sculpture. The waitress removed these adornments, wiping the table with the cloth that left behind a high sheen of grease. We had an excellent dinner of homemade noodles, green vegetables, yak meat on the bone, and red chilies. It seemed sensible to remove the latter, although they certainly added to the flavor. We could have as much milk or jasmine tea as we desired.

That night we stayed at a road mender's house in the semi-attached room they rented out. The main house was occupied by a woman, her husband (although he was absent, probably off trading for the summer), her gaggle of kids, and her mother. In a corner of our room's courtyard was a pony corralled off by great gnarled roots and branches. The charge was $1.25 each, a little more than my mother paid for lodgings in Paris in 1929. The room was comfortable, though not clean, with cigarette wrappers on the floor, greasy pillows and the usual lead-heavy duvets. The floor was dirt, as were the walls, which were covered with fabric that had been tacked over the mud brick. There were candles, but we had our flashlights. There were the usual low benches along the walls for sleeping and plenty of hot water, enough to wash up a bit and have tea. In the smaller court before the main house was a seriously vicious black mastiff on, thank God, a very short chain.

The road mender's house.

Since they had a boom box in their living room, I thought they might have an outhouse so I asked. One of the children with an exceptionally intelligent face took me out through the gate and showed me where to squat off the road, a little protected by shrubs from the occasional traffic. In the morning we wanted more hot water but were most unwilling to walk by the dog. Dorje, bleary eyed in his hangover, leaned into the second court and peered around to where you could tell by the loop of the chain that the dog was in his stone house. Dorje didn't go into the court but called in to the woman who came out with water.

The terrain was getting more barren. We went over Pusi La, which is 4,600 meters. There were no villages but black, yak hair tents, road workers' huts, and low scrub instead of fields.

A tent but not of yak hair.

It was also getting colder. We had to wait behind a truck that had unloaded a pile of dirt, which men were shoveling to make it level.

There were yaks scattered about the brown hills and views of white peaks in the distance. The next *la* was a 16,000-foot pass.

A nomad tent and temporary corral for sheep by the side of the road. A yak hair tent seems to be very thin with the sun poring through it, but if it rains the fabric thickens and repels the water.

We came into an official checkpoint at Raga. A Chinese soldier in a vest, all straps in the back and all pockets in front came over and opened my door saying something I couldn't understand. At this point, Dorje intervened in Chinese to say that he had the permits. As they walked off together, I noticed Dorje had a pack of cigarettes in his hand. I suspect the soldier had come to my door more out of curiosity than officiousness. While we waited for permission to drive on, I saw a Western young man with a diffident look hanging out among the China Post trucks. I motioned him over to talk as it seemed to me I shouldn't get out of the car at the checkpoint. He was an Australian, however, a very different Australian from whining Sean who found the Chinese selfish and dirty. He was hitching on one of the mail trucks. He wanted to go to Kailash; but since he hadn't realized he needed a permit, he was going to go all the way to Ali, get the permit, and come back. At the moment, he was stuck since they had been waiting for three days for a part for the truck.

I asked, "Why don't the soldiers send you back? Surely what you are doing is against the rules."

"We seem to have some sort of agreement where I ignore them and they return the favor. I'm not sure, but I think it has to do with my being on a China Post truck which is a sort of official vehicle. It's all mysterious," he added cheerfully.

I found I was a bit envious of him, traveling so adventurously without a companion. He made me think of Heinrich and Gunar on my previous trip to Kailash. He had an air of freedom about him that was almost tangible, an aroma in the air. Poor Sean, the other Australian, would never inhale that perfume.

Dorje was kept a long time in the checkpoint station. When he came back without the pack of cigarettes, he was worried because one of the officials who had been from his village had told him, "You're really lucky that I was the official in charge because one of your papers isn't in order." We tried to reassure him, telling him that his fellow villager was just putting on a swank to show off his power, but Dorje was unnerved. Tibetans living under the Chinese are always fearful. They live at knife-edge since an official can always claim they have done something wrong or a stamp or signature is missing, and they will have no recourse.

Coming into Saga, the next town, we saw soldiers sitting, swinging their legs like kids, along the top of the wall that surrounded their camp looking bored. We ate in a place whose inside dining room was very dirty but had a delightful tarpaulin-covered terrace. While we ate, a group of Tibetan girls sat with us under its shade, watching us intently as though they suspected we might chew with our ears. Rachael and I had been memorizing bits from a Tibetan phrase book. We tried out our minimal knowledge on them, telling them our names and asking them theirs. Over and over we pointed at ourselves, said our names slowly and then pointed at them expectantly saying, "Ming?" name. They didn't respond and didn't seem to understand what we were trying to do.

To our astonishment, one young woman with high cheekbones and a little indentation in her chin wearing a brown chuba over a pale blue silk blouse burst into tears. We were appalled but couldn't figure out what we had done to upset her. Possibly just our alien presence had been enough to bring on her tears. Her friends calmed her down and then asked in sign language if we wanted to buy the necklaces she was wearing. We were astonished by this offer. At that time, no one tried to sell you her jewelry over lunch, although it might well happen today. We shook our heads in confusion, saying, "Mindu" which is "No," in Tibetan. This seemed to cause them as much confusion, if not more. I don't think they understood our "Mindu."

Often people just presume that they will not understand anything you say. Once on the island of Sulawesi in Indonesia I memorized the phrase in Indonesian, "Where is the Post Office?" and said it to a man in the street who responded, in English, with great courtesy, "I don't understand English." Having presumed that I was speaking English, he hadn't tried to understand what I was saying. Probably these women were operating under a similar assumption. For Rachael and me, this was a definite low point in our international relations.

Tenzin was expert at choosing the right spot to ford at rivers, but once at a deep one our rear wheels became wedged in rocks and the motor sputtered. Dorje wriggled out the front passenger window, quite a feat of nimbleness, onto the hood to lean down and do something to the wheels so they went into four-wheel-drive. We emerged snorting triumphantly from the riverbed with Dorje as our clinging hood ornament.

The land became more barren and more majestic as we approached the area of sand dunes, which formed wind-sculpted crescent shapes. There were yaks, sheep, and goats grazing around black tents out of which, at the sound of our motors, poured children who either waved or threw stones quite indiscriminately. The latter seemed to be hurled without animosity. It was just an alternate greeting.

At Zongba, a town that at that time had been largely overwhelmed by the encroaching sand, we stopped for dinner, afterwards passing a place I remembered from my first trip with the old and the new bridge in the midst of sand dunes. Now the Himalayas spread out their white arms, embracing the horizon. They looked like great icebergs run aground.

The line of the Himalayas stretches its arms from horizon to horizon.

We slept for the fairly high price of 30 yuan at Paryang. The young woman and the old woman who ran the guesthouse were covered with turquoise, whether real or not I didn't know, wearing headdresses, bracelets, earrings, and necklaces. If they had tried to sell them to us I wouldn't have been surprised since they looked like they were making a purposeful display. Mama, who talked in a whisper and yet possessed a great deal of charm, showed us about. The women's toilet was spotless but up a flight of stairs, which I didn't really look forward to maneuvering in the middle of the night. The duvets were particularly nice here, looking brand new and covered with a brightly printed silky fabric. As we looked down from our window into a little inner court where they kept a vegetable garden, its perimeter outlined by beer bottles with their necks in the earth, a dog, who must have been desperately hungry slunk in to warily snatch a couple of cabbage leaves.

I was feeling a bit smug. Though any stair would get me panting after four or five steps, there were no blood scabs in my nose. This was undoubtedly due to traveling protected in a car, rather than in a dust cloud in the back of a truck.

The next day was a mélange of Hindus in Land Rovers, towering Himalayan peaks and dead yaks and sheep. We were passed by a number of Land Rovers going in the opposite direction full of Indians, scarves pulled down over their foreheads and dust masks covering their faces. Either side of the road was strewn with the skeletons of yaks and sheep from the previous winter's snows that had been exceptionally heavy causing starvation among the herds. It was pathetic to see those dark shapes in the now lush grass. An occasional dog would come by to sniff, deciding there was nothing there.

After fording a stream we stopped for lunch in the midst of a nomad camp. A boy and a grandmother came to beg. The restaurant was a half-built, windowless little one-room house, whose striped plastic tarpaulin serving as a roof made a sharp cracking noise when the wind slapped at it.

The restaurant that rented us their fire.

Their menu had two items, *tsampa* and yogurt. We asked if we could use their fire and heated up one of Rachael's fully prepared meals that only needed to be warmed, not cooked. It tasted delicious. I have found that the delectability of meals in Tibet is often in ratio to how much effort one has had to put out to prepare them. I had chicken casserole and Rachael had spaghetti and meatballs. The nomads were curious about us but we couldn't answer their questions.

I committed a solecism that caused more laughter than offense. Getting up, awkwardly, from my cushion on the floor I turned my bottom toward the company. As we left I gave the grandmother some yuan but could not find the little boy. We also paid the owners of the restaurant, for the use of their fire, five yuan.

We had their yogurt for dessert, which was delicious. Dorje took away some in his water jar but with the potholes and ruts it foamed up, overflowing onto his hands and feet. We laughed watching him lick it from his hands.

We came into a bare area of red and soft, mineral green mountains, very beautiful. Dorje and Tenzin spotted animals for us, which we could sometimes, but not always see. There were two antelope, small with fine antlers, a fat marmot, tailless mice and a handsome, brown, fierce-eyed hawk that let us get quite close to him. My favorites, however, were the hares, like American jackrabbits, which scattered before us. Their big bottoms had the loveliest bounce as they loped off the road.

Tenzin and Dorje had been discussing fish for days, peering into rivers we forded. At one they sighted some and stopped the car. We piled out greatly excited. They rolled up their pant legs, took off their shoes and Tenzin took off his socks as well to wade into the river very quietly and cautiously.

How to fish with a rock.

We watched them heave big stones at the fish, the Tibetan method of fishing. They managed to stun three but the others immediately headed for deeper water. They gutted their catch neatly and laid them out on the dashboard to dry. The fish would be sold as medicine to ease childbirth pains or heal boils or blisters.

The fishermen and their catch.

In reading about Tibet I had run across references to the Tibetan relationship to water and fish. It is mysterious. Tibetans neither, as a rule, fish nor eat fish. No one seems to know why; although it is true that for them water is connected to death. This may be the basis of the general Tibetan avoidance of the consumption of fish. I read about a Neolithic site in the Chamdo district by a river that showed no signs of the inhabitants fishing. This suggests the avoidance, although not a prohibition, of eating fish, still existing in Tibet, dates to very early times. The disinterest in fish as food is unrelated to Buddhism, being a mysterious local custom of unknown origins. All of which makes it odd and contradictory, if not paradoxical, that fish then should be considered medicinally good for childbirth pains. The men were elated at their catch.

Oddly there was no smell drifting into the backseat from the drying fish. The smells of Tibet, or any place one travels, are part of the experience. For instance, for me Bangkok is an alternation between the essence of drains and jasmine. In New York City, as you turn a corner, suddenly, the breeze will bring the perfume of the sea to you. The other odor I associate with New York occurs on a searing August day after a sudden shower, an intense aroma of hot dust on concrete.

Smells may be subtle but they have a strong emotional impact. Six months after my mother died, I passed a woman in an aisle of a New York City pharmacy who was wearing my mother's favorite perfume. I was rooted to the spot with my entire body and mind shouting, "MOTHER." But we are also judgmental about odors. I met a girl from Wyoming on a train going to Fargo who told me she had just seen the sea for the first time in her life. I asked her how she had liked it.

"It was beautiful to look at but it had the most awful stink."

"A stink, a bad smell to you?" I asked.

"Yes. It smells of rot and things decomposing."

Having grown up with the sea at my doorstep I found this a novel but obviously true assessment.

"And a cow or horse barn, how do they smell to you?"

"Oh, they smell wonderful. Such a pure, clean smell."

"Even though it is the smell of shit?" I enquired. She'd obviously never thought of that connection.

For some reason, while every house, every temple and every Tibetan carries the fragrance of yak butter, one never smells sweat from a Tibetan only from Westerners. Why this should be true, I don't know. One either likes the odor of yak butter or one doesn't. To me it has a dairy fragrance. When I get the first whiff on arriving I feel I'm home. The other odor that is part of Tibet for me is the dry, desiccated smell of dust on a wind.

Arriving at Lake Manasarovar, we climbed out of the four-wheel-drive to gaze across the deep, dark sapphire of the lake, to the white cap of Kailash.

Lake Manasarovar, the sacred lake that neighbors Mount Kailash, holy to Hindus, Böns and Buddhists.

Dorje took us to the village I had stayed at with Dawa and my first group after we had finished our *khora*. An elderly couple, their toothless faces brown and wrinkled as baked apples, a Tibetan Darby and Joan, owned the primitive guesthouse.

Bits from the walls and ceiling of mud brick flaked quietly down on us. Rachael tried to light the Volcano stove she had brought from England. It refused to function but the stove she had bought from the Viennese girl in Lhasa worked. I cooked a miserable dinner of dehydrated macaroni and cheese. The problem was that it was not really cooked. The macaroni was more than al dente; it was al rock. I had forgotten that at altitude you have to boil things much longer because the boiling temperature is lower. This, not surprisingly, led to a hiss and spit catfight. Exhaustion and a bad dinner are fine ingredients for a quarrel.

We were delighted with the chambermaid who brought us water. She looked like she was dressed for a ball in a glorious, green brocade *chuba*, long earrings of dubious coral and freshwater pearls, both probably plastic, brushing her shoulders. Below these she wore many necklaces of pearls, the black and white beads that have a mysterious significance for Tibetans, turquoise, plus a stomacher, a wide belt, sewn with rows and rows of cowry shells brought from exotic Indonesia's shores, which she knew nothing of. She was cheerful and interested in us and asked, by gesture, that we be frugal in our use of water since she had to haul it up the hill.

Our chambermaid with a bucket of water she's just walked up from the river.

There was something that looked to me like a sheepskin coat slung over the door. I removed it thinking it would keep the door from closing firmly. That night a tremendous thunderstorm awakened us, flinging the door open with a bang. We put a stone against it to keep it from winging itself wildly open and shut. There were enormous blasts of lightning on the horizon, as though someone was cleaving the dark with a two-handed sword of light. The next morning I realized that the "coat" was a piece of sheepskin used to wedge the door closed. This confusion made me smile. I added it to my list of cultural misunderstandings I have had. In the morning the mountains were salted with fresh snow.

I asked Dorje to walk with me along the road because I wanted, if possible, to locate the house I had stayed in on the previous trip.

When I recognized it, he asked a neighbor about it and its people. They told us the house was empty, that the people had gone away but offered no further information.

When Rachael and I talked to Dorje about our itinerary he was paranoid about the military presence in Kyunglung, even though he wasn't sure it was there. Rachael pressed him about our getting to Kyunglung; she was quite insistent. She seemed to feel that she could will things to happen. I was furious at her for pressuring him and didn't mince my words.

Having been smug the day before about having no sinus trouble or blood scabs in my nose, I woke to an altitude sickness attack of the kind that leaves one feeling lousy with aching sinuses and a nose full of dusty scabs. Rachael made the superhuman effort to talk about our spat the night before. I was most grateful to her for making the attempt since it was beyond my abilities at that point. Indeed, it hadn't even occurred to me to do it. We were able to talk a bit about getting on each other's nerves, which helped for a while.

The next morning we drove into Darchen for breakfast meeting, over our Nescafe and tea, a grey-haired American woman, who had walked to Chuku monastery, the first monastery on the *khora*, intending to spend two nights there acclimatizing before crossing the pass, Drölma La. After the first night the monks had insisted that she leave the monastery hostel because they were expecting Hindu pilgrims. These pilgrims filled Darchen; we watched them shivering in bright, light cotton garments with parkas over them.

The American had slept in a tea tent beyond the monastery wrapped in one blanket on top of a mud covered concrete slab. We noted the existence of the tea tent since it meant there was a fire we could use rather than struggling to light our own.

Before the pilgrimage season, the villagers of Darchen have a lottery. The winners set up big tents, roofed by heavy white fabric with Tibetan symbols stitched on them in blue, along the pilgrimage path. There is a stove in the center with a smoke-pipe going out through a hole in the roof on which they make tea or boil water for instant noodles, packages of which they sell. They make simple meals of vegetables and rice. The entire family spends the season in the tent, situated near the river. The children have the arduous job of hauling water up from the river in pails, the mother churns yak butter tea and the father tends to the fire and the money. There are usually benches around the perimeter of the tent, covered with hand-woven rugs on which pilgrims can sleep for a modest fee.

Darchen seemed a little cleaner than last time but was still a very unattractive town. We asked Dorje to find out if anyone knew if Hema and Jay were in town or ahead of us. He was told that they had been there but had turned back, unable to deal with the lack of oxygen. Although the altitude defeated them finally, at least they tried and had time with the mountain, seeing her, experiencing her atmosphere.

Dorje hired three porters for us: Norbu age thirty, his tiny sister, Drolma, thirteen, who walked under the huge heap of their sleeping bags, and Loto Ponzo, age seventeen, a *mani* stone carver by profession, intelligent, helpful, full of fun and enamored of zipping zippers. I fell for the two youngest on contact.

Our porters ready to start the *khora*, the sacred path of pilgrimage around Kailash.

With our three porters we started walking the scrawl of the nondescript, packed-earth path that is the sacred *khora*. Up and down we wound over the small barren hills. While we could still see Kailash, on our right, clouds hunched around her. Then she disappeared behind her ridges and a light rain began to fall leaving no trace in the dust at our feet, not a good omen with which to begin the *khora*. Dorje did not accompany us, as he was required to by Chinese regulations, preferring to stay in Darchen and drink.

But still we set out very merrily with our young companions. It took us an hour to reach the prayer flags and *mani* stones of Chaktsal Gang. We put up a string of prayer flags apiece with enthusiastic help from all three porters; then it was over an hour to the two-legged *chörten*, *Chörten* Kangnyi, wearing a fringe of discarded clothing, earrings, shoes, bracelets, and other items witnessing the discarders' willingness to change. Wind poured down from the pass, herding flocks of black clouds that made the last hundred yards to the *chörten* a walk in which we forced our way leaning against the wind. We took refuge inside it, waiting for the rain, which slashed down, cold and vicious, to stop.

When it eased we started up to the sky burial site I had not even known existed on my first circumambulation of Kailash. Loto Ponzo sheltered with our bags in the *chörten* while Norbu, Drölma, Rachael and I walked in misty rain up the escarpment to a plateau where sky burials for monks take place. We ducked, as the rain increased, under an outcropping of rock.

While hunched under the ledge I saw there was a group of Tibetans further down the trail below us. One of the women pulled on a black and white rain jacket, which she had extracted from a little pouch. With her was a woman in Western dress, blue jeans, and a third, older woman in a *chuba*. Behind them laboring up the slope was a man bearing on his back a large woven plastic bag in a bamboo carrier, made like a large, lattice work, rectangular manila folder. Rachael saw a booted foot dangling from the bag. They were taking a relative to the site for a sky burial, probably the sisters and the mother of a monk who had died.

The rain eased but didn't stop. We were all in a line leaning into the rock under the shallow overhang. Bored, Rachael and I, by motions, told Dawa and Drölma, to stay under cover until we returned, since they had no rain gear or change of clothing. If they got wet they would stay wet and as we climbed it would get colder.

Kailash, and below, the escarpment of Drachom Ngagye Durtrö the sky burial ground for monks.

I reached the top of the escarpment first, not something that happens often, and the band of Tibetans with their burden followed Rachael. While sheltering below us, they had had an opportunity to look us over and to realize we were Westerners. They did not look pleased. As we all heaved ourselves over the rocks at the top of the escarpment they looked decidedly unhappy. At the top of the ridge is a large, open, flat area covered with cairns and, I presume, the clothing of the dead, or perhaps the clothing of mourners, as well as half-moon shelters in which it seemed likely sky burials take place, dry wall structures of loose stones. Victor Chan in his guide book comments on a horrendous smell here, but I did not notice it this time.

The Tibetans went into one of the half-moon shelters with their burden peering apprehensively and sadly over its edge at us. Rachael whispered to me that we should leave. I knew she was right but I did want, so badly, to see a sky burial. However, it was obvious that we were not going to be welcome at this one. I wondered if our reception would have been different if our porters had been with us. Though we only spent a few minutes looking about us, I carried away with me the haunting image of stones around which sweaters had been buttoned, jackets zipped, so that they looked like headless people, not in any way scary, just homey people in worn jackets and sweaters.

I know it is intrusive and bad manners to want to see a sky burial; but my culture, American culture, is neurotic about death, having all kinds of euphemisms for it—my father used to say, "One of these days I'm going to disappear." People talk about "passing" or "the departed" as if there is some invisible door through which people exit. Rarely do people simply say, "He died." Indeed, people will do everything possible to avoid the words "dead, died, death" as though that will make the fact of death invisible.

We lipstick and rouge our dead, dress them up as if for a party, an odd denial. Americans don't seem to feel that death is natural—if they could just eat perfectly correctly, perhaps be vegetarian, exercise enough, take the right supplements, death would go away. Attempting not to share in these odd reactions to death, along with the way we die in hospitals surrounded by machines rather than friends and relatives, I have gone to many foreign funerals and cremations and read about how other cultures deal with the finality of death.

In Bali I, along with many other tourists, was happily included in funeral and cremation ceremonies. Foreigners and Balinese followed the long lines of women tightly wrapped in bright fabrics, pupas in brilliant cocoons, with pyramids of fruit on their heads, the procession led by the shroud wrapped corpse being carried on men's shoulders to the cremation fire.

Tourists are also welcome to Sulawesi funerals where I decided not to watch dozens of buffalo and pigs getting their throats cut. Pigs do not take this quietly, embedding their squeals in your memory and conscience. People are sometimes buried temporarily until the family has accumulated the huge amounts of money needed to buy the water buffalo and pigs to be slaughtered at the wake. At one of these funerals

I went to, the coffin had a little window in it. I found myself gazing in at a friendly looking, wrinkled, white-haired woman I would have liked to have talked to while I gave the family a present of cigarettes, my contribution to the funeral.

I have witnessed cremations in India, in Calcutta when working at Mother Teresa's Home for the Dying Destitute, and in Nepal, on the Bagmati River, at Pashupatinath, outside Kathmandu, where cremations occur on concrete plinths set into the river. Sitting on the opposite bank watching the cremations is a serene way to spend an afternoon. The white shrouded body is laid on top of an open cube made of pieces of wood stuffed with hay. The eldest son pours ghee, clarified butter, into or around the body's mouth. Then he spreads hay over the body before lighting the pyre, the final act of a good son for his father.

Though it must be hard for the eldest tending the fire, it also must leave no doubts about the reality and finality of death. Often he must rearrange the body so the feet or head is consumed. He is present for death as we are not; he is a participant.

I am puzzled that there is no odor from the burning. Is it because hay burns quickly and fiercely at a high heat?

Some people are very matter of fact about death. Isak Dinesen in *Out of Africa* notes that, "The Kikuyus, when left to themselves, do not bury their dead, but leave them above ground for the Hyenas and vulture to deal with." I like that she capitalizes Hyenas, an animal that gets very bad press, and agree with her that, "The custom has always appealed to me, I thought that it would be a pleasant thing to be laid out to the sun and the stars, and to be so made one with Nature and a common component of a landscape."

I suspect Tibetans and Kikuyus have such customs because they do not consider themselves different or superior to other animals, do not think they are separate from the earth but are part of "the system" of nature. They have, therefore, a much more factual relationship with death than more "civilized" people. It also may be that they do not see life and death as separate states but as a continuum. Civilization is wonderful, particularly for women, but there is no doubt that it inserts all kinds of ideas, attitudes and customs between life's realities and us. When a child is horrified that vegetables grow bigger and better with cow shit in their diet and a housewife is frightened to buy meat that isn't in a Styrofoam tray covered with plastic wrap, something has gone wrong.

When I went to Tibet in 1992 you could sometimes attend a sky burial; but now, because of bad behavior by tourists and travelers with cameras, the Chinese have forbidden foreigners to attend, to, I suspect, the great relief of Tibetans.

Water burial, which I have read about but never heard of anyone seeing, may also involve cutting up the body so fish can eat it easily, but I have heard that it is rarely done now because of the obvious problem of pollution. To go back to the mystery of Tibetans not eating fish, perhaps if you feed your dead to them you don't want to eat them, since it might cause you to unknowingly consume your grandmother. But that still doesn't explain why fish would ease the labor pains that bring life into the world.

We ambled down from the escarpment, picking up Norbu and Drölma along the way, to find Loto Ponzo standing, a cheerful, grey sentinel in his sheepskin coat, of which he was immensely proud since it was both warm and somewhat waterproof, by the *chörten*. His coat actually resembled those very expensive sheepskin coats for women, cut to the natural drape of the hide, that sell at Saks Fifth Avenue. He would have been fine on Fifth Avenue in January, except for the jaunty little pork-pie hat he wore. That would have been an anomaly. The rain started again; we took refuge again, waiting about fifteen minutes for it to pass.

When it did end the world about us had that delicate, newly made feeling that land has after a rain. It was peaceful yet exhilarating. We walked by the river toward Chuku Monastery passing a line of old, half tumbled down *chörtens* and a *mani* wall composed of stones carved with the Tibetan mantra, *Ohm, mani padme Hum*. The air was fresh, rinsed of dust by the rain.

We heard a marmot call. Two stood before their holes whistling to their neighbors down the valley. They were uninterested in us, turning this way and that, their dark paws at their sides, like stout middle-aged men, but if a dog appeared they were down their burrows as though sucked in by a vacuum cleaner.

We walked to the bridge that crosses the river, the La Chu, to Chuku Monastery, setting up camp smack on the path. I suppose we were too tired to notice we were doing this. Norbu, Drölma and Loto Ponzo helped with the tents as though we had given them a new toy, then climbed up to the monastery where they would spend the night.

Once our tents were up we visited another tent we could see further up the path, hoping it would be the tea tent with a fire the grey-haired American woman had slept in. It wasn't. It was inhabited by two pleasant Tibetan men who were trying to start a fire under their kettle, set up on three stones, with kerosene soaked cotton spills and wood shavings. It was gratifying to watch someone else struggle to get a fire started. It made us feel less inept.

One offered us sweets. Rachael thought he was trying to sell them to her, a cultural solecism; but Westerners aren't used to generosity from people who have less than they have. I thought of my misunderstanding of the "sheepskin" coat on the door. After ten times in Tibet, I can't get through a trip without a cultural glitch, though straining every psychic muscle to do the right thing. The next day we realized the men were prostrating themselves around Kailash, and were moving their tent each day to a new location.

Back at our tents we lit our stove. A dozen antelope on a narrow ledge of a rock-face opposite the monastery lifted soft noses to the evening breeze, their slender legs fragile against the arid rock. The only other wildlife was a pair of hopeful dogs creeping closer to us. The meal, resuscitated, dehydrated macaroni and cheese again, was not quite cooked through, although better than the last time. I had yet to learn how long it would take to cook things at 16,000 feet. Truthfully, I never did learn.

We scurried back to our tents when the wind came up, bringing rain in its train of black clouds. Rachael had brought two tents, one a single-person, the other a pup tent. We were going to alternate between the two tents each night. That night I got the tiny pup tent, which I had to wriggle myself into feeling like a snake trying to reenter her sloughed skin. In the wind it felt as though it would take off. Rain rattled against it; dust sifted in, but it was dry inside. Thunder surrounded us. Once that passed, I slept only to be awakened periodically by grand choruses of dogs. At one point a pup that had been trying to endear itself to us sent up an aria of howls, a lone adolescent voice singing to the moon. Then there was silence and sleep. Suddenly, in blackest night, I woke to the shrieking rabble of a dog fight. Shortly after, in graying darkness, I heard people mumbling mantras in the cold dawn as they passed, beginning their *khora* in the chill air before full light. It was a susurrus of prayer brushing against my tent wall.

I crawled out of my tent to find Rachael throwing up, a serious sign of altitude sickness. When I urged her to drink water, something she found difficult to do, she said she was afraid it hadn't been boiled long enough. Certainly the night before the water we used for our lousy dehydrated meal, had only reached luke-warm. I offered to go up to the monastery and buy boiled water, since she was too sick to light the stove or instruct me on its intricacies.

Before leaving I ate some pieces of sausage, from Fairway in New York, put a granola bar in my pack, with the remains of a chocolate bar. Rachael said hopefully, "You'll be back in twenty minutes?" I said nothing, knowing it would be much longer. I thoroughly resented Rachael for not drinking enough water and, therefore, making herself ill. But her objection was real, the water could be contaminated, so I didn't have any choice except to climb to the monastery.

Chuku Monastery and the rocky climb up to it.

The climb was a hellish workout. I had to stop periodically to get my breath back, my heart rate down. The path was a maze through boulders. I counted up to fifty steps, then stopped to pant or I would count five switchbacks, then stop to pant. My progress was that of an inchworm doing a mile. Two men coming down, instructed me about where and which way to turn but I got lost anyway since the hill and the boulders hid the location of the monastery. Luckily Loto appeared when I had almost reached the top or it would have taken me a half hour to locate the monastery kitchen, a dark cavern aromatic with grassy smelling smoke from the yak-pie fire. There was a dusty window at one end looking across the river to the escarpment that was topped by the sky burial site in one direction and framing a stunning view of Kailash's white dome in the other.

Keeping warm in the cave were four monks, a younger man, and Loto. The head monk patted the place beside him on the bench in front of the window. His hair stood up on his head in wild locks. His front teeth were missing. One of the other monks had an eye missing.

Rather than a bevy of monks, although they were wrapped in their red robes, they made me think of the notorious bandits that used to rob pilgrims around Kailash. I took out our water bottles, explained our need by gestures, and also asked for butter tea and *tsampa* for myself, the climb having left me wobbly with hunger, despite the granola bar and chocolate I had consumed on the way up. We were very social, talking with our hands and faces.

In the midst of our conversation a boy, perhaps five years old, tore into the kitchen, obviously the ward of the monks. His hair was cropped close along the sides of his head with a great black cockscomb of dust-stiffened locks curving over his head, a Tibetan Mohawk. While I had four bowls of butter tea, excellent butter tea, and *tsampa* which tasted just fine, he climbed in and out of my lap, zipped and unzipped my various zippers, investigated my pockets, emptied my pack, was a total nuisance, and generally behaved like a happy five-year-old.

Meanwhile the monks heated up the big, black stove with Loto working the bellows to get the water boiling. I realized that we needed bellows to get more oxygen into our stove fire, but we had not seen any for sale in Lhasa. These were made from the black and white furry, deboned, hind leg of a goat. I gave the head monk ten yuan. He flipped it disdainfully across a wooden chest, not as an insult I think, but in contempt for money. They insisted I give to the one-eyed monk, which I did. The head monk half-jokingly offered me the boy for free, as he swarmed around my knees like a dozen kittens, but it was only half a joke. I refused the gift. I wrote a note for Rachael and sent it down by Loto with the two full water bottles. I was feeling very happy to be on my own without Rachael. This time it, unlike the pen buying exploit, really was an adventure.

I asked the monk if I could see the chapel. A small butter lamp lighted the room crammed like an attic with things indistinguishable in the murky light. The main effigy was an alabaster, I think, statue of Nangwa Thaye, also known as Chuku Rinpoche for whom the monastery is named.

In all my reading I have been unable to discover who Nangwa Thaye is but Victor Chan does tell the legend of the discovery of the statue. A woman pilgrim, finding the statue in a cave close to the monastery, thought it should be moved to sacred ground. She and others tried to lift it but, although it was small, not much more than a foot high, it was so heavy that they could not shift it. The woman sat down next to the statue and respectfully explained to it that she and her companions wanted to transport it to the monastery where it would be honored. They then had no difficulty lifting it into her basket in which she took it to its present location. The statue, cocooned in rich brocade, was adorned with necklaces given by women pilgrims. Peacock feathers glimmered, in the light of the sole butter lamp, gold and blue behind it. In a corner were a pair of old, yellowed elephant tusks, which purportedly belonged to the sacred elephant, Sala Rabten, who it is said, lived and meditated in a cave nearby.

The head monk deciding that, although undoubtedly odd, I was okay, poured into my hands some liquid from a metal teapot kept on the altar, which I hoped was tea and not unboiled water, to drink and put on my head. The wild child, following us into the chapel, got some too, drinking and pouring it over his head with quiet dignity. All his wildness evaporated once he entered the chapel. He became quiet, reverent, almost sedate, but smiling in the flickering light of the butter lamp before the altar. He had already the beginnings of a spiritual life which did not make him grim and earnest but full of laughter and delight. That aspect of Tibetan Buddhism is fascinating. I come from a religion where the spirit is grim and tortured, Saint Teresa's terribly, physically painful contacts with her God. I much preferred the Buddha's laughter as evinced in this untamed five year old.

I thanked the monk and started down the path thinking it would be an easy, swift walk but found I had to stop to get my breath back from time to time even going down hill.

As I descended I saw Rachael and the porters taking down the tents. I commented to her, once I got down, that if one gets out of breath descending a hill it probably means one is not acclimatized. Pilgrims peeking into her tent had driven her to distraction. They were, of course, just curious as to who the foreigners were, what they looked like, and what they owned. Since we had camped smack in the middle of the path, this was inevitable.

We started slowly, taking many rest stops along the way. The younger porters and I began to get to know each other without language. Drölma and I walked together working out alternatives to linguistic communication such as sniffing at each other; I was sniffing because my nose, while not as badly infected by dust as on the previous circumambulation, ran pretty continuously. We made raspberries at each other or she imitated my panting. I patted her shoulder and she patted my bottom, a thing Tibetan women do to each other, although I was quite startled, and offended, the first time I was patted. Since it was a nun who did it, I decided it probably wasn't a pass. It was an excellent day for communication.

I learned to say, "*Milarepa saya sacho*," ("Milarepa ate nettles.") by pointing at nettles and saying "Milarepa." I discovered that Tibetans lift their voice at the end of words, which may be another reason why the girls at the restaurant the day before didn't understand us. Loto sang folk songs or perhaps popular songs, since I wouldn't know the difference, along the way. I sang, because it was the only thing I could think of, "Amazing Grace," very slowly because I had to portion out my breath among my words and steps. He immediately picked it up and whistled the tune. It was the right song in the right place. Despite its Christian, regulation denigrations of self, it had the right spiritual voice.

We came to the tea tent the American woman had slept in, run by a man and his wife who had a charming baby and an older child. They had a picture of the Dalai Lama, a large one, hanging in the tent, but the periphery of the tent was not outlined by rug covered benches, as is usual. That made clear why our grey-haired acquaintance ended up sleeping in a blanket on a piece of cement. The picture of the Dalai Lama was explained by the fact that we had seen no military presence since we had left Darchen. They let us cook on their stove. I made, quite edible, dehydrated vegetable soup, with some of the homemade noodles Sonam had bought us. Loto, Drölma and Dawa had butter tea and *tsampa* with slices of Fairway sausage. They seemed to enjoy it.

Walking by the river we gazed up at the fantastic shapes at the top of the ridges on either side. The mansions, cathedrals, palaces and pavilions looked down at us, their mystical, mythical inhabitants, if they existed, invisible to us. Along the river, where the land was green with grass, we passed black, yak-hair, nomad tents, the animals with their long tails and long belly hair grazing around them. We could see through the tents' fabric, but if it rained it would thicken and repel the drops. The yaks were attired with glowing necklaces of brass bells that jangled and saddle blankets of rich hued rugs; the herders, resembling Native Americans, were decidedly handsome.

Yaks and horses along the river beside the *khora* path.

We finished our day crossing the Lha Chu River precariously on stones, as I had done the last time despite the bridge up ahead. We were across the river from Drira Phuk monastery in the meadow before the two ridges framing the north view of Kailash, as beautiful as I had remembered her.

Kailash beyond the prayer flags honoring her opposite Drira Phuk Monastery. This year she had little snow on her rocky crown.

A plume of snow blew off the very top of her snowcap. Already encamped were a large group of Austrians who had passed Rachael while she was waiting for me to descend from Chuku Monastery. She had told me about them but I hadn't realized what a large group they were. They had bright orange tents and all the luxuries—Sherpas, a kitchen tent, a dining tent, and most wonderful of all, a toilet tent. Rachael and I watched them like orphans, tattered children, faces pasted against the window of the rich folk's home.

We went to the tea tent down by the river where Loto, Norbu and Drölma would sleep and I cooked something, not very well. I seemed to do better with lunch than with dinner, probably because by dinnertime I was aching with exhaustion, hardly able to think much less cook. But it was nice to sit in the smoky, yak-butter-smelling tent in the dark with the porters, Rachael and the tent owner. When we came out, Kailash was a pale glimmer, a ghost mountain against the stars.

That night I had the larger tent. Rachael must have had a hard time in the pup tent. Shortly after we crawled into our sleeping bags a storm, frenzied as a snow leopard attacking sheep in a corral, charged down from Drölma La. Great claps of thunder bounced off the surrounding peaks and ridges, resounding, reverberating in the chalice of rock we were in. It was like being inside a bell while it was striking. As enormous bursts of lightning illuminated the tent, I peeked out of the flap to see the rocky crevices of the opposite mountainside lit up with eerie, livid light.

Unfortunately my tent faced away from Kailash. I would have loved to see her in that spectral light. Hail, the size of cranberries, rattled down, furiously punching the tent and leaving a rolling layer of frozen bits on the ground outside, a scattering of white pebbles. Later there was a gentle, soothing rain that whispered down caressing the tent with soft fingers. No dogs. But in the morning small drifts of hail surrounded the Austrians' yaks. The dawn was cold but beautiful; Kailash was feathered flamingo pink with sunrise.

Yaks and one of the Austrians' orange tents as dawn clothes Kailash in light.

Yaks and prayer flags in drifts of hail the morning after the storm.

Unnerved by the ferocity of the storm, I went to the Austrians to ask if they intended to go over the *la,* the pass. They said, yes. I trusted their judgment; they are mountain people, so when Norbu asked if we intended to continue the *khora* I told him yes.

We didn't get sorted out until 9:00 a.m., which meant we took off in the midst of the Austrians. I watched them walk. They divided themselves into groups, walking according to speed, single file. I knew

I couldn't keep the pace of the first two groups, who were almost as fast as Tibetans, striding along effortlessly.

When the third and fourth group started I couldn't believe the snailness of their pace. They were a slow motion film. I tried to follow their rhythm, but at first it was difficult to go so slowly. I would automatically hurry up. I found I fit nicely between the slowest, and next to the slowest group.

Kailash disappears among her ridges as the *khora* climbs to the pass, Drölma La.

Once I forced myself to settle into that pace I no longer had to stop to pant. My heart was no longer a drum under frantic fingers. I needed to pause a couple of times on the "staircase" part of the ascent to the pass, but there was no dishonor in that because even the Tibetans pause there it is so steep. It is that unrelenting angle, after all, that caused them to build the rough staircase.

Yak climbing the last steep rises to the pass at 18,600 feet.

I wended my way through and over the area where there were gray boulders with glacial melt clucking as it ran under them, an area I find frightening since one might slip and find one's foot trapped between rocks. I recognized the place where the pass seemed directly ahead, warned Rachael that it was a false slope and resigned myself to the further climb.

Little, long beaked birds, with creamy breasts and pale brown backs, hopped beside the path. They let us come quite close, indifferent to our presence. The Kailash area is a no kill zone, so humans would never have hunted them. They would only fear other animals.

Approaching the big scoop of glacial boulders at the top of the pass, we heard cracking and then the rattle and roar of minor avalanches from the glaciers on the ridge across the way.

Our young woman porter carried my water bottle. I couldn't even manage that as we approached Drölma La.

The steep walk was companionable since, pausing for breath one was passed by two who then, further on, had to stop for breath and, therefore, were passed by the one they had just gone by with nods, and smiles of recognition. The family from the back of our truck passed us. I looked at the wife for any sign of weakness but she was striding right along. Even the children were carrying their own daypacks as we climbed to the pass. We had a reunion of smiles, nods and "*Tashi dilays*." There was much "Helloing" and "*Tashi-dilaying*" as we headed for the great display of prayer flags. I went up to the top of the pass with relative ease.

In Dharamsala, India, I heard the Dalai Lama, when giving his annual speech on the Tibetan New Year, urge his people not to use the expression *tashi dilay*, to say "hello," since it is losing its old meaning in its new use. It was particularly used as a greeting when people wished each other good luck on the New Year. *Tashi* means luck. *Tashi dilay* variously spelled *tashidelay* and *tashidelek*, is used by foreigners in

Tibet as "hello," since there is no "hello" in Tibetan and foreigners are used to having such a greeting. Before this, conversations started between Tibetans not with a greeting but with questions such as "Where are you going?" or "Where have you come from?" Because we are used to doing things in a certain manner, we force our way on a culture we enter, rather than adapting to that civilization's mode. We do this without thinking and the old fabric of custom is changed.

As we climbed to the pass I became aware that among the pilgrims there was a strikingly beautiful Tibetan woman with a haughty bearing whom I'd seen the night before in the Austrian camp. She was noteworthy for her beauty and her heavy turquoise jewelry, both emphasized by a scarlet, woolen scarf wrapped around her head in a sort of loose turban. Now, for the occasion of going over the pass, she was wearing a Lhasa lady's hat, its brim a froth of cream-colored chiffon with a dotted veil.

A solitary yak taking the sun at the top of Drölma La.

At the top, triumphant and exhausted, we were all sitting about among the prayer flags rummaging for something to eat in our backpacks. There were prayer papers under foot, printed with the wind horse and prayers, which had been tossed in the air to celebrate topping the pass and *khatas,* wound around rocks, or tied to the strings of prayer flags that almost covered with their bright colors the rock into which the Drölmas/wolves disappeared. A tall woman with cheekbones like sparrow wings, cunning eyes and something unpleasantly sly in her manner stood before me and pointed at Norbu's *tsampa* bag, which was lying beside me. I could tell by her gestures she was asking for a handout. Somehow, through grimaces and gestures I explained it was not my *tsampa* bag and she playacted her embarrassment at her mistake. Rarely have I encountered a Tibetan woman I have felt I did not trust, but this was one. I was uncomfortable in her presence but could not have told you why.

Norbu arrived; she begged *tsampa* from him and he filled her bowl without looking at her. We were having similar reactions to this woman. It is quite unusual for someone not to have her own personal bag of *tsampa*. Rachael and I offered our porters bits of sausage. It now turned out that they hadn't liked it and had just been being polite in their previous reactions. So we gave them granola bars. I think they actually did like those but they may have just been being polite again. I made a note to myself that while I was quite all right with ritual generosity, as here at the pass, I was not, however, good at spontaneous generosity which involved thinking of other people.

A handsome young man with a whacking great silver ring centered by a black and white stone sat down next to me putting his hand into my daypack to see what was there. He did not intend to steal; he was just curious. Still the trespass upset me. I gave him a severe, incomprehensible lecture, although he knew from my tone of voice that he was being scolded. He went away insulted, which at first was all right with me, but as the day wore on I knew I had lost my temper, anger entering to push out fear, on holy ground and that did not feel good.

The hardships of climate, altitude, unfamiliar food and odd lodgings that Tibet offers tend to expose you to yourself, make you aware of your selfishness, lack of compassion, quickness to anger, or intolerance. Rarely, perhaps never, have I left Tibet without wincing over a behavior of mine. On this trip I kept returning to my excessively vehement lecture to this young man with contrition.

Also nearby was an old, regal man, a tatterdemalion, who was humming away at his mantras with a soft smile on his face. Serene happiness radiated from him like the purr of a contented cat.

We came down quickly; I was ahead of everyone but Loto, who leapt like a mountain goat from rock to rock. This meant I didn't hear Rachael calling for help. She was badly frightened by the woman who had begged *tsampa* from Norbu. On the cliff-edge path, grinning and gesturing that she wanted money from Rachael, she barred the narrow trail. When she heard others coming down the path she turned her back on Rachael and hurriedly went on. Rachael was most relieved.

Down from the pass, there are make-shift bridges over streams along the *khora's* path.

After wending our way through the boulder rubble the mountain had cast off and then down the steep, slippery, pebbled path to the river, we had tea and more sausage in the tea tent at the bottom, which sits surrounded by broken, green, beer bottles and discarded plastic instant noodle bowls. We discussed whether to stop for the day and camp here, where the porters could have stayed in the tent or go on.

Foolishly we went on. It meant a ten-hour day of walking, which was too long.

Loto strayed to the wrong side of the river; it was late afternoon before he could cross back. The Austrians passed with their entourage, which, it turned out, included the striking Tibetan woman who had worn her Lhasa lady's hat on the ascent.

Now, bareheaded, she rode a regal, white horse, her jewelry, long loops of pearls, turquoise and coral for earrings, all real, not plastic, I suspect, with matching necklaces gleamed in the warm afternoon light against her perfect bronze complexion. Her black *chuba* was of the finest, soft wool set off by the high collar and belled sleeves of her scarlet, satin blouse, which was fastened tightly at the wrist with little buttons like peppercorns. Her long black hair slicked back into a tight bun, showed off her long neck. Her hair may have been in a bun but she, it was apparent, was no schoolmarm. There was a sexual magnetic field around her. The horse, as elegant as she, had bells all along its reins that chimed as she rode and a magnificent saddle-rug woven with scarlet and gold dragons. She was queenly and sublime. Not Guinevere but Eleanor of Aquitaine. A nursery rhyme from childhood came to mind:

> *Ride a cockhorse to Banbury Cross,*
> *To see a fine lady upon a white horse.*
> *Rings on her fingers and bells on her toes,*
> *And she shall have music wherever she goes.*

Her husband, owner of the yak herd carrying the Austrians' baggage, was as handsome as his wife, as proud in his carriage. They seemed to have appeared from an illuminated manuscript or, although it's the wrong culture, an illustration from *A Thousand and One Nights*. I couldn't help but stare. I wanted to hold them in my mind forever. But asking for a photo seemed on a par with asking the Queen of England to pose for a snapshot.

Later, coming upon the Austrian's camp Loto and I went to ask if he and our other porters could stay with them overnight. With the two tents Rachael and I could stop anywhere but where would Loto, Dawa and Drölma sleep and eat? The Tibetan in charge gave us a severe "No."

A little further on we stopped again to have a conference but there was nothing for it but to keep on going.

The river, the Zhong Chu, along which the *khora* path winds its way.

When we got to Zutrul Phuk monastery, we were staggering with fatigue; I had been foul humored for hours. At this point Rachael and I were barely talking. She was, understandably, mad at me as I had not been helping with the tents. I let her and the porters put them up and take them down. I wanted her to disappear off the face of the earth and, I'm sure, she returned the feeling. I plodded through a swamp of self-pity.

In any book about mountaineering, you usually find mention of some horrendous, but utterly ludicrous quarrel at some point in the uphill proceedings. Robert Byron in *First Russia Then Tibet* gives one of my favorite examples of this sort of conflict from his time in Tibet. But what today's readers don't realize is that at that time in the early 20th century not only were these men living with the tensions due to lack of oxygen but since there was no sun block their faces, exposed to high altitude sun and wind, burned, blistered and developed running sores.

> *M., his face dripping, unshaven, and crinkling with nausea as it opened to receive a piece of tinned sausage, spoke the first reproach that I had everknown of him: "Why have you brought us to this horrible place?"— as though it were any more my doing than his. Whereat G., employing the dogmatic tone of an Early Father, announced: "I am going straight back to Phari." It was that tone that saved us. "You can," I said resentfully, though ten seconds before I would have followed him. "I'm going on. Any how I rather want to see Lake Dochen." I had no such desire; but as we should reach it that morning, it seemed the nearest incentive. "Well?" we both inquired at once of M. "I'm so wretched," he replied, mopping his face and pushing away the sausage, "that I'm indifferent. But I don't like not keeping to my plans." "Grotesque weakmindedness!" snarled G.; and to me: "If you want to see Lake Dochen, GO and see Lake Dochen."*
>
> *Thereafter no more was spoken.*

This is the sort of interchange one is apt to have where the altitude mangles your spirit and leaves your sense of humor flayed.

Loto, realizing how tired I was, once he came back across the river, kept close to me, for which I was grateful. My eyes stung and watered from the dusty wind; my nose ran. Misery was paramount. We came into Zutrul Phuk monastery at 7:30 in the evening dead beat. They wanted forty-five yuan, over six dollars, to stay in the muddy, monastery guesthouse, an absurd amount. We put up our tents slightly to the left of a patch of broken beer bottles, watched by three dogs, none in prime condition. I crawled into mine simmering with resentment at Rachael and at myself for not insisting that we stay at the tea tent we had stopped at when we came down from the pass.

In a haze of rage, I decided I would tell Rachael that I had decided to call the rest of the trip off. I would return to Lhasa and find something else to do with the time I had left.

Dimly, I sensed there was something wrong with my thinking and pulled an AA book from my pack. What I read had nothing to do with my situation but it instantly altered my mental perspective. It shifted immediately, dramatically my angle of vision. It was as though my rage had been a close-up cinematic shot and the tiny reading I did caused my camera to pull back to a long shot. In close focus, there was only me. The long shot allowed in other people and with them a different perspective. I badly needed that half-minute contact with my world of sane thought and spiritual insight to get me back in balance, keep me from behaving idiotically, a blessing for us all.

We walked to a tea tent run by the loveliest of lone women with long braids. I presumed her husband was trading on the border for the summer, while she and her two sons made tea and boiled up packages of ramen noodles for pilgrims. Her youngest, perhaps five years old, was a fantastic little boy with an expressive face. We had intense, animated conversations with hands, faces and nonsense sounds produced with varying inflections.

Then he told his mother something and she went to one of the chests on the periphery of the tent coming back with his costume, which she must have made for him, a robe of blue and silver brocade, sashed at the waist in which he looked like a little emperor and knew it. He moved regally around the tent graciously receiving tribute, giving peremptory orders, sternly consulting with invisible counselors. The entire tent became populated by the orderly crowd of his court with not a word spoken, just hand gestures, graceful flickers of his fingers, incisive downward motions of his palm, wonderful, and kaleidoscopic facial expressions.

After dinner, snuggled into my sleeping bag I suggested to whatever Fates or Norns may be that such a talent find its way into the light it longs for in this world. He made me think of how Tibetans often call Westerners "gods" which we interpret to mean that we are superior. However, the "gods" to Tibetans are those who live privileged lives, are physically larger, and have longer life spans. Privilege is not a blessing since because of these apparently special gifts the "gods" are less likely to find their way out of *samsara*, the world of getting and spending, into *nirvana*, the world of spiritual peace, believing, mistakenly that they are impervious to *samsara's* corruption.

Between reading my AA book and spending time at the court of the little emperor this "god's" mood had changed; the world had become an acceptable place even with Rachael in it.

On waking, I found my rib muscles were not sore as they had been at the end of the previous circumambulation. I had learned to walk at altitude thanks to the Austrians' example. I felt elated, triumphant.

We had breakfast with the emperor, his mother and older brother. At first he was in ordinary dress, or should I say dishabille, a grubby, once white, split-pants outfit with a pussycat appliqué on the front. Before we left, he changed into his imperial outfit transformed again into a dignified princeling surrounded by his court.

As we folded our tents, I was clumsily helping, the elderly man in tatters I had seen at Drölma La watched. I realized suddenly he was a holy man of some sort. He motioned his approval of the tents by sticking his thumb up in the air. In a moment of openness I was able to be generous and give him a small offering to Loto's joy.

Sometimes I do get it right; then I am filled with simple happiness. My realization that this was the right moment and the right man for generosity filled me with a hope that I was changing despite scolding the young man who had put his hand in my daypack. Maybe I had balanced that lecture, caused by fear, with my appropriate gesture to the holy man. At least I had not lost it all over Rachael. That showed some improvement, if not perfection, despite all the angry, resentful thoughts milling in my head. I hadn't thought to give the necklace to Pema; Rachael had. I admired generosity in others and longed to be more readily generous.

At Zutrul Phuk monastery there was no monk, just a young man, and several Austrians manipulating copper rods, maybe trying to measure spiritual energy. The young custodian was fussing with a *khata* hanging from a pillar. We went to see what he was doing; he was trying to get a snouty-nosed beetle from the *khata* onto a one yuan note so he could then take him out doors where he would be able find things to eat and not die. It took the man twenty minutes to affect the transfer.

Having seen the alabaster image of Milarepa in its swaddle of scarves, we walked back into the main chapel. The Austrians had packed up their copper rods and left. After leaving a contribution we did, too.

Suddenly, as we came down from the temple onto the main path we, to our right, heard growling, barking and squealing. I assumed it was a dogfight but, when I turned, saw a dog had a marmot in his mouth. It was struggling fiercely to free itself, screaming and twisting so that it would be able to bite the dog.

Loto appeared and in a series of graceful leaps, with a triumphal look, hurled a stone at the dog, sending him off yelping. The marmot sprang free throwing himself at Olympic speed into a sequence of furry croquet hoops toward and then down his hole. I'm sure he quivered for a long time in his burrow.

The poor dog, disgruntled, slunk off to the monastery. Although the *khora* is a no-kill zone, it seemed unfair to me. Was the dog supposed to become a vegetarian?

On the walk beside the river the yaks carrying the Austrians' baggage passed us again. The woman, my Tibetan Eleanor of Aquitaine, rode one in a high saddle, almost a chair, her pearl and coral earrings swaying to the rhythm of the yak's stride. Her husband herded the animals from the back of his white horse, its tail knotted up to keep it from trailing in the dust. Horses' tails are part of their beauty to Tibetans and, therefore, are not cut in Tibet and Mongolia; indeed, I have read that thieves will not steal a horse whose tail has been bobbed because it reduces its value. He doubled up his reins and snapped them at the yaks or drove the horse into them to keep them in order. They were all, yaks, horses and humans, a handsome sight.

We crossed a series of landslides on a hard packed path less than a foot wide but it was firm and not too frightening despite the hundred-foot drop to the river. Loto waited for me at the end of each of these paths which were not much wider than my foot. Luckily heights don't bother me much.

We passed two men sitting by the side of the road who turned out to be the drivers for the Austrian group's four-wheel-drives. I felt sad that the Austrians had not used Tibetan drivers. The Nepalis offered us some circular bread, which was excellent. In return I offered a Mars Bar that looked as though it should have sued me for physical abuse. I was struck by how much more sophisticated and worldly-wise these Nepalis were compared to the Tibetans.

Drölma urged me to sing "Amazing Grace." I would sing a phrase and then she would try to imitate what I had said, learning the entire first verse before we got to Darchen. Between singing lessons, Loto taught me the Tibetan obscene finger gesture, which you do with your left pinky. It is the same as our middle finger gesture, just a different digit. I suspect the reference is, "Yours is this big."

Through these interchanges as we walked along the dusty path, I was conscious that the *khora* was ending. We came to the place where one looks out to the Barga Plain and the white massif of Gurla Mandata. This is the end I thought to myself, but there was too much going on around me with Loto Ponzo and Drölma chattering and singing about me. I could not concentrate.

As we came to the end of the *khora* there was a checkpoint manned by a Chinese in civilian dress. It was a jolt after being in the sacred Tibetan world for four days to reenter the controlling, militarized Chinese domain. The man came out to ask me where our guide was. I casually said, "Oh, he went ahead to see if the truck has arrived," thereby saving Dorje's unworthy skin as it turned out.

Loto caught up with us at this point and expressed his vehement disapproval of charging for the circumambulation, which he let us know he felt should be free to foreigners and Tibetans alike since spiritual things should have no price tag on them. He made the little finger, obscene gesture at the tollhouse.

A few bends further on, we ran into our truck driver's family waiting by a truck, which we assumed was ours; it wasn't. However, we all piled into the back anyway, holding onto whatever we could for a bucking bronco ride to Darchen where, in a tent labeled Lhasa Restaurant, we ate delicious yak and vegetable momos, meat or vegetable filled dumplings, while Tenzin pantomimed, with disgusted disapproval, how Dorje had been drunk every night we had been on the *khora*.

The Lhasa restaurant in Darchen where Rachel and I gorged ourselves on momos.

Since this is sacred territory, his drinking was obviously a worse offence than it would have been on profane turf. He had had a choice between participating in something sacred, something that offered the possibility of *nirvana* and something that definitely was not only attached to *samsara,* but would drive him further into that delusional state. He had chosen the latter, taken the wrong turn on his road.

The tent community at the edge of Darchen. It houses everything from healers to prostitutes.

On the edge of Darchen, sheep skins for sale from a tent.

It was certainly a blessing that I had sobered up before I started seriously traveling in Asia. The thought of what might have happened if I had been drinking and traveling is really frightening, particularly since I was given to freely expressing my opinions, of which I had an infinite number, when under the influence. Not something you want to do in Lhasa with Chinese spies in every nook and cranny.

A penitent, hung over Dorje went down to the river to bring us water so that we could do our laundry. His eyes were red, but not from the dust. We tipped Drölma, Norbu and Loto fairly extravagantly, saying a fond, although sad, good-bye.

Scrubbing my socks, I thought about Loto and my son back in the US. He had dropped out of college, as I had at the same age, and then returned. He had made a bad marriage and gotten free from it as I had. Our culture, our economy, allow us to make mistakes and then, like a tipping boat, set ourselves right again. We are privileged "gods." Loto had little maneuvering space in Chinese ruled Tibet, no opportunity for an education unless he learned Chinese. I could also understand that being "gods" meant that we were disconnected from some realities of life, such as death, our relationship to the earth replacing those relationships with our obsessive bonds to transient things—money, social structures, our association to man created things.

. . .

The next morning in the car my throat clogged, constricting painfully with unshed tears as we drove out of Darchen. I was puzzled thinking, as I had the first time, that perhaps it had to do with parting from the porters to whom I had become attached. I felt like a bare-root transplant, one of those shrubs mailed from a nursery that looked vulnerable and unclothed with its root system's fragile tendrils exposed to the air. Leaving Kailash and dirty Darchen was rending, although there was no possibility that this was a part of the earth where I could take up residence.

But I said nothing to Rachael; I certainly was not going to cry in front of her. Pride fought tears. The tension between us was strong. But I was mystified by the recurrence of my dry tears and puzzled over it as I craned my neck to watch Kailash diminishing out the back window of our four-wheel drive.

We went on from the *khora* to find Kyunglung, a place Rachael had, I suspect, heard of through her acquaintance with Charles Allen who in the year of our journey came out with his book *The Search for Shangri-La* in which he tells of his brief exploration of Kyunglung in the Garuda Valley. It is supposed to be the earliest Tibetan city, yet is not believed to have been inhabited by Tibetans but by a people lost to the mists of history more than 2,000 years ago. It is only mentioned once in Victor Chan as "the famed Bönpo shrine of Kyunglung, where the pre-Buddhist religion supposedly originated." He does not mention, at all, Guragem, a Bönpo monastery we camped near on our way. I was in equal portions interested and dubious of our enterprise. It can be, because of Chinese rules, regulations and surveillance, impossible to get to places in Tibet.

But first we went to Tirthapuri, a monastery that forms the last stop on the Kailash pilgrimage. It is an odd place of red and white stone embedded in a green, grassy landscape beside the Sutlej River that flows from the vicinity of Kailash down into India.

Horses in the river's meadows of the Sutlej.

The main temple, *gompa*, of Tirthapuri against red and white streaked cliffs.

The monastery is dramatic with white cliffs to one side, yellow and red cliffs to the other. There were two caves; in one people dug up yellow earth with sacred, medicinal qualities. The main attraction of the second was two stones—one with the footprint of Padmasambhava, the other with that of his consort Yeshe. I am fond of Padmasambhava, Guru Rinpoche, because he tamed the bullying, anti-social deities of the Bön faith. We found our hitch hiking family here, looking tired—he limped; she was spotted with patches applied by various monks. The children had found a kitten and stuffed it into an empty, yellow plastic, yak butter sack. They carried it about squealing with delight. The kitten looked resigned.

Prayer flags across the Sutlej at Tirthapuri Monastery.

Continuing to Guragem, a Bön monastery, through a grassy landscape with clusters of houses where horses graze, we turned into canyon country, badlands eroded into steps, tufa cliffs looking as though they were melting. Guragem, by the Sutlej River, is spectacular.

The temples were on the valley floor with a line of white and red *chörtens*. There was a line of rooms for pilgrims but Dorje discouraged us from staying there saying it was dirty. What was apparent was Chinese influence. Banners printed with Chinese characters were draped here and there; Mao smiled over an inner door. Tibetans put such things up as a way of reassuring the Chinese. The temples were new, brilliantly decorated—murals, small and large statues. Unhappily, there was also a pair of snow leopard skins stretched on wood frames. To the uneducated eye, mine, they looked much like Buddhist temples. I had been told that the Böns, finding themselves out stripped by the Buddhists, had adapted elements of Buddhism in their temples. If the other product outsells you, make yours as like the best seller as possible. The temple complex was rebuilt from its Cultural Revolution ruins in 1989 to 1991.

Guragem, the Bön temple with its prayer flags and lines of *chörtens*.

The meditation cave of the abbot of Guragem.

What was spectacular, and non-Buddhist, was high on a red cliff, reached by rocks and stairs, a meditation cave, its red outer wall splashed with white. It had been the meditation cave of Drenpei Namka a Bön monk and doctor. The present occupant also acts as a doctor to his parishioners.

Rachael went up but I was having such terrible trouble with my eyes that I sat down and closed them hoping to ease the pain. I had never had dry eye syndrome before and didn't know what it was. Tibet is so parched it is quite natural to have this problem. I tried to write while a Bön woman pilgrim sat in front of me, staring at me firmly.

When Rachael came down, wildly enthused by what she had seen, we went to talk to Dorje about getting to Kyunglung, finally persuading him to return to the green area to negotiate for horses. We climbed into the Land Rover, drove to the first house and hailed a man with a number of missing teeth but a pleasant manner. At the end of a long conversation we had hired either two or three horses and the man to take us to the river. If the river was fordable we would go on to Kyunglung.

As a lagniappe we got to see the inside of the man's house when he offered Dorje and Tenzin, our driver, a drink, possibly fermented mare's milk since it was white. The windowless house had a dirt floor, a cylindrical stove with a pipe going through the roof. There was a bedroll, dishes and cooking utensils, a spare life.

We came back to our beautiful campsite, the green meadow dotted with yellow and pink flowers beside the river. Two young women, Tuti and Kapa, hitchhikers on their way to Lhasa, whom our men had picked up in Tirthapuri, had made a yak dung fire in which they cooked potatoes. We all sat about having a good time eating, lounging and joking. Sonam was flirting with the girls and I accused him of it. Then I had to explain what it is to flirt. They all thought it hilarious and true. But with evening, a demon wind arrived sending us into tents, the girls into the back of the truck, the men into the Land Rover. There was flirting but nothing more. Kapa saw to that.

The horseman, Sawa, arrived at 9:00 but we were disorganized until 10:30. We started among heavily eroded tufa hills, climbing through sandy soil seeing hares and once a fat bellied lizard. The horses were docile but stubborn. Following the Tibetan dictum, "A gentleman rides his horse uphill but walks him down," we rode up and led down.

Riding toward elusive Kyunglung.

We climbed from a plateau to a pass leading to a second plateau. Behind us, around the first plateau, we saw badland shapes, beyond green and red mineral streaked mountains, while behind those deep colors stretched the Himalayas white arms.

The mineral colored hills.

We ascended ridge after ridge. The horses, stopping to heave, were as breathless as I had been on the trail to Drölma La.

My horse, Buster, as I decided to call him after looking and finding he was definitely male, considered the best strategy was to stand permanently. I would then flail him with heels and slap his neck with the lead. Sometimes he would start as if waking from a sleep. The horses snorted at the dust climbing to the last pass. We crossed a mesa, stopping at the cliff edge.

Sawa seemed to consider the trip finished but we had brought no water and he had only a small container full. Below I could see green meadows by the river, across which we supposed was Kyunglung, our destination. A half hour of talking, working with the phrase book, got

Sawa to go down. I suspect he knew all along what we wanted but had to be talked into it.

It was an unnerving trip down. Sawa took Rachael's reins and the packhorse leaving me to negotiate Buster who, quite sensibly, was terrified from time to time. Having to negotiate my feet on a narrow path, a twisting channel of slipping stones, while calculating the appropriate distance between Buster and me, was exhausting.

I would misgauge the distance from time to time to find Buster's nose in my rump. There were narrow passages between boulders or only a foot of path on a sheer edge. Buster invariably baulked at these places. I quite understood.

Cliffs and hills slippery with loose stones.

It was a nerve wracking, exhausting descent; we camped on the green banks of the Sutlej. Behind us rose cliffs pocked with caves that had obviously once been inhabited. It was also obvious we were not going to cross the river to Kyunglung. The Sutlej ran swiftly and high on its banks. But it had been a good adventure to get this far.

The next morning I asked Sawa, with phrasebook in hand, if there was an easier path back since the thought of going up that path was more than I could face. He said yes and we took off along a gentler path that rose slowly, gradually to the first barren pass. It was brown country, dusty, sandy, liberally sprinkled with loose stones. It took us to a mesa from which we could look down on the plain below. What vegetation there was clung low against the earth. Hares, short-eared, were not particularly alarmed at our presence. I loved watching them lope away with a little bounce. It was a beautiful, if tiring ride. We had changed horses. I rode Milady, as I called her. She needed a good deal of encouragement to rise above an extremely slow walk. Back in my tent by the Sutlej I found I had a series of yellow-brown bruises on the inside of my thighs from the rawhide knots that keep the stirrups in place.

In the afternoon we went up to the meditation cave. The abbot guided us about. Not only was it a steep climb but once in the structure ceilings were low and without constant caution you bumped your head. It was a spectacular view down to our camp and the river. The monk gave us rich butter tea, which we needed. We took pictures of him and the chapel.

The abbot/doctor in the meditation cave at Guragem.

From it one looked down on the Bön temples. It is filled with pictures of past and present prelates, one with Chinese officials, a prayer wheel, one old one of yak skin, and paints for dying yak butter statues. He explained how the written prayers were folded into the wheel so that when you turned it, counter clockwise, of course, since it is a Bön prayer wheel, the prayers still read forwards. The chapel itself is a hodgepodge of images, most less than six inches high, many enclosed in prayer boxes draped with necklaces of glass, silver, turquoise, amber and coral. The statues are on silver pedestals decorated with coral and turquoise. The boxes, the *kos*, are exquisitely ornate in gold and silver. There is such a plethora of images before one that it is impossible to absorb, but even here there were slogan banners in Chinese.

The view down to the Sutlej from the cliff side meditation cave.

He, the abbot, was leaving in the morning to do bardo for a dead parishioner but pilgrims arrived whom he had to spend time with. The next day we saw him, a swirl of red robes, peddling his bicycle, the front basket filled with necessities for the bardo. We left too, continuing on the road to western Tibet.

Obviously, doing the *khora* had not yet changed me enough to consistently alter my attitudes or behavior toward Rachael. But I was aware both were wrong and needed to change. I didn't try to justify my actions.

On our return trip to Lhasa weeks later we again stayed at the road mender's house. This time he was home. He had a prosperous life running a general store, a four-bed hotel, where we stayed, or renting a room in his house. He had several cows and his wife a lettuce patch. They had a cassette player with flashing lights and a collection of silver edged and covered wood bowls. This time we had the afternoon off. Not surprisingly we went our separate ways. Rachael walked to the village. I wandered down the road with nothing specific in mind, toward some black, yak hair tents, despite the dogs and yaks about them. I stopped to watch some nomads heave a mysterious but heavy parcel onto a wooden cart.

A cart being loaded on the road near nomad tents.

As I neared the tents a woman popped out of one, waving me in. I gestured my fear of the dogs. She threw stones at them.

It was not a super tent. By this time on our western journey we had seen both ordinary tents and one out of *Good Housekeeping* with a floor of river stones, chests and rolled rugs around the perimeter blocking the wind, an impeccably neat fireplace, a beautifully appointed altar and sheep yogurt in a sheep's intestine for sale, which was why we had come to the tent. It was a spectacularly tidy tent with a mistress equal to it in her fine brown chuba and golden yellow, silk blouse.

Here the housekeeping was sloppy, soiled dishes lying about, a dirt floor, few possessions lining the inside of the tent.

But the two women made me welcome. One washed a cup for me, drying it with toilet paper, while the other heated up butter tea.

One was chatty, bright-eyed, vivacious. The other reserved with an aura of thoughtful intelligence. I was delighted just to sit. A nicely dressed woman came in. When I said "Tashidelay," she did not respond. I looked at my two new friends. They motioned with fingers to heads that she was not all there. Meanwhile the butter tea was heating.

I slurped down six cups, emitting a sigh of satisfaction that Chatty found amusing. I was most grateful. They also gave me some soft cheese that was delicious.

Chatty asked in motions if I would take her picture. I agreed but wanted to have their address to send it to them. We were just working this out in pantomime when there was an animal ruckus outside followed by human yelling. They shot out of the tent.

I stayed, inspecting my surroundings. There were various pots and pans, a man's watch of the kind that breaks in three days and a new man's hat with fur lined ear flaps on top of one of the bed rolls at the edge of the tent. Because the smoke was stinging my eyes, I went to look out of the tent, which was fun because you stand at the opening with the tent surrounding you like a heavy skirt.

Looking out of the tent flap at the meadow where yaks graze.

I could not tell what had caused the trouble but watched a dog baiting a yak that lowered his head to charge him. The dog backed off but in a minute returned to nip the knees of the yak.

Serious returned and we sat quietly content. Noticing that the smoke bothered me, she closed the tent flap. This caused the smoke to go straight up to the hole in the tent roof. Chatty returned and we resumed our camera discussion. Serious understood what I was trying to communicate and motioned that she had no address, an interesting and absolutely alien concept, although that's the essence of being a nomad, no address.

I took their pictures, sat a bit longer, and then rose to leave. Serious made gestures asking where I was sleeping, when I would leave, which direction I would go in. I answered as best I could. It was a soul meeting for us. If I had just met Chatty, it would have been pleasant; but something happened between Serious and me without our trying, a recognition of each other.

My nomad friend in her tent.

The next day as we drove round the bend by the tents, she was there, waving at the flap of her black tent. I reached out the window to return the salute.

I did not tell Rachael when she asked what I had done that afternoon of my tent adventure, just saying I had walked along the road. She didn't tell me what she did either. But I didn't want to be accused of leaving her behind while I had an adventure and perhaps she had an adventure of her own. Also I didn't want to one up her—see what I did while you did nothing. I was trying but my balance of temper, grudge and general negativity on a grand scale was precarious under the stress of altitude.

Later in the journey, I was disappointed when I yelled at Dorje because he tried to curtail our trip, a frequent maneuver since drivers and guides often schedule themselves with no time between trips.

The idea of change as part of the pilgrimage had become central to me, not that I didn't think of Aunt Liz, but the emphasis was moving away from mourning. The goal of the pilgrimage was beginning to become centered on who I wanted to become, choices I should make in order to change from a fearful, angry, ungenerous person, to someone more open, available to other people, more ready to absorb what I learned from travels and life. I had not lived up to my model, Sonam, whom I saw briefly when we returned to Lhasa, but I knew that I could now focus on my fears triggering my anger; try to cultivate awareness of others to become generous. If I was constantly self-centered, I would not even be aware of an opportunity to be generous.

When I told Sonam how difficult it was to retain my good humor on the trip and treat Rachael well, she smiled at me and said, "Do you know that we believe that everyone has at one time been our sister, our mother, our aunt, our brother, our father. Think of Rachael as your beloved aunt." Good advice but not easy to follow. However, trying to think of others, as part of one's family seemed a good exercise. The more distant I feel someone is from me, the easier it is to ignore them. I once heard Professor Thurman at Columbia University tell in a lecture of trying to think of Donald Rumsfeld as having been his grandmother. I don't know how successful he was at this enterprise.

Although unhappy at my failures on this trip to behave the way I would have liked to, I was also elated knowing I was not in a closed space but in a vast landscape in which I could construct whatever I wished, but there was no doubt that that construction, like the many temples that Milarepa built under Marpa's command, in penitence for murdering his relatives, would be done only with hard and persistent labor.

PART VI

2002, The Year Of The Water Horse, Acquiring Credit For Twelve Circumambulations For The Exertion Of One.

Rachael emailed me after New Years 2002 asking if I wanted to go to Kailash that summer for Saga Dawa, the anniversary of the Buddha's Enlightenment. It's a moveable feast falling on the full moon of the fourth lunar month and, as I have mentioned, gives you credit for twelve circumambulations when you only circle the mountain once.

I love these tricky little short cuts and dodges that religions come up with. An Orthodox Jew may travel on the Sabbath if he puts a pot of water under his seat since it is only permitted to travel over water on that holy day. Obviously one cannot get off a boat in the middle of an ocean in observance of the Sabbath. This practice seems to flout logic. An all-seeing, all-knowing god can be tricked by putting a pot of water under your train seat?

Another one. When the Nepalese, under Bahador Shah in 1789 attacked Tibet their triumphs in enemy territory meant that their supply lines became dangerously attenuated. Bahador told his generals to have the men eat yak to solve the problem. The men refused, saying that the yak was a form of cow and since they were Hindus they could not eat cows. Bahador going to the chief Hindu prelate in Kathmandu ordered him to proclaim that a yak was not a cow but a deer, which he did. The soldiers then ate yak meat.

It has been suggested the Tibetan twelve-for-one exemption probably lies with an abbot or other cleric who had neither the time nor the interest in doing repeated circumambulations of Kailash. Circumambulating in the Year of the Water Horse, he designated that year for the crash course circumambulation.

Friends asked, "Why travel again with Rachael? You two didn't do that well last time." Under the conditions of Tibet I would snap at my best beloved and for a trip of this arduousness you take the companions you can get. Then there was my need, my hunger, to return to Tibet. Companions, good or bad, were not as important as my desire to walk the *khora* again. I thought ruefully that if I didn't spend time with people at close quarters, how would I lose my fear of them? Also this appeared to be another spiritual opportunity to change my behavior.

Once again I didn't think about the dynamic of temper due to lack of oxygen, nor about what might be the psychological consequences of mixing Rachael and me in with the unknown ingredients of a couple of men which might make things better but might make them worse.

Rachael arranged our group's trip with a Nepali agent she had used before, Bikram, who provided Sherpas—this term designates either a particular tribe or any Nepali tribal men that accompany a trekking group—tents, a cook and made arrangements, through a Chinese agent, for the necessary Chinese permits.

She had done some research, finding sites that sounded interesting— Tsaparang, Tholing, Kyunglung, Shalu, Chung Riwoche and the Khorja Monastery. Some I knew and had been to on my first trip to

Kailash, Tsaparang and Tholing, and others when Rachael and I traveled together on the last trip. The complex of caves at Kyunglung, we had attempted, but had found that there was no way to cross the river, there being no bridge. Since it was spring, the river was in spate due to the amount of glacial melt at that time of year making it impossible to ford. Shalu was a monastery I had been to on my first Kailash trip.

However, the last two I had to look up in Victor Chan because, not only hadn't I seen them, I had never heard of them. She wanted to go to Chung Riwoche which Chan describes as a temple similar in design to the wedding cake of the Kumbum at Gyantze. Its distinctive feature is its statues which are still intact, while the ones at the Kumbum were all destroyed during the Cultural Revolution and have been replaced by modern ones of which Chan disapproves. It is certainly true that they are gaudy. In the same town is Tangton Gyalpo's suspension bridge of iron links. We would also go to the Khorja Monastery, a Sakya institution not far from Darchen outside of Parang, a town on the Nepali border.

We would attend Saga Dawa, but then leave the Kailash area to explore for a week, returning when the path would be less crowded with pilgrims who had come to the festival.

While not as cheap as my solo trips, it sounded much more comfortable. Bringing our own sleeping bags, down jackets, and trekking poles, we would enter Tibet through Nepal, which I hadn't done since my first trip in 1992. But we would fly from Kathmandu to Lhasa, not go by bus as I had on that first trip. We would not have to supply our own food or cook it. Of course, I wanted to go. I was also looking forward to having another visit with Sonam.

Meeting in Kathmandu, the group consisted of Rachael, me, Tom, a thin, precise, man retired from a cashmere firm in Scotland, and a painter, Alex, who possessed a laugh which caused all in his vicinity to crane their necks to check out where that big noise was coming from. I wondered how we would feel about each other two weeks into the trip.

Due to food preferences we broke naturally into two groups: Alex and I who ate almost anything and liked chilies, Tom and Rachael who preferred familiar things without chilies.

Nepal was at that time in the midst of a conflict verging on civil war between, at first, the elected government, but that in 2005 was dismissed by King Gyanendra, and the Maoists. Although terrible things were happening in the countryside—a friend who was working for an NGO teaching children, was relocated from western Nepal when, in the village next door, an official bled to death having had his arms cut off by Maoist guerillas in his front yard—but Kathmandu was largely undisturbed by the Maoists who were operating in the countryside.

The four of us met with Bikram in his Kathmandu office. I immediately liked and trusted him. He had also arranged for us to meet with the Chinese agent responsible for all of our permits. Bikram struck me as straight forward, rather hearty, tolerant and good humored. On the other hand the Chinese agent I thought sly and slithery. A small, wiry man in glasses, he looked at the floor all through the meeting, never making eye contact with any of us as we talked.

Bikram had told us to ask any questions we wanted at this meeting. I was interested that Tom arrived with a written list. It seemed to me this suggested that he wanted to be in control in a situation where one was unlikely to be at the switchboard. A number of his questions had to do with food. He wanted to be sure that we would have meat every day. While I sympathized with this desire, having an overwhelming craving for protein on these treks, it seemed to me inevitable that there would be meatless days. I can't say that I consider the little Vienna cocktail sausages out of a can I have had for dinner on one trek as meat.

The next morning we were driven from the Kathmandu Guest House to the airport where we stood guard over the heaps of our personal luggage against queue jumpers, a species that is indigenous to the Kathmandu airport, until everything had been weighed and labeled.

Then we went upstairs where, Alex and I, having taken to each other immediately, had tea and Pringles for breakfast while we waited for our flight to be announced. This snack was a good thing since China Southwest Airlines had cut back on its food. They served us a roll and a chocolate wafer bar that tasted like chocolate flavored dust.

At the new Lhasa airport, clean, filled with light and tapestry rugs woven with mountains, at that time four hours outside of town, we found ourselves mummy-wound with red tape going though line after line for baggage inspection, baggage X-ray, customs forms in triplicate and then passport inspection and immigration forms, also in triplicate. As we exited, shaking loose from the last mortal coil of bureaucratic tape, our guide, Thubten, a cheery, plump young man who immediately told us, with great excitement that his wife was expecting their first baby, met us. Our lanky truck driver, a Tibetan Abe Lincoln, named Jamyang, wore, to our amazement, an ancient Western suit of heavy, slightly shaggy from years of wear, brown wool, short in the sleeves so that his knobby wrist bones were evident. It was the one time he wore the suit; he must have felt it was the appropriate dress in which to formally welcome us. We were to find that Jamyang had hidden depths. Our four-wheel driver wasn't there, foreshadowing our future with him. Bikram, acting as our *sirdar*, our trek organizer, would come overland from Nepal, meeting us in Shigatze with the truck full of supplies, tents, the cook, the cook's assistant and another Sherpa to give general help.

I was exhilarated by the familiar drive to Lhasa; the very familiarity was cause for happiness. Snow streaked the high mountains. The fields on either side of the road, moist and dark as plum cake were already plowed.

Yaks plowing in their red pompoms and bells.

There were great herds of sheep crossing the road and huge convoys of army trucks carrying supplies and men, who looked in their teens. Thubten, when I asked, told me you have to be eighteen to be in the Chinese army.

We stopped at the roadside Buddha on the cliff-face, which this year was faded. He had not been repainted yet with his glistening orange and blue.

Cliff side Buddha in need of repainting.

As on the last trip, a nomad stood opposite with two elegantly saddled yaks for any who might want to ride or take a picture. We gave him no custom.

As we entered Lhasa we passed huge complexes of Chinese buildings before whose gates, in sun, wind and dust, uniformed guards stood at attention on platforms barely larger than their feet. There were also from time to time large, elaborately grandiose concrete gateways with nothing beyond them signaling a future project. That contrast between the ostentatious gate arch and the barren, arid Tibetan land beyond was an iconic image of Chinese imperialism. Once on Beijing St., formerly called Happiness St., more changes appeared.

There was a glitzy, new Post Hotel near the main post office and stores selling Chinese jewelry, testifying to the increasing number of Chinese immigrants. Opposite the Tashi One restaurant, old Tibetan buildings were being knocked down. Chinese and Americans have in common a lack of admiration for the old, feeling everything must be modern, even if that means ugly.

We were greeted at our hotel, the Shingbala, on a side street near the Jokhang, by our female, Chinese agent in a severe brown, 1950's suit, well tailored and not shaggy from wear like Jamyang's. The parking lot in front of the entrance was strung with Chinese red lanterns giving the entrance a festive air. She took our passports, showed us the restaurants in the hotel and departed without a smile. There was a grimness about her that recalled the floor concierges who ruled the old Soviet hotel corridors.

The contrast with Thubten's warm, personal welcome was stunning. One of the differences between Chinese and Tibetans is that Chinese are often earnest and wooden faced; smiling at strangers is not a cultural habit. Tibetans smile easily and often, making Westerners feel at ease.

The hotel was clean, had plenty of hot water, good toilet paper and real wall-to-wall carpeting instead of the customary red felt of many Chinese hotels. No messages about smoking or paying for furniture were on the walls or in folders on the desk. Nothing was the matter except that it was Chinese in both its ownership and ambience meaning it was efficient, but cold and cheerless. We wanted a Tibetan hotel with Tibetan atmosphere, but it hadn't occurred to any of us to ask Bikram to put us in a Tibetan hotel. We felt guilty staying in a Chinese hotel.

The twinge of guilt, however, did not, at least for Alex and me, seem to extend to our choice of restaurants and food. We ate superb twice-cooked Sichuan pork and chicken with ginger and honey at the hotel's Chinese restaurant. A friend has said, "The Chinese cook best; Tibetans pray best." Those statements make an excellent demarcation between Chinese and Tibetan but also draw a neat line between *samsara*, this ephemeral, apparently real world and *nirvana*, the world of the spirit.

We found out, after we had eaten, that our dinner at this particular restaurant was not included on our plan. The menu offered sea slugs and ostrich at 12,000 feet. We discussed where people could be raising ostriches in China. Alex's gargantuan laugh attracted the attention of Tibetans at two tables near by. Their presence made us feel less guilty about eating in a Chinese restaurant. They kept turning to look at him when his laugh burst out. They obviously admired it.

When I told Alex about the nose problems we would encounter at higher altitude, he countered by telling how as a young man, thoughtlessly entering a London party with finger in nostril, he was greeted by his hostess demanding, hand out, palm up, "Put it right there, this instant."

In enjoying Alex's company I was feeling a bit envious of his young wife. "Why," I thought, "can't I find someone like this." I have lived long enough to know that the problem is not "men" but my choices. There is absolutely nothing wrong with men. They are fine. I am the problem. Because I quite automatically choose what I know, the familiar, not the healthy, not the grown up, I always choose a variation on my father.

I had had no idea that my father was an alcoholic until my mother, in tears one day, when I was teetering on the cusp of adolescence at thirteen, had told me. Days before she had discovered his cache of bottles in the chicken coop. She explained to me she might divorce him and sitting in the basement, in the sweet hot smell of ironed linen, at the mangle, an ironing instrument used for pressing sheets and men's shirts, she wiped her eyes and asked, "If I decide to leave him, will you want to come with me or to stay with him?"

She was really distraught but the question landed splat, like a half cup of hot lava burped out of a volcano smack into the middle of my little pubescent life. I didn't like or trust her but I knew very well that my father was even more untrustworthy. I went for a walk, which did not help at all. Thankfully I never had to choose. I am very grateful for that, although, many years later, after my mother's death, he did end up living with me.

Once she knew that he was an alcoholic she suggested, having read, as had the entire American world, Jack Alexander's article in the *Saturday Evening Post*, that he go to AA, then a burgeoning institution. He would not go being convinced of several misconceptions, primarily that a real man did everything by himself without any help, ever. Absolute self-sufficiency was his code. This, while not an unusual male attitude anywhere, is in the U.S. a cultural ideal, sanctified by Ralph Waldo Emerson as propounded in his essay, "Self-Reliance." It has filtered down into popular culture through such dubious icons as John Wayne and the Marlboro man. He certainly didn't believe in the idea that "No man is an island entire unto himself," that John Donne proposed. Also since my father was socially inept, as are many alcoholics—too friendly with a drink and chilly without one—I suspect he was terrified at the idea of joining a group.

I may poke fun, but one of my thoughts while being driven to my first AA meeting was that it probably wouldn't work because there were other people in it. They would be cliquey, mean and spiteful. My fear of people, inherited from him, or perhaps just a side effect of my alcoholism, surfaced immediately at the thought of joining a group.

On the other hand, my mother may not have been entirely enthusiastic about AA, viewing it from another perspective. Who would populate those meetings? Bowery bums? Déclassé outsiders? Would there be women? Would those women be after her husband? What if the neighbors found out he was going to AA? Would people look at her differently, would she be less middle class if her husband was known to be an alcoholic? So she may not have pushed him very hard.

But she had no idea, since she never read anything about alcoholism, except the Alexander article, what she was up against. Fighting a brontosaurus with a hatpin, she simply couldn't comprehend that he was not able to control his drinking. She thought he wasn't trying hard enough, that he was weak willed. She could not grasp the utterly alien idea that he could not have "A" drink, since "A" drink set off a chain reaction of obsession ending in his passing out.

Her solution was to control his drinking for him since he couldn't do it himself. She allowed him to drink in the cordoned off area of the weekends. How he must have longed for the weekends! When they went to Europe they always had a bottle of wine with their meal. I have her letters praising the wines they drank in France and Italy. Since one drink kicks off the addiction, those dinners with two or three genteel glasses of wine must have been pure hell for him, a very refined torture.

At thirteen, however, my problem was that I had no real idea of what was meant by the word alcoholism. I had noticed throughout my childhood, alterations in his emotional weather. He was often angry and unapproachable. Suddenly his climate would shift to warmth bordering on a display of affection, and he would become wildly talkative. Since he was a classic, silent Swede these times were always astonishing, as though after months of dark, somber weather, the sun shone blindingly on a snowscape. I didn't know if I had done something right or wrong. Of course, I didn't know that I had nothing to do with it at all. It was the genie stirring up his magic in the bottle.

On those dark days my mother would use me, a little apologetically, as an emissary.

"Would you ask your father, he's in the basement, if he could come fix the toaster? The lever won't stay down. If I ask him he'll yell at me. He won't yell at you."

And no, he didn't yell at me but his words would come out like black, cold, sharp-edged, clinkers of coal. My father lived in dooms of gloom. I suspect that his doom echoed with voices telling him how inadequate he was, how he never had a chance because he hadn't gone to a university; how everyone was against him.

He had graduated from Pratt in Brooklyn when it was a technical school, not yet an institute and had not yet acquired its strong reputation. If some man at a Westchester cocktail party innocently asked what university he went to, or worse, what his fraternity was, my father, struck dumb, shrank into himself and had another drink. He was convinced that the people who "made it" were actually all frauds, phonies, just "Personality Boys" who had no substance. The successful were in my father's mind corrupt. To be successful was to be immoral.

It never occurred to him that what he had accomplished was extraordinary. He came from a Swedish-Danish immigrant family who, discovering that he had a talent for drawing—at eight he could draw a horse few trained artists could improve on—could not imagine that such a talent was worth anything. For his family it was just an aberrant factor in his character. He had to seek out his own education and pay for it because to them an education beyond high school was not just a luxury for the rich but something a bit incomprehensible. There was fear around the idea of education. It would change your child into someone alien to you, perhaps make him or her superior to you so that they would no longer be able to love and respect you.

He worked for all the important architects in New York from the 1930's to the 1970's—Cram to I.M. Pei. But faced with a fraternity member or university graduate he metamorphosed himself into particularly fine grade of dust before his imagined image of their imposing chariot wheels.

Another possible factor is that he was raised in the Baptist faith, a tenant of which is that the more successful you become the more distance is created between you and God, I suppose because you are apt to lose your gratitude toward your creator, thinking yourself solely responsible for your success.

Whatever was the case these inadequacies or beliefs fueled his drinking. Unfortunately, his attitudes toward the successful, toward success itself, I inherited along with his alcoholism. If you want to make a psychological problem worse drinking and drugging will not only magnify it but will give it a few new twists and contortions that were not in the original. My father rarely, or maybe never spoke to me about his attitudes toward success, although his feelings about successful people were apparent to me. But one of the things I have discovered is that the unsaid parental message, like high-grade fly paper, adheres to your psyche with greater tenacity than the openly declared one which you can fight off because you are aware of its existence.

After dinner with Alex, I walked to Sonam's shop, passing the Yak where I had stayed on my first trip to Tibet. As I entered the shop young Pema gasped in surprise, put her arms around me, and said, while holding me gently, "Sonam died ten months ago." I felt as though I had slammed my head into a low ceiling beam.

She told me Sonam had been able to go to the United States for tests and had been hospitalized there. Then she had returned to Lhasa where she was again hospitalized. Finally they sent her home, putting her on, what sounded to me like a morphine drip. I asked what she died of, a Western question; Pema gave me the impatient Buddhist look, meaning, "Why ask that?" Sonam had died of stomach cancer.

Buddhists consider the Western preoccupation with the cause of death an absurdity. What is the point; the person is dead.

Resting my head on Pema's shoulder as we continued to hug, a kaleidoscope of thoughts, memories, and visions streamed through my head. I had lost a woman I loved. I saw her sitting behind the curtain in her shop, with her little straw, Uigher hat on her lap, twisting its white string ties around her fingers or rocking back and forth with the terrible pain of her laughter, as she told me how she had survived the invasion and then the occupation of Tibet, the Cultural Revolution, three successive cultural traumas in thirty years of Tibet's history. I suddenly realized, quite inconsequentially, that never had I seen her in a Lhasa Lady's hat with a broad brim and a veil.

Pema and I sat, as Sonam and I had, behind the curtain where the sewing machine and bolts of fabric were kept. Sonam was in our silence. Pema offered me the usual fragrant jasmine tea.

She broke the silence, "Did you know about her jewelry?"

"I know the cadre broke her pearl necklace," I responded.

"No, I mean her traditional jewelry."

"No, I didn't know that she was able to protect that from the Chinese."

"Yes, she buried it near a house her family had owned out in the country which was destroyed by the Red Guards during the Cultural Revolution. When Mao died and her husband returned they went out to the house, dug the jewelry up and brought it back to Lhasa."

"How lucky her daughter is to have that as an inheritance.

"Yes, her daughter has it now but once, about three years ago there was a woman, an English woman who was traveling with a German man. They wanted to get married and they wanted it to be a Tibetan ceremony. They had been together, having met somewhere on their trip, for a year. She came into the shop because she wanted us to make a *chuba* for her to be married in.

"When Sonam realized that the woman was getting married in the *chuba* we were making she took the couple to the Jokhang to meet the abbot who arranged the wedding. Then she offered to lend the woman her wedding jewelry.

"On the day of the wedding she dressed the English woman as a Tibetan bride and they walked, the bride, the man. What do you call him?"

"The groom."

"The groom, their friends, all walked to the Jokhang together. Everyone from the shop followed behind them. It was a wonderful wedding. We had good fun."

I hugged Pema again, telling her I would be back before we left on our trip to Kailash. That story was for me the epitome of Sonam. Give. Give to strangers. Cast your bread upon the waters. It is not that there is enough so, therefore, it is all right to give, but because you give there is enough.

As I walked back to our very Chinese hotel I thought of how much of Sonam's story I did not know. I had no idea how she and her husband had come to start their *chuba* shop. I did know she had grandchildren whose education she worried about, and a very bright daughter in school on a scholarship in the United States. But my relationship had been exclusively with her. What was most important to me was that she had told me her story because she wanted it to live. I too want it to live beyond the confines of Tibet. But I had lost not just a friend; I had lost my spiritual lodestone who had helped to keep my compass true.

I stopped by the Internet shop where Alex was emailing, serenaded by explosions and gunfire, among Tibetans hunched over all kinds of digital games, to tell him the news. He gave me a hug. When I arrived at the hotel I went up to Rachael's room and told her. She gave me a hug as well, but I was overwhelmed by Sonam's death, with no idea how to cope, since I had imagined us seeing each other every few years, growing old on opposite sides of the globe. Rachael, recognizing I was lost in the labyrinth of my grief, wisely suggested I talk to Thubten about the possibility of some sort of ceremony.

He proposed we go to the Jokhang, give a money offering, asking the monks to pray for a good reincarnation for her or, if already reincarnated, for a good life. This gave me a focus and I asked him to arrange the ceremony for us.

The haze of juniper incense obscures the front of the Jokhang.

Rachael and I each bought three *khatas*, offering scarves, as Thubten instructed, and went into the Jokhang that evening, entering the majestic two-story inner court, an atrium, which contains the largest statues. In this enclosure, the red robed monks in long rows chant, many doing the wonderful, growly, deep-throat singing.

Towering over us was the sixteen-foot statue of Guru Rinpoche, who started the renaissance of Buddhism in Tibet in the 8th century, forcing Bön deities to protect Buddhists and Buddhism. He has piercing eyes and a rippling black moustache.

Next to him is a thirteen-foot gold and copper Chenresi, the deity of compassion, with eleven faces whose thousand hands reach out to suffering beings. The Dalai Lama is the *tulku* of Chenresi, known in India as Avalokiteshvara (try saying that ten times very quickly), and in China as Kuan-Yin. Avalokiteshvara and Kuan-Yin float between the sexes, sometimes being portrayed as male and at other times as female. Being the *tulku* means, as I understand, that the Dali Lama embodies the idea of Chenresi, the ideal of compassion. Tibetan spiritual ideas are frequently alien to the Western mind, the spiritual vocabulary far more intricate than in the West and often impossible to translate.

The air was heavy with the odor of yak butter lamps burning in the chapels surrounding this enclosure. The monks filed in, leaving their sandals outside the enclosure in little cupboards around the perimeter of the chanting area. They settled onto benches, arranging their robes around them, teasing their companions, throwing bits of paper and laughing, boys in a schoolroom before the teacher arrives. Then they composed themselves with the arrival of the senior monks, their chanting accompanied by the rattle of small drums, the thump of a big drum or the clash of cymbals. Among normal tenors and baritones sounded the big, dark swell of deep-throat singers, the sleek back of a whale rising and submerging in the sea. I stared up at the cornice encircling the court. In the evening gloom, the grinning row of white, wooden, snow lion figures, with cheerful, denture smiles had a Disney quality.

We bowed to Guru Rinpoche to Chenresi and sat a little self-consciously. While we waited, two men distributed money to individual monks giving the remainder to the head monk. The monk who was organizing the blessings signaled to us; we went up and down the red robed rows of monks handing out money under the eyes of Chenresi and Guru Rinpoche. Rachael had no money left, while I ended up with a fist full.

I felt incredibly nervous during all of this, fearing I would commit some awful solecism in the middle of the ceremony. The head monk looked at what I handed him with surprise; apparently I should have given more money to the individual monks. This made me even more nervous.

Thubten herded us around the periphery of the enclosure, past chapels glimmering with butter lamps, some closed by massive curtains of linked steel rings, the chainmail a giant might wear. Tibetans darted about with plastic bags of yak butter spooning offerings into lamps. Others dug into their woven plastic bags filled with *tsampa* scooping out the flour and depositing it in basins placed near figures and paintings as offerings and for the use of the monks.

Thubten had had Sonam's name inscribed in gold on a scarlet strip of paper. He led us to the Jowo Sakyamuni Chapel, the holy of holies in the Jokhang, handing me the scrap of paper with the curling Tibetan script on it, that felt like my last contact with Sonam. Although I hadn't written it, it seemed to be my last letter to Sonam.

The doorway to the chapel is a great, golden mouth of light, because of the number of butter lamps burning within and the darkness of the outer corridor. The Jowo is a statue of the Buddha purportedly made during his lifetime, part of Princess Wencheng's dowry, the Chinese Emperor's daughter who married the first historical king of Tibet, Songtsen Gampo.

The image sits on a platform framed by writhing silver dragons. The heat from the masses of butter-lamps in the chapel was palpable as I stepped in under the arch of the dragons, the smell of yak butter overwhelming. Within the entrance I handed the red slip of paper with Sonam's name in gold to the monk standing with a large bowl in his hands. Above gleamed a silver sphere, a centuries old gift to the temple from a descendant of Genghis Khan.

The monk was carefully burning the names that were handed to him one by one. I wanted to stop, to stay by him to see her slip of paper ignited, the flame curl around the script of her name, transforming it to a dark figure of smoke, but there was a crush of pilgrims at my back. I had to keep moving, circumambulating the Jowo, climbing the steps to touch my head to his knee padded by many offerings of *khatas*, and laying my own *khata* on it before completing the circle. I was aware of the tall figures that line the outer walls of the chamber, some with benign faces, some fierce, but all protective of fragile humans.

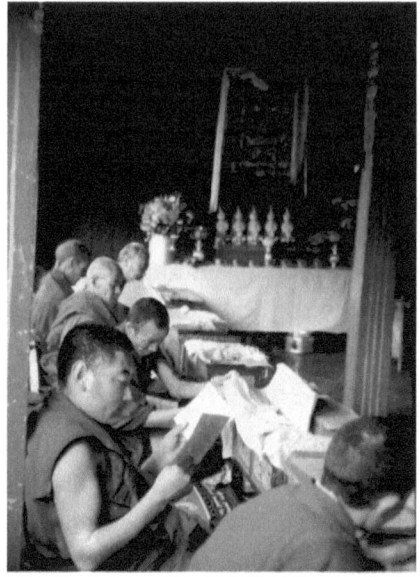

Monks at the Jokhang looking at mantras they will be chanting.

Once outside the chapel I looked back at the Jowo on his plinth. He is five feet high and represents the twelve-year-old Buddha; his impassive, gold face has brilliant blue eyes. Beside me, near four guardians, which according to legend came from the emperor's court in China, an old man, face deeply lined, looked into the chapel, twirling a prayer wheel, its barrel encased in ornate, silver repousse. His gaze, full of love, was focused on the Jowo. Watching him I thought that he would remember when the Jokhang's courtyard was made into a pigsty during the Cultural Revolution and the chapels became offices for cadres. In my mind he was a connection to Sonam and her suffering.

I felt better, a little less rocky and confused, although my throat was sore, tight with unshed tears. She was gone into darkness, into the light of yak butter lamps, into another life but I was left with my dry tears.

Women among rows of butter lamps at the Jokhang.

I hoped in her next life she would have less cause for tears and that if she had them she would be able to shed them with ease.

Thubten took us upstairs to the roof where there was a new souvenir shop.

The roof of the Jokhang with the Potala in the distance.

I sat on a wooden bench. Rachael went off to photograph people prostrating themselves before the temple in the square down below.

Looking down from the Jokhang's roof on the prostrators and their mattresses.

Women were pounding *arka* into the roof of the temple as they sang. "One, two three…." The leader said sharply and they began a new song, a perfect requiem for Sonam.

The golden roofs of the Jokhang.

The Dalai Lama's apartments are kept ready for him in the Jokhang.

Thubten asked me if I would speak English to a small girl. She was Tibetan, about seven years old, accompanied by her grandmother. If you cannot get an education through the usual channels you have to use your imagination. This child's family obviously was doing that very well. I asked her age. She asked me where I came from. It was all the usual rather stilted discourse that one has between people who know neither each other nor each other's language and yet, under grandma's watchful eye, it was also an affirmation of my bond with Tibet, the link I had to it through my friendship with Sonam.

The next morning I gave Pema the *khata* I had worn during the ceremony and told her what we had done.

"I am glad," she said.

I hugged her again and left to join the others who were wedging themselves, their bulbous daypacks, water bottles, and cameras into the car. We were going to be so tightly packed there would be no worrying about who was taking up too much of the seat.

We four left, with Thubten, crammed into the four-wheel drive, through the dramatic Kyi Chu gorge for Shigatze, coming out on a broad plateau between mountain ranges. Farmers plowed fields with yaks or *dzos*, a cross between yak and cow, adorned with red tassels, pompoms, bells and *khatas*. Some yak's horns were elongated with "falsie" extensions. Their dark shaggy bodies, against the pinkish-grey clods in the dry fields, made a fine contrast of texture and color.

Yaks in their finery waiting to plow.

There were a number of cable ferries connecting the riverbanks. Since the road is well above the river, we looked down on the boats laden with carts and trucks holding bouquets of pilgrims in bright colors also headed for Saga Dawa. Tom longed to go on one of these cable ferries but it wasn't possible on this trip. There was a view up stream, surreal in its bleached aridity. A stretch of the river winds through the valley's flat bed, ending in a pale congress of dry mountains of various shapes in delicate pastel shades.

In Shigatze we visited Tashilhunpo's shrines. In the main court I saw hemming the edge of the roof a line of roof pounders making Sonam suddenly present in my day as I remembered her pounding *arka* into roofs in Lhasa.

Roof pounders above the central court of Tashilhunpo ready to begin singing and pounding.

Tashilhunpo in Shigatze. The structure that looks like an outdoor movie screen to the right is a sort of easel on which the huge applique tapestries of the monastery are displayed at festivals.

The main court of Tashilhunpo Monastery in Shigatze.

Rachael's Nepali agent, Bikram, had booked us into digs more modern and elegant than the Orchard Hotel where we had stayed in 1999. Our new hotel was a modern high-rise that gave us an impressive overview of the monastery. I thought that if there were a sky burial I would be able to just stand at the window and watch it.

Rachael and I went to bed early, decorating the bathroom with laundry since this would be our last night in concrete. The next night we would be under canvas. We got to bed fairly early despite two calls, one from Bikram, saying he and the Sherpas had arrived with the truck from Nepal, and one from the hotel manager issuing a preemptory directive to us that we must eat breakfast in the hotel. These breakfasts are invariably composed of cold, dry, plasterboard toast, two hardboiled eggs and instant coffee, the Chinese idea of a Western breakfast. Not terrible, but Thubten's younger brother was working in a restaurant in town where we would be able to get a much better breakfast, which we were looking forward to. We didn't eat in the hotel. I suppose the hotel manager receives a black mark from his superiors and their bean counters when guests don't breakfast in the hotel.

The next morning meeting Bikram, handsome, friendly, with his no nonsense manner, we drove off from Shigatze in high spirits, with our newly arrived Nepali staff, a caravan of one four-wheel drive and one blue Chinese truck steered by Jamyang who had replaced the Nepali driver. The truck was full of supplies, equipment and Sherpas as well as lots of dust.

We were to go to Shalu Monastery, one of Rachael's extras, but the road was closed since they had just resurfaced it with tarmac, which was still soft. They were allowing no one on it until it was "set". This was a disappointment since I had not been to Shalu since my first trip to Kailash in 1995 when I had not known why it was an important place to see. Shalu has on its walls the only large collection of fourteenth century murals in Tibet. My disappointment was not as great as Rachael's. She seemed to take it personally, appearing seriously and visibly upset. However, after a discussion, we went to Narthang, a *gompa* none of us had heard of before, passing donkey carts and in the distance green villages plumed with willow trees.

Low stone mountains showed the edges of thrust where slabs of sedimentary rock were heaved up and twisted sideways.

As Eskimos have many words for snow, Tibetans have a number of words for mountains. In Tibetan low mountains are called *zari*. Peaks are *ri*. *Kangri* means snow peaks. Everest is a *kangri*. Grasslands are *pangri*.

Narthang was a monastery surrounded by stupas, which at one time had been covered with delicately sculpted terracotta tiles. Then came the Cultural Revolution. What remains are the rubble heaps of those stupas, looking like middens, surrounding the new buildings put up after the Cultural Revolution. Old broken roof tiles shimmering with blue glaze, terracotta lotus leaves, broken curves and arabesques that once formed the base of the stupas rest on these middens, their artistry a poignant contrast to the rubble beneath. Flat stones were carved in shallow relief with images of the Buddha, Mahakala, the bull-headed deity, and graceful Green and White Taras, the goddesses who were formed from Buddha's tears.

In 1959, there were, according to one count, 6,259 monasteries, in 1976, at the Cultural Revolution's end 8, today, 1,400. During those ten years of Mao's chaos, statues and other art in gold and silver were often melted down, the metal sent to China. Other objects undoubtedly entered the European and American art, black market.

Narthang was also a publishing center with famous woodblocks used to print the *sutras* as well as the *Jakata Tales of the Buddha,* the stories of the Buddha's previous lives. A few of these woodblocks survived the depredations of the Cultural Revolution and are kept in one of the buildings. As I stood looking at them a Tibetan man in Western clothes but with prayer beads wound around his wrist slipped yuan notes in between the blocks and touched his head in reverence to them. Raising his head from this respectful gesture, he looked at me and asked, "You from where?"

"The United States," I answered.

"You believe?" was his next question.

"I don't know what I believe," I stammered back.

"Me too," he said with a happy smile. "Me too. Like Buddha don't know if god," and he moved on to the next room of relics rescued from the Cultural Revolution.

I looked after him musing on the problem of believing in the unknowable while keeping that thought distinct and pure, uninflitrated by wishful thinking, tradition, fairytales—the unknowable and belief. The idea that you do not have to know in order to believe is a difficult concept.

Our exchange made me think of my father and his unmilitant refusal to believe. His had been a quiet disbelief. In the world I had grown up in the word "atheist" usually meant simply someone who didn't believe in god and by extension someone without any sense of the sacred or of the spirit, and, perhaps also, neither morals nor ethics. Certainly my father had morals and ethics to the point of being moral bound by them, as though he were an ethics weight lifter. But I have come to understand that definition is not necessarily true. The atheist may not believe in god but often what she or he is rejecting is the formality of religion, the elaborate, towering manmade structures superimposed over the simple essence they so often mangle and obliterate with rules, codes, and excellent business policies.

While my mother followed the priestly regulations of that extraordinarily baroque construction called the Catholic Church, fearing Hell, rather as I, as a Ph.D. student, sweated my way through the arcane laws of footnotes, fearing my Ph.D. advisor, she seemed unaware that there was an ineffable something, flayed, fragmented, having difficulty breathing as it smothered under the heap of rules.

Terrified and horrified, as were many women of her time, by the idea of sex she went obsessively from parish to parish in Westchester county trying to find a priest who would not tell her that it was her duty to have sex, if her husband wanted it. Poor thing, she was looking for a loophole and no priest would give it to her. It was her duty to obey the regulations. Religion was simply a rulebook to her.

My father came to religion from a totally different direction. A friend one Thanksgiving gently and with humor questioned my father about his beliefs. I think he was glad to have the turkey to attend to as he struggled to answer what he knew were questions motivated by true interest.

"I just don't like being told by people who don't know any more than I do what to believe, how to believe. They are self-made authorities not real ones. No one "KNOWS," he said emphatically severing a leg from a thigh.

The friend gave him a sympathetic look and said, "I think you belong to the one, true church of Howard Swenson."

I remember being very proud at the honesty and directness of his answer, which to a large extent became my answer. However, my mother told me a story, both funny and interesting in its perspective, that she learned from my Danish grandmother which suggests that my father's antipathy for religion may have started early in life from a different conception.

One Sunday an Important Person came to his Sunday school class and asked condescendingly, "Which of you want to go to Heaven?"

All hands shot up except my father's.

Horrified the teacher and the Important Person asked why he didn't want to go to Heaven.

"Because there's nothing but girls in Heaven. All the angels are girls," my father replied sullenly.

"Why do you think that?"

"Because I've never seen an angel with a moustache," my father answered.

My father, once he was able, grew a moustache and wore one all his life.

But whether my father's opinions of religion were the result of female angels or disbelief, or repulsion at the edifices created by organized religions, I think he would have agreed with the physicist Richard. P. Feynman who wrote:

I don't feel frightened by not knowing things, by being lost in a mysterious universe without having any purpose, which is the way it really is so far as I can tell. It doesn't frighten me.

Leaving Narthang we decided to skip Gyantze this time and head straight to Lhatze. We passed low mountains, deep finger thrusts of erosion in their sides. Two yaks, red tassels dangling from their ears, butted heads in a field, not fiercely, but in a companionable, playful way.

We climbed out of the car to photograph another pair of yaks pulling a harrow a young man was standing on to force it more deeply into the earth. Brocade straps with bells jingled on the necks of the yaks; tassels nodded in their ears. With no command, they stopped at the field's end when he came to try to talk to us.

He admired my Khampa belt of leather pouches with silver trim, bought on the Barkhor. Tom offered it to him jokingly for 10 yuan. After he returned to his team, Rachael had a sudden thought and handed me a postcard of Kailash. Seeing it in my hand, he sprinted back to us with a huge smile. I was sure he thought it was a picture of the Dalai Lama but if he did, he showed no disappointment. He took it from me with both hands and touched it to his forehead.

Small white scars of snow were etched on the mountains. Smelling dust I tied on a white cotton mask bought in Lhasa, but it was too uncomfortable to wear all the time, although I knew it would help keep my nose from drying up.

We stopped in Lhatze; the huge speakers were belching gunfire and explosions as they had the last time we were there. We were delighted with the box lunch our newly acquired cook had made—hard-boiled eggs, small, cold potatoes and cold curried cauliflower—certainly an improvement over the half-cooked macaroni and cheese I made on our last trip, and the dried ramen noodles I'd chomped on during my first trip. While we ate in the car, children and adults came to our windows to sell quartz crystals of all sizes. One grotty tot with snot shimmering on his upper lip begged for food. I gave him an egg. But he and the others became bored with us and left. I don't think he was really hungry. He was just interested in the game of getting something from the foreigners.

Lhatze's white tile store fronts.

Before arriving in Karga, where Rachael and I had eaten at the truckers' restaurant with the yak vertebra as the table's centerpiece on the previous trip, we sighted the turn off leading to one of Rachael's extra sites, Chung Riwoche. It was supposed to be a temple, of the same, tiered architectural variety as the Kumbum in Gyantze, but according to Victor Chan, our ever-reliable authority, its statues had survived the Cultural Revolution and were still intact.

We stopped for a conference of Nepalis and Tibetans. One or possibly two, of our petrol drums had developed leaks. Should we stop or go on? We drove a little further to where a small stream ran through a shallow depression giving the spot some slight protection from the wind. Tibetans and Nepalis, united to stop up the holes in the barrels. Then they raised our dining tent, our individual little yellow tents, and the wonderful toilet tent with its dug out hole to squat over, its center pole being of great assistance in rising from your squat. It is wonderful to see your home grow up magically in an unknown location. I couldn't wait to get into my tent; I was beginning to shiver with cold, and all that was keeping my chilled spirits up was the thought of getting into my down jacket and eating something warm in the dining tent.

The next day, on the road to Chung Riwoche, we saw the mud brick and stone remains of pillars built to hold telegraph lines to a defunct army post. They brought home the fact that there is no wood in this part of Tibet. The lines had been removed and the pillars were slowly disintegrating back into the dust from which they had been made. The post must have been moved to some other part of Tibet.

We passed a massive, mauve boulder to the side of the road with a shrine behind it; prayer flags were draped over them both. Further along the dirt track we maneuvered around a little house-like structure occupying the middle of the road full of *tsatsas*, some painted red. We got out to admire them. I thought of the *tsatsa* Heinrich had given me, which I still have, although I feel guilty about it now that I know we shouldn't have taken them since they were someone else's offering. I think that our action was like a Tibetan wandering into a church, admiring the flowers on the altar and taking them back to her hotel room.

Beyond we drove past a village whose houses sat along the banks of a meandering, narrow stream that came winding its way down a mountain. Its trees were walled in to keep goats and sheep from tearing their bark. In urban areas, Tibetans cut tin cans and put them around trees to protect them but here, not having such luxuries as tin cans, they made dry stonewalls to shield the slender trunks from the always voracious goats and sheep.

Then we entered a badland of odd formations from which stones protruded from the compacted dirt matrix like gigantic mussels attached to piers. This opened up to flat land by the river. At the edge of a town, with a white-washed *chörten* with a gold spire that looked new, we became stuck in a mudlicious puddle. Farmers preparing fields had created it by diverting a stream into the road to form a reservoir until they were ready to release it to irrigate their newly planted furrows. This made it clear that though the road was used by cart, horse and pedestrian traffic, it was not often that a car came along.

It took a half hour to get out. The Land Cruiser driver, Temba, a youngster we later nicknamed Temba the Terrible, when he embezzled our gas money, hit the accelerator churning the wheels wildly in the mud, digging the car deeper. I, being American, and therefore, feeling I knew about and had a kinship with cars, kept telling him to put stones under the back wheels but he certainly was not going to listen to some foreign woman.

Village teenagers tried lifting the car out, while standing up to their knees in the puddle. I was terrified one would slip under the wheels. Finally they did put rocks under the rear wheels but not until Temba had ground the car down into the mud so far that water was within an inch of going up the exhaust pipe. The village teenagers had a good time hauling rocks, vying with each other as to who could haul the biggest and throw it into the puddle, making a great, muddy splash, from which they all sprang back in unison.

While this splashing was in progress, Alex and I visited the *chörten* at the entrance to the village; when we returned the car was clear of the deep puddle. We paid the young men and continued to the next village where we hesitated before yet another puddle. The women who came in from the fields to try to talk to us claimed it was dangerous. Alex selflessly rolled up his trousers, and waded through, finding deep holes. We discussed going forward, daring the puddle, or driving through the newly plowed and harrowed field, or turning back.

Rachael was in tears since this was the second time one of her plans had gone awry, the first having been Shalu. I found myself thoroughly annoyed at her, whether for her tearfulness or for her inability to accept defeat gracefully I am not sure. But worse than that, I found myself feeling smug and superior to her. I was worried at this early sign of my spiritual decomposition.

We all very much wanted to see the temple but Tom, who knew more about plowing than the rest of us, for some reason, said it would be immoral to mess up a field that was ready for planting. The labor of preparing it would have to be done all over again and money would not help repair the damage we would do. We also thought we might be just as likely to get stuck in the soft, newly plowed earth of the field and it seemed likely that in the next village there would be yet another puddle to deal with.

In 2010 I got to Chung Riwoche, although it took a number of trips before Bikram, our Tibet agent and I figured out where it was and how to get there. We drove on a totally different, equally bad, dirt road hair-pinning down curves where the outer verge of the cliff-edge road had collapsed, forming small, but in a car, potentially fatal, landslides of dirt, gravel and stones of all sizes. The driver was not happy but we kept moving, hugging the inside of the tight curves or walking when it was too scary in the car. There had been heavy rains that summer resulting in landslides.

Riwoche, beside the Tsangpo River, was once an important town with several forts. Now it is a scatter of houses with willows. A man came up to my window to ask what condition the road down was in since it is the lifeline to the main road across Tibet.

Although externally not as pretty, or delicate as the Gyantze Kumbum, indeed it has a lumpy look, the temple does have the same, layered structure. Inside, the statues are, as reported by Victor Chan, delicate and graceful. They are small and seem to dance in their postures, very different from the gaudy, static replacements in the Gyantze Kumbum. Gyalpo Tangton whose bridge is outside is represented by a piece of his rustless iron on top of a stone, some small links made from his iron, his shoes—he had small feet—and a picture of him as a wild haired old man, indeed, "The Mad Man of the Empty Land."

On this first attempt to reach Chang Riwoche, having abandoned our objective, we drove back to the main road with Rachael sullen and moody, stopping at a teahouse in Karga to reassemble our forces, reunite with the truck, which we had left behind, and adjust to our defeat at the hand of nature.

The teahouse was inhabited by a pretty waitress with whom a number of truck drivers were flirting and a woman who was strolling around with a sheep's backbone in one hand, a knife in the other cutting off hunks of dried meat. As we drank our tea a young woman came in with her father. She was obviously taking him to Saga Dawa. Both had on brand new Chinese sneakers, although their clothes were worn.

My father had gone to live with his brother after my mother had died but that didn't work because he had disliked his brother's wife and made scathing comments about her taste in furniture. The morning after he had been drunk and taken off his clothes in the middle of their living room his brother, also an alcoholic but not yet that far along the downward path, called me to say my father had to go. I was not surprised having been sure this was going to happen.

My son had just left for college; I was simmering with resentment at having to take in a new child. I talked to my landlord who rented my father the garden apartment in the three-story Brooklyn brownstone I was living in. Some months after he moved in he suggested that he buy me the house. It was a calculated bribe that I would take care of him in exchange for owning the house. This was not necessary. I would have taken care of him anyway, not with kindness or good humor however. I was much too angry with him to do that.

He kept his half-gallon of Smirnoff in the cabinet above the sink. I couldn't comment on that since I was drinking upstairs and fighting hard to stay blind to the fact that I too was an alcoholic. It was not a happy arrangement.

When we went out to dinner at the local Italian restaurant he would rapidly order a succession of double martinis. These threw him into a hysterical, frantic gaiety. Watching his desperate, false happiness wrenched me about like the tail of a child-tormented cat. He would then eat practically nothing. I was terrified he would pass out and I would have to ask the waiters to help me get him into a cab. Then how would I get him out of the cab and down the stairs into his apartment?

But what was really painful was watching him move from being morose to a state of artificial gaiety. In desperation I finally told him that I would not go out to dinner with him if he drank. I never drank with him. I did that alone on my own.

Once he moved into the garden apartment below me, I took him around the neighborhood, introducing him to shops, from Chinese laundry to supermarket. I was not going to take care of him as my mother had. I had a full time job; my son had left for college. I wanted to enjoy my freedom. In actuality this meant being able to drink the way I wanted to. I found he needed constant ego support. He wanted to be told that every decision he made, no matter how small, how banal, was right. I refused to give that reassurance.

As we walked from the Chinese laundry to the dry cleaners I said, "I wish you were a little more content, a little happier."

"Well, then why don't you make me happy?"

"I can't make you happy. Only you can make you happy," I answered cringing at the smugness of my own voice, which sounded to me like that of a particularly self-righteous social worker.

"Don't give me any of that psychological talk," he snarled back. "I've got enough mental trouble."

Watching the young Tibetan woman pour her father's butter tea from the shiny Chinese thermos with its floral decorations, I had a wave of guilt over an argument we had in the supermarket at the check out—I can no longer remember the content—where I found myself shouting at him, "You don't give a damn about what is actually going on. All you care about is surface, appearance, what will the neighbors think. Truth is of no interest to you."

He was desperately embarrassed as he kept trying to hush me, but I was rabid with rage and would not be hushed. I luxuriated in his discomfort; it was my revenge.

When he died I was newly sober. I kept going to meetings and saying, "I know I ought to feel terribly sad about my father's death and grateful that he bought me the house I live in, but all I feel is rage at him because he preferred his bottle to me and because he never protected me from my mother's beatings and abuse."

One day when I was fifteen or sixteen, I had had an argument with my mother of, I'm sure, the sort you have at that age. She had shouted at me, "How dare you talk to me that way. You are impertinent," and slammed me across the face with the back of her hand. In a state of volcanic hate I went off to my room to find that I could move my nose back and forth. She had broken it. I went to my father, showed him how my nose was no longer anchored and said, "I think I ought to go to the hospital and get it set."

"No," he said, "what you should do is not talk to your mother like that."

I realized then that he was afraid of her too, that he would not be able to be my ally.

Once he did support me against my mother. I had received my divorce and was giving myself the treat of a trip to Denmark, my first trip to Europe since I had traveled there with my now ex-husband. I wanted to go to my grandmother's island of Bornholm off the coast of Denmark.

Her love, before she died when I was ten, had been a radiance in my life. I wanted to see if I could find her house on the island as well as visit the castles, archeological sites and museums on the other islands and the peninsula.

My mother, who was in Fargo at the time helping my Aunt Liz move from the family house, which we had sold, to an apartment, called while I was visiting my father in Chappaqua. After he had talked to her, he handed me the phone.

"You have no business going to Denmark. You need to save that money. You're going to be very sorry some day soon that you did this. Who do you think you are, Mrs. Big Bucks? You earn a meager salary and have a son to support. You're irresponsible."

She then put Aunt Liz on the phone. Hesitantly, in a soft voice, Aunt Liz said, "Dear, do you really think you should make this trip?"

It was obvious Mother had bullied Liz into supporting her. Aunt Liz was my rock and the betrayal was too much. I burst into tears, an event rare as Haley's Comet.

Suddenly, my father yanked the phone out of my hand and started yelling, "What are you doing to her? You leave her alone." Then he slammed the receiver down.

I was as amazed as if a tabby cat had suddenly metamorphosed before my eyes into a fanged, charging lion, all claws and wild mane. I was particularly astonished because he had not shown much enthusiasm for my trip to Denmark, making mildly contemptuous remarks about it, asking in a deprecating manner if I was "looking for my roots." He had told me I was wasting my time going to Denmark rather than going back to England or France or Italy where there was a thick impasto of his idea of culture. Yet here he was suddenly intervening, guarding me from my mother's scornful attack. I knew and he knew that he was going to pay for protecting me.

My father had, in his youth, had a period of adventurous travel. After journeying through England and France, he had, with a couple of friends, taken a train through Spain crossing the Gibraltar Strait to Morocco on a ferry going on to Tunis and Algiers. But this was as far as he ventured from Europe returning across the strait to spend a couple of months among the hallowed architectural monuments of

Italy. I suspect his alcoholism and its accompanying fears cut him off from adventure. Even traveling with my mother he was not comfortable. He wanted his own bed, his own house without the possibility of alien surprises.

He was, in his outlook, firmly Eurocentric. My interest in places other than the three or four European countries that had contributed their genius to the architecture he most admired struck him as bizarre. Even Scandinavia was outside the sacred circle. He didn't think there was anything much to see beyond Europe. When my mother returned from her round-the-world trip, with a friend who was the wife of an up-scale travel agent, and showed him slides of temples in Thailand and Nepal, he was repelled. He found them garish and tawdry, crude, the opposite of his beloved, austere, gray Gothic cathedrals, although they, some hundreds of years ago, had once been just as brightly painted.

I too love gray Gothic cathedrals. It is part of my love for him but I was also enraged at him, a deeply imbedded anger that has given me a bitter distrust of men to add to my distrust of my mother. I was furious with him for not being the image of what a "man" should be that I picked up from American culture. Our culture seems to me to be hard on men, forcing them into a narrow concept of manhood, causing them to believe that emotional expression is feminine, and often depriving them of esthetic outlets.

Our vision of what constitutes a "man" may be reflected in the disproportionately large population of gay men in the arts. We consider the arts a slippery slope for heterosexual manhood and therefore many heterosexual men avoid the arts. I don't know, but my father as an artist may have felt pressure from these attitudes. Faulkner had to fight against the Southern idea that writing was a feminine activity. What we would have lost if he hadn't had the strength to fight.

I may have expected my father to be John Wayne. Certainly he had some of the same characteristics—silence and the insistence on self-reliance. Wayne was the beaux ideal male image of my childhood, the man who always won and was always morally right. My father was not, as most of us are not, some one who triumphed, or was successful in a large way. I felt a man should be successful even as I was absorbing his anti-success idea. I am amused now at how I was able to simultaneously believe contradictory ideas, and not even notice it. But how incredibly unfair, however, to expect a parent to be a fantasy invented by your culture!

Yet it was his death in 1981 that gave me the money to start my travels. As I parked on my Brooklyn street, having just finished my five day drive across the U.S. from California where I had been teaching, a neighbor leaned in my window to tell me that my father had died two days before. Weeks later another neighbor told me that seeing him drop to the sidewalk around the corner on Atlantic Avenue, he had gone to help him up, asking if he was all right, did he need help. Of course, my father answered, "I'm fine." In pain I can't imagine, he walked around the corner and dropped again in front of the house just as the firemen were coming into their station across the street. They saw him and rushed to resuscitate him, but this time he was not "fine"; he was dead. After a sad funeral, attended only by my neighbors, I flew out to Fargo.

I buried his ashes next to my mother's in the Fargo cemetery on that huge openness of plain where the sky with its ever-moving panoply of clouds is the landscape. The fact that the cemetery was right next to the airport runway struck me as a happy portent. I splurged on a tour to the USSR. You couldn't do it any way other than on a tour in 1982 unless you were fluent in Russian. We started in Moscow, flying south to Samarkand, Khiva and Bukhara in Uzbekistan, all part of Russia at that time, before flying east to Ulan Bator in Mongolia, also then a part of the USSR. His death gave me the financial liberty I needed to travel.

I had already ventured to Nepal with the anthropologists from Idaho but there were pauses of years between my trips since I had to scrimp and save for them. He gave me the means to the freedom I had been straining toward over the years to travel solo. I wasn't going to be able to travel luxuriously, not even middleclass hotels would be possible, but I was going to be able to travel every year.

Outside of Karga, on a flat area near a stream, we camped, looking out of our tents at the mountains. Children and puppies came to investigate us. When I got up to visit the toilet tent in the night, snow was drifting down lazily from the stars, draping the base of the tent in a white *khata*. In the morning all was powdered. We drove toward Sangsang passing nomad tents, flocks of sheep, yaks and longhaired goats with the snowy line of Himalayan peaks in the background.

Before Sangsang we came to the road-mender's hut where Rachael and I had stayed in 1999. We stopped for nostalgia's sake but also because I had with me pictures that I had taken of the family. But they were not in the house. There was only an old woman with her loom in the courtyard, where the pony had been. She didn't recognize the people in my pictures. This was disappointing because Rachael and I had been hoping for a little reunion.

As we talked to the elderly woman through Thubten, a young woman and man walked up the road. When they saw the pictures they recognized the people who, they told us, had left the road-mender's house, moving to a village we could see from the road.

Blushing and giggling, the young woman admitted that she was engaged to the young man who was wearing a single, handsome coral earring and a white sheepskin coat in the traditional manner, off one shoulder. That morning her mother, in honor of the engagement, had given her a conch shell bracelet, an heirloom, for her wedding. Her brown arm enhanced the shell's white sheen. Tibetans treasure conch shells and cowrie shells being, as are all humans, attracted to what is exotic, what is not available in one's environment. Looking at her bracelet I thought of my carefully kept Tibetan prayer beads, carved from yak bone, cherished on the same basis and those delightfully gaudy blinkers and tassels for a donkey my mother had bought in Sicily.

I gave her the pictures to give to the family. We didn't have time to go to the village.

When we stopped for lunch, pilgrim trucks decorated with wind-whipped prayer flags passed us. These were flat beds without the prairie schooner covering over them that my truck on my first trip to Kailash had had. People were standing, unprotected, on their belongings in their best clothes braving wind, cold, sun, and dust; they waved, smiling at us. We were all on our way to Kailash for Saga Dawa. On the road there was a celebratory air about us, both Tibetans and Westerners.

We stopped at a 16,000-foot pass with a view out to a white barrier of mountains. The tailgate of a truck, which must have come loose or fallen off a passing truck, had been set up on end and wound with prayer flags and *khatas*.

To our intense annoyance a party of Chinese in a Land Rover passed us. Because they were Chinese, they were able to travel unencumbered by a guide or a truck and were waved through check points. We were momentarily jealous of their freedom, not that we weren't happy to have our Nepali staff, but the thought of traveling without all the restrictions and red tape the Chinese impose on foreigners at the constant checkpoints looked liberating.

Pausing for a leg stretch by a wood and wire suspension footbridge festooned with prayer flags I watched three men sitting cross-legged as they fished over its edge. I presumed that what was caught would be used for medicinal purposes. Hanging from the underside of the bridge I noticed a sheep and a yak head. I asked Thubten why they were there. He told me they had been hung by a herder whose sheep and yaks had been stricken by disease. The heads were to mollify whatever demon was causing the illness. Bön practice, which frequently involves animal sacrifice, often coexists quietly with Buddhism, as Halloween and the Yule Log live companionably with Christianity.

We camped outside of Saga with truckers and a couple of Westerners in a small meadow by a stream.

The next morning we passed some unidentified ruins picturesquely situated on an island in the middle of a small river as a number of horsemen beautifully accoutered with fine carpets under their saddles, hand forged stirrups and silk shirts billowing their bright yellows and blues in the wind passed us at a gallop.

A ruin on an island by the side of the road. It may be a ruin due to the Cultural Revolution or due to an invasion from Nepal in the 18th century.

At Zhongba, a village with a scattering of truck-stop motels and restaurants, Thubten took us to a monastery just outside the town up on a hill where the main temple held a large statue of Padmasambava, also called Guru Rinpoche, smiling under his rippling black moustache possibly with satisfaction at having subdued the Bön demons and having reestablished Buddhism. Our monk guide was accompanied by his spoiled, pet goat, which wanted its head rubbed and butted against you gently until you gave him the attention he wanted.

Often women are excluded from the protector chapel, but that, for some reason, was not true here. The chapel's pillars were painted with skulls and male heads on bloody neck stumps. The main figures were Palden Lhamo, Tibet's protector wearing a necklace of severed heads, astride her mule, bull-headed Mahakala and an old man I had never encountered before, his white beard dripping off his chin like icicles.

Although I didn't recognize him at the time, I later discovered that he was Tangton Gyalpo, "The Madman of the Empty Land," bridge engineer and creator of Tibetan opera. His other notable accomplishment is that he recognized Samding Dorje Phagmo, the highest female incarnation in Tibetan Buddhism.

Sitting on some rocks near the temple and monastery to eat my lunch of curried cauliflower and hard boiled eggs, I watched a boy and a girl about eight years old, playing among some heaps of dried mud bricks and big pieces of wood, building materials for the renovation of the *gompa*. The girl, intense but also full of giggles, was ordering the boy around. He followed her instructions, hefting bricks into crude walls and lifting some long broken pieces of wood across the walls he'd set up. She criticized his efforts, which annoyed him, but when he was finished she threw a blue piece of plastic she had been carrying under her arm over the beams and the two of them happily crawled into their little home made shelter.

I considered these two with nostalgic eyes. Between the ages of six and eleven, I had had a true love with the improbable but delightful name of Billy Bliss. He had lived up the road from me in a house whose stone foundation was the burned out chapel of the abandoned estate we all lived on, once the property of the president of the Grand Central Railroad. Our house had been the cow barn; others lived in houses reinvented from the dairy or from houses built for the men servants or the butler.

The Blisses were the exact opposite of my family, liberal, easy going and nonconformist. Mrs. Bliss was an early woman pilot; her house was a messy haven full of children, cookies and toys. My mother sniffed at the mention of her name since her house wasn't up to Mother's decidedly Austrian standards of cleanliness.

Billy and I had acres of woods to wander. We had a swamp to investigate in our fathers' goulashes making sucking noises as we clopped among the tussocks and filled our mothers' Mason jars for canning with frogs' eggs to watch them hatch. There was the hill, behind the Bliss house, where we could ramble among the old, gnarled apple trees, from whose fruit the Blisses made cider.

After World War II, when Chappaqua began to bloom into an affluent suburb, high school kids, and maybe adults as well, abandoned their defunct cars along the road that led up the hill where they would slowly rust and rot among the apples trees twined in winter with the orange and red fruits of bittersweet. Those bare vines with their sharply bright seedpods always recall Billy. I keep a few branches in the house in winter.

Billy protected me from my schoolmates who bullied or made fun of me, finding me odd because of the long stockings my mother made me wear as well as for my love of classical music, and even worse, opera. I read and liked serious books. I was a nerd. I tried to listen to the Andrews Sisters but couldn't figure out what people liked about pop until the 1960's when the Beatles, the Doors and a plethora of groups created lyrics and music that were politically topical. While he was alive Billy kept me safe, kept my classmates at bay.

Billy and I walked home every day from school through a small forest made musical by a tumultuous rock bound creek. There was a place where a flat stone among fir trees on the edge of a cliff allowed us to sit and look down at the water tumbling between the rocks. Sometimes we would scramble down to the creek. I wanted to create a little pool by damming the water flow. I moved some of the rocks but Billy did most of the labor with me ordering him about. He, not surprisingly, took offence at this. I remember walking home enveloped by his annoyed silence. I knew I'd done the wrong thing but I also knew he would talk to me the next day. I had absolute trust in our relationship. It was the only relationship in my young life, outside of that with my rarely seen Danish grandmother, and my Aunt Liz, where I had this trust. With these people I knew I was loved without strings or expectations. How astonishing that one can be loved for just being one's self, unconditionally.

My mother had nothing good to say about Billy, her main complaint being that he wasn't "that smart." I didn't understand then that my mother automatically judged everyone and everything in front of her, usually negatively, unless the person was rich because she desperately needed to feel superior.

One winter day, returning from school, Billy, though I fought hard, over powered me and washed my face in snow. I didn't talk to him the rest of the way home and didn't wait for him at the end of my drive to walk to school the next morning. Puzzled and upset by my behavior, he asked his mother why I was angry with him. "Doesn't she know I love her?" he asked. She in turn, amused by the situation, told my mother who told me. The next day on the way to school Billy received an indignant lecture about love not being a reason to wash anyone's face in snow. He continued, however, to be puzzled by such an incomprehensible female attitude.

One day we climbed a maple in my front yard; we spent a lot of time up in trees. I was about to step onto a branch when Billy told me it wasn't safe. I glared at him, taking it as a dare. Stepping onto the branch I fell twenty feet flat on my stomach to the stones below. I didn't, amazingly, break any bones; not only was the breath knocked out of me but the doctor was afraid that I had ruptured my spleen and would die. No one told me this but they did tell Billy, who came to see me.

I was sitting up in bed, cheery and bright, if still finding it difficult to breathe in a regular way. He was white faced and apologetic. I, puzzled at his contrition, told him he had nothing to apologize for, that I had been stupid.

Every summer we walked through the woods to the swimming pool in the next town, unless there was a polio alert. Billy proposed on one of these trips that we each take a crap and then compare sizes. Nothing about the idea struck me as wrong, although if I'd thought about it at all surely I would have known my mother would have been horrified. I thought the idea was funny and went behind a tree. Billy walked a discrete distance away and went behind another tree. We compared. My shit was larger; I won.

How odd that the act was done in absolute privacy, although the result of the act was then on public view. Humans are really very peculiar.

Later that summer I went with my mother to Fargo to visit my gaggle of great aunts. While I was there I received a letter from Billy's mother telling me that he had died. Appendicitis. I remember the pattern of the kitchen tablecloth that I stared at—red and white gingham squares. I was numb. I was uncomprehending. How could he be dead? Old people died. I understood that, but Billy was young, a year older than I. The physical sensation was as if I had swallowed something, much, much too large and it was stuck in my chest. It was indigestible and I was just going to have to carry it around. I decided that maybe once I was back in Chappaqua I would understand, that my incomprehension had to do with place.

On the first day of school I walked to the end of the drive and waited for Billy, knowing he would not come. His absence spread around me growing more and more vast like a flood inundating the landscape, altering it forever. After a few minutes, Eddy, Billy's older brother, came along. He was in high school, the only person I have ever known who could walk anywhere, on a potholed road, on a rocky path, crossing a brook on stones while reading a book. He looked up from his book, nodded at me, and I fell in silently beside him.

Walking home alone after school that day, I did some hard eleven-year-old thinking that distilled into two ideas. One was that it was very important that I remember Billy because his parents would die, Eddy would die and no one would remember him. As long as Billy was remembered he would be, sort of, alive. This idea, which at eleven, I thought unique to myself, I later found beautifully expressed in Thomas Hardy's poem, "His Immortality."

The second thought was that Billy, by dying so young had lost his future to death; it had been stolen from him. I could repair that devastating damage by living two lives, instead of one. I would lead a boy's life and a girl's life.

I have kept the promise made that day to Billy. I have led *our* lives.

There is terrible pain in my memory of Billy, but there is also a great hive of sweetness because the relationship is still there. Death, although powerful, can not erase that. I have learned that is what we finally distill from loss. It requires time, but what we end up with is a sweetness that makes the pain bearable.

As I gathered up the eggshells from my lunch, I could hear the young pair behind the blue plastic drape giggling together. More trucks passed with pilgrims packed into them, heads wrapped in scarves, mouths and noses covered with white cotton masks against the dust on the road that passed the monastery. Climbing into the Land Cruiser, we were all actively nose picking. Dust and dryness had lined our nasal membranes with blood scabs. Alex was in the very back of the four-wheel-drive asleep and snoring, possibly because of a clogged nose.

A nomad tent and temporary corral for sheep by the side of the road.

We came to the two bridges, one a replacement for the other where the view of the Himalayas, all peaked and rounded snow shapes, runs horizon to horizon, a magnificent, white, rickrack barrier.

The line of the Himalayas.

On my first trip to Kailash in the back of the truck these bridges had been surrounded by sand dunes, which my companions, sliding down from the back of the truck tried to run up. I hadn't had breath for such activity. The dunes since that trip in 1995 had moved further west leaving the bridges clear of sand.

We camped near Payam. Getting up in the middle of the night to go to the toilet tent I stood for a moment in the cold darkness that smelled of dust. Above in the night's absolute silence, the Milky Way was a white road of glistening pebbles across the sky. In the morning the mountains were clouded over.

Little birds in flocks fluttered across the road at which Temba honked to make them scatter to safety, yet he was petulant when we ask for a photo stop. Never, in my visits to Tibet have I seen a dead animal on the road until my most recent trip. Taking any life diminishes your merit and imperils the quality of your next life, setting up a future of bad *karma* and a lower incarnation. You might return to earth as a maggot. Tibetans always brake for an animal in the road. As we set out again, I saw out the window a frightened, silvery fox move swiftly away from the road into black hills tufted with yellow grass.

It was a day of dust devils, small ones like a series of beige scarves, which appeared to be plucked from in front of the car by an invisible hand, then big ones, which one preferred to see in the distance, tumults of red dust lashing themselves in a frenzy, hysterical penitents. There were also very small ones, long like a bar, low to the ground, churning fiercely toward the car's wheels, apparently full of animosity, wanting to bite the tires.

The road to Maryum La and Kailash.

We arrived at the huge spider web of prayer flags at the top of Maryum La, in time to glimpse Gurla Mandata and Kailash's white cap as evening came down to darkness.

The colorful spiderweb of prayer flags at Maryum La. Beneath are the little cairns of stones that people build both here and along the path of the *khora*.

I felt a surge of joy, of homecoming. When we did the ritual circumambulation of the fluttering flags, a Tibetan man, unpacking a portion of small paper squares with the flying-horse on them, lost control; a huge number of little papers whished into the air like a storm cloud of sparrows.

Besides prayer flags with the wind horse on them you can buy inch thick stacks of small papers printed with the Wind Horse to throw in the air at sacred sites.

In *Travels in Tartary, Thibet and China, 1844-1846* the authors, Huc and Gabet, a pair of French Lazarist priests, who were sussing out the territory for missionary work, encountered a monk who asked their help in supplying travellers with horses. Thinking that they were being asked to give up their mounts they protested that they had only a horse and a little mule. The monk whom they nicknamed "the Lisper" replied:

"'...what we send to the travellers are paper horses." And therewith he ran off to his cell, leaving us with an excellent occasion for laughing in our turn at the charity of the Buddhists, which we thus learned consisted in giving paper horses to travellers. We maintained our gravity, however for we had made it a rule never to ridicule the practices of the Lamas. Lisper returned, his hands filled with bits of paper, on each of which was printed the figure of a horse, saddled and bridled and going at full gallop. "Here!" cried the Lisper, "these are the horses we send to the travellers. Tomorrow we shall ascend a high mountain, and there we shall pass the day, saying prayers and sending off horses." "How do you send them to the travellers?" "Oh! The means are very easy. After a certain form of prayer, we take a packet of horses, which we throw up into the air, the wind carries them away and by the power of the Buddha they are then changed into real horses, which offer themselves to travellers."'

It is interesting that Tibetan Buddhist spiritual practices turn outward, offering help to strangers. One of Buddhism's ideas is that things exist because of the relations between them, therefore, one should always be cognizant of the needs of others rather than of oneself, be aware of the interlace of relationships. Before and after meditating one dedicates any value the meditation may have to be for the benefit of "all sentient beings." Yet, Tibet as a nation, to perhaps its eternal detriment, turned inwards isolating itself from the world. Tibet is an excellent, and unfortunate, example of what happens through isolation. It became a country locked in the mold of its old ideas, some of them excellent, some of them long out dated, with no new information, with no contacts or friends in the world, except China.

As an alcoholic I had a similar pattern. Because of my fear of people, I lived an isolated life, drinking alone. By the time I came into AA I had very few friends. My brain, like my father's, by itself believed it was right, that it needed to be self-sufficient with no dependencies. To ask for help was to me to admit intolerable weakness. Tibet also believed that it was right, that it needed nothing from the external world. Groups in the monasteries, anxious not to lose their power and control, discouraged outside contacts and ideas. That situation or mental attitude enabled China to swallow Tibet whole. You could certainly say that I was swallowed as entirely by alcohol, as Jonah was by the whale. But there is another dimension to being open rather than isolated. A spiritual life, I have come to believe, involves being with others, being of service to them, hearing them, being available to emotional connection.

One of the dangers of isolation is that the person or country is apt to believe that what and how it thinks is normal because it has no basis for comparison. Since getting sober I have come to realize I need to know people who think as I do and people who think very differently from me, that I need a reference not just to like-minded people but to unlike-minded ones. Any brain or country left with no one but itself to talk to will produce some very odd perspectives. We grow and learn through contact with other people. Science has burgeoned through the communication between scientists all over the world. Researchers add to each other's knowledge helping to prove as well as disprove theories and experiments. Isolation is a bad idea for both individuals and countries.

We attempted to camp on the plain outside of Darchen but there was no site with water nearby. Within Darchen, Chinese officials insisted that we had to camp in a compound fenced off by a wall of concrete blocks, a dung heap with loudspeakers blaring Chinese messages and music. After Alex commented that he had not realized that he needed a cholera shot, I christened the site Cholera Corner. The stench was fecal and overwhelming.

The wall around Cholera Corner. Our truck is the one to the right. Looking like a cloud, Gurla Mandata is in the distance.

In the evening, we discovered that the shallow trench crossing our camp was where the contents of the public toilet were flushed out once a day. After dropping my toothbrush in the dirt, I soaked it in iodine, the bacterial and viral possibilities being endless. I had a brown toothbrush for the rest of the trip. Tibetan travel misery was full upon us. We picked our noses, were slowed by altitude sickness in a mild form, and suffered from self-pity with our chapped hands and faces.

Walking the tent city Rachael found jewelry shops and, more interestingly, a very smiling, very pretty woman, whom, it slowly became apparent to us, was a prostitute. Her toes had been amputated because of frostbite. She was eager to display these to us, although it wasn't clear whether she was charging a fee for this exhibition. Her manner was similar to that of the sly woman who had begged for *tsampa* and barred Rachael's way on the path down from Kailash on our last trip. Noticing this similarity I wondered if the *tsampa* borrower had been a prostitute. It would explain why Dawa had been so uncomfortable around her, avoiding eye contact.

At the other end of the social and spiritual spectrum, the tent where monks were performing ceremonies was so crammed it would have been offensive, if not physically impossible for us to thrust ourselves in. I stood outside for a while listening to the chanting, feeling the descent into unknown depths of the deep voiced singers, punctuated by bells and drums, feeling in an emotionally misty area between

Gregorian chants and this Buddhist chanting, no longer alien but gently reassuring.

As with my mother, my father had gifted me with positive and negative presents. Music had been one of the positive ones. On Sundays when my mother and I had left for church he would push the big piece of furniture containing the combined record-player-radio, it was called a radio console, over to the French doors that opened onto the flagstone terrace, stack the turntable with vinyl plates threaded with Chopin's Etudes, crank the volume all the way up and mow the lawn, a dark lock of his hair falling over his forehead.

Bach made him happy. Mozart entwined him in melodic strings of rapture. I have a photograph of him, blissfully passed out, a smile on his face, in a chair at the end of a party. My memory is that Bach's partitas were playing in the background. Looking at that picture I don't feel angry; I don't think, "You were a rotten drunk." I feel great waves of fondness, a glow of affection. Is it then surprising that I have had a perennial attraction to addicts? I am also angry with him but that has more to do with his not supporting me against my mother and the passivity of his character, which may or may not have been connected to his alcoholism.

I grew up surrounded by these lovely classical noises supplemented by Saturday afternoons of the Metropolitan Opera emanating from the radio. I feel the silky cover over the speaker of our big radio console against my cheek as I leaned against its fabric, as though I was trying to climb into the speakers. The sound enveloped me, enclosing me in a capsule of voice and orchestra. Bizet's Carmen was my favorite opera and heroine, although I couldn't understand why she chose that wimp Don Jose. The matador was so obviously the right man. I thought, as I suspect many children do, that adults were, despite their obvious superior factual knowledge, a little dumb. I, of course, would not grow up to be a dumb adult.

Often the things my mother had given me would be taken to a new level by my father's additional gift. My mother gave me Strauss's waltzes. My father gave me Mozart's **Don Giovanni**. My mother gave me Rudyard Kipling's **Kim** and Robert Louis Stevenson's **Treasure Island**, but he urged me on to Conrad and Melville. She gave me the Catholic Church. He, an atheist who designed Catholic churches, gave me the alternative of doubt.

These were the good things, a fascination with music, literature, art, which led to long discussions in my high school and college years about how it was possible, or impossible to tell the difference between what was popularly acclaimed in one's time as being great but was actually just fashionable, and what would last beyond its time. How would Christianity have been different if Augustine had been the leading thinker in the Catholic Church rather than Paul? The negative side of our relationship had to do, of course, with the effects of his alcoholism, his passivity, his inability to protect me from my mother, his silence that shut me out, his fears that ignited his rages.

With a final rattle of small drums like rain pelting on a tin roof, the ceremony in the tent was finished and people came bursting forth to wander around Darchen's garbage dump of human and yak shit, noisy and crowded. But the people were fascinating—a woman's belt dangled metal medallions set with turquoise; men sported cowboy hats and brocade jackets; snotty nosed children wore stocking caps; shops sold odd assortments of stuff: glass jars of mandarin oranges, shiny steel bridle bits, batteries, stirrups, flashlights, ballpoint pens, needle and thread.

Because it was the Year of the Water Horse the tent city
at the edge of town was much larger than usual.

Rachael was interested in a belt, huge with engraved steel plates on stiff leather. I urged against it since, to me, it looked like one of those kidney belts men wear in New York City gyms.

The river in Darchen where people wash and fill their
water bottles. Along with the expected varieties of
pollution there are also batteries that have been thrown
into the water.

Tom and I went out beyond the mud brick gate that marked the entrance to Darchen to sit on a couple of rocks and talk, while trucks, five at a time sometimes, came in spewing long plumes of dust behind them loaded with excited, happy pilgrims.

Trucks of fellow pilgrims along the way.

We discussed the distinctive architectural visions caused by how differently Eastern and Western religions perceive worship. In the West worship occurs exclusively inside. In the East it is often performed outside with people walking around stupas, *chörtens* or mountains. Somehow we moved from such metaphysical abstractions to talking about the fact that Rachael had a new boy friend.

"I do hope it works," I said. "She has really wanted to be in a relationship and they seem to have running marathons in common."

"Well, they certainly didn't seem to be able to keep their hands off each other when I saw them at the airport," Tom said indignantly. "It was disgusting and embarrassing to have to be around them."

Taken aback by his attitude I commented, "I disagree. I think that's lovely. And it gives me hope that this is really going to work for them. That kind of physical attraction is a good place to start things off. I think all those prohibitions about people touching in public are a bad idea. I know in the U.S. people always leer about what is called, PDA, Public Displays of Affection. But what I love about Spain, France and Italy is the way young and old hold hands walking down the street or exchange a fond kiss. I like coming around a corner in a supermarket to find two people clasped in each others arms next to a pyramid of canned soup."

Tom gave me a sour look.

We walked back to Cholera Corner in silence. I was thinking about Les.

Once I had been divorced I made a conscious decision not to marry again. In the words of an acquaintance of mine I had decided, "my picker was broken." When I sobered up I thought maybe my selection apparatus would improve. But when I look back over more than forty years, both drunk and sober, since my divorce I feel like Macbeth watching the ghostly line of Banquo's kingly descendants parading by. What they all have in common is alcohol. It is that ineluctable addiction attraction.

In my Banquo procession there are a few standouts. A wonderfully kind and generous African American who worked in children's TV, yet did the cooking on weekends while I labored on my masters and doctorate. A sober ex-alcoholic, a high powered lawyer, with whom I lived for eight years, who was so delicately, emotionally balanced that he would yell and be on the verge of physical violence if someone casually brushed up against him in a theater. When we went to couples' therapy, far too late, the therapist told me he had never seen anyone, who had not served in Vietnam, with such a bad case of post traumatic stress, yet this man had never been in a war or near one. Discouraged, when that affair broke up, I quit for a long time.

But finding that I wanted someone to go to the movies with, cuddle and make love with, talk to, I tried web sites which yielded either a wizened elf who had posted Gary Cooper's brother's photo or a man who apologized profusely for standing me up twice. I gave up again.

A woman friend, with a complex three continent history, gave a party for her sister who was visiting from Argentina in the Delegates Dining Room of the UN. I was seated next to a slip of a woman in her seventies, I was then in my sixties, who told me how she had met the man she was with in the elevator of her building in which he also lived. He was listening in further down the table looking abashed but pleased.

"Then one day, after maybe a year, he asked me to move in. I said to him," for emphasis she waggled a long slim, exquisitely manicured finger back and forth, "No, no. I don't want to be a wife. I want to be a sweetheart."

"Why," I interrupted, "that's exactly the position I've been looking for."

"Turning her big eyes on me appraisingly, she said, "I was just talking to a young woman at this party who told me her father is looking for someone."

"If you see her, point her out to me."

She scanned the room intently and then led me up to a young, longhaired woman with a beautiful oval face at another table whom I recognized as someone from the gym that I belonged to.

"I've found someone for your father," announced my lunch companion to the woman's astonishment.

I introduced myself and gave her my telephone number. About a month and a half later, when I was close to giving up hope, I received a call from a man who introduced himself as Les.

"My wife almost married a man named Moore, but she settled for Les," he told me.

I was immediately won over by his combination of pun and corn. Les was a plump, Jewish lawyer in his eighties. He had never made a lot of money because he was always helping someone who had less than he had. I liked his Brooklyn accent, which he was a bit ashamed of. I felt it gave him a certain authenticity, an earthiness of place. I quickly discovered that the two things Les was always up for were food and sex, although up wasn't part of the sex we had. But there are many ways to make love and we worked the spectrum.

We always ate at good restaurants, preferably close to my apartment so that there would not be a lot of time wasted between his two favorite activities. He loved the Swedish meatballs at Aquavit and really, to my astonishment, did not want me to cook for him. The one time I did cook he dutifully ate but I could tell that though he liked the food, he was not happy. He wanted to take me out.

Les talked about his wife who had died of breast cancer some years before. She had escaped the Holocaust, just barely. I didn't understand the depth of his loss until we went to a movie about Jews who had gone to sub-Sahara Africa before Hitler came to power, thinking it might be a place to start their own nation. When we came out of the movie, we sat in the little park behind the Lincoln Plaza Cinema. As we talked about the movie, he suddenly broke down completely. I held him until his sobs softened, envying his tears.

I never felt any jealousy toward his wife, although I have known women who insisted that their lover's marriage was bad out of competition with a woman long dead. It seemed to me Les had a good marriage. She had her time. I had my time. I was amused, however, when going out to his house in Dobb's Ferry I saw that in her closet he had saved a small collection of what, I suspect, had been her favorite dresses, all by well-known designers, which I am sure he had been proud to buy for her and she must have enjoyed wearing. Les, I realized, was attracted to women who liked to dress, who enjoyed having style and he noticed what I wore. As I got into a taxi beside him one day he noted, "Those are really sexy boots." Seeing those dresses gave me an odd feeling of kinship with his wife.

After our first three dates, as we were sitting next to each other, appropriately, on my grandmother's love seat, I thought, "You like this man but can't make up your mind about him until you go to bed with him. That's the only way you will know. Jump in."

Just as the thought was finishing in my head Les turned to me and said gently, "Is it too soon?" Another thing I loved about Les was that he knew how to say difficult things elegantly.

"No," I responded and we went upstairs to bed, starting a wonderful affair that death ended abruptly.

Les was an amazing experience for me, perhaps unmatchable. He was the first adult male I had ever been attached to. My husband and my former lovers, as a therapist had pointed out, had almost all been boys. My father was certainly a boy. Being with Les exposed me to myself in unflattering ways. I could clearly see my pockmarked psychic landscape full of neurotic acne scars. My selfishness stood out like a rash of rosacea. I was always fearful of how I was perceived. Did others, particularly if I was in bed with one of them, think I was all right? What I meant by all right was not particularly clear to me. It was obvious that Les was pretty sane and that I was frequently nutty. He, through his gentle directness, taught me to be open which I had difficulty doing having lived with people who were always busy hiding something.

Even more wonderful than his talent of saying difficult things sweetly, was his astonishing generosity. Les always put himself last, not because he thought he was less than other people, but because that was truly where he wanted to be.

When we had been together for two months I found I owed a sizeable chunk of money to the IRS. I had it, but it was going to make my life difficult for a while when I paid.

"Honey, why don't you let me take care of this?" he said, in a charmingly paternalistic tone, when I complained about it to him. I have to say the tone appealed to me, and made the offer extremely tempting. But I was also dumbstruck.

"Les, I've only known you two months. I can't take three thousand dollars from you."

Again and again he offered to pay for large expenses, although he was certainly not a rich man. I would turn him down. Finally one day he looked at me severely and said, gruffly, for Les, "What are you afraid of? I can't make a slave out of you."

The other area in which I was not able to accede to his desires was in sleeping. Les wanted, such a lovely wish, to sleep with his arms around me. I couldn't bear that. It was too confining. It brought up in a directly physical way all my fears inherited from my mother about being trapped by men, about their constricting my life.

I was, amazingly, able to explain to Les that I wanted to sleep in his arms but could not do it. "Can we try it and then I will move away if I need to?" That I could say that directly was a gift from him. We tried but I could feel the fear turning into irrational panic in under five minutes. However, I was able to say to him, "I love sleeping with you. I feel safe with you."

I did not tell him, however, too embarrassing, that I can get the same panic when my trainer tightens the straps on my feet before I use the rowing machine.

Gradually I realized that I had a man who was absolutely committed to me. He wasn't going anywhere. He was here to stay. That frightened the living daylights out of me. I had always thought, although I had not been aware of this until I knew Les, of men as temporary phenomenon in my life. Being temporary made them safe. If they weren't going to be around long they couldn't take away my life. I realized that I was going to have to come to terms with things I had never approached inside myself.

Les was fourteen years older than I. I had always feared going with men who were my senior because I thought they would boss and control me. But Les was the good Daddy I had never known I was longing for.

In the middle of one of our weekends Les went home early, not feeling well. I called him several times a day. He called me several times a day. I was worried. He went to the doctor who found nothing. I asked if I could come out and stay with him, help him, cook for him. His sense of manhood wouldn't allow that. I received a bouquet of roses, each bloom a different color. It was beautiful.

When I called to thank him, he was excited that I had received the flowers and wanted to know if I liked them. His thoughts were not on himself, although he must have been feeling terrible. Les was an astonishing union of love and generosity.

The next day I called. No answer. Probably he was at the doctor's. An hour later his daughter called me. A neighbor had found him dead, sitting by the telephone.

I was also lucky that his family accepted me. I have known many women who have been excluded from the funeral of the man they were lovers with. I, most definitely a gentile, was a participant right through the Orthodox Jewish funeral. This experience gave me a great admiration for the Orthodox funeral with its simplicity and directness. I will always be grateful to his daughter and granddaughter for their inclusion of me. It made me feel that though the time had been short I had been a part of Les's life. It certainly helped me to mourn. They were my comfort. The hollow thuds of the shovelfuls of earth on Les's coffin, however, made me more determined to exhume my feelings, although I did not cry.

Walking back to our tents, Tom and I passed the Darchen telephone office, a hub of Tibetan guide activity. Thubten emerged from the office as we passed with a big grin on his face. He had called his wife in Lhasa and reported back to us that all was fine with her pregnancy. We were all delighted to be included in the progress of the coming baby.

Yaks among trucks in Darchen waiting to be hired.

The next morning trucks roared out of the tent city at 4 am in the dark loaded with pilgrims headed for the *tarbouche*.

Trucks loaded with pilgrims on their way to see the raising of the *tarbouche*.

We left at 8 am, getting lost because Temba, who was being exceptionally idiotic, couldn't find his way. All he had to do was follow the other trucks and four-wheel-drives but he was seized by an attack of individualism and wanted to drive his personal route.

Rachael kept saying, "Just drop us here. We'll walk," putting me in a panicked snit since it would have taken me an hour to get to the *tarbouche* if I had had to walk.

I totally lost my spiritual and every other kind of cool descending like a yak dropped from a cliff on Temba, yelling, pointing at trucks passing in a dust cloud, using terms that undoubtedly improved his vocabulary. For a miracle, he drove toward them, joining the long line, which crested a ridge to swoop down into the hollow where the *tarbouche* and two-legged *chörten* lay.

We were on a dusty track up to the *tarbouche*, jammed with Land Cruisers and trucks. To one side a long line of men, women, and children walked toward it whirling prayer wheels; some big ones, that would tire any arm, were carried in leather holsters on the hip. The line was over a mile long, snaking along the narrow path, the brilliant colors of people's clothes looking like a curve of blooms trailing across the dusty, grey, rocky land.

Chinese police directed traffic. We and other Land Cruisers jumped the queue like people in the scrum of a cancelled flight coming in sideways to the airline counter. We waved at people on the trucks; they waved back.

Temba parked by an outdoor, female john encircled by a chest high plastic tarpaulin that Rachael and I were delighted to see. Inside a sort of wide, wooden ladder with broad rungs had been laid over a newly dug trench. Rachael and I, taking advantage of the facilities, were stared at by Tibetan women who needed to know we did it the same way as they did.

Rachael took off to photograph something. Alex and I walked to the great, multi-colored, flag-fluttering spider web with, at its center, the pole of the *tarbouche* lying aslant, its wood wound with *khatas* and ropes of primary-colored prayer flags people handed up to policemen who passed them on to the chief officiator to be attached.

The *tarbouche* being wrapped with prayer flags and *khatas*, white scarves. There are Chinese police, or army in attendance.

He was dressed in an ornate, yellow brocade coat and a red hat with short, red fringe hanging from it that swayed as he went up and down an aluminum ladder tying prayer flags and *khatas* onto the *tarbouche*.

The ladder is to help the Tibetan standing on top of the *tarbouche* go up and down for more supplies of prayer flags and *khatas*.

All of this sacred activity was carried on not in an atmosphere of solemnity but with laughter and joking.

The man who ties the prayer flags and *khatas* onto the *tarbouche*.

A nomad woman in a sun shade viewing the *tarbouche*.

Monks of the Gelugpa order, of which the Dalai Lama is the head, in yellow cockscomb hats and other monks in red, wedge-shaped hats, of the Sakya order, surrounded a prelate who circumambulated the pole praying and blessing people from beneath a red and yellow umbrella held carefully over his head by his monks.

This was not to protect him from the sun. The umbrella has a hierarchical significance in Asia. The Thai king, when on his throne, has seven umbrellas of diminishing size over his head.

Alex and I settled on a couple of rocks protruding from the dirt on the hillside above the *tarbouche* among Tibetans who, judging by their clothes and their hats, came from all over the country. We all sat listening to the horns, drums and cymbals that accompanied the prelate as he walked around the *tarbouche*.

Above us on the hill side were elegant nomad women from, Thubten later told us, Payang, a location I cannot find in Victor Chan but perhaps I'm not spelling it right, in high circular sheepskin hats with, in the center, poufs of brilliant brocade.

The crowd above me watching the progress of the *tarbouche*. The hats signify the area of Tibet the women come from.

The curly fleece of the sheepskin formed a cuff around the pouf. Their jewelry was sumptuous–pearl and coral earrings, turquoise and coral earrings, silver bells dangling from their flint cases, belts with monster silver buckles, necklaces of amber, coral, silver, pearls.

It's hard to get a view of the inside of one of these hats.
They are lined with brocade.

Here she is front view. Notice her silver amulet box
hanging around her neck and her sumptuous apron of silk
and wool.

The day before in Darchen I had seen a woman in a silver net that fitted over her hips, an open linked garland of a hundred dangling, tiny, silver bells. Two women were admiring, and surely enquiring, the name of her jeweler.

Alex, who was good with children played peek-a-boo with two boys and I joined in. A man seated nearby showed us proudly a saddle he had just bought, carved from wood with a high curved front, not really a pommel, covered with a thin plate of steel adorned with gray-green, enameled medallions. His saddle rug was of beige wool blooming with yellow flowers.

The Chinese police, hugely outnumbered, were visibly nervous being surrounded by around 3,000 Tibetans either sitting or circumambulating the *tarbouche*. But the thoughts of the Tibetans were on the festival not on the Chinese. Some stood up below us, obstructing the view. People around us and above, threw little pebbles at them to make them aware so that they would sit down.

Woman with her prayer wheel watching anxiously as the *tarbouche* goes up.

On such a celebratory day, as for us at Christmas or Easter in the West, dress is important, flamboyant and rich. Dressing up adds to the festivity of an event and shows that one is honoring and commemorating it. There were a huge variety of hats among the men—fox fur hats, hats with red fringe dangling from the brim, baseball hats, cowboy hats, and red felt hats, shovel shaped to shield the eyes.

In her superb hat and earrings she is totally focused on the *tarbouche* being raised.

Woman wore sheepskin wimples with long tapered ends, cartwheel sheepskin hats with fur on the lower side, brocade on the upper side, bonnets, resembling the old Dutch bonnets of Holland were of embroidered wool and brocade, short stocking caps, scarves folded into turbans, city felt hats and, of course, Lhasa ladies hats with veils and/or flowers. Braids were extended with multicolored yarn or silk strings in shocking pink or turquoise blue. Women in dark *chubas* wore silk blouses in canary or sunrise pink or robin's egg, all the gradations of the spectrum. Nomad women wore *chubas* with primary colored blocks along the hem-red, yellow, and green.

The men were also in *chubas*, below the hip jackets, worn off one shoulder, deriving from the custom of keeping your bow arm free to draw an arrow, in wildly colored brocades, silver, lavender, scarlet and black, trimmed in real or imitation snow leopard. One man wore a knee-length jacket of maroon brocade with gold medallions, lined with black, curly sheepskin.

The *tarbouche* surrounded by Tibetans.

Two trucks parked next to each other, side by side would haul the *tarbouche* upright.

The *tarbouche* being raised. The two trucks doing the raising are hidden from view.

People around us on the hillside chanted mantras and shouted when the steel cables connected to the *tarbouche* jerked. It was important that it be absolutely straight up, a tilt to right or left would mean a year of difficulties or disasters. The nomad women sang softly. When it was upright there was a pause while all concentrated on whether it was indeed straight or not. Then with a whoop everyone, shouting, chanting, and laughing, rushed down to walk or run the *khora* around it.

Wildly happy Tibetans converge on the *tarbouche* to circumambulate it.

The police tried to control people but it was impossible with such a joyous crowd. At the *tarbouche's* base stood a blue suited policeman with a battery-operated cattle prod, a representative of Chinese power, but I didn't see him use it.

I did the *khora*, sliding under prayer flag ropes, knocking my camera's lens cap off under the crowd's feet. As I straightened up among the ropes and flags a man handed it to me with a grin. People pried slivers from the *tarbouche*, sacred treasures to take home for the family altar.

I saw a Western man with a monster camera standing over a Tibetan who was prostrating. I was infuriated. Would you photograph someone deep in prayer in St. Patrick's?

When the people doing the *khora* became fewer, a dozen horsemen on fine little horses, bells and tassels on their brocade covered reins, raced round and round the *tarbouche*. Leaning low over the necks of their mounts in jackets shot with silver and gold, the red fringe on their hats streamed out. People shouted and cheered them on.

Watching the horses near me was a Tibetan woman I can only describe by an old Victorian term: she was obviously "a woman of quality". She wore no exceptional jewelry. Her tan *chuba* and shell-pink silk blouse were sober, conservative but they were perfectly tailored. She was exceptionally tall with an air about her, wearing a worn but intricately embroidered hat of the Dutch bonnet variety. She had presence, her dignity intrinsic and having nothing to do with adornment.

I approached a tent where monks were giving blessings. The crowd started backing up. I became trapped in mid-lane so that the monks stream out on either side of me, laughing at finding an abashed foreigner in their midst.

As Alex and I wended our way back to the car we found women selling trinkets on a blanket. We each bought a bowl of green stone or perhaps some kind of glass, not jade, translucent and trimmed with cut metal. My seller asked $100 as a starting price but settled for $10.

A woman with silver bells dangling from her belt.

Rachael arrived looking as though she had been caught in a light snow since where she had been sitting people had thrown celebratory handfuls of *tsampa* into the air as they chanted. Even as we left, people were starting on their circumambulation of Kailash; with 3,000 or so attending it was going to be a very crowded *khora*. Probably delaying our circumambulation was a good thing.

We drove to Lake Manasarovar where our yellow tents were perched on the shore, like cabanas at a resort. Next morning we headed to Khorja Monastery near Parang, one of the places Rachael had found in Victor Chan's book that neither of us had been to before. This one we got to with no difficulty unlike the other two that we hadn't been able to see—Shalu on its newly tarred road and Chung Riwoche on its deeply puddled road.

Purang, also called Taklakot, is a small town on the Nepalese border, which was a traffic jam of Chinese military trucks. Our destination, Khorja Monastery, is a red cube of a building, red because it is a monastery of the Sakya order. It is a branch, so to speak, of the main Sakya which I saw on my first trip to Tibet, the temple with its towering pillars that were single, tree trunks each wrapped in its own myth—one a gift of Kublai Khan, one delivered by a tiger, and one delivered on the horns of a black yak. This monastery sits, handsome and regal, on the banks of the Map Chu, known in the west as the Karnali River.

The main chapel has, in a cupboard, fragments, lovingly preserved, of an old bronze statue brutalized during the Cultural Revolution. However, the wall murals, which were slick with grease from the yak butter lamps, had not been damaged. I have been in temples in Lhasa where the eyes of the Buddha and deities in the murals were gouged out during the Cultural Revolution.

A young monk was energetically running a souvenir shop in the midst of the temple, reminiscent, as Tom noted, of Christ and the moneychangers. I don't think Buddha would have approved of this activity either, but I suspect he might have handled the situation with a joke rather than a whip.

From the ceiling of the protector chapel hung large animal puppets, companions, we were told, of the protectors—a wild yak, a man, a tiger — beside them were the lumpily stuffed skins of a real snow leopard and a wolf, dangling eerily in the dark above us.

The next day, following our decision not to circumambulate immediately after Saga Dawa to avoid the crowds, we drove to Tholing and Tsaparang, lonely remnants of the Guge Kingdom. Although I had been there twice before I was looking forward to seeing them again. There is always something I have forgotten or not noticed on a previous visit. Sometimes doors that were closed and locked on one's last visit are unexpectedly open without explanation. I thought fondly of Annalisa telling me of these on my first trip to Tibet. She had felt the resonance of these sites without having seen them.

The multicolored mountains on the road to Tsaparang and Tholing.

These two locations are important in Tibetan history because they were a sanctuary for Buddhism when it came under attack after the third Buddhist king, Ralpachen, was assassinated by his Bönpo relative, Langdarma, who succeeded him and attempted to eradicate Buddhism while reestablishing the Bön religion. Buddhists under his persecution fled to the Guge kingdom.

Buddhism's hold on Tibet was not at first very strong. Bön practices and prelates were, like pagans in early Christian Europe, ready to rise at any sign of weakness on the part of the new, official religion. The Bön returned to power through the assassination of Ralpachen, in 838 AD, by his elder brother, Langdarma, who persecuted Buddhist monks, killing many and uprooting the Buddhist communities, harassing them until they abandoned their villages. They moved west, a flood of refugees, to Tholing and Tsaparang, in the Guge Kingdom, a stable Buddhist state near what is now the Tibetan border with India.

This story ended with another assassination. Pal-dorje, a Buddhist ascetic, rode to Lhasa on his white pony stained black with coal dust, wearing a robe, black on one side, white on the other, hiding in his sleeve a bow and arrow. He danced before the Bön king, Langdarma, in front of the Jokhang temple. The King, fascinated by the magical dance, drew closer. Pal-dorje shot a poisoned arrow from his concealed bow, killing Langdarma.

Pal-dorje then leapt to his saddle and rode through the river washing his pony white. Reversing his robe he escaped, a stranger on a white pony in a white robe.

King Langdarma's persecutions scattered the Buddhists. In the 10th century, under King Yeshe Ö, the Guge Kingdom became a Buddhist center of a hundred monasteries. But Tsaparang and Tholing are also interesting because the citadel and monastery are the location of an early attempt at religious tolerance that did not work.

Antonio Andrade, a Jesuit missionary from Goa in India, was the first Westerner to visit the kingdom in 1624, the first Westerner to visit Tibet. He was welcomed by the King and allowed to talk about Christianity. This angered the Buddhist community and may have been a contributing factor to the destruction of the kingdom. In 1630 the Guge was invaded and conquered by Ladakh, an area now a province of India.

The drive to Tsaparang and Tholing astonishes in a land over-endowed with magnificent scenery.

The southern horizon is filled side to side with the white immensities of the Himalayas. Suddenly the earth gapes, you look down into a labyrinth of badlands in soft greens, grays and dusky roses.

The view down into the badlands where Tsaparang and Tholing are located, with the white rickrack of the Himalayas beyond.

As you drive down balconied mansions, cloisters, pavilions, castles, villas, and pyramids rise above you in the badland maze.

One of the strange shapes in the badlands. There are an infinite number of them.

Another shape looming up on the dirt road in the badlands before Tsaparang.

The first Westerner to describe this landscape was Ernest Lothar Hoffman, a man of German and Bolivian descent. He lived in Capri after fighting in World War I, converted to Buddhism, studied in Sri Lanka, took the name of Lama Govinda, was initiated into several Tibetan sects, and married an Iranian woman, Ratti Petit, with whom he traveled to Tsaparang and Tholing. They minutely recorded the paintings and statues in the temples and chapels. Because of Lama Govinda and his photographer wife, who took the name of Li Gotami, and ended up in America on Alan Watts's houseboat in San Francisco, we have a record of what existed before the Cultural Revolution on this site.

At the end of these badlands is Tholing, a monastery and temple in the town of Zanda Xian above the Tsangpo River, a big army post. Here the military usually bully and humiliate the guides. We could see that Thubten was tensing up. He was normally easy going and smiling. But there was nothing we could do to help him with the military. He had to go to the office to arrange passes for us to see the temples. Often a guide will turn surly at this point. This was not true of Thubten but he returned to us more solemn and silent than he had been.

At dinner one night on my previous trip with Rachael to this area, a Tibetan boy of, perhaps, five stood before me making a series of terrible faces, obviously feeling he was striking a blow for justice. I wondered what he had been taught in school about Westerners.

Among the temples, is a building in the form of a mandala, which according to the glossary of Tibetan terms in Victor Chan's *Tibet Handbook* is "a symbolic, graphic representation of a tantric deity's realm of existence". It is used in meditation. Graphically it is a circle inside a square with a deity at the gate of each of the four sides. In meditating you enter the mandala mentally at one of the gates and move in your meditation toward the center.

The mandala temple at Tholing with red and white towers.

The mandala temple still in ruins from the attacks on it during the Cultural Revolution.

One of the mud brick towers of the mandala temple with its bird house finial.

At that time the building was locked, although when I pushed the doors to the full extent of their binding chain I could see where a row of images had been replaced by what looked like a row of bullet holes.

I took this photo by wedging open a chained door of the mandala temple with my foot. These are the spaces formerly occupied by Buddhas destroyed during the Cultural Revolution.

The limbs of the images were scattered in the dust below. Mandala paintings on scrolls or on walls in temples are common but this building in Tholing is the only instance I know of where a mandala has been rendered as a building.

The crenelated ramparts on the cliff edge of Tholing looking toward a ruin I have never visited.

The Lhakhang Karpo, the White Chapel, was not as damaged, containing 15th and 16th century paintings. Women, perhaps *dakinis*, with nipped waists and grapefruit breasts smile benignly, if a bit vacantly, with Tibetan chain-mailed warriors fighting on the walls below them.

One of the pillars of the Lhakhang Karpo, the White Chapel, carved from a deodar trunk which must have been carried over the Himalayan passes from India. The building may be 11th century but the murals within date to the 16th century.

Tsaparang, a few hour's drive from Tholing, has survived better than Lama Govinda might have guessed, although concrete picnic tables and chairs have been built on the path up the mountain by the Chinese. It reminded me of places like Mystic, Connecticut in the U.S., which have been "improved" for tourism until they acquire a plastic sheen, not that Tholing is that highly, polished but the picnic tables, which I have never seen used, probably because they are unshaded under the hot, glaring sun, exuded a whiff of Disneyland pretension.

Tsaparang, the citadel of the Guge Kingdom.

Looking up at the citadel of the Guge Kingdom, Tsaparang.

We dodged in and out of tunnels Lama Govinda had discovered when he was searching for a route to the crown of the ruins.

To get to the top of the Guge citadel one walks part of the way through tunnels built as an escape route for the royal family. This is a view from that route.

You also walk on the outside path passing the chapels.
This is the great wooden door of one of them.

Visiting chapels with exquisite 15th and 16th century murals in shining gem colors, we panted to the top of the citadel. In these murals the detail astonishes. Each delicate figure is dressed in a fabric distinct from her or his fellows. Each face is unique. Colors are as saturated as the day they were laid on the wall.

This is an illegal photo I took when the guard's back was turned. I did not pay the exorbitant fee the Chinese charge but only took one photo. This a mural of the Buddha's disciples praying before him.

Most statues are gone, due to the Cultural Revolution ably assisted by time. A pair of fierce faced guardians remains, their straw stuffing hanging out of their bellies, making them look as though they have been disemboweled. Alex and I stood in the gloom looking at the floor where gently smiling heads of dainty deities with sharp little chins, pink complexions, shiny onyx hair and lively, blackberry eyes lay in the dust. The big Buddhas of these magnificent halls, as well as the little Buddhas that used to cover the walls in their hundreds, are almost all gone. But what once existed remains in the photographs of Li Gotami.

That afternoon Alex and I wandered around Tholing investigating various structures we hadn't seen, except at a distance. Our objective became a large red and white stepped stupa standing alone on the largely treeless flat. It's dusty layers dominated the area. When we got to it we, of course, had to circumambulate it. What else could we do? In going around we surprised an older woman in a Mao cap also circumambulating with her prayer beads. She was ensuring her family's spiritual future with her steps and prayers. Her shy smile, the irony of her Mao cap above her prayer beads was perfect closure to our day.

The striking red and white stupa at Tholing.

Circumambulating the stupa, reciting her mantras, she ensures the spiritual well being of her family.

Tirtapuri was full of pilgrims. The *gompa* flickering with butter lamps supplied with yak butter they spooned out of plastic bags. At the hot springs women washed their hair, to my horror in laundry detergent. As I was observing these ablutions a handsome, not young Tibetan man, came up to me and offered his sexual services. I was totally taken aback. His wife was not. She, a few yards away, made what were obviously caustic and disparaging remarks while glowering at him. I quite agreed with her.

The Tibetan Lothario who made a verbal pass at me in front of his wife.

At this point, as I was trying to figure out how to kill off a pass without language, Alex showed up at my shoulder. The Tibetan man deciding he was my husband, immediately made friendly overtures to him. This pleased the wife no end, me as well and amused Alex into a fit of hilarity.

The uninhibited Tibetan making friends with Alex to his vast amusement.

The next day we camped by the Sutlej River at Guragem, a Bön monastery partly on the flat and partly, spectacularly, in red and white caves up on a cliff.

The cliff hermitage of the Bön monastery at Guragem. We started from here on rented horses for Kyunglung.

Here we hired horses to go to Kyunglung, which Rachael and I, in 1999, had not been able to get to because the river was too high to ford. I wanted to go there because, like Kailash, it reaches back into the mysterious past of human spiritual experience. The troglodyte caves are of pre-Buddhist origins and, perhaps, were occupied by people of an unknown belief earlier than the Bön faith, who may also have circumambulated Kailash.

Rachael and I were excited, triumphant. This time we would get there; we had the necessary permits.

Our horses loaded with our bags going to Kyunglung. At this point my camera began to go wonky but then it recovered more or less.

My horse was a chestnut colored lady, obedient, perky, nipping her fellows, particularly those younger and smaller. A colt traveling with its mother was always dodging her. We passed shepherds and flocks. In places the grass had been stripped by rain or wind from the hills, as if a coverlet has been pulled off. Underneath were rocks of celadon and rose familiar from the badlands, making it clear that the loss of grass cover would turn this area into badlands as well.

Coming down to the river we could see the town of Kyunglung on the opposite bank. Bikram was dubious about the place where Thubten intended us to ford the river. The water, frigid, glacial melt, was belly high on the horses. Thubten tried riding into the river. His horse backed and filed. But, to get to Kyunglung it was going to be necessary to force our mounts into the river.

Deciding to ford the Sutlej River.

Fording the river.

My horse and the colt's mother carried people; others transported luggage, tents, and cooking equipment. I crossed on my lady, who, I was told, had no name. It made me feel sad. Crossing was scary since in places she had difficulty with her footing. The foal dived after his mother, neighing pathetically, to swim across the strong current.

Another shot of us fording the river.

In the town people only nodded at us solemnly; children ran and hid. This should have alerted us. The white walls of houses had red stripes and their gates were adorned with yak horns. A Tibetan soldier of the Chinese army stopped us. He examined our papers retaining our passports. There is something about having your passport taken from you that induces instant paranoia. Again we should have scented trouble but where would he go with our passports? It seemed unlikely that there was some sort of official office in this little town.

The soldier motioned us along a path that passed large *mani* walls our horses paced around clockwise. We came to ruined *chörtens* and smoke blackened caves that were inhabited. One woman, dressed in red robes, looked like a nun. There were herders, their charges wandering the meadow that squelched down to the river, and three mastiffs that were enthusiastic about murdering us until the shepherds called them off.

We turned a corner.

First sight of prayer flags and red *chörtens* at Kyunglung.

Broad bands of colors pocked with the dark mouths of caves rose up like the curved wall of an amphitheater across the river.

The great multicolored cliffs of Kyunglung punctuated by caves inhabited 2,000 years ago as a city and then more recently as a monastery. In the foreground is a *mani* wall covered with stones carved with Bön mantras.

To the right, it was spanned by a bridge of wire and wood garlanded with prayer flags, the humble replacement for one of Tangton Gyalpo's bridges. Kyunglung was magnificent in its striations of colors, all Rachael and I could have dreamed.

My bottom was sore from the ropes that crisscross my saddle strapping two of our bags onto my nameless horse. I was exhausted and covered in horsehair because the animals were shedding their winter coats. They were also on a diet of new spring grass that made them fart incessantly and shit emerald dung.

In the westering sun the irregular stripe like registers of the cliffs were on the right rose and grey, on the far left ochre and slate blue with a big band of rose and grey paling as it descended to the river. A side valley was striped vertically with brilliant red, almost orange, and white rock. Exhausted, we ate dinner and crawled into our tents as sunset turned the sky behind the cliffs the color of plum jam. Both view and light were spectacular. We thought, as we fell asleep, that tomorrow we would have an exciting day exploring. We had arrived at the Silver Palace of the Garuda Valley, as Kyunglung is named.

We were awakened at seven the next morning in a soggy mix of snow and hail by a chagrined Thubten coming to announce that last night's soldier and an equally young police man had arrived demanding we leave immediately after breakfast. They wanted to confiscate our film.

Somehow Thubten got us out of that one. The cliffs were not as beautiful in the grey morning light. I have gone back to Kyunglung a number of times leading groups, but I have never seen the amphitheater of colored cliffs as beautiful as they were that night with the plum tinted sky behind them.

Regretfully we left Kyunglung stopping in town at a house with yak skulls over its gate where Thubten had to negotiate our fine with the police and the military. This was paid to a couple of middle aged, stolid looking Tibetans wearing sweaters in shriekingly bright colors one of whom was carrying around what looked to be a walky-talky. Obviously, they were the office and were in touch with Chinese headquarters.

Rachael was not as upset by the failure of this plan, perhaps because as least we saw the cliffs of Kyunglung. Our failure was, therefore, I think, an honorable miscarriage in her mind. Alex and I asked Thubten how much the fine had been and gave him the money. It didn't seem right to let him bear that charge, with a baby about to arrive, even though, most likely, it would have come out of an emergency fund.

Coming back to the river, it was obviously too high to ford. We climbed a hill so steep I had to lead my lovely chestnut lady up. At the top we stopped, looking down on a thin wolf visibly frightened by our staring. It is the only wolf I have ever seen in Tibet. It ran, stopped, looked up at us; ran, stopped looked up again, finally running until it was hidden from our intrusive sight. More hills followed. Some I had to lead her up, scrambling over boulders, all of which were odd and fascinating in their composition. Both she and I stopped and panted from time to time. It was nice to have her company in that activity.

Finally we came to the top of the plateau and I rode. I kept singing in my head, "I was out in the desert on a horse with no name…" which was literally true since my lady had no name and what I was riding through was desert.

I was able to dismount with grace but since the stirrups were chest high, and I could not get my toes to that level, mounting was an undignified scramble. I used any available rock as a step, knowing that my clambering ascent to my saddle was a source of amusement to the staff both Nepali and Tibetan. Finally we saw the formations that signaled we were approaching Guragem.

There is a Tibetan saying that a gentleman rides his horse up the mountain but never down. So as we descended endlessly to the river I led her. She balked a few times, but never over rode me. Twice she stopped, rubbing her soft nose against my shoulder in protest. At last we reached the river.

The Sherpas led our horses up over another hill to the fording spot. We, Alex and I, walked by the shore, on a crumbly path of gravel, dirt and unstable stones a foot wide that horses could not manage. The river was swift, grey with silt, and deep. I found that I was angry that Rachael and Tom had gone ahead without us. There was no reason why they should have waited for us, but I was in a high altitude temper and reason was not of interest.

We seemed to walk a mile on this treacherous footing with wind slashing at us, brewing up a storm and finally spewing icy rain into our faces. Toward the end two Sherpas met us, taking our daypacks. When we arrived at the ford the horses had already taken the equipment, Rachael and Tom across. Jamyang, the truck driver, who had enjoyed riding my lady across the river as they took all our supplies to the other shore, restored her to me. We all crossed safely. I was in a foul mood.

The next day Temba the Terrible announced he had no fuel to get us to the border after our Kailash circumambulation. We discovered, via Thubten, that the fuel money had gone to pay Temba's gambling debts. He probably thought we'd pay again. The result of this betrayal was, rather illogically, a general disintegration of the group. Our psychological crumble may have started when we were thrown out of our camp at Kyunglung. We had been tense up to this point but had been able to treat each other civilly. I went into a total spiritual disintegration.

Tom and I got into an argument about something. I had been fermenting for a fight since the day before when I felt, quite irrationally, that Rachael and Tom should have waited for us before crossing the river. I can remember talking to him in a tone of voice a kindergarten teacher might use to a fractious pupil. I cannot for the life of me remember what the argument was about. He yelled and threw a map at me, shouting that he intended to sue Thubten's agency. Luckily Thubten, a good Buddhist, just kept saying, "Yes."

There was much drama with Alex storming out of the dining tent after the map-throwing incident. I was quite annoyed that he did this. I wanted him to stand shoulder to shoulder with me and shout at Tom. Some how Rachael did not participate in this *opera buffa*. As one traveler in this part of the world has understated, "People are easily irritated at high altitudes." But once I got my balance back, I was thoroughly ashamed of my self-centered indulgence in temper.

Since we were headed to Darchen to do the *khora* anyway we decided that we, meaning Rachael, would call Doris Lee, the woman in the brown suit, our agency liaison, to tell her our fuel money was gone, that forty-five percent of the Cruiser's gas was missing and Temba was refusing to give us rest days.

I was grimly, if also secretly, shame-facedly, pleased that Rachael would have to do this since with my fear of people I would have been thoroughly intimidated by my memory of Doris Lee looking, in her severe brown suit, like the Matron in **One Flew Over the Cuckoo's Nest.** Confrontation makes me want to disappear. On top of that I was not pleased with myself over these emotions, yelling at Temba on the way to the *Saga Dawa* ceremony at the *tarbouche*, my fight with Tom or my general emotional condition but I could not seem to get a hold on myself. I kept justifying my behavior to myself, an empty exercise. I felt I had sprung a spiritual leak.

Temba had been selling off our gas since we had stopped up the barrels near Karga, at the turn off to Chung Riwoche, as soon as we had discovered that the gas was leaking out of the drums. That leak made a good excuse for any loss of gas. Thubten also admitted that often drivers get bored and want to go home, arranging their return in any way they can, a lack of gas being one ploy. I can understand that foreigners would only be interesting in the short term.

In penance for my spiritual collapse, when we broke camp at Guragem the next morning, I collected all the trash around us-others, and ours- and, feeling virtuous, deposited it in our garbage pit which would be filled in before we left. After breakfast I saw a neighborhood dog, equally proudly, pulling everything out with all the delight of a bargain hunter at a sale. It made me laugh, something I badly needed to do. We started for Darchen, a cranky group, unanimously glaring at the back of Temba's head. It was nice to have him as the focus of our general ill temper.

In Darchen, Rachael, having corralled a grim Temba, went to call Doris Lee in Lhasa. She explained the situation and Ms. Lee asked to speak to Temba. She told Rachael, when Temba handed the phone back to her, that she had instructed him to find enough gas. Somehow, while we were on the Kailash *khora*, he did.

We were again in Cholera Corner but more distant from the public toilet channel, near the official rental tents on concrete platforms, inhabited by Hindus from India, many of them *sadhus*, Hindu holy men, with their hair up in a top knot, with long beards wearing orange cotton *dhotis*, not suitable to the climate of Kailash. The women wore saris and *shalwar qamizes*–tunics over trousers–topped by down parkas. They started their *khora* the day before us. Both Hindu tent community and trekking-tent community were much reduced in size. The jewelers and many of the sellers of glass jars of mandarin oranges had packed up and left.

I came out of my tent the next morning to find Jamyang, our truck driver, sitting cross-legged in the back of the truck. Beside him was a mysterious sack. He was intently gazing at the passers by. As I watched he called out to a little girl with a baby strapped to her back. She came over, gazing up at him. He leaned out of the truck offering her a little hand knitted jacket in blue and white, just the right size for the baby. While she stared he pulled out of the sack several other items in the size of the child she had tied to her plus a blouse that fit her. Minutes later, looking thoroughly stunned, she walked off with a bundle of baby clothes and two or three items for herself.

A barefoot boy came by with his mother. Jamyang motioned them over to the truck, dug into his pack and the boy had socks and shoes that he stared at in wonder as he and his mother walked away, he still barefoot, holding them in his hand. Jamyang was a Tibetan Father Christmas.

I went to find Alex and the two of us watched Jamyang stop people with children and rummage in his sack, always successfully, for clothes for them. Alex affected by Jamyang's generosity, offered him half of his merit in going around Kailash since Jamyang was going to have to stay with the truck and Land Cruiser. Merit can be given away but the receiver must pay a token amount. Jamyang paid one yuan. It was Jamyang who would have to stay with the vehicles since we were not entrusting our belongings to Temba while we circumambulated.

Rachael, Tom and I, testing our walking and breathing abilities, climbed to where prayer flags were strung across a ravine above Darchen. In the distance was Gyandrak monastery, mysteriously forbidden to us by the authorities that year. On my next trip, there was, equally mysteriously, no prohibition. Walking back we heard, then saw, a military helicopter above, a nasty, black insect flying over these peaceful, sacred sites.

The next day, I started walking the anonymous dusty, finger-trace of path before me scrawling its way up and down small hills. I began the *khora* early with Alex, conscious of my slowness. By now I recognized the way which though sacred was also most anonymous in its scuffed surface. For a while Kailash was on the right, Gurla on the left, then Kailash was eclipsed by her ridges.

When we saw Kailash again at Chaktsal Gang, the heaps of rocks, yak skulls, *mani* stones and prayer flags, were larger than usual because of Saga Dawa.

Because it was Saga Dawa in the Year of the Water Horse the quantity of prayer flags and *khatas* was overwhelming at Chaktal Gang.

I added strings of prayer flags. At the *tarbouche* pilgrims sang and danced as they waved *khatas*. Unfortunately, they finished just as we reached them.

Chörten Kangnyi, the two-legged *chörten*, was so draped in flags and *khatas* that you could not see the entrance.

Chörten Kangnyi hung with sheep heads, *khatas* and prayer flags.

I ducked under them to find the passage floor strewn with sheep heads and skins, Bön offerings. There was a definite stench.

The odiferous goat and sheep heads hung inside Chörten Kangnyi, the two-legged *chörten*, by Bön pilgrims who do the *khora* counter clockwise. Their odor was vivid when I walked through the *chörten*.

Hanging from the left side of the exit was a bouquet of rams' heads and tails laced together like braided onions in a Western kitchen.

Alex and I emerged eager for air unperfumed by drying, dead sheep, to pass the *tarbouche,* its base littered with beer bottles. I don't think drinking would occur here if the Dali Lama were in Lhasa.

We started the climb to the sky burial ground with its eerie, numinous aura. Staring about us at the top, Alex noticed that some one had erected a windsock in the midst of the boulders and half-moon stone fences. It was totally out of place, yet in the right place, a symbol of our breath's wind one concentrates on while meditating, vanishing into death. Humans are in passage, our breath as transient as wind.

Cairns and stones were draped with discarded clothing so that the whole site, as we glanced around, looked as though a crowd of silent people were waiting.

Clothing litters the sky burial site left as offerings which will increase your chance to be reborn in the Paradise of the Dakinis. Sometimes people lie down to visualize their death.

Bracelets left by pilgrims at the sky burial site for monks and lamas.

As we crossed a ledge of maroon stone I looked down to see a discarded bamboo litter at my feet. It was a sort of open work, woven folder of split bamboo, large enough to hold a body, exactly like the one Rachael and I had seen on the last trip, a foot dangling out, when coming to the burial site. This one, having served its purpose, like the clothing on the rocks, had been cast aside.

A litter at Drachom Ngagye-Durtrö, the sky burial site for monks and lamas, on which a body has been brought.

There was, this time, the smell Victor Chan mentioned, not strong, but an odor that speaks clearly to the human heart: the perfume of mortality, disturbing, perturbing, stirring what we keep still and unacknowledged in our depths. Death's fragrance awakens a fear we are desperate to avoid.

Alex and I descended an almost vertical path on the opposite side of the site from where we had entered. Iced over at one point, it was a long, precipitous way down. I was glad of his presence. We slipped cautiously over the ice on our bottoms, scrambling down for lunch opposite Chuku Monastery beside the row of ruined *chörtens*.

As we were munching our way through our curried cauliflower and hard boiled egg lunch, Alex, who has a sense of humor that glitters like cut glass in strong sun, said, "Do you know any good limericks?"

I confessed, "The only one I can recall, and I can't recall all of it, is, 'There was a young lady from Natchez, whose clothes were in shreds and in patches.' But I've lost all except the last line which is "so wherever I itches I scratches."

He then proceeded to recite between bites of hardboiled egg and curried cauliflower a limerick which that premier pilgrim, the Wife of Bath, would have appreciated:

Oh the ferocious old Bishop of Chichester

Would preach 'till the saints in their niches stirred,

But one morning at matins A choirboy in satins

Made the Bishop of Chichester's britches stir.

This almost caused me to tumble off the rock I was perched on.

Invigorated by both lunch and my attempts to memorize the limerick, we tried to cross the river on stones, getting wet feet. Finally, we walked to the bridge. The path to Chuku Monastery had been improved since my trip to get Rachael boiled water but it was still a long, hard slog up to the temple.

There was a new entrance with steps. Two women motioned me into a side room for tea, also offering dried meat but I needed to catch up with Tom, Rachael and Alex on the terrace that looks out to Kailash through a ripple of prayer flags. Although it was now a week since Saga Dawa, there were still many pilgrims.

Inside Chuku Monastery.

The chief monk was not the man who'd been there three years before. This new one was much more official and not as raffish as the previous man. I tried to talk to the present head, wanting to find out about the boy and the monks who had been there, but he couldn't understand me. I felt sad at losing my connection to the wild child and his parental group of monks cum bandits.

He opened the chapel for the pilgrims and us. The alabaster statue was there but to the left was a wooden figure I hadn't seen before and it wasn't something you could overlook since it was waist high and orange. It was a vibrant portrayal of the fierce manifestation of Padmasambava, the eighth century sage and missionary, who created the first temple in Tibet, Samye, and tamed the Bön deities, making them protect Buddhism and Buddhists. This statue was totally different from either the one in the Jokhang in Lhasa or in the little temple in Zhongba. All deities come in two forms, benevolent and fierce. I had not seen a fierce representation of Padmasambava before. People clung naked, in all kinds of attitudes, to his multitude of bright orange arms. I could feel their desperation. It was a disturbing image.

Another innovation was a mirror in the skylight of the temple. We took turns, pilgrims and we four Westerners, standing with our backs to the altar looking up at the mirror to see the dome of Mount Kailash reflected above us, an image as deeply peaceful as the naked clinging forms on Padmasambava were agonizing.

Kailash seen from Chuku Monastery.

Among the pilgrims were some much in need of help, one man with a terribly curled and split harelip and a monk with a half-destroyed face and badly crippled hands. Leprosy? Whatever it was it had twisted lips and nose into a Goya grotesque. I didn't think to give to them and was angry at myself later.

At Chuku Monastery this hand carved ladder and a satellite dish make a contrast in eras.

Coming down from the monastery we walked along the relatively flat path through the valley with, high above, the fantastical crests of cliffs on either side; as we climbed, the stream chattered beside us. Passing pilgrims greeted us. When the cliff walls drew closer to the river, we saw our campsite facing the Lha Chu, a little corner of Kailash visible behind us, the ground pink with flowers of a plant that spread out tentacles clutching the earth tightly against gusts channeled down from Kailash.

Flowers clinging precariously to the earth along the path of the *khora*.

We had no tables or chairs, since metal is forbidden on the circumambulation. I have asked why and been told that the mountain does not like metal. Yak men will not load tables and chairs on their animals. Returning to my tent after dinner, I watched a magnificent herd of yak pass on the path, fine carpets on their backs, red tassels dancing in their ears.

A waterfall across the Lha Chu from our camp descended, a narrow white ribbon down the dark stone until the wind blew it into a vapor cloud that floated away. The next morning it had been transformed into a rippled, satin ribbon of ice.

Alex was feeling the altitude, so we started late, joining the line of pilgrims who passed us invariably asking for Dalai Lama pictures, which I didn't have and which were now illegal.

The mountains on the left marched along beside us in smooth, perhaps, igneous peaks. Ah, those missed Geology classes.

The cliffs, snow covered this year, on the walk to Drira Phuk Monastery from Chuku Monastery.

I reflected with a feeling beyond sadness, a kind of anguished despair as I climbed, "Someday, a soon someday, I'll be unable to return. I'll be too old." I thought of Sonam, glad she did her Kailash *khora* many years before she died. I thought of Liz, my sadness at not being at her death. But I could rejoice in how lucky I was to have known them. I also rejoiced that I could walk this path. I was happy in anticipation of arriving at Drira Phuk monastery and seeing Kailash head on.

I'd planned to do the *khora* thinking of Sonam, dedicating it to her, as my Aunt Liz, when I could actually think, had been part of previous *khoras*. But Alex was talking of his daughter's difficult marriage.

"They have a perfect right to be nasty to each other if they want but they don't seem to realize that in harassing each other they are hurting their children."

"How do you feel they are injuring the children?"

"Oh, by saying the usual spiteful things. And they use the children in their anger toward each other. Ronald, Angela's husband, insists that Beth's nail biting is due to Angela not being firm with her. He is forever grabbing Beth's finger out of her mouth so that she cringes and then he yells at her mother. Robin a year or so ago was a very bouncy little boy, wanting to tell you all his ideas at once. Now he just sits in front of the TV and grunts at you."

"That sounds really bad. But I don't see what you can do except, of course, take them on outings and get them away from their parents."

"I do that as often as I can. I take them to the zoo and to plays. But their day to day grind is doing terrible things to them."

Listening to him, admittedly a bit unwillingly, I thought I was doing, perhaps, what Sonam would do in these circumstances, therefore, doing the *khora* in her image. Part of Sonam's practice of compassion had been to listen deeply, intently to what you said. One knew this by the quality of her responses, which were never superficial. I tried to pay complete attention to Alex, to think about his difficulties as though they were mine. I was attempting to follow Sonam's example. It was, not only, a way of remembering her but a way out of my self-centeredness. Being alone in my head, a comfortable state for me, activated that ego focus.

We came to the point at which a prayer flag web across from Drira Phuk monastery marks the dead on view of Kailash's north face.

Kailash seen from the roof of Drira Phuk Monastery.

Small brown and white birds flew back and forth across the path, one only five feet away, the little dark horns or tufts on his head quite visible. With no killing there is no fear. Then, looking up from my feet, there she was huge against the blue sky's enamel, her mantle of glinting snow draping down to the black lines of her raw and ragged ledges.

At the small prayer flag web, people were prostrating. I could not imagine having the strength and yet these were not young people. For me just carrying my daypack all day, even though it was at most five pounds, was a major triumph.

Alex and I visited a tea tent near the web whose proprietor asked, through gestures, for socks. I promised, through gestures, that I would bring him a pair later. He made us butter tea in his churn, then lay down on his carpet-covered bench for a smoke.

Kailash looked, in afternoon light, as though wrapped in strips of glossy, white satin. Rachael and Tom went to Drira Phuk monastery; Alex sketched; I sat on a rock writing in my journal, looking at the mountain then down at a marmot twelve feet away, leaning out of her hole, a tenement housewife resting her elbows on a window sill. She seemed to enjoy her view of Kailash as much as I.

Later Thubten accompanied me to Drira Phuk Monastery. I contributed five yuan, receiving from a monk a *khata*, blessed water poured into my hands and grains of barley. His room was hung with pictures of the Tsurphu *Karmapa*.

Through Thubten I explained that I had met the *Karmapa* when he was five or six, before he was ordained, although that is not the right word, and again when he was eleven, leading his monks in chanting at Tsurphu. I also visited his monastery in Sikkim just before he arrived there, after walking over the mountains out of Tibet. This information was greeted with smiles and made me again recall Annalisa, my trip with her to Tsurphu on my first journey to Tibet.

We searched the cave for the imprint of the *dri*, a female yak, which guided Götshangpa, the first circumambulator of Kailash. Tradition says on a pilgrimage to Lake Manasarovar he stopped at the entrance to the Lha Chu Valley to make tea but each stone he chose to prop up his kettle had mantras carve into it. A heavy rain began. Out of it came a *dri* who led him to the cave around which the monastery of Drira Phuk was later built. The *dri* was actually a *dakini*, a spirit that aids humans. I couldn't find the impression of the *dri* on the ceiling.

Back at camp, I rummaged in my big pack for socks and delivered them as promised to the tea tent man. They were immediately put away, not on. I was offered in payment a big bowl of instant noodles, which I refused, then tea, which I accepted.

The tea man taking a nap in the tea tent after putting away the socks I brought him.

The next morning in cold and dark, Kailash luminous in snow, we started the climb to Drölma La, the pass. Already pilgrims streamed up toward the pass. Alex, felt physically stronger, but was still worried over his daughter.

"Maybe it would be better if she just divorced him. Maybe it would be better for the children. I just don't know"

I sympathized with the pain of his powerlessness.

"All you can do is love her and love them."

No one tells you parenthood is never ending. We wove through boulders, then over them. I listened to Alex, praying I wouldn't slip as a pilgrim strode by us, passing his prayer beads through calloused fingers and murmuring mantras.

A little girl who danced about us, mocking our difficulties, adopted us temporarily. But she had to keep up with her parents, not spend time with slow pokes. I gave her a picture of Kailash and off she went. She might have been a *dakini*. Certainly her lively spirit helped keep ours up on the difficult climb.

That day and the next we saw Tibetans suddenly stop to lie down by the side of the path and sleep. They were doing the *khora* in a day, a feat I find unimaginable. We came to the jog in the path where stones have been laid in a rough stair and started to the top of the first ridge, a killer. I warned Alex of the second ridge, the hidden one full of boulders, which comes next. Kailash disappeared behind her ridges on our right.

When we stopped to catch our breath on the stair, trying to stand out of the way of passing yaks, Alex told me, "Robin is beginning to stutter. I think it is because his father yells at him so much."

The family sounded as though they were operating in an emotional pressure cooker possibly without a valve. Alex could do little but listen to his daughter, and take his grandchildren out of the house, a frustrating situation.

"It is truly terrible being powerless to help those one loves," I said.

The top of Drölma La fluttered prayer flags, *khatas*, abandoned clothing, and wind-horse papers. One man opened a pack of cigarettes and threw them into the web of flags. We tied our flags to those already there. I handed out dried apricots. Tom handed out postcards of Kailash. Alex and Rachael handed out their lunch. As an offering, I cut two inches from my waist-length braid. I haven't cut my hair seriously since I was a freshman in college. This was an easy offering, not requiring any real sacrifice, which made me feel I was cheating a bit but since Tibetan women do it, I'd decided it must be okay. I suspect the wind just blows it away but perhaps a marmot or a raven gets lucky and uses it for nesting material. That thought pleased me.

Drölma La, the pass at 18,600 feet strewn with *khatas* and prayer flags.

We came down the cliff-edge path; the Tibetans' wild cries echoed off the perpendicular rock, "*So, so, so, so,*" and "*La, la, la.*" "*So, so, la, Gyalo,*" which means, I have been told, victory to the Gods. This is the same formula that Dorje and Tenzin would recite as we drove over *las* on our previous trip.

A group of pilgrims sang songs that others on the trail picked up. The song would get softer and softer, slowly dying out, melting into the sound of the wind but then someone would start it again and the voices would swell again in the narrow channel between mountain and mountain, echoes ricocheting off cliff faces, filling them with melody. Some men sang falsetto.

We wended down through another field of boulders to the narrow path carpeted with little stones that rolled beneath my feet, debouching at the tea tent in a meadow that sloped down to the river, the Zhong Chu. The meadow's green coverlet of grass glinted with the domes of plastic, instant noodle bowls and the green shards of broken beer bottles.

Alex and I bought a thermos of butter tea. Thubten stopped by our table with a lady of many braids and few teeth asking us to share with her. She offered us *tsampa*. I appreciated Thubten instructing us. I wouldn't have thought to have asked her to join us even though I had had the example of Janet on my first trip giving her leftover noodle soup to the hungry young men in the restaurant near the Jokhang.

We walked two hours from the tea tent passing people lying down to rest, many sleeping peaceably on the hard ground, and talked to a group from Kham who had, for twelve days, done a circumambulation a day. I wondered if there is anything fitter than a fit Tibetan! We glimpsed Kailash, the last sight of her on the *khora* her ridges rumpled with snow, and camped by the river before reaching Zutrul Phuk.

The next morning, walking on to the monastery we found it in the midst of a thorough renovation with new statues being installed. A young monk was holding a ceremony for a family accompanied by the temple's drums, and cymbals. Alex and I bought a thermos of butter tea at the tea tent below the monastery, but no young emperor in his costume, holding his imaginary court with his mother and brother in the background were there this time.

Remembering Thubten's instructions, we shared with an elderly woman accompanied by her tall, stalwart son. They were a fairy tale pair. He was the son who in the tale would stand by his mother bringing her old age to comfortable prosperity. It felt good to have asked them to join us in the tea thermos but what I wanted was to be able to lose my self-centeredness enough to know when to give tea or money or whatever was needed spontaneously.

It was a cold and misty morning. Tom said that it reminded him of Scotland. Clouds wreathed the mountains on either side of the river. We had little company; a few Bön were going in the opposite direction. But there was one elderly woman alone in a dusty brown *chuba*, leaning on a slender stick, which she had acquired from somewhere. It was obvious that her feet hurt in her ragged Chinese sneakers; still, she out distanced me with no difficulty.

Sheep grazed on the slopes of wide meadows running up the sides of mountains. At the gorge whose sides are slashed with red earth, the blood of the Soul Yak, pilgrims were digging for, I think, obsidian or the type of clay considered to be medicinal, the *sana*, I had seen people digging for when I was walking with Jemi on my first journey to Kailash. Alex and I found a few pieces of obsidian, but their significance was different for the pilgrims. To us they were just black rocks, nice but not sacred.

Across the gorge was a single strand of prayer flags. Just beyond, we turned a corner and there was Gurla Mandata, Kailash's neighbor mountain, huge and white while before her was the open lap of the Barga Plain burnt brown by the sun. I thought to myself, "The end of the *khora*," and felt a little sad that it was finished.

As we sighted Gurla, a Chinese man mysteriously came from behind us, small and neat in a charcoal grey, shiny silk suit and sneakers; dangling from his right hand was a camera neatly velcroed into its case. Where had he come from? He certainly hadn't risen early to do the *khora*. What was he hurrying to take a picture of? Perhaps he had already taken a picture of something and was hurrying away? He was obviously an official, not a pilgrim.

Then we came upon two girls by the path selling beer from a plastic bag. The Chinese man bought a beer going off, perhaps, to his office at the checkpoint at the *khora's* end. The toes of the younger girl peeked from torn socks. Alex played "This little piggy" with them to her delighted giggles. She stuck her tongue out at us in a sort of quick snake-flick, the courteous Tibetan greeting, showing she was polite. She was adorable; her hair in little rubber banded bunches all over her head.

The young beer seller at the end of the *khora* with her hair in tufts.

We found our truck, which took us to Lake Manasarovar for a rest day of laundry and napping. That night two donkeys, perhaps a mating pair, danced and sang about Rachael's tent miraculously leaping over the guy ropes, never tripping, never pulling down the tent.

Leaving the next day I had no reaction as Kailash disappeared behind us. The lack of any response left me bereft. I felt as though traveling to a foreign town I had sent a friend living there my hotel phone number but she never made contact. I thought that, perhaps, I imagined my earlier emotions or had been overly impressed by them. Perhaps even in such a small group there was enough Western influence to keep me from the unnamed experience I had had before. Perhaps I had been right, that my emotion had come from my contact with the porters and since our bags had been carried by yaks, the source of my emotion, the porters, had not been present.

In the four-wheel drive, tucked into my corner against the window, I contemplated change. I was beginning to realize that I needed to concentrate on process, that what I was involved in was/is not a matter of a goal and a finish line. Have I changed? I thought I had been more patient than before, despite my outburst at Temba but the interchange with Tom was definitely a black mark. What would I change?

I thought of Thubten's gentle instructions to share butter tea and of the lack of generosity in my family. My father's drinking and difficulty earning caused us to clutch at things. But my mother had, I think, learned to grab early in her life. She was always fearful that she would not have enough, not get whatever it was that she wanted or that something she possessed would be taken from her. She gave only when she had to and largely, grudgingly since it was a duty, to the Catholic Church.

The landscape changed, growing greener as we approached the pass that would take us down to the river and the Nepali border. We were leaving the barren heights, the world of ascetic rock, of the Changtang plain behind. That external change from dry to wet connecting to my thoughts on generosity somehow brought me the idea that perhaps my inability to cry was a lack of generosity toward myself, a withholding, an emotional miserliness.

On either side of the road clumps of white primulas were blooming in the long grass. We were about to dive into the chasm down which the river plunges and the road twists between high, walls where water spouts, drips and falls hundreds of feet. I thought as we entered those cliffs that whatever I wanted to change, whatever emotions I wanted to release, I was on a spiritual journey. I could only change through growing spiritually.

While there is talk in AA of "spiritual awakening" and of the occurrence or non-occurrence of "a white light experience," in New York City there is a meeting for atheists and agnostics. There is no set of rules for belief. I could relax. I didn't have to believe in anything prescribed.

We were now traveling between the dark walls of the chasm streaked with the white plumes of falls, sun glittering on the wet rocky faces of the cliffs. What I hadn't thought about until now was that I had internalized the ideas I had been taught in my childhood about god and while I had rejected that idea I had not thought beyond it. Just rejecting that concept did not get that god out of my life. I believed vehemently that I was not a candidate for reentry into the Catholic Church. Even as a child I had been dubious about what I was told.

I had no desire to reinstate the long bearded Catholic God the Father inherited from Judaism, but made gentler by Christ. I might just as well have Odin, a Scandinavian psychopath, in charge. The advantage of that Norse god would be that at least with a sociopath in control I would have a rational explanation for the inane cruelty of the world that the Russian novelist Dostoevsky found so troubling, particularly when it tortures and kills the young and innocent.

I also objected to the version of Christ we have in contemporary Christianity who is not female friendly, although the original may have been. There is a Gnostic gospel in which the disciples complain to Christ that he prefers Mary Magdalene to them. Christ responds saying, "When a blind man and one who sees are both together in darkness, they are no different from one another. When the light comes, then he who sees will see the light, and he who is blind will remain in darkness." Quite a put down for the apostles. Certainly not a parable the Catholic Church in its ineffable masculinity would find acceptable.

What I hadn't realized until now in the dark channel between the cliffs of the chasm flashing with bright water was that rejecting an idea of god does not remove that idea from your life. You can't just destroy; you have to build; you have to replace. I had not thought outside of the box. My thoughts about god were firmly inside the Catholic box of my childhood all neatly wrapped up in the tissue paper of my catechism. I was lugging around my old god in my old baggage. I thought looking out at trees clinging to the sides of the abyss it was time to dump the old luggage. What would replace it? Maybe a firm belief in nothing?

I knew enough about Buddhism at this point to know that when asked by a disciple if there was a God, Buddha's response was, "I don't know. Do *you* know?" This was the response that the man I had talked to at the Narthang monastery had been referring to. This strikes me as the definitive answer to that question. I also admire the Dalai Lama's statement that if science discovers something that casts doubt on a scriptural passage, the scriptural has to give way or be reinterpreted. The idea that for a religious leader scientific fact supersedes scripture is not a concept much accepted in the West.

I couldn't accept Buddhism, although I admired it, because it is largely a celibate, male-dominated religion. I became even less sympathetic toward it when I discovered that, at least in Nepal, to be reincarnated as a woman is considered an inferior reincarnation to that of being reincarnated as a man.

I also read June Campbell's book, **Traveller in Space: In Search of Female Identity in Tibetan Buddhism**, which tells of a high ranking monk who used women sexually for tantric rites without the woman having any choice in the matter. But less scandalously and more ordinarily the usual patriarchal prejudices are evident in Buddhism. Nuns are required to take vows which monks are exempt from. These forbid nuns from criticizing monks; require nuns, even those who are ordained for many years, to rise in respect to monks with less ordained time, although monks need not rise for nuns who have been ordained longer than the men. Both monks and nuns must be present at the ordination of a nun but only monks at the ordination of a monk. This seems typical of the subordination of women in all religions. However, Buddhism has given women, the feminine, a certain amount of room and recognition, perhaps more than Christianity with that ultimate token figure, the Virgin Mary. The highest female incarnation in Tibetan Buddhism, also probably a token, is Samding Dorje Phagmo, "The Thunderbolt Sow of Soaring Meditation" whose monastery is on a ridge above Yamdrok Lake. Tangton, "The Madman of the Empty Land," the bridge builder cum opera composer, portrayed with an icicle beard in the truck stop town of Zhongba, was the first to recognized this highest female incarnation.

Wisdom is represented in Tibetan Buddhism as feminine, which must be joined to the male attribute of compassion, but compassion is also present in those feminine spirits, the *dakinis*, and the *taras*, both green and white. Wisdom, female, and Compassion, male, are often shown in painting and sculpture in, *yabyum*, what is referred to in technical jargon as "sexual congress." This representation of the spiritual in sexual terms is often a bit hard for Westerners to adjust to.

Having started with my "Something" substitute for the word "God," I decided that I might have to live with the indefinite indefinitely. I had been comfortable with that until now when I realized that despite wanting to move on I was still retaining my old received ideas given to me by Catholicism.

Now coming down to the town of Zangmu and the border at the river I knew that it would at least be an intellectual adventure to move from the "something" idea. To do that I was going to have to examine my emotions and thoughts about what I considered a god to be. I had been told in AA to make my own god. This sounded to me as though I was being sent out to find somewhere in LA a Build a God Shoppe. However, it was a relief to be among people who were not fussing about what they cannot know and instead paying attention to what they can do. What I could do was change so that I could be more generous, and perhaps generosity would open up my emotions I thought, as we drove through the narrow streets of Zangmu made narrower by trucks parked and waiting to go through Chinese customs into Nepal.

PART VII

2004, Encounter With The Mountain

I was guiding, Anna from Israel and Sophie, a New Yorker. We saw no Himalayas flying from Kathmandu into Tibet, just a few white heads above the cloud quilt, disappointing, even though one of those heads was Everest.

Anna had been my student many years ago when I taught in California. She had impressed me because she had decided that once she graduated from college she would go to Israel to live permanently. I found this out when she came into my office one afternoon and burst into tears.

"What on earth is the matter?" I asked, fumbling for a Kleenex.

"My parents are mad at me."

"Why?"

"I went to Israel for a year when I was in high school. I loved it. I was so happy there. I decided I would go back after I graduated from college and live there. I just told my parents last night and they don't want me to go," this ended in a crescendo of sobs.

"I think that's a very exciting idea. But is this really the first time you have ever done something that your parents have not approved of?"

"Yes," followed by a shuddering sob.

"Well, I think you had better get used to it. If you have a normal life, you will do many things your parents disapprove of. Don't worry about it too much. They will adjust."

Possibly because of that conversation we had stayed in touch. She was now in her late thirties, overweight, although in good shape from exercising regularly. She had a sense of humor that seemed ineradicable by hardships, (oh my, I wish I were like that), a sweet face with an enviable peaches and cream complexion. She was taking the trip as a space in which to think about a possible career move, returning to school to get a Ph.D. in order to teach. She had served her time in the Israeli army and like most Israelis, had done a lot of rough traveling.

With Sophie, shapely, in her fifties, I had a different, a less fortunate history. She was recently divorced with grown children. Reentering the wage earning world in mid-life she had become a real estate agent. We lived in the same building. A few years before when I had put my apartment on the market, Sophie had wanted, to be my agent. I was very uncomfortable with this idea. It struck me as incestuous that someone living in the same building would be your agent. Friends in other buildings where this happened had complained to me about how trammeled they felt by being forced to use the live-in agent. Too close for comfort, too many conflicting interests. But I had not had the courage to say no. I was afraid of a confrontation; I was always afraid of confrontations. What I did was very foolish and cowardly. Because I wanted to preserve our relationship I did not say no to her and the result was to seriously damage the relationship I thought I was trying to preserve. I diddled about when I should have been direct.

When I finally got to the point of saying, "No," our relations had become decidedly strained. Not a surprise. She felt I had behaved badly. I had known I should talk to her about it directly. That I did not was pure, inexcusable cravenness. It was my fault. The tension between us was still there, which made it a little puzzling that she wanted to go to Tibet with me. But again, a trip to Tibet is not like a trip to Florence where one would have so many people interested one could pick and chose companions. Going to Tibet you go with those who want to go or else you have no one to go with.

I had known a few upper middle class, middle-aged New York matrons who, on losing a partner through death or divorce, had decided to do a physically challenging journey. Usually they were the oldest in their group but made up for the age gap in determination and perseverance. It was a rite of passage from the married life to the single life that I could understand and admire. Ceremonies of passage are not just for adolescent boys. Such a rite may be a useful and stabilizing ritual at any time in life. There is no obvious connection, as the crow flies, between the physical demands of a Tibetan trip and living a single, middle-aged life in New York City but proving one's self in one area gives confidence in another.

Sophie had naturally curly hair, nut brown as her eyes. She had traveled, but always in comfort, to well known, accessible places in Europe on walking tours or by bicycle. I worried that Tibet, difficult, dusty and largely without amenities would not be her soul match. Having a soul match with the country you are traveling in is not absolutely required but when the journey is as physically and psychologically arduous as it is in Tibet it helps to have a deep desire to see and be in that place, to feel a connection.

I was not particularly worried about guiding. I had been a sort of secondary guide on my first strip to Kailash with Arthur and Ben since I was the one with the knowledge of the sites, Tsaparang and Tholing, we went to after circumambulating Kailash. I had been the guide when Rachael and I did our first trip since I knew the territory of the first half of the trip and was also knowledgeable about how to set up such a trip within Tibet. I was cognizant as well about the intricacies of relationships between guides, drivers and clients. Not, I have to say, that having that knowledge ever does one a great deal of good when the guide, driver or both decide they want to go back to Lhasa early. Having a good Tibetan agent, which we acquired through Bikram on the second trip with Rachael solved that problem. I organized this trip through Bikram. Also, I was by this time, with all the reading I had done knowledgeable about Tibetan history. The religion and its intricacies I found to be more difficult to comprehend.

Even before we left Kathmandu Anna was having horrendous digestive track troubles, not the way you want to feel at the beginning of a trip in Tibet. But before we left Lhasa, we each had a bout of dysentery acquired from a huge water dispenser at the Kathmandu Guest House in Nepal that was clearly labeled "Potable Water." We had, too trustingly, filled our water bottles from it.

We landed at the airport that had once been four hours outside of Lhasa, but now, because of the tunnel the Chinese had blasted through the mountains, was two hours from the city. That tunnel was a major technological event for Tibetans in the area who had never seen anything like it. It gave them a wary admiration for the Chinese even as they disapproved of the damage done to the earth.

The baggage people were so lackadaisical about getting luggage into the building that most of us went out to get our cases from the cart on the runway ourselves. Since we three all had huge cases of the duffle bag variety, there was a lot of dragging, shoving and kicking of luggage with pauses to pant because the 12,000-foot altitude was beginning to affect us. I could feel the headache hovering, waiting to descend on me with its claws out and took two Tylenol which made it back off.

Rigsum, our guide, tall, lanky with long shiny black, black hair and blade sharp cheekbones, met us as we exited the tedious hassle of immigration and customs. He was a hyper-gregarious young man who took to Anna on contact. They flirted and teased throughout the trip. It was fun to watch. She used her sense of humor to try to induce him and the rest of our staff to quit smoking, stealing their cigarette packs and secreting them in either her daypack or mine. Rigsum, who was not an academic type, was taken aback and quite openly disapproving when Anna told him she was thinking of going back to school.

While his English pronunciation drove us crazy from time to time, Rigsum was not only good at naming the gods on altars, the basic Tibetan guide skill, but had a complex web of friends able to answer almost any question and if they could not Rigsum was also ready to interrogate strangers to discover whatever we were interested in. He was so charming and funny people were always willing to help him. At any town in Tibet, Rigsum had a friend and, therefore, a strand of his information web.

On the drive into town there were many long, low greenhouses, made from plastic sheeting that looked like silvery caterpillars, in which all kinds of vegetables burgeoned. When I first went to Tibet, vegetables were root vegetables, period, with the occasional squash. Now there are tomatoes, eggplant, cucumbers, bokchoy and even lettuce. This was one of the good things the Chinese have introduced to Tibet. The mountains, decked out in new snow were looking their best.

We stopped with a miscellany of other cars at the Buddha on the cliff who looked newly painted. On the other side of the miniscule pond at his feet, was a clutch of kitschy cottages the Chinese had erected for people to stay in. Empty and already deteriorating into tattiness, they were a blotch on this sacred place. Eagerness to exploit the next touristic opportunity vitiates what brought the tourists to the place to begin with. We do it; the Chinese do it.

The self-manifesting Buddha on the cliff outside of Lhasa
newly painted, surrounded by *khatas* people have
snagged on the cliff face.

The string of ugly glass and tile buildings with grandiose gates and guards on tiny platforms had lengthened since my last drive into the city.

In Lhasa we stayed at the Yak, as I had requested, having learned from my previous trip with Rachael that I wanted a Tibetan hotel. Whether the Yak was still a Tibetan hotel or had been sold into Chinese hands I could not determine but it was not the old Yak, in which the police had come to my room, of dirt floors and smelly bathrooms, but a refurbished version and this version was, even as we stayed there, being knocked down for a yet newer version. The right wing was being demolished; the one facing Beijing St. was already gone.

The old rooms of the Yak being destroyed with a sledge hammer. Each has a painting on its wall.

The new rooms were prettily painted with Tibetan mountain scenes, *chörtens* and grey bearded hermits. There were similar paintings on the walls of those rooms being wrecked concrete block by concrete block with sledgehammers. They were valued so little no one gave a thought to their destruction. The floors were concrete and the bathrooms, sufficient unto the day, were en suite and certainly less odiferous than the old communal ones.

I hurried off to Pema at the *chuba* shop. Her delight at seeing me made my heart levitate, a helium balloon of happiness. I had brought her a little cosmetic case with rouge and lipstick. I was sure she would give it to a friend or her sister immediately. I had never known her to keep anything I had given her, except once, a pretty perfume bottle. I had also brought her a sweater, a more practical present. But the gift was unimportant since it was just a way to express my affection for her.

Anna went to bed exhausted and sick, while I, happily anticipating her delight, took Sophie part way around the Barkhor. She was horrified, repelled by the dirt, the odors of drains, manure, and yak butter, which Lord knows, were strong. All her comments as we walked were negative ones about the dirt and the odors. Her reaction made me aware of the dust and dirt I had come to take for granted, although even initially I had not been horrified. I was too fascinated by the strangeness of what I was seeing, too involved in my curiosity to be appalled.

Girls happily watching the tourist traffic on the Barkhor.

On the Barkhor, a boy in big gloves.

It isn't just that many people see dirt where I see another way of leading and seeing life, the dirt is there and one has to acknowledge it, but there is more than dirt and odor. It's all in what you decide, or are predisposed to focus on. I didn't know if this bias was a result of the American super germ hypochondria or just a personal reaction.

My mother ate things that fell on the kitchen floor and expected that I would too. She was not a germ fusser, which may give me an edge in this situation. But I find it disheartening to take people to a place that fills me with fascinated interest, joy and awe and have them see only dirt, unpleasant odors, and disorder. Focusing on these negative factors means you never make it into the embrace of otherness. Sophie's reaction confirmed my fears that this was not her soul place but, on the positive side, while repelled she also later asked questions, which showed that she was interested. She at least had a willingness to be open to new experiences.

There was a woman, with her two-year old son, doing her *khora* around the Barkhor by prostrating through the pedestrians, a dusty business since the street was largely unpaved. She had tethered him to her wrist with an old, grubby *khata* but, to keep him amused, had bought him a bright red, plastic drum on a handle, a child's version of those used by monks. It had little balls attached on strings which when you twirled the stem beat the drum. He was entranced and twisted it so the balls tapped out an erratic rhythm. Her hair was matted with dust, her clothes grey with it and her child cheerfully streaked with dirt but her expression of faith through her prostrations seemed more important to me than dust.

Ahead of us were two elderly men, the essence of Tibet, in sheepskin lined *chubas*, hands behind their backs, prayer beads slipping automatically through calloused, dirt ingrained fingers as they strolled together mumbling mantras companionably and looking at the merchandise in the stalls. This seemed to me a junction where the material, *samsara*, and the spiritual, *nirvana,* joined.

Between stalls on the Barkhor a man plays the complex and mystifying dice and shell game.

One of the stalls to my horror and distress was full of mutilated bits of Buddhas, hands, arms, decorative pieces of brass, obviously stolen, ripped from temples.

The next day Rigsum, who had been talking nonstop about the women in his office since he had picked us up at the airport, took us there to meet his "sister" and the other coworkers he had told us about. The "sister" was charming with good English and was definitely crazy about him. She had brought him lunch, which she had made, bought him a pair of pants and was lending him her ivory prayer beads for the circumambulation. She was, obviously, determined. But there was also no doubt that the female population took to Rigsum like jam to peanut butter. She was going to have a lot of competition I thought.

In the next few days we did Lhasa's sites—Drepung monastery, the Potala where the Dalai Lama's quarters had been stripped, since my last trip in 2002, of the beautiful religious objects that used to be displayed there; the Norbulingka, the Dalai Lama's summer quarters had been similarly stripped. I could only hope that the objects, made of silver and gold, had not been melted down or sold to collectors in the West. Perhaps they were being reserved for a museum displaying the exotic art of Tibet. There is often in mainland museums a floor dedicated to the art of "minorities," some of which have become so minor that they are close to nonexistent.

The windows of the Potala rising above you.

The Chinese sense of their relationship to Tibet was epitomized for me when I spoke to a woman working for one of the few NGOs in Lhasa. She told me that the Chinese government had contacted the American government to learn how we have dealt with the Native Americans. They consider us a role model to be followed. That sends chills down my spine.

The next morning we went to Drepung monastery, for me always a massive confusion of gods. There were lots of pilgrims with their bags of *tsampa* and yak butter. They passed me on the stairs, which I climbed with much labor made more difficult by the insistence of beggars of all ages along the way. A boy and little girl vied for my attention. To get her to leave the field to him, he kicked her neatly in the shins, setting her howling. Then I really would not give to him.

Rigsum took us off on a little path to the left of the main *khora* that goes around the monastery to see some women hermits who live near a big boulder painted with the image of, I think, Tsong Khapa. They kept rabbits; a white one was loping around the entrance to their cave. There was as well a charming, small, grey cat on a leash that they had provided with a pillow. She did not like her leash, complained to us about it and, I am sure, would have liked to spend time with the rabbit. The cave they lived in was swept clean, with everything they needed neatly arranged. The floor was covered with what looked to me like Astro Turf, certainly a practical cave rug.

Buddhist figures painted on stones near the hermitage cave.

In front of the nun's hermitage cave at Drepung Monastery was a reflector to heat water for tea. A cat was using it to warm itself beside some flowers.

When Rigsum explained that we were going to Kailash, they expressed their delight and blessed us. In contrast to the tidiness of the nuns' cave, a little gulch, with a stream running through it, which we crossed by a bridge to get to the hermit cave, was full of broken beer bottles, plastic bowls from instant noodles, cartons et al.

In one of the multitude of buildings we visited, we were acquired by two little girls in dainty handmade, leather short boots, soft as butter, and the same color. They took our hands and walked with us.

Their mother, in a beautifully tailored *chuba*, asked, Rigsum translated with amusement, "Are you going with the foreigners?"

"Yes," they replied in unison.

"Well then, don't bother to come home."

"All right," they responded cheerfully.

They could both count to ten in English. When we parted I delved into my daypack coming up with two yellow balloons, close to the shade of their boots. They were delighted.

I met at lunchtime with the head of our Tibetan agency, a man in his early forties, quick, obviously intelligent. I explained to him that I had tried twice before with other groups to reach Kyunglung but had had difficulty, once because the river was too high to ford and the second time because we had not had the necessary permits. I pointed out that since there was no road or bridge we would have to be prepared to hire horses and ford the river.

He and Rigsum talked together in Tibetan. Then Rigsum called someone on his phone. In a few seconds he was talking to a guide who had been to Kyunglung within the past month by road. He also got the name of another guide who would be at Saga Dawa at the same time as us who knew how to get to the road. I was very skeptical about this but hoped the road was real and not imaginary. Having met Rigsum's boss, I felt quite sure our papers would be in order. He was in personality quite the opposite of the sly and slippery looking Chinese man who had failed us when Rachael, Tom, Alex and I had gone.

Rigsum's boss suggested that when I came to Tibet again I deal with him directly rather than going through Bikram in Nepal. He would supply me with a Tibetan cook and staff instead of Nepali Sherpas, making the trip much cheaper. I had no intention of doing this but I was amused when, later, Rigsum told me, "You don't want Tibet staff. Nepali better." I agreed. I like Tibetans but they are proud, individualistic and lacking in the personality skills that make for good service. Nepalis excel at this.

We went to Sera monastery that afternoon getting into what I think of as "the Mystery Hall", a chapel known as the Tamdrin Lhakhang, *lhakhang* means chapel. From the walls and ceiling hang helmets, armor, chainmail, bows and arrows, shields which, according to Victor Chan, Tibetan soldiers presented to the god of the temple when they had come home safely from war. Also over your head in the midst of weapons and armor is a packed, fanged crowd of snarling, fierce deities glaring down at you out of the gloom. They are masks but in the obscurity above they have the nightmare force of a pack of pursuing demons. This time the hall was less mysterious because it was very well lit, whereas before all these objects, including the fierce deities, their white fangs gleaming, had been just discernable in the dark of the high ceilinged hall.

In the tree shaded courtyard we watched the monks debating. They ignored us, having an excellent time following and criticizing the arguments between the younger orators. I could see in my memory the Italian doctor's wife who, on my first trip into Tibet by bus, had practiced, in a corner of the court, the hand gesture the monks used to emphasize their debating point.

We went to the Jokhang twice, once during the day and once in the evening to hear the monks chant. Rigsum was a miracle of patience, saying the names of gods over and over for us. He pointed out to Anna, having adjusted to her desire to return to school, a statue of Manjushri, the god of wisdom who has a flaming sword in his right hand above his head with which he destroys ignorance and darkness while in his left he holds a blue lotus. "That's the god you need for going back to school, the god of learning, and wisdom," Rigsum told her. From then on Manjushri, with his raised sword, received special reverence from Anna.

That evening we were going to see the chapels on the second floor of the Jokhang and to hear the monks chant. We waited for Rigsum outside near a walled enclosure where there is the stump of a willow purportedly planted by Princess Wencheng the Chinese wife of Songtsen Gampo, the first historical king of Tibet. Next to it is a *doring*, a stone stele, with the Smallpox Edict of 1794 carved into it in Chinese characters. It states that the disease is a plague and tells of various ways to defend the population against it.

The descendant of Princess Wencheng's willow and the stone on which was carved in 1794 instructions on how to deal with a small pox epidemic.

There is a second enclosure nearby with a tall *doring* inscribed in both Chinese and Tibetan. This is the text of the treaty of 822 between China and Tibet declaring peace.

It begins:

"The great king of Tibet, the Divine Manifestation, the b Tsan-po and the great king of China, the Chinese ruler Hwang Te, Nephew and Uncle, having consulted about the alliance of their dominions have made a great treaty and ratified the agreement. In order that it may never be changed, so that it may be celebrated in every age and every generation the terms of the agreement have been inscribed on a stone pillar."

Further down it states:

With great compassion, making no distinction between outer and inner in sheltering good–the single thought of causing happiness for the whole population–they have renewed the respectful courtesies of their old friendship.

It was here, in front of the Jokhang that Langdarma the Bön king who persecuted the Buddhists and drove many as refugees into the western Guge Kingdom, was assassinated by the Buddhist monk, Pal-dorje, as he performed his magical Cham dance.

A patient horse near the Jokhang waiting for his master.

We watched the Barkhor evening scene of circumambulators–stout, stiff-limbed, middle aged Tibetan ladies with pug-faced lap dogs or small, grey, moppy dogs on leashes held in one hand while the other whirled a prayer wheel. There were hordes of children some solemnly circumambulating the *khora* while holding a grandparent's hand, others chasing each other with shrill shrieks around the stalls that sell strings of primary colored prayer flags. Young men in brocade *chubas,* their long black hair twisted up and fastened with barrettes studded with coral and turquoise, slowed their stride beside ragged old women, their grey hair coated with dust, leaning on their slender staffs of willow branches.

When we entered the Jokhang with Rigsum, going through the passage from the first big courtyard, I pointed to a bell hanging in the darkness overhead and asked, " Do you know where that's from? I just read about it in Victor Chan." He didn't.

"It's the bell of a Christian church built by Capuchin missionaries who came to Lhasa in the early 17th century. The church was very near to the Jokhang, although now no one knows exactly where. They were allowed to stay and preach by the Sixth Dalai Lama but they made no converts."

The Sixth Dalai Lama, whose poems are still popular to this day not only in Tibet but also in China, was a bit of an anomaly having not been discovered and, therefore, trained as a monk until he was fourteen, by which time he had discovered girls, drinking and music. He was not interested in giving them up. Tradition has it that he used to sneak out to spend late nights with the ladies in the town below the Potala, now destroyed by the Chinese, drinking wine and singing songs.

Rigsum looked at me in disbelief, saying, "You sure about bell?" He went to check my statement with a monk who corroborated what I had read.

In one chapel there was a rat, very ill, who to our alarm wandered toward us, then away, then back toward us again, causing me to think of the dancing rats that presaged the plague in Europe. Rigsum took the rat's presence matter-of-factly, telling us that there were many in the Jokhang because of the big basins, which the pilgrims fill with *tsampa* making offerings to both the deities and the monks. The damage they cause has to be constantly repaired.

Just as we arrived at the Jowo chapel, refulgent with the light of butter lamps, the great doors onto the main square in front of the Jokhang were opened and the pilgrims who had been waiting came hurtling like an invading army around the fenced space where the monks chant, a wave of bodies across the stone floor, a seething, pushing mass that metamorphosed itself into a ragged line to the chapel with its twin silver dragons guarding the Jowo. Then all was quiet except for the swish of prayer wheels whirling in the grip of work-calloused hands.

The monks arrived, kicked off their shoes, putting them into low cupboards that form the base of the fence around the chanting area that also holds statues of Chenresi and Guru Rinpoche. Some looking bored settled yawning into their places. But when the chanting began, filling the temple with the gruff rumble of male voices, they became focused. The voices were accentuated by the thud of a drum and the cymbals making bright, brass sparks of sound in the dusky light.

Leaning on the chanting area fence, I heard two Israeli girls ask a monk standing nearby what percentage of the admission fee the Jokhang received from the Chinese government. They and Sophie were astonished to hear, "None." Sophie had difficulty believing the Chinese have, and still do, mistreat the Tibetans, although the evidence was certainly all around and has always been consistently reported in the Western press. It was only later in the trip, after a Tibetan, away from any possibility of being overheard, hissed at her, "We hate Chinese," that she accepted this fact.

We went up to the second floor where one can look down into the center of the court where the monks chant seeing the upper part of the statues in the gloaming around the edge of the well. Touring the rooms, a muddle of images, we passed though old, carved doorframes, their designs almost erased by the casual caress of centuries of hands.

As we strolled from chapel to chapel Rigsum and I told the story of how the Jokhang came to be built. It took two of us because the Chinese have cut the Tibetans off from their history and, therefore, there are facts that they are not told, mostly these have to do with Tibet rivaling or triumphing over the Chinese.

"King Songtsen Gampo built Jokhang temple," said Rigsum.

I segued in, "He was the first historical king of Tibet in the 7th century AD. He harried the Chinese right up to the gate of their capital, present day Xi'an, which is now famous for the army of individual, terracotta soldiers made for the tomb of Qin Shi Huang, the first emperor, who unified China in the 3rd century BC."

"Songtsen married Nepali princess, Tritsun, and Chinese princess, Wencheng," Rigsum continued.

"He invaded Nepal in 632. In those days aggression brought wives in peace-making marriages. In 641, the Chinese offered him their Princess Wencheng as a bond of armistice," I interrupted.

"Both women Buddhists and their marriage dowries two Buddha statues. One in Jokhang. Other in Ramoche temple." There was a five-minute hiatus here while the four of us slowly worked, consonant to vowel to consonant, on a word that Rigsum's pronunciation had rendered incomprehensible. It turned out to be "dowries".

"Princess Wencheng also brought with her copies of the Buddhist *sutras*, the scriptures, treatises on astrology, silk manufacture, and medicine. Wencheng and Tritsun converted Songtsen to Buddhism," I added.

When I read or hear this story I always wonder what Wencheng thought on her jolting trip in a wooden wheeled cart, or perhaps a palanquin shouldered by her serving men to Lhasa. Did she dread this marriage to the "barbarian" Tibetan? She must have been used to the best that civilization anywhere in the world could offer, elaborately good manners, relative cleanliness, good and varied food, beautiful clothing. What did she make of the intelligent, powerful man smelling strongly of yak butter who became her husband? She would have been prepared by her upbringing as well as the counseling of the diplomats around her to be submissive and accepting but still it must have been a bit of a shock. However, she apparently, judging by the varied architectural results of her influence, assimilated into her new country, having a strong impact on its ruler.

"Songtsen build a temple in Lhasa," Rigsum continued. "Wencheng decided should be in Lake Wothang."

"There is still part of Lake Wothang in Lhasa. Her choice, although odd, was confirmed when the King had a vision while meditating," I interposed.

" Long pieces of wood put across lake. It filled with dirt. Goats brought dirt to lake. But day's work gone in morning, not there. King and two wives pray. Saw dream, vision. On Tibet huge, demoness sleep, you know like ogre? Monk told King and wife destroy her power build many monasteries and statues on top her. Hold her down," Rigsum said, spreading his hands expressively.

The sleeping demoness with temples pinning her down at various points of her anatomy.

I explained further, "They had to build temples and monasteries at particular points in the vicinity of Lhasa that corresponded to various parts of her anatomy. Once these constructions were completed the building of the Jokhang went forward without any difficulty."

Sometimes I come across, a picture of this demoness—there's a fine one in the Rubin Museum in New York–temples and monasteries firmly pinning down her elbows, knees, wrists and hips as she sleeps peacefully. I imagine her snoring gently through her fangs.

It is paradoxical that Tsongsen, definitely a warrior king, having become with his army a sufficiently serious threat to the Chinese empire for them to offer him a princess to marry, should then have adopted a religion that is pacifist by nature. The Chinese did not lightly offer their princesses to people they considered barbarians. But these particular barbarians were at the gates and a princess must have seemed a suitable bribe to get them to enter the gates peaceably.

The next day we went to the Norbulingka, a complex of summer homes of the Dalai Lamas in a park, which seemed to be in better condition than the last time I had visited. The resident geese were all clustered on their one, feather-strewn island honking conversationally at each other. The lilacs had just stopped blooming and the roses were budding. Around the fountain in front of the present Dalai Lama's house there were pots of nasturtiums, petunias and a daisy like plant. Marching up the steps like stiff, green uniformed soldiers wearing red busbies were extraordinary, tall cacti covered with flamboyant scarlet blooms.

Norbulingka, the summer home of the Dalai Lamas with temples and quiet pools full of noisy geese.

Inside, many of the objects I had seen years before were gone and a rope had been put up so that one could not see the mural that shows the present Dalai Lama, his family, cabinet members and the foreign dignitaries who visited him. I pulled Rigsum aside and enquired if it would be all right for him to ask the young guard to let us by the rope so we could look at this very intriguing painting. Rigsum asked, but the guard obviously had orders to keep people from seeing it. Tibetans who were going through the building craned their necks to look at the one picture of the Dalai Lama still on public view in Lhasa. We did see the mural that tells the story of the monkey monk and the ogress.

When our car dropped us back at the Yak, I suggested that we go to the Snowlands for lunch. To my surprise Sophie said, "Why would we go there since you are the only one who's hungry." It seemed a little early for an altitude attitude.

I could feel my irritation growing toward Sophie. The challenge of change was grinning at me like the Cheshire Cat. I wished Sonam were there to talk to about my rumbling righteous anger toward Sophie. I knew she would tell me to think of Sophie as my beloved aunt. But I felt so justified, so entitled. It was prodigiously tempting to lash out and be spiteful. St. Teresa of Ávila said that her God was always right there telling her what to say as she negotiated with the men who opposed her projects. It would be nice to have such an entity in one's life, someone who has worked out the tactful, appropriate answer, I thought. But first I would have to have a god.

I absolutely believe in evolution, in those facts that are all around us in the breeding of dogs and cattle, in the manner in which bacteria and viruses select into new strains resistant to our antibiotics or antiviral medicines. I don't think though that these facts eradicate the possibility of the other way of considering the world, through the spirit. It is important, however, not to get the two confused. One's beliefs are not facts except perhaps to one's self.

It is unfortunate that most people perceive evolution as an elimination of god. This, I think shows a certain lack of both imagination and flexibility. There is no reason why we have to choose one or the other.

I am not an atheist, certainly not of the Richard Dawkins evangelical atheist variety, who has made a religion of atheism. Those who write against him are just as shrilly sure they are right, being right being more important than the existence or nonexistence of god.

However, there seems to me to be something else going on here. It may be that we perceive life as something to be lived in either of two ways, which we consider, for reasons that I cannot fathom, mutually exclusive. One is living by the "facts", i.e. evolution, natural selection, the survival of the fittest, although the meaning of those phrases is a bit murky. For instance, in a cave in the Zagros Mountains of Kurdistan, Iraq a number of skeletons of Neanderthal men were discovered. One, whose age has been established to have been between forty to fifty, which would be about eighty years today, had a withered arm, was probably blind in one eye and crippled in other ways. These were not recent injuries and would have kept him from contributing to the hunting and gathering of his community. He certainly was not among the fittest, yet he had been so precious to them that they had helped him to survive. He may have been a shaman, a wise man. His fitness for them was probably spiritual not physical.

My thinking here may seem wooly minded to some and blasphemous to others but I do think it is useful to keep a clear demarcation between facts and the spiritual and not muddle the two up together. Facts can be proved. The spirit is a whispering, echoing, reverberating creature, luminous and numinous.

Not having St. Teresa's politic god to tell me what to say I kept my mouth shut. We did go to the Snowlands and Sophie was delighted with the food, which was a great relief. I was pleased that I did not reciprocate with any snippy remark of which I am quite capable.

Someone had given the Snowland's owner, to my delight, a copy of an article I'd written for *The Wall Street Journal* about where to eat in Lhasa, which they had laminated and posted outside their door. Unfortunately the Snowland's owners have since become supporters of the Dorje Shugden sect, an anti Dalai Lama group, and so I no longer eat there.

After lunch we went our separate ways. I walked to a shop on Beijing Street where Anna had reported seeing some interesting Tibetan hats, not Lhasa Lady's hats. Despite being a bit guilt stricken I bought a fox fur hat. The fur wraps around in a band forming the base of the hat and there is a pouf of soft, pale yellow brocade in the center. I found a piece of embroidery for a friend and then took a last walk around the Barkhor since we were leaving the next day.

I came across a pair of monks, one a bit of a yuppie in a fine wool robe and sunglasses with the label still attached (Tibetans do not remove labels) who with his more humble companion, was trying out bells at a stall with, I presume, much discussion of the quality of tone as they worked their way through those on display ringing them one by one.

That evening I went to visit Pema. I was now 68; it was more than a decade since I made my first trip to Tibet in 1992. How much longer would I be able to do these treks? I had brought the yak bone prayer beads carved with little skulls that the abbess of the Lhasa *ani gompa*, the nunnery, gave me on my first trip to Lhasa. I went into the back of the shop pulling them out of my pocket. I did not really want to do what I was about to do, but I felt, despite my large reluctance that it was the right thing.

Cupping them in the palm of my hand I said, "These were given to me by the abbess at the *ani gompa* almost ten years ago. I'm getting old and I don't know how many more times I will be able to come to Tibet. I want you to have these. I wouldn't like them to be stranded in America when they belong here."

It was rending to give them up, even as I write I think of them longingly, but I knew that in my part of the globe they would just be a curiosity. Here they would be used. I was also trying to get myself to both understanding and accept that my time in Tibet was finite, as a prelude to understand that my time in the world was finite.

Pema draped a *khata* around my neck. We hugged and said goodbye.

The next morning we three, with much panting, hauled packs down two flights, bump, thump, bump. They were very large bags. Anna's looked like a giant sausage on wheels that, of course, fell off during the trip. Rigsum our guide and Rigsum our driver hefted them into the four-wheel drive. Later when we joined up with our truck outside of Lhasa we discovered that our truck driver was also named Rigsum. It made things easy on the memory. We decided they were Rigsum 1, the guide, Rigsum 2, the four-wheel drive driver, and Rigsum 3, the truck driver.

Anna found us breakfast, since the restaurant next to the Yak was not open early in the morning, tasty steamed pork buns from a tiny place next door to the massive portal of the Yak. I think they were made there in the shop, not at the Kirey Hotel's steamed bun factory down the street that had provided me with hot water for my shower on a previous trip. We bought more for Rigsum and our driver.

While we ate in the car heading out of Lhasa, Sophie told us that she had washed the soles of her shoes, "Because I don't know where they've been," as though they had explored Lhasa on their own while she slept. We giggled at her, which she took in good part.

All our Tibetan staff were named Rigsum but we also had, in the truck that met us outside Lhasa, (trucks carrying tourist paraphernalia were no longer allowed in the city) Nepali staff headed by our *sirdar*, Karma Lama, a short, compact, dedicated man. I worried about our two teams getting along. Would there be conflicts? That would be deadly for the trip. Only once did I hear a disparaging remark by one team member about the nationality of the other team.

With the truck behind us we drove a little east of the capital along the Tsang Po River, which when it turns south, cutting through the Himalayas into India via an extraordinary gorge that has only recently been explored, becomes the Brahmaputra. We were going to the Yarlung Valley, the locus of the original kingdom of Tibet, to visit temples and, the tumuli of the Tibetan kings before we set out for Kailash. On our way we turned off the road through a pompous modern Chinese arch with nothing around or on either side of it and followed the dirt road to stop at a dusty, nondescript village that I had read about in Victor Chan.

Our campsite by the Tsang Po River in a grassy, sandy spot. Despite the road hidden by the trees, it was serene to be beside the river's flow.

The temple's structure dates to the 4th century. The central shrine moved us all to a still sadness. There were, along its walls, vacant arches of ornate *toranas*, horseshoe shaped frames, great, flame like nimbuses made from clay, marking niches where statues of Buddhas, some twelve feet high or more, lived before the Cultural Revolution. These frames were now reliquaries of emptiness.

The paintings on the walls of the *khora* around the main chapel date to the 11th century and were unlike any I had ever seen in Tibet. Tucci, an Italian who was the first great, Tibetan art expert, believed they were painted by craftsmen from the far west of China, at least as far west as Kashgar, who had been influenced by the Greek artisans who followed in the train of Alexander the Great's invasion that inundated the borders of India.

There are large Buddhas painted all along the walls, these are surrounded by people, worshipers, and saints, usually men. But the faces of these men are different from those in the murals in the Jokhang or Drepung; these have big noses, high foreheads, sometimes baldpates, and twiddly little moustaches. Their jewelry is elaborate, their robes float and swirl on some invisible, ethereal wind and prancing among them are deer, lions and elephants.

Looking at these paintings I realized that I have never seen a bald Tibetan, shaved heads on monks, yes, but no one bald or balding. The faces look Persian or Middle Eastern. Sophie and I were engrossed by these murals while Anna and Rigsum 1, neither much for art history, went outside to wander the tiny town.

We drove on eastward but needing to pee asked Rigsum 1 to have Rigsum 2 stop. There was not much cover so we walked down into a gulch that hid us from the road. It was only as we climbed back up that we happened to glance overhead and saw a man fixing the lines at the top of a phone pole.

Getting back into the car, Anna accused Rigsum, "How much did you charge him? I'll bet you called and said I'll deliver three pale bottoms just under your pole at 3 pm."

We all thought it was ludicrous and hilarious that after taking so much care to go into the gulch to crouch we would have been plainly visible from above.

We camped at the side of the Tsang Po in a grassy, sandy spot. Across the river, faun colored, peaked sand dunes edged the water. Over them rose barren mountains, just discernibly pale green with the first spring grass and above, higher, white-topped mountains shouldering clouds. Our tents were set up when we arrived and we were, under Karma Lama's direction, served a snack of lemonade and pineapple cream cookies. Such little luxuries help one survive altitude and clogged noses.

The next day we visited the Yumbu Lagang, the only castle remaining in Tibet, rebuilt multiple times. Its foundation may date back as far as the 7th century, to the time of Songtsen Gampo, Tibet's king who married both the Nepali princess, Tritsun, and the Chinese princess, Wencheng. It was a testing climb up to the castle but there were horses and a yak available if you wanted to ride. A young, Chinese woman rode the yak, giggling and shrieking at the difficulty she was having because, not being a multiple-armed Indian God, she couldn't hold on, as well as hold her purse, and her parasol, which impedimenta was apparently necessary to her.

The Yumbu Lagang, the only castle remaining in Tibet.

I walked the *khora* around the castle with Rigsum 2, the four-wheel-drive driver, and Rigsum 3, the truck driver, finding two little caves on one side with *tsatsas*, heaps of them, some in boxes which I was told are given by families. I was also told that it is not all right to take them, which brought up memories of Heinrich and my illicit *tsatsas* displayed on a shelf in my library.

Above and below the prayer wheels *tsatsas* are line up or heaped up. They are small clay figures of dried clay given as offerings.

Inside we walked up and up to the top floor very slowly. Here there were new images because the eight old ones had been stolen–art theft is prevalent in Tibet, a persistent threat to the culture–and a superb view across the patchwork of fields, in modulated shades of spring green.

We drove on to the barrows of the Tibetan kings. I find the method of arrival of these monarchs to their new homeland quite distinctive, since I come from a cultural background where kings arrived with sword in hand. Nyatri Tsenpo, the first Tibetan King, shinnied down from the sky on a rope to Mount Yala Shampo in the Yarlung Valley.

His thirty-third heir, Songtsen Gampo (605-649), who with his Chinese wife constructed the Jokhang in Lhasa, raided the Chinese western borderlands, disrupting trade on the Silk Road. He also invaded Nepal, acquiring the western Bönpo area of Shangshung that centuries later became the Buddhist kingdom of Guge with its capital in Tsaparang near the hermitage area of Kyunglung.

It was warriors like Songtsen and his father, Namri, who caused the Chinese to build the Great Wall. They were the barbarians the Chinese feared and their fear made them send him Wencheng. Along with his two foreign wives, Songtsen also had a Tibetan wife who provided him with an heir but that is all we seem to know of her.

Wencheng's marriage to the king of Tibet is part of China's rational for maintaining its right to occupy Tibet. They claim inheritance of Tibet through the distaff side.

In Songtsen Gampo's barrow tomb are buried the king, his two foreign wives and his two principal ministers, Gar and Thönmi Sata.

The barrow of one of the Tibetan Kings in the Yarlung Valley.

The poor Tibetan wife certainly gets short shrift in all of this. Some how not getting buried with your husband strikes me as worse than being cut out of the will. Contemplating this exclusion I found myself thinking gratefully of Les's daughter and granddaughter for including me in his funeral.

At the tumuli of the Tibetan kings, huge earthen barrows long since robbed of any precious contents, there were many Tibetan pilgrims because this is a sacred place. They seemed to be mostly women in *chubas*, shimmering silk blouses and hats ranging from plain straw to one jaunty Lhasa Lady's hat without a veil but with a wreath of bright flowers around the brim.

We walked up a steep flight of stairs to the top of the barrow to see the renovated chapel with paintings and statues of deities and protectors. On the way down as we passed them, women pilgrims commented, Rigsum 1 translating, on how big our bottoms were, not just Anna's, which she admitted was large, but all of us. Sophie and I were a bit put out since in our culture our bottoms would be considered small. We received friendly pats.

On either side of the road where our car was parked the grass was a vivid green and nestled in it were wild iris, delicate lavender and white petals curling away from a spotted center.

Purple, wild iris blooms along the verge of the road and in the meadows in the Yarlung Valley, petals curling away from a spotted center.

As we were about to get into the car, an elderly woman approached us with crystals for sale. We three said, "No," automatically, without a thought, but Rigsum 1 bought her least attractive piece that she would otherwise, possibly, have never sold since it wasn't even stone; it was plastic. This inventive form of charity that does not belittle the receiver amazed me. I realized I would never have thought to do what Rigsum did. I am much too self-centered to have the imagination to think of another person in that fashion. It was an instance of the ingenuity of Tibetan compassion and generosity that Rigsum bought what was least saleable allowing her to have lunch, which she might otherwise not have been able to have.

With Rigsum wearing his plastic crystal on its black cord around his neck we drove on to Trandruk monastery built by Songtsen Gampo in the 7th century. The *gompa* is a small replica of the Jokhang in Lhasa. A watery mythology similar to that about the Jokhang surrounds it. Princess Wencheng wanted to build a monastery on this site, which was inhabited by a five-headed dragon in a lake. Songtsen agreeing that this was, despite the lake, an auspicious place spent days in retreat gathering sufficient spiritual power to summon a huge falcon, a *tra*, which lapped up all the water in the lake and defeated the dragon. Thus Trandruk was founded.

Trandruk Monastery, originally constructed in the 7th century, with two elderly visitors sitting by the entrance. The *tarbouche* for the monastery is in the courtyard.

I had been to Trandruk once before but this visit affected me more, perhaps because the temple was familiar. The chapels, courtyards and corridors were full of elderly men and women twirling prayer wheels and passing prayer beads through gnarled, heavily veined hands as they moved reverently through its multiplicity of chapels and courts. Their lined faces were beautiful in the flickering light of the butter lamps which were sometimes overhead, sometimes at waist level and sometimes lower, illuminating their old faces from various angles.

When you are beyond working age in Tibet you are not thought of as useless. You become the person who labors to fulfill the spiritual needs of the family as the others toil to fulfill the material needs. Through saying mantras, prayers, meditating and performing *khoras* around sacred sites you store up merit for the family. You are an important and useful component of the household.

We climbed a stair to see a famous *thangka* portraying Princess Wencheng, the founder of the temple, in a mosaic of pearls ranging from pink to grey to white to black. When I had seen this before I had had to stand in front of it for a number of minutes before I could make out its subject, the Princess portrayed as a White Tara. Somehow I got focused on the little bubbles of pearls in their gradations of hues rather than on the overall picture. Next door was another chapel but this one had a peacock that emitted a mechanical cry. It and its cry were a non sequitur for me in this environment.

We drove on into Tsethang, a fairly large town with many Chinese immigrants changing its architecture and ambience, to see the monastery and the nunnery. The former has a very pretty garden, a serene place to wander in and from its roof a charming view over the old Tibetan town.

The nunnery, Sang Ngag Zimche, is tiny and also has an atmosphere of serenity. The nuns saved their convent from the Cultural Revolution by building a high stonewall around it with no entrance. They sealed it up. When Mao died the walls came down and they reentered their home.

We stopped in Tsethang for Rigsum to go to the market to get us a chicken for dinner. He came back with the chicken but also with a bag of peaches, which in the back of the car, we rubbed clean on our shirts, the juice running off our chins and down our arms to drip stickily off of our elbows.

We came back to the campsite to do our laundry while the cook turned the chicken into a luscious stew with tomatoes. Our location was idyllic; although there was a road not far away on which we could hear cars zip by from time to time. I concentrated on the water's silken flow.

Since there is little wood in Tibet a boat is made out of yak hide and inflated.

Nights by the river were illuminated by a moon slice and a splendor of stars, the Milky Way's fluid stream of white made closer by altitude and the thinness of the air. Getting up to go to the toilet tent was not a labor but a somnambulistic stroll through velvet dark with a soft glory of light above. Birds animated our mornings, skimming in the air or paddling among the reeds. Rigsum 1, proudly announcing that he knew how to swim, did a dog paddle in the river close to shore. He was braver than we were, afraid to dare the current and the muddy bottom. We left our beautiful campsite reluctantly but it was time to head to Kailash.

As the tents came down and the Sherpas packed them up with the other equipment Sophie ran to help, lifting the folding dining chairs up to the man in the back of the truck. I could see that the Sherpas didn't know what to do about her assistance, which they didn't want. First, it went against the Sherpa/client social divide and second they knew what order they wanted things to come into the back of the truck and she didn't. But they said nothing and neither did I. I felt that at least so far I was dealing well with Sophie.

We took the road for Gyantze and Shigatze passing Yam Druc Lake, Scorpion Lake, fed by unknown sources with no known outlet. The Chinese hydroelectric plant was still there and operating, although they had to pump the water back up at night to keep the lake from emptying. The road was rough because they were improving it, putting in culverts to take off the water coming down from the mountains. We stopped for a picnic by the side of the lake, a flawless turquoise clasped in a setting of mountains in snows shiny as pulled taffy and were joined by a pair of Tibetan sisters and their father. We ate together, travelers, Western and Tibetan, the crew and all—curried potatoes, chapattis like leather gloves with peanut butter and jelly and hard-boiled eggs. Those who could speak each other's language talked; otherwise we smiled, happy to be in each other's company.

Yam Druc Lake, always an astonishing shade of blue, is still having its water pumped back up at night after, during the day, it has passed through the hydroelectric plant.

We passed the two glaciers close to the road. At the second there was a fearsome scrum of ragged women and children begging vigorously or selling rocks and crystals. Taking refuge in the car, we waited for the truck to catch up while watching a Japanese family with an earnest, tripod bearing father, a Chinese group of business men in buttoned up dark suits, and a lone Italian leaping from his four-wheel drive to take a photo, then leaping back and speeding away. We found out later that he only had three days in Tibet and was trying to cram in as much as possible.

When the truck arrived I was told that it was having some kind of gear difficulty. But our next incident as we drove along the side of a stream was to find the lone Italian, his driver and guide hunched over their rear wheel trying to change a flat. We stopped to help, drove on and within a couple of miles had a flat ourselves. He stopped for us. The spare tire in place we went on as the stream widened into a river of startling blue green.

In Gyantze we didn't camp but stayed in a miserably cold, barely adequate hotel. We would have been more comfortable in our tents. I shared a room with Sophie who commented on the odor in the bathroom, "We must be above the kitchen. It smells like they are making turnip soup." I thought for a moment about telling her, "No, it's just bad Tibetan drains." But decided that was not information she really needed. However, she was absolutely right; that was what it smelled like.

The parking lot with prayer wheels outside Gyantze's famous monastery.

Gyantze was worth the odor. The parking lot outside the Pulchor Chode, the monastery, was full of pony carts parked at random angles, the ponies happy to drowse in the warmth of the sun. Inside it brimmed with pilgrims prostrating and carrying butter lamps. The murals on the walls on the first floor are almost totally obscured by centuries of yak butter smoke. Monks chanted with drum and bell accompaniment, the senior monks wearing tall, ceremonial hats like a series of licorice buns edged in gold.

There were three sand *mandalas* in vibrant colors, one with thunderbolt daggers in bronze sand that the monks were working on. These were similar to Navajo sand paintings one sees in Arizona and New Mexico. The Navajo call their sand paintings, "the place where the Gods come and go." They are used in healing ceremonies. Tibetan sand paintings are usually of *mandalas* representing the realm of a tantric deity. I may be wrong but that sounds to me very close to a "place where the Gods come and go."

Both Tibetan and Navajo paintings are destroyed soon after they are made. For Tibetans, this symbolizes the transitoriness of life; among Navajos it is because the painting, having absorbed the illness of the person for whom it was created, has become toxic.

We went into the dark protector chapel where masks of fierce birds and beasts with open red mouths hang from rafters as though about to swoop down and carry you off to a sulfurous realm. There are paintings on the walls of sky burials, arms and legs strewn about among vultures, ravens and kites. I revisited the picture of the man having his eye pecked out by a vulture I had seen for the first time years before. The statues of the protectors had their faces and upper bodies draped with *khatas* or curtains hanging over the doors of their chapels; only their vigorous lower limbs could be seen. I knew one of them shielded Palden Lhamo, the protector of Tibet.

Buddha's eyes gaze down from the top story of the Kumbum.

At the wedding cake Kumbum, on the third level, I found the god holding his smile between his hands and asked Rigsum 1 the question I had always yearned to ask a Tibetan, "Who is the god holding a set of teeth between his hands? Is he the god of toothaches?" But to my immense disappointment he didn't know and, unfortunately, I didn't urge him to ask the guardian monk or one of his fellow guides. I still have no more information.

A painting of Avalokiteshvara on a wall of the Kumbum. He, but sometimes she, has a thousand arms with which to reach out to all sentient beings.

The Gyantze Kumbum.

The Mountain Will Decide

The statues in the Kumbum were destroyed in the Cultural Revolution. This is one of the replacements, a bit gaudy.

An elderly woman turning prayer wheels at the monastery in Gyantze.

The golden roofs of Shigatze.

We drove to Shigatze to see Tashilumphu monastery, the huge Buddha and the burial *chörtens* of the former Panchen Lamas. The pictures of the boy who is the Chinese choice for the next Panchen Lama were still on display. But this time we went into a low ceilinged chanting hall off the big courtyard with rows and rows of little Buddhas painted on its walls. I had not been here before. That hall and the chapels off of it are less imposing and more intimate than the other chapels in the monastery that are very arresting. The best is the Drölma chapel whose main image is of the White Tara who has seven eyes, two on her hands, two on her feet, the usual two, and one in the middle of her forehead. The Drölma and the White and Green Taras are related in some fashion I have never quite grasped but I do know that the two Taras were born from the tears of the Buddha when he wept upon seeing the suffering of mankind.

We went back on the road heading to Lhatze, although I had stipulated to Bikram, that I did not want to stay the night there. It was years since Rachael and I tried to sleep in the Meteorological Hotel while the gigantic speakers of the DVD shop across the street spewed bomb detonations and machine gun fire but the memory had remained green.

However, to my surprise, we did stop, at Rigsum's suggestion, just as we entered Lhatze, parking before a low Tibetan building with a sign reading Farmer Hotel, a place I had never noticed. It was a charming, Spartan, Tibetan hotel around a courtyard bright with paintings and flowers. The proprietors kindly plied us with butter tea, which Anna could not deal with but Sophie managed well.

The inner court of the Farmer's Hotel in Lhatze where Rigsum took us for lunch.

As we sat around the courtyard sipping tea, the family's youngest daughter, about four years old, paraded about in the all-together wearing a small pink plastic basin on her head as a hat. After her hair was washed, she was rubbed down briskly with a towel, which she objected to very vocally. To compensate for this indignity we gave her hair clips and balloons.

I have no idea what Duixie Dancing is nor have I ever seen it. Could it be an invention of the Chinese tourist office?

At our camp that night in a canyon by a river, which was also close to the road, trucks geared up and down the hill, sweeping our tents with their headlights, but it was much better than the cold, cheerless room smelling of turnip soup we had been in at Gyantze. Anna noted with amusement in the morning that going to and from the toilet tent, she had heard an orchestration of farts and snores coming from our tents that she was sure she contributed to upon returning to sleep. Sophie bridled a bit at this.

Anna over our morning porridge and eggs told us, "My sister and I had to share our room with my grandmother when she visited. We complained to Mother, 'It's disgusting. She farts and snores all night.' But Mother said, 'You wait. You'll fart and snore some day too.' The day has come!"

As the Sherpas and Rigsum were handing things up to the truck after breakfast, Sophie hurried over to help. Rigsum turned on her, to my surprise, I thought one of the Nepalis would do it, and said, "No help, please. We know what we want do this." Sophie looked a bit crestfallen but accepted his instruction.

I had warned Anna and Sophie that despite our best planning, Bikram's knowledge, and the Tibetan agent's expertise, something would go awry. The next day awryness arrived. Our truck, near a road workers' camp, the workers seemed to be mostly women, once again developed gear trouble. We sat for an hour and a half while the men worked on it. They stopped passing trucks, asking for a particular kind of nut and finally after four or five vehicles a Chinese driver of a passing gas truck came up with the right nut.

Meanwhile we sat in the car periodically surrounded by road workers, who with shouldered picks and shovels, peered in at us through our rolled up windows. We stayed in the car, not because we didn't want to fraternize, but to shelter from the constant wind and accompanying dust. Most of the road workers had scarves pulled up over their mouths and down over their foreheads under their hats. Only their eyes were visible, bloodshot from the dust. Bored with staring in at us, they moved on to stand around the tipped up cab of the truck where the real excitement was.

When we started up again, the truck could only go in second gear, meaning we, in the four-wheel drive, were far ahead. Arriving in Zhongba, which I recalled from my previous trip, Rigsum 1 and 2 conferred. They decided we should stay in a truckers' motel to await our truck that, along with our camping equipment, contained the precious cargo of Karma Lama and our Nepali staff.

The parking lot outside the truckers' motel in Zhongba before the snow storm. That is not our truck on the right. Our truck was gnashing its gears somewhere on the road to Zhongba.

The room, we were all in one room, had, as do all Tibetan hotel rooms, rug covered benches around the perimeter for beds, a dirt floor swept clean and a stove in the center which we lit and warmed ourselves around that evening. It was cozy waking in the night to look over drowsily and see its soft glow. Since going to the bathroom meant going to the second story porch outside our door, then down to the courtyard cum parking lot and then up again to the outhouse, which resided on its own platform, I commandeered a basin for peeing purposes.

Our room in the Zhongba truckers' motel. The kettle is always on the stove for some kind of tea.

Two women, who looked like mother and daughter, from Kham in eastern Tibet, were running the hotel while their husbands traded around Tibet from village to village for the summer. The kitchen, its old cabinets painted with scenes and deities, had both a dung fire stove, with a fragrant blaze in it and a new gas one. Those kitchen cabinets, considered old fashioned and generally undesirable in Tibet, sell for thousands of dollars in Bangkok antique stores.

Long, stiff, raggy strips of dried meat dangled like laundry from a clothesline in the kitchen. The women filled a large basin with the meat, looking like holey, starched, maroon socks, for the two Rigsums who ate it with *tsampa* and butter tea, letting me nibble. I hadn't had dried meat since I had hitched across Tibet after leaving the truck at Lalung La, on my first trip with Heinrich, Chiam and Gunar. I had cups of butter tea with Sophie, which perked us up. You do need that animal fat to give you energy.

Since we had nothing to do but wait, I took them up to the temple and monastery, which I had seen on my last trip, silently thanking Thubten for having introduced me to it. The same goat greeted us, wanting us to rub his head with our knuckles but I didn't see his monk friend around. The temple swarmed with men building up the outer wall, doing repairs, and replacing doorways. We visited the big Padmasambava, the main image, with his lithe black moustache and the protector chapel with Palden Lhamo, Mahakala and the old man with his icicle beard whom I recognized this time as the suspension bridge builder, and inventor of Tibetan opera, Tangtong Gyalpo.

My donation of ten yuan to the chief monk obviously disappointed him. The next morning I was surprised and delighted when Sophie decided to donate ten US dollars. He was a little more outgoing at her gift but Buddhists believe you take away merit from the giver if you are effusive over a gift. Often in Thailand people will not open a gift in front of the giver. The economics of merit: you can have it now in thank-yous, or later as a deposit on a better incarnation.

We returned to our motel through thickening snow; it was the 31st of May; there was no sign of our truck. We walked along the dirt road inside a room carpeted with skirling white and walled with drifting flakes. As the snow thickened the room became smaller; visibility was shrinking. On the Changtang plain there is no month in which snow is an impossibility.

For dinner we ate instant noodles to which the women in the kitchen added pickled vegetables. Sophie bravely tried a Chinese snack in a red plastic sausage-shaped container, available all over China and Tibet, like potato chips in America. It was foul. We snuggled down in our sleeping bags around the glowing stove while Rigsum 1 and 2 went off in the heavy snow looking for our truck, having been told by the driver of a vehicle full of wool bales, that ours had made it over the pass. I could sleep knowing the gear had held to the top of the pass.

In the morning we breakfasted in our room around the still warm stove, very cozy. I discretely disposed of the basin's contents, scrubbing it with detergent. The parking lot was full of trucks that arrived in the night, including ours. The mountains were limed with snow on the side the wind hit. We couldn't leave until the men had made yet another appraisal of the gears.

While that was going on Anna stole Rigsum's cigarettes so he wouldn't be able to smoke, an ongoing game. Sometimes I hid them in my daypack, since Rigsum had taken to burrowing into Anna's to find his missing property.

We passed the place with two bridges, the old suspension and the new concrete, then the sand dunes, which had moved about ten miles since my trip in 1999. In the distance was the long line of the Himalayas, a white fence of mountains along the horizon. I could not pick out the group of peaks that Gunnar had thought was the Annapurna Massif. Wind was ceaseless and the dust horrendous. We gazed at dust devils dancing tarantellas usually in the distance while munching on heavenly, dried mangos Anna had bought at Costco in California and sausage I had brought from Fairway in New York.

The unbroken line of the Himalayas running from horizon to horizon. In those days the roads were not paved. Their texture was definitely stiff, wide wale corduroy.

More awryness befell us. The four-wheel drive having become bogged in sand had to be dug out. Further on after getting stuck, our truck was finally hauled out by another truck, all with the wind howling and filtering dust in even though the windows were rolled up. Our noses were dry and a bit scabby but nowhere near as bad as they would have been without an ointment that Sophie brought and kindly shared.

We lunched in a spot wreathed by used toilet paper from Western and Hindu groups wafting in the wind. As we finished our boiled potatoes, eggs and fried bread washed down with warm orange drink we saw a four-wheel drive go by towed by a Chinese gas truck.

It was from a Hindu group with, as Rigsum 1 told us, "bad *karma*." He went, immediately to talk to their guide whom he knew, keeping us current with travelers' gossip. He reported back that one of the group's members had died the night before of altitude sickness at age fifty-five and his wife was also very ill, possibly dying.

After the Chinese investigated his death, he would be cremated using yak dung, cooking oil and bald tires. But to die on the way to Shiva's mountain, Kailash, is a good death. Still I felt sad about the bald tires, cooking oil and yak dung, a long dry way from the green ghats on the Ganges where he might have been cremated had he died at home.

Our awryness reappeared (at least it wasn't bad *karma*) next in the form of a blow out. We stopped for lunch, eating while the men fixed it despite trouble with the air pump.

We had to give up on our first campsite for the night because of a lack of water. We had just passed through a checkpoint where the soldiers were unpleasant to us, the Nepalis and the Tibetans in a screaming wind. There was no prejudice against any particular group in their ill temper. They hated us all most even handedly.

I occasionally have compassion for the Chinese soldiers stationed on the Changtang plain. Being usually from the south of China they are accustomed to a wet, mild climate. Perhaps these men treated us with surliness because of the weather. Certainly as far as they were concerned they were at the back of beyond stationed among barbarians. We ended up camped next to a little inn and didn't eat until 10 pm, crawling into our sleeping bags in trembling exhaustion. Is it any wonder altitude causes irritability?

The innkeeper was a woman with an adorable, precocious, show off of a daughter who was a born comic if a bit scruffy. Mama was carefully dressed and heavily bejeweled but spent most of her time carting water from the river in a plastic milk jug tied to her back. She was gracious but apprehensive that her spirited daughter might give offence.

The next morning walking toward the toilet tent, I ran into Sophie coming out with a roll of toilet paper sticking out of her pocket.

"Don't take the toilet paper out of the tent," I said. "The next person might want it."

"But I don't have any toilet paper. I didn't buy any before we left Kathmandu."

"Just ask Karma Lama for a roll any time you need some. He has a supply."

I had no idea that I hadn't told her to ask Karma Lama and was thoroughly annoyed with myself, although it did explain the shortage of toilet paper that had occurred from time to time.

Around one, we stopped by the Tsang Po River where there was a confabulation of tents. The tent tea house Rigsum chose for us served butter tea and little deep-fried dough twists. However, I suspected we were there because the young woman running the tea tent was particularly attractive. She was from Kham in eastern Tibet, her braids woven with turquoise and coral. Each year her men bring her out and set up the tent for her for the season. There was a little boy, not hers I think, with whom I conversed in raspberries and cheek popping noises.

We stopped at this tent city of restaurants and hotels on our way to Kailash. Rigsum had his favorite place based on the looks of the owner.

This yak's head served as an advertisement for one restaurant. They claimed it was a wild yak's head. I hope not. Small solar panels supply electricity for a dim bulb or two at night or to run a mixer for yak butter tea. It's easier than the old fashioned churn.

The proprietress of Rigsum's favorite restaurant helping him with some warm water to wash his hair.

The dust and wind were so terrible, so exhausting, that I asked Karma Lama, our *sirdar*, for washing water in the evening. This is something of a no-no in trekking etiquette since heating the water delays dinner. Knowing this, I told him the water needn't be hot. Even so we received at our tent doors basins of hot water that felt heavenly on our gritty skin and for which we were hugely grateful. Such little things like Sophie's ointment and these basins of hot water made a monumental difference to us in days filled with discomfort that chafes the spirit like rough canvas abrading sensitive skin.

Sophie complained of the wind, which she found frightening. When you have never experienced this, it seems as you lie in your tent, that the invisible force battering at your cloth wall is malignantly intent on uprooting every tent peg and that it will do just that leaving you exposed. We weren't talking much by this time, not from antagonism but exhaustion. But whether frightened or worn out, we were there.

I thought of a couple who had come to a slideshow I gave in a town in Illinois. The woman had gushed at me over dinner, "Oh I think what you do is wonderful. I could never do it. I wouldn't feel safe." This was after the Oklahoma City bombing. "But you aren't safe here with people planting bombs and shooting people."

I managed not to go on to say what was on my mind, "Is the point of life, to be safe?" I thought that whatever our shortcomings as individuals or a group we at least were doing well with not feeling safe.

The next day in a dust cloud we headed up to Maryum La. At the top of the pass you have your first sight of Kailash. Our truck labored, coughed, gagged and sputtered out. Our four-wheel drive was then hitched to the truck to pull it and we, feeling the car was doing more than its share, walked. Moving very slowly, as we were, kept animals from being startled by us. We saw a pair of female antelope, legs dainty as chicken wishbones, staring at us with big dark eyes as we panted up the road. We did well until it started to snow; the cold was intense. It must have been below freezing.

I am apt to think I have hit the nadir of discomfort on a trip to Tibet only to be lowered through a trap door into the strata beneath, in this case the snow and descending temperature. We walked back downhill a bit, standing and waiting for the car in that temperature was out of the question, as the truck, miraculously, roared by us, the Nepali crew cheering and waving triumphantly as they passed. We climbed into our car, happy to be inside and warm, or relatively warm.

We saw the first lake, which I always mistake for Manasarovar until corrected, and then shortly thereafter had our first sight of Kailash. We stopped at the web of prayer flags on which Sophie commented, "They look very pretty at first, but then they get dirty." I wondered if she thought they should be taken down and washed. I rummaged for my prayer papers with the wind horse on them, which we threw into the wind, a blizzard of paper wings. Rigsum 2 did at least ten prostrations without even breathing hard.

We came to a checkpoint full of tourists and pilgrims of all nationalities with a pool table in front of it. I was dying to take a picture of the pool playing Tibetans with Kailash in the background but, since this was a military post, I was stopped as I raised my camera.

A pool table within yards of the police/army check point for going to Darchen and the Kailash *khora*.

Lake Manasarovar looked solid, a big blue plate. Then we saw Gurla Mandata, a giant's body under a rumpled white sheet and, on our right Kailash's peak. We drove into dirty Darchen pluming dust. Rigsum 1 deposited us in a teahouse for lunch. I got one cup of butter tea, only one, because they didn't believe I liked it. Rigsum 1 went off to deal with officialdom and get our permits.

As we ate our instant noodles and drank tea we overheard a good looking man with an Oxbridge accent talking to a group of ten, two of whom were Hindus I'd talked to at the checkpoint. He urged them to pay an extra 480 yuan, about US $70, each for a campsite near the *tarbouche*, pointing out that camping at Cholera Corner, not that he called it that, could be dangerous to their health, which indeed it could be. He also warned them that the price of yaks had gone up.

Hearing this, I was worried that we would have to pay extra but perhaps that was true for his people because they were are large group. We were charged 120 yuan, US $15 for our group to camp near the *tarbouche* and nothing beyond the usual for yaks. However, we didn't get to our campsite until eight in the evening because we had to wait in Darchen for the Chinese official who was out at what would be our campsite, fining people who were there illegally and sending them back to Cholera Corner. He had no assistant and, therefore, had to do everything himself.

A herd of yaks on the edge of Darchen with the long, white body of Gurla Mandata across the plain.

Sophie and I wandered around Darchen. The tent city was small and uninteresting with one jewelry tent whose entire stock had been made in Nepal, the other tents contained horse accessories, household goods and wound up cylinders of prayer flags. Women necklace sellers, heavily adorned with their own products that were also from Nepal followed us about. They were short on customers. Generally, they reacted well to, "Mindu" "No."

Part of a herd of yaks waiting in a desolate corner of Darchen to be hired as pack animals on the *khora* around Kailash.

Sitting in the car waiting to go to the *tarbouche*, I pulled out my down jacket. It was seriously cold. We watched in a dystopian silence of cold and dust as yaks meandered from their herd for a nibble of grass only to be shooed back to their companions on a trampled grassless bit of turf. Finally Rigsum 1 arrived with our permits; we drove joyously off. Our tents were already up and by the time we had arranged ourselves inside them dinner was ready.

We were able to camp close to the *tarbouche*.

In the morning people gathered at the *tarbouche* handing up prayer flags to be tied on to it for the Saga Dawa festival. After breakfast I went to hand up ours and to circumambulate the pole with Tibetans who prayed and whirled prayer wheels.

The *tarbouche* wrapped with *khatas* and prayer flags. I brought some for the occasion.

People gathering for the raising of the *tarbouche*.

Then I sat on a rock behind an elderly Tibetan woman with a cane. She was accompanied by a sweet-faced young woman, probably her granddaughter, wearing, to my astonishment, lipstick that matched her red scarf. A fashion statement on the *khora*. I pled and pled for a picture of her lovely face and after many refusals I was granted the privilege, although she pulled her scarf up around her cheeks and down over her forehead so that much of what I wanted to photograph was in shadow.

The girl and her grandmother at the raising of the *tarbouche*.

There were far fewer people at this Saga Dawa than at the one I'd been to in 2002, the year of the Water Horse. There seemed to be more old people, but there were also lots of children racing around. In the crowd I noticed two European women in *chubas* speaking fluent Tibetan to their companions. I envied their linguistic ability.

The Saga Dawa gathering was not as large as it had been for the Year of the Water Horse.

There was also a tall European, a Germanic looking man, with a blond-grey goatee, dressed in an extravagant brocade *chuba* trimmed with sheep's wool. Something about Tibet, its remoteness, its reputation for the mystical, for being a "magical mystery tour" causes people to act out their fantasies. He was certainly acting out his sartorial fantasy. He even kept his small digital camera in a handsome Tibetan shoulder bag of two layers of leather in contrasting colors, the top in dark brown cut out in patterns to show the yellow layer beneath. Where would Thomas Carlyle have placed him in *Sartor Resartus,* possibly among the dandies as "he is inspired with Cloth, a Poet of Cloth," who perhaps thinks to change his inner self by acquiring the outer covering of what he thinks he would like to be. Humans have a terrible time accepting the idea that character cannot be applied from the outside in. Look at any "individualistic" teenager.

I cannot pretend to be superior to him as I write this since I feel I should apologize to Tibet which, like a magnate, seems to acquire the iron filings of spiritually free floating Westerners. I am certainly among them. The Tibetans are aware of this as is the Dali Lama. When he preaches his tone is completely different if he is talking to us rather than to his own. With us he is jovial, with his own a strict father. This reminds me of the parish priest of my childhood, Father Brady. All the town's Protestants would say to us, "How lucky you are. Father Brady is such a sweet and humorous man. So understanding." Not to us. We and our mottled, moldy souls were his responsibility and he was as severe with us as the Dali Lama with his own.

Nomad women in their primary colored capes.

You may bring your horse to the Kailash *khora* but you would not ride him on the circumambulation because he would get half the merit.

The officiating monks were more in evidence than the last time because there were far fewer people. One monk's job was to carry the big mouths of the long, long horns around while the players held the other end as the monks circumambulated the *tarbouche*. Before they were sounded, the monk laid them gently on the dirt and stood aside. There were also wind instruments sounding like clarinets, decorated with tassels.

The monks under their umbrella observed by a Chinese official.

The horns being carried around by assistants to the officiating lamas. Their hats resemble Western bishops' miters. Perhaps it is the other way around. Western bishops' miters resemble the hats of lamas.

A smart young Tibetan woman in hat and sunglasses.

The great horns which require a blower at one end and a carrier at the other.

The *tarbouche* was pulled up slowly with stops and jerks; they even lowered it once to start over. I was afraid it might drop to the ground. Rigsum 1 was distraught. There might be a bad year ahead. No horses raced around the raised pole. Rigsum had the honor of putting up one of many taut spider lines, which stretch out to hold the *tarbouche* in place. But he felt that the problems in raising the pole presaged a difficult year.

The *tarbouche* being raised. You can see one of the blue trucks that is pulling it by backing up.

Among those circumambulating the pole was a colorful young couple from Ali, the town far to the west of Tibet that Heinrich had been headed toward when he left us in Tholing on my first journey to Kailash. She had on a cartwheel hat of sheepskin with a brocade center. Her handsome husband wore a green *chuba* closed with a silver belt whose buckle was a monster with a turquoise in its mouth. His wide brimmed hat was of the same green brocade as his *chuba*.

Anna plotted like a diplomat working on a delicate treaty to get a picture of them. She pleaded and offered the young woman a handful of hair clips, ties, and bands. Finally the woman shyly gave in. The husband acquiesced a bit reluctantly as well. They were a magnificent pair. You could see the yellow canary feathers at the corners of Anna's mouth as she clicked the shutter. A bit of a romantic, I hoped it was their honeymoon. But I don't know if Tibetans have honeymoons.

Chaktsal Gang, the two-legged *chörten*, draped with prayer flags and *khatas*.

Once the *tarbouche* is raised women open their bundles to sell jewelry almost all of which is made in Nepal.

I asked Rigsum 1 if he could find out anything about our chances of getting to Kyunglung, since there were many guides with whom he was friends at Saga Dawa. Among them was supposedly a guide who knew the location of the new road to Kyunglung. I explained again that this was my third attempt and told him how we had, on the last trip, forded the river on horseback and then been chased off by the police and army young men after they had allow us to camp overnight.

He consulted his fellow guides. As we headed toward our campsite, he told me that there was now a bridge and a road. We wouldn't need horses. I gave him a look of disbelief and told him jokingly that I thought his friends were hallucinating. There had been so much prevaricating and so many misfortunes around my attempts to get to Kyunglung I didn't know what to believe.

At our campsite, we did laundry, diluting freezing river water with hot from a kettle Karma Lama had had heated for us. As we scrubbed socks and underpants we were approached by the fourteen-year-old daughter of a herder camped behind us. Her father had brought his yaks to rent as pack animals to people doing the *khora*. She was strikingly pretty, with big black eyes framed by lashes that seemed long as a giraffe's, in a nomad style *chuba* with great swatches of primary colors along its hem and a mint green silk blouse.

She had burned her wrist cooking for her father and brother. Sophie put ointment on the burn and showed her pictures of sites in Tibet in the *Lonely Planet Guide,* which the girl, to Sophie's surprise, took away with her thinking it a gift. Rigsum 1 straightened this out.

As a consolation prize, I gave the girl hair ornaments and a picture of Mt. Kailash. I was interested that, despite my pointing to the mountain and then to the picture, she was insufficiently experienced in what pictures are to be sure that the thing on the piece of paper was Kailash until our men backed up with words what I had been trying to express with gestures. She had held Sophie's book upside down while looking at the pictures. This meant that the pictures conveyed nothing to her except pretty colors.

How amazing to live exclusively with reality, no reproductions. We, to the contrary, live with more reproductions than reality via television, YouTube and all the manifestations of the net. Virtual reality is often our reality. Our world has moved further and further into second hand experience. I was recently sent a virtual tour of an Italian cathedral in which I could get as close or as far from paintings and altars as I wished. I was able to look at objects closer than I would have been able to if I had been physically in the cathedral. Soon people may feel they don't have to travel. Why go to all that bother when you can just sit at your computer eating potato chips and gazing at images? And, you would be safe at home.

While Anna and I sat in our dining tent writing before dinner, the yak girl came in, patted our faces and stroked our hair. We were curious entities to her, three traveling women, waited on by men, the reverse of the order in her world.

The next morning we left early; we planned to return to do the *khora* after we had been, as in 2002, to Tirtapuri, Guragem, and hopefully this time Kyunglung, if that road and bridge existed, then Tholing and Tsaparang.

The yak maiden had her wrist smeared with ointment a last time by Sophie and then stood beside her great, hairy beasts, loaded with foreigners' packs and tents, waving to us.

The drive to Tirtapuri crosses a flat, dusty plain with barren mountains on either side. We saw a number of antelope herds flicking their white tails as they leapt across the sere landscape that wore the pale green silk of new grass. Fording a river we saw a truck, nose down in the water, being hauled up, rear end first by its four-wheel-drive companion.

The road was good. Sophie commented on its smoothness. "Good roads may make this country more hospitable." How different Sophie's and my reactions were to Tibet. I treasure the Tibet's lack of good roads, lack of hospitality. One of the things I like about Tibet is you have to earn your experience; you don't just purchase it. It doesn't cajole you with smiles and softness. Tibet takes words like "majesty," "awe," "magnificent" and reduces them to banalities. It greets you from the strength of harsh barrenness, the aesthetic of rock. Grit and wind are its ministers; silence its voice.

Sophie's comment suggested to me again that she should not have come to Tibet; perhaps her place was Provence or Tuscany.

At Tirtapuri there was a wire across the road, an innovation; we bought a ticket for the temple from a cheery Tibetan woman. Tirtapuri was the total opposite of what it had been in 2002 when it had overflowed with people. This time it was empty. A few foreigners were relaxing in the hot springs but there were no Tibetans.

The *mani* walls at Tirtapuri.

We climbed to the caves on the white and red striped cliff face. In the *gompa* I bought a butter lamp lighting it for the success of the trip trying to put to rest my worries about Sophie, possible conflicts between the Tibetan and Nepali crew and hoping my temper and my ability to zip my lip would continue to hold.

The white stupas of Tirtapuri.

We camped beyond Montser, a mud-brick town with puddles and pool tables where we searched for vegetables finding one store with boxes of daikon, a few tomatoes, onions, potatoes and cabbage. I was and am still baffled by the presence of daikon, a Japanese radish, in the middle of the Tibetan plain. Walking about town, looking into shops as though on a fashionable promenade along Fifth Avenue, were two young Tibetan ladies in *chubas*, high heels, hats, gloves and dust masks.

The next day we arrived at Guragem, a Bon monastery and *gompa*; I felt at home camping under its high, cliff-cave hermitage where we had camped on the last trip with Rachael. Rigsum 1 talked to a Bön monk. Indeed, there was now a bridge across the Sutlej, to Tibetans the Elephant River, just behind the monastery.

Cliffs along the Sutlej River near the hermit cave at Guragem.

We crossed it following a road beside the river where on one side soft hills swelled in the pale green of early grass while on the other rocky hills piled up their blocks of stone. We would drive on over these to Kyunglung. What took us a day's labor on horseback on my previous trip with Rachael, Alex and Tom, now took at most two hours.

The road to Kyunglung.

It was true, however, as it had been last time when we had arrived on horses, that there were few smiles in the village. Rigsum 1 talked to two men who pointed us toward the meadow I had camped in before. No policeman stopped us, or took our passports, nor did anyone show any interest in us. We were not charged for staying in the meadow but we didn't have horses this time.

Looking up at Kyunglung.

We arrived at the line of *chörtens* and *mani* walls that precede the site. Last time the caves had been full of people and sheep; this time all was empty. But the badland cliffs were magnificent as ever, their panorama so extraordinary in coloration as to make you wonder if someone had slipped just a little LSD into your water bottle.

I leapt from the car and followed the first path I found which took me up to a hot spring, more warm than hot, with blue pools of water in hollows before grottos hung with white icicles of lime deposits. There was a whiff of sulfur.

The warm springs at Kyunglung form basins and stalagtites.

While Sophie inspected the caves under the line of *chörtens*, Anna and I strolled down to the bridge of wire and wood, hung with prayer flags that I had planned on crossing last time. There used to be one of Tsongsen Gyalpo's bridges on this site.

The bridge across the river to the troglodyte cliffs of Kyunglung.

The original bridge was one of Tsongsen Gyalpo's never-rusting, iron-link bridges. It, undoubtedly, was also bedecked with brilliant prayer flags.

I was not going to risk being sent back before we did at least a little exploration. On the other side of the river were *mani* stonewalls, many of whose stones were white marble.

Anna, ahead of me, became trapped in a sheep and goat traffic jam. They trotted down the hill above the bridge in packs of twenty or more to eddy around her still figure. She might have been a boulder for all the notice they took of her. We walked along the line of decaying red *chörtens*, some broken into by treasure-seekers. *Mani* stones were all over among oddly shaped and colored stones under foot.

The red *chörtens* at the base of Kyunglung's cliff.

One of the *chörtens,* which has been broken into by treasure seekers.

The conglomerate, if that's what it is, maybe it's just clay, was a pinkish, pebbly dough with occasionally, medium sized boulders wrapped in it.

The rock of Kyunglung.

We passed a little penis-like structure to the last *chörten,* laboring as we climbed a hill of loose sand into which we sank, but it gave us spectacular, slightly vertiginous views of the amphitheater of organ pipe formations rising over our heads, and multicolored tiers of canyon walls around us.

We separated on the way back, Anna following a sheep trail over stones by the river; I went up to the warm spring where hay had been left for horses roaming in the area. Many of them, small but handsome, were grazing in the hills and meadow. Was my horse with no name, which I rode last time, among them? I had no way of finding out.

We gratefully ate Spam for lunch. If you were alive during the Second World War and find yourself grateful for Spam you know you are desperate for protein. We were at that point in the trip when meat becomes scarce. One day seeing a chicken scratching by the side of the road, we yelled at Rigsum 2, "Hit it. Run it over for dinner." We were joking, mostly.

After lunch we explored caves on our side of the river, clambering among smoke stained hollows, shelters for shepherds, until we arrived at the top among heaps of *mani* stones and yak horns. The area was littered with the detritus of yak and sheep bones, shoes and bits of clothing. This was mildly disturbing, although I am not sure why it should have been. It suggested that animal sacrifice might be part of the local rites. Was this the residue of Bön rites? Was the area Bön not Buddhist?

Kyunglung is reputed to have been a Bön site of hermit activity. Its neighbor, Guragem, is a Bön monastery. Perhaps, like the Kailash *khora,* it is multi-denominational. Its spiritual history recedes through known and unknown religions into the dark tunnel of time.

Returning from our explorations we washed, and then walked down the squishy meadow to sit on some rocks. Rigsum came with us and sat on a rock in front of Anna who braided his hair into little pigtails. He hated having straight black hair and wanted to get a permanent when he returned to Lhasa. He was hoping that the braids would put a wave into his hair. They didn't. I was a little surprised that he didn't want to become a blonde. For people in the East two of the most amazing things about Westerners is our body hair and the fact that our hair comes in different colors. In Thailand, these days, there are a lot of Asian redheads.

We watched the cliff face shift through a glory of shades and shapes created by shadow as evening drew on. There are places whose spiritual component is connected to the total lack of any trace of humanity—The Horse Head nebula is one of my favorites. But there are other places where that strange drive humans have to make contact with the incomprehensible has created a spiritual aura. For millennia people came here out of a desire to reach out to the ineffable. All the dark mouths of those empty caves speak of that yearning.

I had gone, early in my sobriety, to do a reading at the University of California Davis, staying with a fine, fellow poet, Wendy Barker. One morning over breakfast I had posed the question to her that, I didn't believe in anything and, therefore, could not have a spiritual life? She had looked at me in surprise and said, "But don't you realize you are spiritual? It is obvious in your poetry."

Before I had not been able to feel my emotions, now I discovered that I was numb to my spirit. Not only was it invisible to me, but also I had so firmly linked god and the spiritual, like love and marriage in the song, that I had not given thought to the idea that you could have the spirit without the god. The word "spiritual" makes me queasy since it brings to mind California mushroom mystics and the crystal toting inhabitants of Sedona, Arizona, New Agers.

I saw one of these leaving Tibet one year. He was in the Lhasa airport with a two-foot crystal wrapped in flannel and velvet. The Chinese had him produce a passport for it showing that the crystal had come from outside of China. I cannot imagine why he had brought it to Tibet.

I am repelled by what I consider easy, druggy spirituality, the misty romantic variety that thinks of mysticism as an escape from life. To me mysticism is the grounding rod, firmly buried in the earth of everyday life, with the spirit, the lightning flashing down. I have huge respect for the gritty, hard working mystics of Catholicism, Judaism, Buddhism, and Islam, for the unknown authors of *The Cloud of Unknowing*, the *Kabbalah*, the Sufi mystic Rumi, and the Buddhist mystic Milarepa. It seems to me that they weren't engaged in a self-indulgent daydream. They had the discipline of St. Teresa of Avila who, washing her clothes next to an old blind nun who kept splashing soap suds into Teresa's eyes, decided not to snap, snarl or even comment.

The spiritual isn't about visions but about living everyday life, a discipline of the mind and the emotions.

St. Teresa and St. Francis caused consternation in the Catholic Church because they renounced the comforts and elegance of the cloister. I have not been interested in that part, or the mortification of the flesh that was part of Catholic sainthood and of which the Buddha disapproved in the Hindu mystics of his day. I find it difficult to believe in a god who would give you something and then expect you to mistreat it. What parent would give a child a puppy and then tell him to beat it and starve it as so many saints beat and starved their bodies? The body seems to me to be much like a puppy, full of delightful, visceral excitement, vivacious, ebullient and eager to do all sorts of things it probably shouldn't. My wonderful lover, Les, ate coal from the scuttle as a child. That's the sort of thing the body does.

Catholicism has a sadomasochistic urge built into it, a desire for victimization. To show your love of the Christian god you must suffer, bleed and possibly die as a martyr. Early Christians actively sought death, suffering was something to be proud of and certainly the Christian saints and martyrs were amazingly creative in the extraordinary variety of ways in which they were tormented. But mysticism to me is about living in contact with or at the least having an awareness of the spirit.

As I tried to think my way through this, it was as though I were attempting to put together a jigsaw puzzle without knowing what the image would be when it was finished, and not at all sure I had all pieces necessary to complete the puzzle. Also I might have pieces mixed in from some other puzzle.

Early the next morning we crossed the bridge decked with prayer flags which swayed under our feet to climb up the cliff hoping to reach the ruins of the monastery at the top. We took Anna's route over the stones by the riverbank, passing the *chörtens* and then went up a little valley to caves I'd seen the day before. Anna picked a good initial route.

The badly eroded caves that pock the cliffs of Kyunglung.

We climbed to the first strata of caves whose roofs and walls were blackened from shepherds' fires. But the niches and shelves carved out of the walls long predate the shepherds. Views across to both the organ pipe walls of the canyons and down to the river were powerful with the feeling of the presence of humans believing, seeking. Rigsum, Karma Lama and the rest of the crew joined us. They loved scrambling up and down, into and over.

Cave walls were heightened and enlarged, but all is in ruins now.

Looking out from the heights of Kyunglung at the organ pipe formations on the surrounding cliffs.

With Rigsum 1 leading, we ascended carefully to the next level. We were climbing, I think, on tuff, a soft volcanic stone that crumbles. Whatever was under our feet was obviously fragile and friable. We stayed away from edges that might disintegrate under our weight and collapse. At this new level there was a shallow cave with a line of dots, about the size of an American quarter, contained between two horizontal lines across its center and above a blue ceiling. I had heard rumors of paintings but this was the first I had seen.

The cave with the line of white dots on a red stripe for decoration.

We scrambled again to the next level, each climb being steeper than the previous, to find a larger cave of the same shape with painted Buddhas separated into niches by interlacing, green vines, as though each sat in his own private bower. The painting was simple but elegant, particularly the twists and turns of the vines whose leaves enclosed smiling Buddhas.

The Buddhas in their vine niches, the same vines painted
in French 14th century manuscripts.

When I returned home, I showed my pictures of this cave to a friend, a scholar in French and English Renaissance literature. She said to me, "In book illuminations of the 14th century in France there are vines exactly like that." Did they originate in Christian 14th century France, or in Buddhist Tibet? Another mystery, but the world is round. We may well underestimate the extent to which people traveled in earlier times.

Attempting to get to the next level we slid through holes and clambered over walls to a place where to continue we would have to go over a wall dropping down seven or eight feet on the other side. I called a halt here since, although we could certainly get safely down, how would we get back up? I had visions of the Sherpas trying to hoist us up.

Looking up to the monastery at the top of Kyunglung.

We investigated caves on this level. I found a sort of stone bowl, what in the American southwest one would call a metate, a hollowed stone used to grind grain. Coming out of a cave I caught Rigsum 1 and a Sherpa writing on a bare wall with a stone. I had a fit. Not taking me very seriously, Rigsum 1 teased me by threatening to hurl a grinding stone over the edge for the pleasure of watching it shatter.

Wheels worn from grinding grain.

Having decided to give up climbing any further we watched as a group while Rigsum 1, mountain goat like, tried to get to the ruin of a monastery at the top. He was stymied just below it at a twenty-foot wall. But I felt no disappointment. I had seen two caves with paintings and we had found many small mill stones we imagined hermits using to grind their daily barley. There were some carved pieces of wood that were once doorframes and caves enlarged with mud bricks into chapels, now roofless and empty. I certainly felt content, after three tries, to have explored an area holding in its silence the memory of an unrecorded spiritual beginning.

Kyunglung from bottom to top, a Swiss cheese of ruined caves whose history is largely unknown.

On the way back down to the camp we ran into another sheep and goat traffic jam, the flocks herded by a woman and man on chestnut horses. Once in camp we packed up and drove to Montser, which is pronounced rather like "monsieur" although the temptation is to pronounce it monster.

Rigsum 1 was searching for a telephone because he wanted to report our success in getting to Kyunglung and what we had seen. I am amused that I have served in Tibet the purpose that sightseeing visitors always serve everywhere, to introduce locals to their own interesting places. What New Yorker would go to the Statue of Liberty without a visitor to take to it? I introduced my Tibetan agent to Kyunglung, to Chung Riwoche and its many chapeled kumbum like the one at Gyantze and to Tangton Gyalpo's bridge. The last two he checked out before I arrived for my trip. When we met in Lhasa he was excited and enthusiastic admitting he had not known about them before.

I trailed behind Rigsum to the back of a store, hoping for butter tea. Instead I found two little boys pulling maggots out of a leg of lamb. They collected them carefully in a bowl watching them wriggle with lively interest but no disgust. Our culture forms our judgment of what is unpleasant, revolting, or acceptable. The children thought the maggots were just interesting; I could feel my gut going automatically into a clutch as I looked at them and then quickly looked away.

We camped outside Montser where in freezing rain and snow we pulled on our down jackets. It was well below zero. The tents of other groups were near us but in that weather I had no desire to go exploring. However, an Indian/American woman had more courage, or perhaps more boredom. She entered our dining tent to exclaim with astonishment and wonder, "Oh, you have chairs and a table!" Her group was so poorly outfitted that they ate on the floor of their dining tent. They had no salt and pepper and for breakfast were served last night's leftovers. They also put up and took down their own tents. This was a level of budget touring I had not known about.

The next morning, having asked permission she arrived with a bowl to have some of our cornflakes with warm milk, because, she told us, it reminded her of her Indian childhood. It hadn't occurred to me that middle-class Indian childhoods included cornflakes. I thought you had chapattis for breakfast. She was good company and full of laughter particularly over the difference between her group and ours on the material level. Perhaps, I suggested, she would have more merit from her more difficult trip.

On our way to Zanda and Tsaparang we saw wild donkeys, which, with no fear of humans or cars, grazed frighteningly close to the road. After an army post, a grey grim complex that looked like a prison, we turned directly into the multicolored mountains. It was snowing and the road became mushy. This was worrying because the road, unpaved, was narrow and often at cliff edge. Mushy cliff edges collapse. We stopped on a curve to look out at a troupe of mountains I had seen on other trips colored yellow, red and green, as though a child had been busy with her crayons. We climbed up to the grassland plateau and then slalomed down on S curves to the badlands winding our way through its spires, castles, cathedrals and villas.

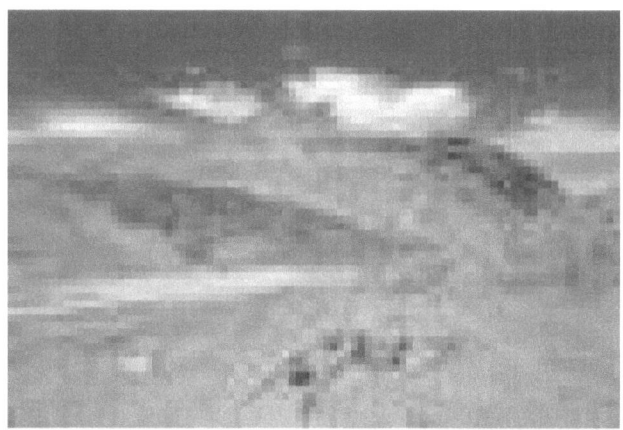

The multicolored mountains on the road to Tsaparang and Tholing.

Looking across the badlands to the white ridges of the Himalayas.

Zanda, since I last saw it, had been transformed into a Chinese town with no Tibetan architecture except for the original temples and other religious monuments.

A small stupa at Tholing.

The beautiful red and white towers of Tholing.

White bathroom tile, the preferred Chinese facade material, was everywhere. We stayed at the Military Hotel, a dire hostelry with exceptionally cement like beds, sand filled pillows, and a toilet odiferous from fifty feet away. Buying a pee basin helped.

We discovered the door lock on our room didn't work when a young Chinese soldier, filled with "satiable curiosity," popped it to find himself facing three very angry Western women who immediately, slammed the door in his face. To complete our misery, the hot water thermos leaked drearily all over the table.

After eating our boxed lunch on the steps of the hotel, the room was too depressing to eat in, we went off to Tsaparang passing through a town, I have never known its name, which I think of as the "pirate town," because the first time I went through it in 1995 in the back of the baby blue truck, they stopped us demanding a fee for going through their village. The seven other members of our party, Arthur and Ben were trying to climb Gurla Mandata, the mountain near Lake Manasarovar, decided it was my decision. I understood that the villagers needed the money and we had the money. However, it did seem to me that they were going about this the wrong way. I said that we refused to pay. After all they could have offered to sell us something. We got out of this because another truck arrived and they transferred their attention to it.

We were not held up this time and saw all the chapels in the citadel including the little *mandala* chapel on the top that is dark as a dungeon being windowless, but we had brought flashlights. I had never been inside this chapel before as it had always been locked but it is, I believe, the chapel that gave Lama Govinda his moment of spiritual connection so that he was able to leave Tibet feeling he had accomplished what was necessary. He had felt at peace.

The pile of the citadel at Tsaperang, hardly discernible from its rock.

A beam with a carved dragon protruding from the building at the top of the citadel.

I wonder what the mental processes were that had taken him from his experiences in the First World War, which I presume were the events that set him in spiritual motion, to his interest in Buddhism, to his move to study in Ceylon, now Sri Lanka, and finally his engagement with Tibetan Buddhism. What were his objections? What caused his rupture with Christianity? What had he been searching for? Had he known what he was seeking?

My own objections were pretty typically female and of my time. In my mind gods and husbands are similar in their tendency to restrict. They both are inclined to be control freaks. My lingering resentments had/have to do with the actions of religious organizations: the Baptist proclamation that a woman is subject to her husband (speaking of restrictions), the protection of Southern Baptist pastors who rape girls as told by Christa Brown in her recent book, honor killings in Islam and the Catholic Church's long refusal to confront the international molestation of boys by priests. I am always amazed that women continue to belong to religions that din into their ears the incessant message, "You are bad. You are to blame. You are dirty." The abuse of power by institutions or individuals that proclaim their superiority to ordinary people seems worse just because they consider themselves superior to those they abuse. The thought of receiving absolution from a priest who has sexually abused a ten-year old boy makes me want to throw up.

Religions are frequently founded by very tolerant, exceptional men who set things out simply. Then other, more ordinary, people, people interested in power, in control, in being right, in money, come along and start playing with the originator's ideas. The original concepts begin to twist. Mohammad did not institute most of the restrictions on women practiced in many Moslem countries. Those rules and regulations were developed by the misogynist clerics who came much later. The apparently innate fear some men have of women is often behind some of these twists.

Over time, a lot of time, I have lost some, if not all, of my resentments toward Catholicism. I can go into a church, Catholic or Protestant, without feeling uncomfortable or defensive. I react to them as if I were going into a Masonic Hall or a Veterans of Foreign Wars meeting room. My feeling is, "This has nothing to do with me." I was not put on this earth to set any church right.

I have a fondness for Lama Govinda because he was a searcher, a seeker. I have noticed that addicts, not that Lama Govinda was an addict as far as I know, seem to be seekers. Often while still addicted they bounce from religion to religion, belief to belief, looking for some place to hang their spiritual hat. Some consider this a failing, a sign of our lack of stability. While still addicted what we don't comprehend is that we need to invest ourselves in our belief. I met people in Tibet who were aware of a connection between their religion and their lives. You could see they were, not all of course, trying to align life with belief day by day. That's a pretty exalted occupation.

Like Lama Govinda I was looking for a spiritual core, a center of some sort. I wanted a contact, such as he had had in this dark chapel, a confirmation.

My trips to Tibet nudged a door open or at least ajar. The fact that I returned again and again might have suggested to me that I was seeking something, if I had been paying attention. People asked me often why I returned to Tibet. I had no real answer for them. There are "whys" that one cannot find an answer to. In my case I think I had/have a deep internal compass that was absolutely determined in its direction.

My traveling had been a quest to slay my dragons of fear, to be willing and able to feel my emotions, to change myself. It was a spiritual exploration. Walking around the mountain was a further draw for me. Again I have no clear explanation of why, but the idea of pilgrimage with the objective of change appealed to me.

Now I can see that I moved from telling my mother nothing, a zero of silence, to telling everything in AA, to the naught of circling the mountain where the importance of telling disappeared. My progression was from the silence of not telling to a silence beyond all telling.

In the dark little chapel that inspired Lama Govinda, the paintings are arranged in bands on the walls according to subject matter with a mud brick *mandala* in the center of the room. I was engrossed by those paintings in the bottom band that portray the seven famous Indian cemeteries separated in their frieze by dancing girls with shaved pudendums and charming, smiling faces. What's the relationship between cemeteries and shaved dancing girls? These paintings are another language, one I shall probably never learn.

We came down from the citadel to have butter tea with a laughing, toothless woman with whom Rigsum 1 bantered, pretending he wanted to purchase her daughter. She wore an old, worn, white conch shell bracelet on one wrist and a heavy, handsome lion headed silver bracelet on the other.

After a dinner of lamb, noodles and spinach, during which Rigsum 1 chatted up our handsome waitress whose earrings swung tempestuously as she gave him tit for tat, we lay our heads on sand filled pillows in the freezing room of the Military Hotel.

The next morning Anna and Sophie showered at the much nicer Telecom Hotel across the way, which had been full the night before, while I packed, sponge bathed, and wrote.

After a breakfast of pork buns, not as good as those in Lhasa, we went to see the Tholing temple. Two of the temples in the complex had more decorations and statues than before but the old murals were still desperately in need of expert repairs. One could see where water had streamed down the wall causing the old, 15th century paintings to fade and bubble.

The rebuilding of the *mandala* temple was well underway, with the chapels reconstructed but as yet undecorated. We were escorted by a groping monk who incessantly "helped" us over the high sills of the chapels by grabbing various parts of our anatomies, a breast, a bottom, but never an arm.

The chapels gave us heartache with their broken bits left by the Cultural Revolution-a Buddha head with a soft, half-smile here, an expressive hand there, or a pelvis and legs in an exquisitely decorated sarong cut off at the ankles. A foot or two of the original murals remained in some chapels. I wonder why the fury of the Cultural Revolution had been so particularly hot in this largely forgotten valley in western Tibet. The quality of the old workmanship of both paintings and statues is superb. The towers of the *mandala* chapel, shaped at the top like honeycombs, the delight of roosting pigeons, had also been renovated.

We then headed back to Montser for the night passing antelope along the way. Our cook gave us excellent vegetable lasagna but we would have killed for a chicken.

Bounding across the grasslands we started for Darchen and the *khora* the next morning only to be frustrated by our ailing truck, which we had to wait for several times. But the four-wheel drive gave us trouble as well. Fording a river our right rear tire gave out. We lurched out of the watery, stony bed and Rigsum 1 and 2 changed the tire. But when they had finished the truck still hadn't caught up.

Rigsum 1 climbed a rise to look for it. No truck. The two Rigsums and I conferred. We decided we had no option but must head back to find it. Within a few kilometers what we found was Karma Lama walking toward us. If we had continued to Darchen he undoubtedly would have walked all the way there with his water bottle in hand.

We packed him into the car and on the way passed another party's dead truck. Rigsum 3 told us when we arrived at our truck that our clutch was shot; nothing could be done. We left Rigsum 3 and two of the Nepalis in the moribund vehicle. Karma Lama piled in with us again. In Darchen, Rigsum 1 installed us in a guesthouse whose toilet was across the way. I had been there before. Our rooms were very cold but there was nothing better.

We found a room upstairs filled with Tibetan men drinking butter tea and beer where we relaxed while Rigsum 1 ran about getting permits and tried to find a truck to tow our truck. We washed and hung things to dry in the sun attended by a boy of six whom I was convinced was a girl until Anna pointed out his penis poking like a puppy nose out of his split pants. He was very adhesive in his desire for "bonbons." I gave him a balloon but he still wanted "bonbons."

Rigsum 1, a whirl of activity, found a truck to tow ours, got our circumambulation permits and telephoned Ali, where the young couple Anna had photographed at Saga Dawa had come from, to find a garage with the appropriate clutch. He was a wonder and I could see he enjoyed juggling all of this.

He had not been happy with the idea of doing the *khora* in four days being used, as are all Tibetan guides, to a three-day *khora*, but with the truck's demise he changed his attitude and the four days became okay since they would allow Rigsum 3 to get to Ali and back.

I postponed dinner until the truck arrived with the Nepalis and Karma Lama, who, of course, went back in the cab of the tow truck to be with his crew because I wanted us to be reunited with our crew. This for some reason infuriated Sophie; I think it was just a case of altitude attitude. It took them two hours to be towed in. When they arrived we all embraced and cheered our crew. The cook immediately made us dinner. Sophie at first refused to eat but when Anna got them to serve it in the downstairs' dining room she decided to join us.

Over the last day or so of traveling our relationship had reached a new nadir. Her backseat-driving, "Be careful." "Oh dear." "You don't have to pass now." "You don't have to go so fast." "Be careful of this curve." None of which Rigsum 2, the driver, probably understood anyway. But her constant outpouring of instructions made us tense or maybe it was just me. However, since he didn't understand and if he did wouldn't pay any attention since she was a Western woman, there was no need to say anything. But I did. I don't think I was nasty. I just wanted to stop the constant out pouring of driving instructions.

Someone once sent me a cartoon of a woman with a bird's nest of hair and her hat on cockeyed saying, "You know that little voice that tells you not to say things? I don't have one." I cannot remember what I said but it did not make anything better. On the other hand we did not have a big blowup. But I was disappointed that my lip had come unzipped.

Sophie reminded me of a young man I had met in Bangkok many years before who found fault with everything Thai.

"Why," he asked, "don't they close the doors on the buses?"

"Maybe because it is over 100 degrees Fahrenheit and there is no air conditioning?" I responded.

"Why do we have to take our shoes off when we come into the guest house?"

"Because it's the local custom and keeps the floor clean."

"All the children wear school uniforms. They must all be brought up to be conformists."

"Well, probably no more than American children who go to school in uniforms," I replied.

If you don't like a culture or landscape, you don't like it; no amount of explanation helps. He finally admitted he liked South Korea, superficially closer to the US in its business and industrial culture than Thailand that is still, despite the Sky Train and high-rises, an agriculturally based culture. I felt Sophie's juxtaposition with Tibet was similar to what his had been with Thailand.

I too have met cultures I don't like. In Irian Jaya, where I met Rachael, I had been quite unhappy. To me the culture was primitive, in the pejorative meaning of that term; women were considered the equivalent of pigs and traded on an equal basis. I was not fascinated when I was shown the village's god, a long roll of fabric with cowrie shells sewn onto it. I did not find penis gourds and bare breasts intellectually stimulating and was very happy to go home. But I knew I was the problem, not the culture. Perhaps if I had been an anthropologist I would have been enthusiastic about staying in Wamena.

Men gathered round our truck with tools borrowed from other trucks to fabricate a gear from a Chinese army pork can. It worked. The truck sped off to Ali many miles west, with Rigsum 3 at the wheel, to buy a new set of gears.

Having slept in our frigid rooms, we started the next morning from Darchen in gnawing cold with snow wind-driven into our faces, because of this I did not look up as I walked. It was June 10th. I was alarmed but left the decision of whether or not we should start the *khora* to Rigsum 1.

The path's usual dusty script on the earth was buried under two or three inches of snow. The trail was, this time, not so much nondescript, as it usually was, as simply not there. To me the characterless quality of the path and now its "not there" quality seemed appropriate. Spiritual seeking is sometimes, although not always, a pathless enterprise. Others may occasionally mark a turn in the route, like the piles of stones, the cairns, humped with snow along our way, but only you and your internal compass know your way.

The snow wasn't deep but slogging through just three inches is exhausting at altitude. We walked seven and a half hours that day.

One of us on the *khora*. We were walking in a cloud and never had a clear view of Mount Kailash. Walking in two or three inches of snow is exhausting.

I expected us to make camp near Chuku Monastery but we went much further. Somehow Anna had injured her hip so that walking was slow and painful for her. Rigsum 1 helped her along. I had forgotten to wear my sunglasses, which were in my pack on one of the yaks, and had to take three steps with my eyes closed and then two with them open. That was bad enough when it was overcast but much worse when the sun came out. Chiam's snow blindness was on my mind.

Because of the snow we didn't make it to either the sky burial site or to Chuku, nor could we see Kailash. Of the three of us Sophie was definitely doing best. She was out ahead of Anna and me and seemed to be pacing herself well.

The day was made warm and pleasant despite the weather by the two tea tents where we stopped. At the first, just after Chuku Monastery, they poured me butter tea but I had to ask for refills because they were so sure I didn't like it. The tent was full of Tibetans, among them a woman we had seen at Tsaparang who had walked to the top of the citadel in two-inch heels. Now she was slogging along in soggy sneakers through the snow with a stick.

In the tea tent grateful for the warmth even if it is only for a while.

As, outside the tea tent, we pulled on gloves and mittens looking up at ridges shelved with snow under low hanging clouds, we heard a motorcycle. The driver was a man in a *chuba* topped by an Australian bush hat and sunglasses. Behind him was a pretty girl, much younger than he, perhaps his daughter, also in a *chuba* who, when they went up hill, which was most of the time, jumped off to push. They putt-putted off into the distance. They were an unlikely sight in the falling snow.

The second tea tent was a family business, as is typical. Anna dispensed balloons. The elder boy knew about blowing a balloon up halfway and then letting the air out so that it emits an ear-piercing squeak. The younger thought that interesting but was quite content to just exhale into his, then watch it flatten when he inhaled. The adults, all three, were delighted with the elder's game. Anna gave them more balloons. They squeaked them in a balloon orchestra. Other balloons were blown up and loosed to jet about the tent making farting noises. We were all giggling, even the men.

We met Bönpos coming toward us, monks and nuns, the latter veiled in thin red fabric as protection against the sun.

Along the *khora* in the snow.

When we camped, I was exhausted and uninterested in the dinner, which was served in our tents so we could huddle in our sleeping bags against the cold. Part of altitude sickness, for me, is appetite loss. I have thought of starting a fat farm at 16,000 feet. Everyone would be allowed to eat a Snickers bar, or the caloric equivalent, at lunch and dinner plus the regular menu but would have to circumambulate the spa buildings ten times a day.

The *khora* as it follows the river between channels of towering cliffs topped with strange, imaginary temples and pavilions.

Because of the prohibition against metal on the *khora* we didn't have any chairs or a table. That made eating in our tents more acceptable. Our shoes and socks, wet from walking in slushy snow, we left in the kitchen tent next to the fire, hoping they would dry over night.

In the morning they were still damp, but we started walking on the right side of the La Chu, crossing the bridge to Drira Phuk, which was full of young monks. We saw the *dri* chapel and then left since there was much walking to do and it was very cold, I suspect less than zero. We couldn't see Kailash; the view of the north face was clouded over completely. This was a major disappointment to me. Not only did I want to see her but I wanted to show her off to my companions but I think they were so intent on walking up the trail that they just accepted her absence. We started off with snow gently falling through the universe on us from a sky that bellied like a goose feather quilt.

Climbing to Drira Phuk in the snow.

Rigsum 1 guided us, on a path I had no recollection of ever having been on before, up through what I thought was a second sky burial area. There were clothes everywhere. Sweaters were buttoned over upright boulders topped with snow, as though grey, white-haired people were eerie sentinels along the way. Were we walking on clothes from the dead or perhaps garments abandoned to show the willingness to change? I was too tired to ask. Clothes were frozen into the mud and snow beneath our feet.

I found out later that this was the graveyard of the eighty-four adepts, the Vajrayogini Cool Grove Charnel Ground. Pilgrims leave the clothes of relatives or anyone loved by them who has died. It is not a sky burial site, or a real graveyard, this is a bit hard to explain, but a place that Tibetans have designated as being the recreation of a graveyard in India. I find this difficult to understand it is so outside my Western ken.

Our yaks on the path to Drölma La. The red canister provides the gas to cook dinner.

As we were walking over the frozen remnants of clothes I heard the one unpleasant remark from a Nepali to a Tibetan. To my surprise Karma Lama, for whom I had at that point a solid respect, said it. Tibetan women often have little bells attached to their belts or to the case which holds the flint they use for lighting fires. They make a pleasant jingling noise as they walk. As they passed me, Karma Lama said to Rigsum 3 with a sneer in his voice, "Do you make your women wear bells so that you know where they are and what they're doing?" It was an obvious slur on the fidelity of Tibetan women. Rigsum 3 paid no mind; perhaps his English wasn't good enough for him to understand. I hoped so.

At one place on the path we saw a bundle, a sleeping bag, by the side of the path. It turned out to belong to a young man who was assisting another man doing prostrations around Kailash. He expected to complete his *khora* via prostrations the next day, having done it in twelve days. The usual time is a month; he must have been a speed demon. Further on we passed him as he laid himself out at full length over rocks and snowy, frozen clothes.

The climb to the pass of Drölma La.

As we neared our campsite, just beyond the cemetery area, the sun came out, the sky cleared and Kailash loomed over us, her lower ridges brilliantly edged with crushed diamonds of fresh snow. It was horrendously cold, well below freezing, partly because of the altitude. We were going to sleep at about 17,000 feet, not a good idea, but Rigsum 1 was worried about getting us up and over the pass in the snow. I slept in my down sleeping bag, my down jacket, three layers of trousers and my silk cocoon. We ate in our tents again.

This was the best view we had of Kailash on the entire *khora*. It lasted about 45 seconds.

Since we walked so far the day before and camped at such a high altitude, the climb to Drölma La, though not easier, was quicker than usual. We reached the pass before the sun. Although the cold was biting when we started, the effort of walking quickly warmed us. We were so early that for the first time in all my treks to the pass I arrived without Tibetan companions.

Among the cracking of the frozen prayer flags I cut off the end of my braid and laid it on a rock, talisman of my intention to change. I was hoping it would aid me in keeping my temper with Sophie and Anna. I could feel I was on edge, self-centeredly irritable, in the danger zone of temper.

In brilliant sun we tied our prayer flags to the lines already streaming in the sun and wind.

We all put up strings of prayer flags and *khatas* in the midst of the huge web around the rock where the twenty-four *dakini,* having led Götshangpa, Kailash's first circumambulator, to the top of the pass, transformed themselves into wolves and disappeared into the rock.

I took out my Fairway sausage and dried apricots bought in Lhasa for our ritual meal at the top of the pass. It was cold, bleak and grey. Just then a lone pilgrim, the morning's first, arrived. He accepted a bit of sausage, completing the ritual of the ascent of Drölma La.

Coming down from Drölma La to the river.

We started down without being surrounded by singing Tibetans, as I had been the time before. I slipped and slithered on the narrow path; the little stones rolled under my feet almost sending me onto my bottom, which was better than over the edge. We each had a Sherpa walking with us, keeping an eye on us in case we slipped. Somehow mine always grabbed me about a foot and a half before I hit the ground. To my bemusement he always said, "Sorry," after righting me, as though it was his fault that I had slipped.

Sophie objected to having someone help her. Her designated assistor was a young, rather weak faced Newari from Kathmandu. He was not from the mountainous tribal areas of Nepal where most Sherpas come from. This was unusual. Nepalis from the city don't generally act as Sherpas on a trek. She didn't want him around her and a few days later when we tipped the staff at the end of the trip she would not give him anything extra.

It was a long time, a month or more after the trip that she told me that he had, early in the trip, started to try to get money out of her. He was from a middle class Kathmandu family, an only child. When his parents died, he had trusted someone who had promised to double his inheritance. He now had no money, had never worked before in his life, was not used to roughing it and hated living with the rest of the crew, whom he considered his social inferiors. He had told Sophie this and tried first to get money out of her and then to get her to marry him and take him to the U.S. Since he was about nineteen years old this was laughable but it had frightened Sophie who didn't know how to deal with it. When I finally learned all this back in New York City, I was equally astonished and annoyed that Sophie had not said a word at the time.

At the tea tent by the river we discovered the bonbon boy from Darchen. He had been doing the *khora* with his parents who were porters for a French-Canadian couple.

We walked on the path by the river, camping on the right side an hour and a half before Zutrul Phuk Monastery, cheerfully whistled along our way by marmots, whom we couldn't see, but who piped warnings to each other on either side of us. The difficult place was where we had to cross the river by leaping boulder to boulder. But it was warmer now that we were at a lower altitude.

When we camped, bonbon and his mother came by to visit. I offered him an apricot; he ate it very solemnly; not the bonbon he would have liked. In sign language I told his mother that she had a fine son. Her face lit up making her even prettier. Leaving my tent he gave, along with a Queen Elizabeth wave, a smile that would enchant the world.

We had a steady stream of visitors as we sat, first in our tents and then, because at last it was warm enough, on the floor of our dining tent where we wrote. I write, or attempt to write, for two hours every day on my journeys. Even then I never get enough detail down. There is always something left out. Tibetans finishing their *khoras* in time to be in Darchen for dinner stopped to watch us write.

I had planned from the beginning to do the inner *khora,* telling Sophie and Anna that I would be gone for a day, since I had heard and read that the inner *khora* is a one day trek, at the end of our circumambulation of Kailash. But trying to discuss this with Rigsum 1, I couldn't seem to get a straight answer from him, which was disturbing. Every time I asked about it, he would say, "We'll see when we get to Darchen" or "Which inner *khora* do you want to do?" which I found confusing since I knew of only one. However, we started early for Darchen because I wanted to get laundry and packing done before going off to do the inner *khora* the following morning.

We got to Zutrul Phuk in good time. The chapel had been beautifully renovated and the monastery had a little teahouse, impeccably clean with excellent butter tea. The monk who served had his hair in a neat braid down his back, and was continually wiping the tables while spitting on the floor.

We passed fourteen Böns starting their *khora* rather late. The gorge walls splotched yellow, red and green declared their colors in brilliant sun. I paused for a moment at the place where the Barga Plain spread before me and Gurla Mandata raised its white, rumpled mass. I let the others pass me so that I could be alone for a moment at what is, for me, the *khora's* end. I was tranquil but without tears. We were met by the car, which brought us packed lunches that we ate before driving back to Darchen.

On the morning's walk Rigsum 1 and I talked and talked about the inner *khora.* In Darchen we sat with his guide pals and talked more. I still didn't know what the problem was. Perhaps he wanted more pay for the inner *khora* and I didn't offer it? I should have. Perhaps at that point in time he hadn't done it himself? Perhaps we needed special permits? That seemed a very likely answer. But why didn't he or one of the other guides tell me what the obstruction was?

There appeared as well to be much confusion about where and what the inner *khora* is. They talked about the Hindu inner *khora,* the

Buddhist inner *khora*. They quizzed me on whether I had done the outer *khora* the required number of times. When had I done my circumambulations?

Rigsum 1 and his friends keep discussing how many days it would take to get to the *chörtens*. I had no idea what he meant. What *chörtens*, where? It wasn't until I actually did the inner *khora* that I realized he had been talking about the *chörtens* on the ledge on the side of Kailash that mark the apex of the inner *khora*.

Then they started talking about Khandro Sanglam, which was a total red herring. This is a obscure, almost legendary route, known as The Secret Path of the Dakinis, which takes you close to Kailash cutting across from above Drira Phuk and going over Khandro Sanglam pass. It cuts off the corner of the *khora* occupied by Drölma La and is a path, like the inner *khora*, you also are only supposed to do after twelve circuits around Kailash. It takes you across a glacier. I am unwilling to walk on glaciers. Since I had not asked about this route, why were we talking about it? I became more and more confused.

However, I did realize I was not going to do the inner *khora* on this trip for whatever mysterious reason, monetary, religious or bureaucratic. Not only was Rigsum 1 blocking me but also all his guide friends were helping him. I managed to accept my fate with good grace. I had changed enough for that.

As a consolation Rigsum 1 said he would take me, the next day, alone, to see a special view of Kailash. I agreed and went to do washing.

The next morning Anna and Sophie drove off in the truck to Lake Manasarovar while Rigsum 1 and 2 and I went off in the four-wheel drive to see the view of Kailash Rigsum 1 had promised me. We drove up to Gyangdrak Monastery, forbidden on my previous trip. It is on a commanding height with a striated black ridge behind it, snow lining the eroded ledges. It was being rebuilt. The renovated building would be four stories with large ornate windows looking down the valley toward Darchen, then out across the Barga plain. Behind it was a smaller chapel, recently refurbished.

One of the remaining temples at Gyangdrak Monastery.

The *chörtens* and ruins of Gyandrak Monastery.

Men and women working on the construction sang and broke off when their labor became too intense as they hauled up soil and bricks. There were many tree trunks, their bark peeled off, stacked on the ground waiting to take their place in the monastery temple.

A door delicately decorated at the monastery.

Now I have to tell you what happened. Perhaps you won't believe me; you'll think I'm crazy. You might want something bigger, more dramatic than what I have to tell. Maybe I won't find the right words to help you understand. But I have come this far and I have to go the rest of the way, as though climbing the pass, Drölma La.

Walking toward Rigsum's special view of Mount Kailash.

Rigsum 1 and I, leaving Rigsum 2 with the four-wheel drive, started to climb up a series of hills/mountains where there were no paths. Rigsum 1 zigged and zagged, with me panting behind him, over grass tussocks covered at first with minute flowers, little yellow trumpets, infinitesimal purple blooms, round clumps of white flowers with blush pink centers and patches of brilliant emerald moss. I found myself, absurdly, trying not to step on the flower patches, a child trying not to tread on sidewalk cracks.

We got higher, stopping along the way for drinks of water as we topped each ridge leaving tundra behind and entering the realm of rock and scree, small loose flat stones, with occasional patches of grass. My throat began to ache with dry tears, the tears I had experienced on other trips. I was painfully slow, continually out of breath because the climb was difficult and steep. Rigsum 1 was patient. I contemplated with dread what our descent would be like over the slippery scree as I stamped the side of my foot into it repeatedly in order to ascend. As I rammed my foot into the scree it poured its slippery, smooth stones around my foot.

We had, at first, superb views of Gurla Mandata, Namaneni in Tibetan, when we looked behind us. As we climbed it became liberated from the angles of its surrounding mountains. Once it stood clear of those I realized Kailash was beginning to raise its snow-smothered dome in front of us.

After another panting, steep climb we arrived at the top of a ridge that had a promontory of carunculated rock on its top and two *lhatses*, stone cairns. Standing there Kailash could be seen from her dark, river-wrapped foundation to her eye searing white crown. I asked Rigsum 1, "Is this as far as we are going?" He said, "Yes," and pointed to the view. This place with its two lonely windswept *lhatses* paradoxically gave me an intimate sense of Kailash in her immensity.

The two *lhatses* wound with *khatas* with Kailash between them where I prayed at Rigsum's instruction.

Rigsum 1 posed between the two *lhatses* and asked if I wanted my picture taken. I cringed from the idea that suggested to me a trophy photo, but I did take a picture of Kailash by herself.

I took out my prayer flags and a *khata* I had set aside for the inner *khora*, handing them to Rigsum who before he strung the prayer flags around one of the *lhatses* handed the *khata* back to me saying, " Take this and pray."

I did, closing my eyes.

For a few moments I am alone in the soft darkness behind my eyelids. Then something, a thing for which I have neither word nor name, reaches out of the air around me into my chest, grips me, makes a fist around my heart, my lungs. It is not gentle. Imperiously it demands; it commands. The mountain is a magnet pulling at me with enormous force. My throat closes, aching. I, for a moment, fight back, quite automatically, against this something that takes possession of me, this invasion. Then I am able to think, "No, let go. Let it in." I relax. My mind and heart open and empty to make a place for the unknown. All becomes still in my darkness, which is soft, vast and without definition as the night sky. I am secure. I am at peace. There is no struggle. But the force within me is vibrantly alive.

I opened my eyes. I was back in the world blue and blazing with sun.

Rigsum 1 was looking at me oddly but he said nothing. We started down. The descent was as hellish as I had imagined. We slipped and skidded on the small loose stones of the scree. I was frightened. Rigsum held my arm; he made a place with his foot again and again in a puddle of scree so I would have a stable spot to put my foot against his and not slip. The flat stones slithered and tumbled down from around our feet as we might if we lost our footing. Both of us concentrated fiercely so as not to slip.

Finally we reached the line where the rock and scree stop and tundra begins, walking easily to the small, renovated chapel at Gyangdrak where a monk poured water into our hands, giving us the usual blessing that one receives in a monastery. We drank the water from our hands as he poured more over our heads. Again my throat was taut with unshed tears.

The truncated ruin of Gyangdrak Monastery which was being rebuilt.

We drove down to Darchen, then out to Lake Manasarovar where Anna and Sophie were already camped. In the back of the four-wheel drive, where no one could see me, I broke, just a little, tears rimming my eyes but my throat still painful.

I had locked myself away from my emotions from a very young age, denying them burying them. They were dangerous because they made me vulnerable. And here I was at the age of 68 overwhelmed in the back of a dusty four-wheel drive by an emotion I didn't understand, that I could not name but had to acknowledge. It was immense; I felt that it enveloped me. There was nothing to do but sit there and gulp in my painfully tightened throat. I didn't know whether to hope for a cloud burst of tears or for a gentle subsiding. But however painful, my ability to feel had returned and with it a knowledge of my spirit, a sense of connection, of confirmation. I was linked, in touch with myself emotionally and spiritually but also I was linked to something else, numinous, ineffable that those moments in the dark had made me realize I loved.

What is this all about? Why, you ask? I will make an attempt to answer. Certainly you may think me crazy or untruthful or you might think there is some magnetic pole in Kailash that draws me, and others, to her. You might think it was an effect of altitude. Here is, tentatively, what I think.

We are of the earth, dust unto dust, although we have largely lost our awareness of that. If we remain disconnected from the earth our species will die and the earth will go on without us, not noticing our absence. I think there are places on this earth where we can encounter a beauty and a connection, a spiritual link that for each of us is uniquely overpowering. For many it is the sea. It could be the Sahara Desert for someone else. For me it is a mountain inconveniently located in Tibet rather than the Adirondacks. At Kailash I am, who knows why, powerfully connected to the earth. I feel I am of her. Why should this make me cry? Coming home or leaving home often causes you to cry.

This experience does not mean I am special. Lucky, yes but not special. I have not been given a message or mission, told to preach it and save woman and man kind. I simply have had an encounter with a power that I do not understand and cannot explain that I believe communicated with me. Why me? Why not me? I am an ordinary human being. You might believe that I am over imaginative. That's all right. Tibetans would say that in a former life I was a Tibetan who lived near Kailash and am in tears because having come home I must leave again. Maybe.

I do believe that there are places that humans have, through their emotional energy, imbued, as though we are charging a battery, with energy. Kailash, like Kyunglung, has a spiritual history of thousands and thousands of years with humans through circumambulation or meditation putting their energy into this locale. For me both places resonate with our interchange with the earth but Kailash much more so. Perhaps I can explain what I mean a bit more clearly through a Tibetan story.

The mother of a young man, a trader from a remote village, asked him every time he left home to bring her a sacred relic, something small from an unimportant saint. She knew he didn't have enough money for a hair of the Buddha. Just a sliver of a saint's bone for her to put on the family altar was all she asked. On every trip he forgot and then felt guilty. Returning after a trading trip, almost home, he suddenly remembered and cursed himself for his thoughtlessness. Then by the side of the road he saw a fragment of a dog's jaw. He picked out a tooth wrapping it in a *khata* he had in his pack. Feeling like a phony, he gave it to his mother on his return as a saint's relic, thinking that on his next trip he would remember and buy a real one. Then he would substitute the real for the dog and no one would know. She was overwhelmed with happiness and gave it the most important place on the family altar.

When he entered his house after his next trip he found his mother and all the neighbors meditating before the dog tooth, which was emanating rainbows on his family altar.

The Tibetan moral is: Faith can make even a dog's tooth shine with rainbows. In other words, we are the agency that makes things sacred through belief, through faith.

Has this experience changed my life? Yes, but not in any sudden dramatic way. It has increased my belief that the point of life is not money, not stuff, although heaven knows like most people I have lots of stuff, but to know yourself, be in control of yourself, have humility, try as hard as you can to behave well. Change is the fulcrum of life. That doesn't mean one is successful or a saint. It means one tries.

Later on this trip I quarreled with Anna about riding up to Everest Base Camp One in a horse cart. I felt it was a tourist thing to do instituted by the Chinese. She felt it was beneficial to the Tibetans who drove the carts. What was really the matter was that my eyes were so dry, an altitude and climactic effect, that I was in pain unless I closed them. Why couldn't I say what was really the matter? Taking the trip as a whole maybe I was a little more in control of my temper than on previous trips but not by any large margin. Perhaps I managed better with Sophie just because I was aware of the antagonism in that relationship. No, I had not achieved perfection.

Perhaps the real change is not only do I now feel I have a spiritual connection but I understand that these attempts to change go on until I die. What I was looking for, I found. And that could mean that I have duped myself but I don't think so. I will continue to attempt over and over to change my behavior, my attitudes and sometimes I will succeed and sometimes I will fail but the journey goes on into death.

I was and am very grateful to my Aunt Liz who through her death set me on the path. I am grateful to Sonam who showed me the path, accompanying me a little on the way. The two of them have made me into a cultural bigamist.

Coming back to camp, I was in shock from my experience and slept most of the next day. I told no one what happened. I was afraid of people's reactions. Once home in New York I told two friends, one spiritual in a nonstandard way, the other a serious Chinese Buddhist who had had a similar experience. Then I told my son who didn't roll his eyes. Very slowly I realized that I needed to write about it. But how? It was while doing the inner *khora* in 2006 that I began to formulate how to tell this story.

I returned to Kailash in 2007 and planned to go to Tibet in 2008 but the Chinese closed the borders because of riots in Lhasa. I spent my time in Nepal instead, doing the circumambulation of the Annapurna Massif in 21 days. Coming back to Kathmandu from that trek I found myself standing in front of ranks of postcards staring at one with tears rising in my throat and eyes.

PART VIII

2006: The Inner *Khora*

As I walk I look up at that ledge on her side gay with the colors of prayer flags wreathing the *chörtens*. I cannot quite make their shapes out yet but I can see now that I am not looking at a monastery. The top of the slide of debris that fans down from her side looks close, surely only an hour away. The next slopes are steeper; there is less oxygen. I slow to my trailing-behind-the-snail pace.

I'm happy, not exhilarated or hyper, but deeply contented. I feel love in this world of raw rock fissured by ice and snow. Does it come from me to the mountain or from the mountain to me? I inhale it thinking of a talk I once heard the Dalai Lama give in which he said that A may love B while C hates him but that this has nothing to do with who or what B is. Instead it has to do with the perceptions of A and C. My emotions about the mountain I think are like that. They have to do with me not the mountain. The mountain is simply there, simply herself. But my fear vanishes.

Two hours later we climb the fan of mountain debris spreading from her side. In the thin air, trying not to stumble over the loose stones, it is an incredibly difficult ascent. I have no option but to pause to pant even though I am going at a pace slow as a slow-motion film. I count fifty steps, stop, pant. To my left a second fan is topped by what looks like a monastery built of snow-blocks, in reality, snow covered, house-sized rocks fallen from her ledges.

The snow slide with white blocks of debris on top of it.
We rock climbed to the right of the slide, beyond the edge
of this picture.

Abruptly I top the fan of mountain detritus. To my left are the snow-covered house-sized rocks. In front is sheer rock, striated horizontally, pockmarked, dripping water, her wall, her side. I hear our breath, the pop of falling stones. But for some reason, despite the evidence around me, perhaps my ability to think is impaired by the altitude, I don't think house-sized stones might drop from above. I realize we are going to have to climb this wall but all my mental doors are now slammed and locked against fear. Six months later or today I will recall this climb with terror but now I deny fear absolutely.

I fit fingers and feet to half-inch ledges. I've rock-climbed once, in Ladakh, edging, terrified, horizontally above a bellicose river. I now do realize that the outer *khora* with its well-marked path is a beginner's route compared to what is before me.

Someone grabs my right arm; someone pushes my bottom. Yes, they are "helpers." The short man is pulling my arm; the tall one with the moustache and straw hat now jammed down over his eyebrows, is in charge of pushing my bottom up the cliff.

Rigsum and Jigme are spiders, already higher up, clinging to the wall's yellow rock. From the ledge above flutter prayer flags; the ledge above that drips water and drops stones that bound off her wall. On the wet cliff I find a handhold, a foothold to help the "helpers." Stones pop. The rock is slippery. Here, I realize, is where the German-Swiss I talked to at the monastery in Darchen crossed soft ice. But Kailash is kind, lenient with me. The soft ice has melted, leaving a wide damp band of pocked stone through which we cling and climb.

They heave me up the sheer, dripping face, three in a chain of hands. Sun enters the valley below striking diamonds from the stream beside the path from the plateau where we prostrated a lifetime ago.

My arm is pulled; my bottom pushed. I look up, limiting my gaze to six inches, at most a foot, seeking holds. I feel a tug on my left hand the helper below now holds. I turn to see he has one foothold, but his left hand and foot are scrabbling on smooth rock. Losing his foothold he'll swing out into air. Three will plummet, like the stones pinging as they drop from her glacial hem above. It's a long way to death but fast with an incredible view. A breeze blows his straw hat off. It swirls as it wings to where we will fall. He and I smile at each other.

He finds a grip for his left hand, he fits a toe into a hole in the cliff side; we are safe. These seconds seem hours as we cling to the cracked, bare, rock of Kailash's side hearing rocks make percussion noises about us as they plunge from above. One grazes my arm. What injury would a small stone cause? A broken arm? Concussion? It sounds as if someone is shooting at us.

The prayer flags that Rigsum threw down to us as a joke as we climbed to the ledge.

We claw up another foot. Rigsum grins as he leans over the ledge to throw a prayer flag string for us to haul ourselves up on, as a joke. Wanting a picture I ask the "helper" above for my camera in my daypack he's carrying.

At this, Rigsum's smile dissolves as with creased and anxious face he leans over the edge and yells at me, "No, no picture. Come up. Stones, maybe big rocks. No."

The "helper" ahead drops my hand, scrambles onto a graveled depression and then onto the path. Rigsum asks, "You need help?" The "helper" behind delivers a final shove to my bottom. I crawl onto a little basin like depression full of gravel, pull myself to the wall where thirteen mud brick *chörtens* in a row along the ledge in her side wear garlands of prayer flags. The inner *khora's* goal, 20,000 feet. We tie prayer flags to *chörtens*, gazing down and out to Gurla Mandata's white mass.

Offerings on the ledge left by pilgrims of all persuasions.

People have propped offerings on the ledge, a Hindu pilgrim's little, silver Shiva trident, a weathered photo of a young Chinese man with his mother and father at his college graduation. We touch these gently, lay them back on the ledge. There is a luminous connection between us and those who left these objects. We will never know them or they us but we are connected by this journey. I cut off the tail of my braid as an offering assisted by the approving "helpers".

We lean against the wall behind the *chörtens*, eat chapattis, dry Indian flatbread, hard-boiled eggs, drink water. The mountain is silent at my back. But I miss seeing her. The ancient Greeks thought love happened through the eyes, through sight. There's no communication between us this time but that is all right. I relax into my love of her.

Chapattis and eggs eaten, I dig in my pack for my bar of Lindt 80% chocolate from Kathmandu, the last place such things are available. I hand it to the elder "helper" thinking that each will break off a little and hand it on. Tibetans are usually suspicious of Western food so I expect half the bar to come back to me. No. When the chocolate returns to me two squares are left.

The *chörtens* and prayer flags on the ledge at 20,000 feet.

We have accomplished our goal. But we sit for a time inhaling the thin air, looking at the *chörtens*, the prayer flags, her monolithic side. We have completed our pilgrimage.

A view as we came down through scree underfoot.

Lunch finished we walk along the ledge passing the slippery edge where the narrow path we ascended finished in a small basin of gravel. Abruptly the mountain's wall breaks. We slip through an aperture crossing to her other side. There's snow, a slope of scree, loose, slippery flat stones. The "helpers" each take an arm, motion me to dig my heels in. We hurtle down the scree; I sled on my heels between them. At a bump in the mountain's side, we rest. I listen to them talk, hearing "Tibetan, Tibetan, Chocolate, Tibetan, Chocolate." I'm happy.

The mountain's side as we descended.

After our rest they take my arms again. Because scree slides under your feet you often have to run down a slope it covers. I sled between them until we reach tundra where they stride ahead. I follow among yellow flowers and the stream's chortling voice.

Resting on our way down from 20,000 feet.

No, she did not communicate with me as she did when Rigsum and I climbed above Gyangdrak and Selung Monastery but that's all right. I feel our bond. Looking back, above her dark ridges, I look at her majesty rising alone against the sky. The mountain decided.

Walking away from Kailash and the inner *khora*.

It is now some years since I did that *khora*. I will be 80 this summer. I am in training. I am going back to see if I can do the outer *khora* one more time. I may not have the physical strength but I want so much to see her again. I am a child. "Mommy, one more time on the swing. Push me higher. One more time. Please."

About the Author

Karen Swenson was born in New York City on a hot July day in 1936 before air conditioning. Pity her mother. She was raised in Chappaqua, New York, not then the prosperous suburb it is now, and walked to school through woods, up hill only one way. Graduating from Barnard College, Columbia University she became lost for a while in the brambly thicket of a difficult marriage. Finding her way out she spent the 1960's raising her son and teaching happily at The City College of the City of New York in the Basic Writing Program under Myna Shaughnessey. Her first book of poetry, AN ATTIC OF IDEALS, was published in 1967 by Doubleday. She worked first on an MA in American Literature and then a Ph.D. on Beowulf and Old English. When budget cuts ended the curriculum at City College she went on the road and for six years drove a little, red Honda Hatchback back and forth across the US ten times teaching as Poet in Residence at universities all over the U.S. Returning to New York City she taught at City College, Fordham, NYU and Barnard College, very happy to end where she had begun.

She was unable to travel, something she considered necessary to life, until she was in her forties, but once started she faced eastward and became a middle aged backpacker—Iran, Thailand, Cambodia, Laos, Burma, Indonesia, Hong Kong, coming to Tibet in her fifties. Her travels saturated her poems in her 1994 book, THE LANDLADY IN BANGKOK, which won The National Poetry Series. In 1999 A DAUGHTER'S LATITUDE, her new and selected poems, appeared with Copper Canyon Press.

She has been to Tibet ten times and circumambulated the sacred mountain Mount Kailash seven times. In 2008 Tiger Bark Press published A PILGRIM INTO SILENCE including poems about Tibet. She made her last trip to that captive country when she was 80. But she has also been to Saudi Arabia, Denmark, Turkmenistan, Norway, Uzbekistan, Tajikistan, Sweden, North Korea, China, Ecuador and on it goes. Her experiences in all of those places have formed this book.

As she traveled she wrote articles for THE NEW YORK TIMES and THE WALL STREET JOURNAL about the places she visited and the people she met.

In 2010 she moved to Barcelona, Spain where she lives with a cat whom she is trying to persuade to not be feral.

Also by Karen Swenson

An Attic of Ideals (Doubleday, 1967)

A Sense of Direction (Smith Press, 1989)

The Landlady in Bangkok (Copper Canyon Press, 1994)

A Daughter's Latitude (Copper Canyon Press, 1999)

A Pilgrim into Silence (Tiger Bark Press, 2008)

www.ingramcontent.com/pod-product-compliance
Lightning Source LLC
Chambersburg PA
CBHW020512080526
44583CB00013B/568